To Professor Henders

with Best wishes.

Dajin Sun

Dajin D. Sun, MSLS, MA
Ruth C. Carter, PhD, MS, MA
Editors

Education for Library Cataloging: International Perspectives

Education for Library Cataloging: International Perspectives has been co-published simultaneously as *Cataloging & Classification Quarterly*, Volume 41, Number 2 2005 and Volume 41, Numbers 3/4 2006.

Pre-publication REVIEWS, COMMENTARIES, EVALUATIONS . . .

"COMPREHENSIVE AND TIMELY. . . . Describes education for cataloging and classification in twenty-one countries on six continents. It is a significant contribution to our understanding of cooperation in the increasing international world of cataloging and classification. American library educators and administrators alike will profit from reading this book."

Michael Gorman
President
American Library Association

More pre-publication
REVIEWS, COMMENTARIES, EVALUATIONS . . .

"This comprehensive survey of cataloging education outside North America is ESSENTIAL READING for anyone concerned about the current state of education for cataloging around the world. It can be used as a benchmark to assess whether the reader's country is making the grade. This is an opportunity to use an evidence-based approach to promoting the development of viable cataloging education programs in the reader's part of the world."

Ann Huthwaite, M App Sci, Grad Dip Lib Sci, Dip Ed
Library Resource Services Manager
Queensland University of Technology

"ALL OF THE CONTRIBUTIONS HAVE MUCH OF INTEREST, but a few may be of special note. Iwe's chapter about the Cross River State in Nigeria contains a heartfelt paean to catalogers and cataloging that is relevant worldwide; Sitarska's chapter on Poland includes an inspirational statement concerning the need for formal education, rather than only on-the-job training; Raghavan's chapter on India reminds us of the tremendous impact of S. R. Ranganathan on the organization of information; Hallam's description on an innovative mode of instruction in Queensland opens up exciting possibilities for future education; and Bowman's chapter on the situation in the British Isles may serve as a sobering object lesson on just how little cataloging education some schools may find it possible to teach. This book should be of interest to anyone with a serious interest in education for cataloging and classification. It may also be of use to employers who have occasion to wonder about the comparable educational preparation of their international job applicants."

Janet Swan Hill, MA
Professor
Associate Director for Technical Services
University of Colorado Libraries

More pre-publication
REVIEWS, COMMENTARIES, EVALUATIONS . . .

" **A** MUST-READ FOR ALL LIBRARY EDUCATORS. . . . EXTREMELY INFORMATIVE AND VERY WELL DOCUMENTED. I was especially interested in the surveys from Latin America and the Middle East, having recently attended the second IFLA Conference of Experts on an International Cataloging Code, held in Buenos Aires, Argentina, and having been involved with coordinating the third meeting, held in Cairo, Egypt. The historical perspectives by Dr. Barber and Dr. Shaker helped me to fill in the context behind some of the recommendations made in those conferences and thus, I found the readings to be extremely relevant."

Ana Lupe Cristan, MLIS
Cooperative Cataloging Specialist
Cataloging Policy and Support Office,
Library of Congress

The Haworth Information Press®
An Imprint of The Haworth Press, Inc.

Education for Library Cataloging: International Perspectives

Education for Library Cataloging: International Perspectives has been co-published simultaneously as *Cataloging & Classification Quarterly*, Volume 41, Number 2 2005 and Volume 41, Numbers 3/4 2006.

Monographic Separates from *Cataloging & Classification Quarterly*™

For additional information on these and other Haworth Press titles, including descriptions, tables of contents, reviews, and prices, use the QuickSearch catalog at http://www.HaworthPress.com.

Education for Library Cataloging: International Perspectives, edited by Dajin D. Sun, MSLS, MA, and Ruth C. Carter, PhD, MS, MA (Vol. 41, No. 2, 2005 and Vol. 41, No. 3/4, 2006). *Library school faculty and professional librarians from more than 20 countries discuss the international development of educational programs for cataloging and classification.*

Metadata: A Cataloger's Primer, edited by Richard P. Smiraglia, PhD (Vol. 40, No. 3/4, 2005). *"A comprehensive overview of metadata written by experts in the field." (Michael Gorman, President-Elect, American Library Association)*

Functional Requirements for Bibliographic Records (FRBR): Hype or Cure-All? edited by Patrick Le Boeuf (Vol. 39, No. 3/4, 2005). *Examines the origin, and theoretical and practical aspects of IFLA's Functional Requirements for Bibliographic Records.*

Authority Control in Organizing and Accessing Information: Definition and International Experience, edited by Arlene G. Taylor, PhD, MSLS, BA, and Barbara B. Tillett, PhD, MLS, BA (Vol. 38, No. 3/4, 2004 and Vol. 39, No. 1/2, 2004). *Presents international perspectives on authority control for names, works, and subject terminology in library, archival, museum, and other systems that provide access to information.*

The Thesaurus: Review, Renaissance, and Revision, edited by Sandra K. Roe, MS, and Alan R. Thomas, MA, FLA (Vol. 37, No. 3/4, 2004). *Examines the historical development of the thesaurus, and the standards employed for thesaurus construction, use, and evaluation.*

Knowledge Organization and Classification in International Information Retrieval, edited by Nancy J. Williamson, PhD, and Clare Beghtol, PhD (Vol. 37, No. 1/2, 2003). *Examines the issues of information retrieval in relation to increased globalization of information and knowledge.*

Electronic Cataloging: AACR2 and Metadata for Serials and Monographs, edited by Sheila S. Intner, DLS, MLS, BA, Sally C. Tseng, MLS, BA, and Mary Lynette Larsgaard, MA, BA (Vol. 36, No. 3/4, 2003). *"The twelve contributing authors represent some of the most important thinkers and practitioners in cataloging." (Peggy Johnson, MBA, MA, Associate University Librarian, University of Minnesota Libraries)*

Historical Aspects of Cataloging and Classification, edited by Martin D. Joachim, MA (classical languages and literatures), MA (library science) (Vol. 35, No. 1/2, 2002 and Vol. 35, No. 3/4, 2003). *Traces the development of cataloging and classification in countries and institutions around the world.*

Education for Cataloging and the Organization of Information: Pitfalls and the Pendulum, edited by Janet Swan Hill, MA, BA, (Vol. 34, No. 1/2/3, 2002). *Examines the history, context, present, and future of education for cataloging and bibliographic control.*

Works as Entities for Information Retrieval, edited by Richard P. Smiraglia, PhD (Vol. 33, No. 3/4, 2002). *Examines domain-specific research about works and the problems inherent in their representation for information storage and retrieval.*

The Audiovisual Cataloging Current, edited by Sandra K. Roe, MS (Vol. 31, No. 2/3/4, 2001). *"All the great writers, teachers, and lecturers are here: Olson, Fox, Intner, Weihs, Weitz, and Yee. This eclectic collection is sure to find a permanent place on many catalogers' bookshelves. . . . Something for everyone. . . . Explicit cataloging guidelines and AACR2R interpretations galore." (Verna Urbanski, MA, MLS, Chief Media Cataloger, University of North Florida, Jacksonville)*

Managing Cataloging and the Organization of Information: Philosophies, Practices and Challenges at the Onset of the 21st Century, edited by Ruth C. Carter, PhD, MS, MA (Vol. 30, No. 1/2/3, 2000). *"A fascinating series of practical, forthright accounts of national, academic, and special library cataloging operations in action. . . . Yields an abundance of practical solutions for shared problems, now and for the future. Highly recommended."* (Laurel Jizba, Head Cataloger, Portland State University Library, Oregon)

The LCSH Century: One Hundred Years with the Library of Congress Subject Headings System, edited by Alva T. Stone, MLS (Vol. 29, No. 1/2, 2000). *Traces the 100-year history of the Library of Congress Subject Headings, from its beginning with the implementation of a dictionary catalog in 1898 to the present day, exploring the most significant changes in LCSH policies and practices, including a summary of other contributions celebrating the centennial of the world's most popular library subject heading language.*

Maps and Related Cartographic Materials: Cataloging, Classification, and Bibliographic Control, edited by Paige G. Andrew, MLS, and Mary Lynette Larsgaard, MA, BA (Vol. 27, No. 1/2/3/4, 1999). *Discover how to catalog the major formats of cartographic materials, including sheet maps, early and contemporary atlases, remote-sensed images (i.e., aerial photographs and satellite images), globes, geologic sections, digital material, and items on CD-ROM.*

Portraits in Cataloging and Classification: Theorists, Educators, and Practitioners of the Late Twentieth Century, edited by Carolynne Myall, MS, CAS, and Ruth C. Carter, PhD (Vol. 25, No. 2/3/4, 1998). *"This delightful tome introduces us to a side of our profession that we rarely see: the human beings behind the philosophy, rules, and interpretations that have guided our professional lives over the past half century. No collection on cataloging would be complete without a copy of this work."* (Walter M. High, PhD, Automation Librarian, North Carolina Supreme Court Library; Assistant Law Librarian for Technical Services, North Carolina University, Chapel Hill)

Cataloging and Classification: Trends, Transformations, Teaching, and Training, edited by James R. Shearer, MA, ALA, and Alan R. Thomas, MA, FLA (Vol. 24, No. 1/2, 1997). *"Offers a comprehensive retrospective and innovative projection for the future."* (The Catholic Library Association)

Electronic Resources: Selection and Bibliographic Control, edited by Ling-yuh W. (Miko) Pattie, MSLS, and Bonnie Jean Cox, MSLS (Vol. 22, No. 3/4, 1996). *"Recommended for any reader who is searching for a thorough, well-rounded, inclusive compendium on the subject."* (The Journal of Academic Librarianship)

Cataloging and Classification Standards and Rules, edited by John J. Riemer, MLS (Vol. 21, No. 3/4, 1996). *"Includes chapters by a number of experts on many of our best loved library standards. . . . Recommended to those who want to understand the history and development of our library standards and to understand the issues at play in the development of new standards."* (LASIE)

Classification: Options and Opportunities, edited by Alan R. Thomas, MA, FLA (Vol. 19, No. 3/4, 1995). *"There is much new and valuable insight to be found in all the chapters. . . . Timely in refreshing our confidence in the value of well-designed and applied classification in providing the best of service to the end-users."* (Catalogue and Index)

Cataloging Government Publications Online, edited by Carolyn C. Sherayko, MLS (Vol. 18, No. 3/4, 1994). *"Presents a wealth of detailed information in a clear and digestible form, and reveals many of the practicalities involved in getting government publications collections onto online cataloging systems."* (The Law Librarian)

Cooperative Cataloging: Past, Present and Future, edited by Barry B. Baker, MLS (Vol. 17, No. 3/4, 1994). *"The value of this collection lies in its historical perspective and analysis of past and present approaches to shared cataloging. . . . Recommended to library schools and large general collections needing materials on the history of library and information science."* (Library Journal)

Education for Library Cataloging: International Perspectives

Dajin D. Sun, MSLS, MA
Ruth C. Carter, PhD, MS, MA
Editors

Education for Library Cataloging: International Perspectives has been co-published simultaneously as *Cataloging & Classification Quarterly*, Volume 41, Number 2 2005 and Volume 41, Numbers 3/4 2006.

The Haworth Information Press®
An Imprint of The Haworth Press, Inc.

New York • London • Victoria (AU)
www.HaworthPress.com

Published by

The Haworth Information Press®, 10 Alice Street, Binghamton, NY 13904-1580 USA

The Haworth Information Press® is an imprint of The Haworth Press, Inc., 10 Alice Street, Binghamton, NY 13904-1580 USA.

Education for Library Cataloging: International Perspectives has been co-published simultaneously as *Cataloging & Classification Quarterly*™, Volume 41, Number 2 2005 and Volume 41, Numbers 3/4 2006.

The development, preparation, and publication of this work has been undertaken with great care. However, the publisher, employees, editors, and agents of The Haworth Press and all imprints of The Haworth Press, Inc., including The Haworth Medical Press® and Pharmaceutical Products Press®, are not responsible for any errors contained herein or for consequences that may ensue from use of materials or information contained in this work. With regard to case studies, identities and circumstances of individuals discussed herein have been changed to protect confidentiality. Any resemblance to actual persons, living or dead, is entirely coincidental.

The Haworth Press is committed to the dissemination of ideas and information according to the highest standards of intellectual freedom and the free exchange of ideas. Statements made and opinions expressed in this publication do not necessarily reflect the views of the Publisher, Directors, management, or staff of The Haworth Press, Inc., or an endorsement by them.

Cover design by Kerry E. Mack.

Library of Congress Cataloging-in-Publication Data

Education for library cataloging : international perspectives / Dajin D. Sun, Ruth C. Carter, editors.
        p. cm.
        "Co-published simultaneously as Cataloging & classification quarterly, volume 41, number 2, 2005 and volume 41, numbers 3/4, 2006."
        Includes bibliographical references and index.
        ISBN-13: 978-0-7890-3112-9 (hc. : alk. paper)
        ISBN-10: 0-7890-3112-4 (hc. : alk. paper)
        ISBN-13: 978-0-7890-3113-6 (pbk. : alk. paper)
        ISBN-10: 0-7890-3113-2 (pbk. : alk. paper)
        1. Cataloging–Study and teaching. 2. Classification–Study and teaching. 3. Library education. I. Sun, Dajin. II. Carter, Ruth C. III. Cataloging & classification quarterly.
Z693. E38 2006
025.3'071–dc22
                                                                                    2005018358

Indexing, Abstracting & Website/Internet Coverage

   This section provides you with a list of major indexing & abstracting services and other tools for bibliographic access. That is to say, each service began covering this periodical during the year noted in the right column. Most Websites which are listed below have indicated that they will either post, disseminate, compile, archive, cite or alert their own Website users with research-based content from this work. (This list is as current as the copyright date of this publication.)

Abstracting, Website/Indexing Coverage . . . . Year When Coverage Began

- *Computer and Information Systems Abstracts <http://www.csa.com>* 2004
- *Current Cites [Digital Libraries] [Electronic Publishing] [Multimedia & Hypermedia] [Networks & Networking] [General] <http://sunsite.berkeley.edu/CurrentCites/>* 2000
- *EBSCOhost Electronic Journals Service (EJS) <http://ejournals.ebsco.com>* 2001
- *Elsevier Scopus <http://www.info.scopus.com>* 2005
- *FRANCIS. INIST/CNRS <http://www.inist.fr>* 1999
- *Google <http://www.google.com>* 2004
- *Google Scholar <http://scholar.google.com>* 2004
- *Haworth Document Delivery Center <http://www.HaworthPress.com/journals/dds.asp>* 1980
- *IBZ International Bibliography of Periodical Literature <http://www.saur.de>* 1995
- *Index Guide to College Journals (core list compiled by integrating 48 indexes frequently used to support undergraduate programs in small to medium sized libraries)* 1999
- *Index to Periodical Articles Related to Law <http://www.law.utexas.edu>* . . . 1989
- *Information Science & Technology Abstracts: indexes journal articles from more than 450 publications as well as books, research reports, and conference proceedings; EBSCO Publishing <http://www.epnet.com>* 1980
- *Informed Librarian, The <http://www.informedlibrarian.com>* 1993
- *INSPEC is the leading English-language bibliographic information service providing access to the world's scientific & technical literature in physics, electrical engineering, electronics, communications, control engineering, computers & computing, and information technology <http://www.iee.org.uk/publish/>* 1982

(continued)

- *Internationale Bibliographie der geistes- und sozialwissenschaftlichen Zeitschriftenliteratur . . . See IBZ <http://www.saur.de>* 1995
- *Journal of Academic Librarianship: Guide to Professional Literature, The* 1997
- *Konyvtari Figyelo (Library Review)*. 1995
- *Library & Information Science Abstracts (LISA) <http://www.csa.com>* 1989
- *Library & Information Science Annual (LISCA) <http://www.lu.com>* 1998
- *Library Literature & Information Science <http://www.hwwilson.com>*. 1984
- *Links@Ovid (via CrossRef targeted DOI links) <http://www.ovid.com>*. . . . 2005
- *Magazines for Libraries (Katz) . . . (see 2003 edition)*. 2003
- *OCLC ArticleFirst <http://www.oclc.org/services/databases/>*. 2002
- *OCLC ContentsFirst <http://www.oclc.org/services/databases/>* 2002
- *Ovid Linksolver (OpenURL link resolver via CrossRef targeted DOI links) <http://www.linksolver.com>* 2005
- *PASCAL, c/o Institut de l'Information Scientifique et Technique. Cross-disciplinary electronic database covering the fields of science, technology & medicine. Also available on CD-ROM, and can generate customized retrospective searches <http://www.inist.fr>*. 1999
- *Referativnyi Zhurnal (Abstracts Journal of the All-Russian Institute of Scientific and Technical Information– in Russian) <http://www.viniti.ru>*. 1992
- *Scopus (Elsevier) <http://www.info.scopus.com>* 2005
- *SwetsWise <http://www.swets.com>*. 2001
- *WilsonWeb <http://vnweb.hwwilsonweb.com/hww/Journals/>* 2005

Special Bibliographic Notes related to special journal issues (separates) and indexing/abstracting:

- indexing/abstracting services in this list will also cover material in any "separate" that is co-published simultaneously with Haworth's special thematic journal issue or DocuSerial. Indexing/abstracting usually covers material at the article/chapter level.
- monographic co-editions are intended for either non-subscribers or libraries which intend to purchase a second copy for their circulating collections.
- monographic co-editions are reported to all jobbers/wholesalers/approval plans. The source journal is listed as the "series" to assist the prevention of duplicate purchasing in the same manner utilized for books-in-series.
- to facilitate user/access services all indexing/abstracting services are encouraged to utilize the co-indexing entry note indicated at the bottom of the first page of each article/chapter/contribution.
- this is intended to assist a library user of any reference tool (whether print, electronic, online, or CD-ROM) to locate the monographic version if the library has purchased this version but not a subscription to the source journal.
- individual articles/chapters in any Haworth publication are also available through the Haworth Document Delivery Service (HDDS).

Education for Library Cataloging: International Perspectives

CONTENTS

Introduction   1
Dajin D. Sun
Ruth C. Carter

AFRICA

Education and Training for Cataloguing at the University
of Botswana Library: An Overview   5
Rose Tiny Kgosiemang

The Relevance of Cataloguing in a Library Science Curriculum
in Cross River State of Nigeria in This Technological Age   27
J. I. Iwe

The Education and Training of Cataloguing Students
in South Africa Through Distance Education   53
Linda M. Cloete

ASIA

Education for Cataloging and Classification in China   71
Zhanghua Ma

The Status Quo and Future Development of Cataloging
and Classification Education in China   85
Li Si

Education for Knowledge Organization: The Indian Scene   105
K. S. Raghavan

Current Status of Cataloging and Classification Education
in Japan   121
Shoichi Taniguchi

A Study on the Job Training and Self-Training of the Cataloging
and Classification Librarians Working in South Korean
Academic Libraries   135
    Chul-Wan Kwak

AUSTRALIA

Beyond Our Expectations: A Review of an Independent Learning
Module in Descriptive Cataloguing at the Queensland
University of Technology   149
    Gillian Hallam

MARCup to Markup: Education for Cataloguing
and Classification in Australia   173
    Ross Harvey
    Susan Reynolds

EUROPE

Education for Cataloging and Classification in Austria
and Germany   193
    Monika Münnich
    Heidi Zotter-Straka
    Petra Hauke

Education and Training on the Nature and Description
of Documents: Polish University Studies and Professional
Librarianship Schools   227
    Anna Sitarska

Cataloging Education on the Sunny Side of the Alps   269
    Jerry D. Saye
    Alenka Šauperl

Education for Cataloging in Spanish Universities: A Descriptive
and Critical Study   291
    Rafael Ruiz-Perez
    Emilio Delgado López-Cózar

Education and Training for Cataloguing and Classification
   in the British Isles   309
    J. H. Bowman

LATIN AMERICA

The Teaching of Information Processing in the University
   of Buenos Aires, Argentina   335
    Elsa E. Barber
    Silvia L. Pisano

Education for Cataloging and Classification in Mexico   353
    Filiberto Felipe Martínez Arellano

Education for Cataloging and Related Areas in Peru   389
    Ana María Talavera Ibarra

MIDDLE EAST

Cataloging and Classification Education in Egypt: Stressing
   the Fundamentals While Moving Toward Automated
   Applications   407
    Mohammed Fat'hy Abdel Hady
    Ali Kamal Shaker

An Account of Cataloging and Classification Education
   in Iranian Universities   431
    Mortaza Kokabi

Cataloging Instruction in Israel   443
    Snunith Shoham

Continuing Education for Catalogers in Saudi Arabia   461
    Zahiruddin Khurshid

Index   471

ABOUT THE EDITORS

Dajin D. Sun, MSLS, MA, is Assistant Head of the Catalog Department of Yale University Library. Before joining the staff of Yale Library, he held several positions with the University of Pittsburgh Library System. An active member of a number of professional library organizations, Mr. Sun has chaired the Education Committee of the ALA ALCTS Serials Section and the Scholarship Committee of the Chinese American Librarians Association, and has served as a member of the Program for Cooperative Cataloging Standing Committee on Standards. In addition, he has been a certified trainer for the national Serials Cooperative Cataloging Training Program (SCCTP) and has conducted workshops on five serials cataloging courses developed by the SCCTP in the United States. Mr. Sun has been a contributing member of the editorial board of *Cataloging & Classification Quarterly* (The Haworth Press, Inc.) since the early 1990s, and has published articles and books in subject areas ranging from cataloging to the history of contemporary China. His professional accomplishments led him to attend and graduate from the second class of the yearlong Leadership and Career Development Program of the Association of Research Libraries in 2000.

Ruth C. Carter, PhD, MS, MA, holds her PhD in History from the University of Pittsburgh and her MS in Library Science from the University of Illinois at Urbana-Champaign. She is retired from the University of Pittsburgh where she held many positions in technical and automated services, including Assistant Director and, most recently, Head of the Archives Service Center and Curator of Historical Collections. Her national recognition for leadership and expertise has led to receipt of the Bowker/Ulrich's Serials Librarianship Award, her election as president of the Association of Library Collections and Technical Services (ALCTS), and the University of Illinois GSLIS Distinguished Alumna Award. Dr. Carter is completing twenty-one years as Editor of *Cataloging & Classification Quarterly* and has also edited the *Journal of Internet Cataloging* and co-edited the *Journal of Archival Organization.* Additionally, she served on the CONSER Policy Committee, the IFLA Standing Committee on Serial Publications, the OCLC Users Council, and the Pennsylvania State Historical Records Advisory Board.

Introduction

Catalog librarians have been the cornerstone of library services for centuries. Their education and training largely influences the profession's collective ability to deal with the current challenges and meet the future needs for information services. Although studies or reports on cataloging practices outside of the United States have been seen in the library literature from time to time, very little is published about how education for cataloging develops in other parts of the world. Now that there is growing interest and effort to foster international cataloging standards and cooperation, an understanding of how education contributes to the cataloging profession globally would be significant and beneficial.

With this in mind, we have compiled this special volume in an attempt to reflect and capture the worldwide education in the first decade of the twenty-first century for cataloging and classification in its dynamic forms. Focusing on international perspectives, this theme issue is a cross-sectional document for the current status, developments, and trends of cataloging education around the world. It contains 22 papers written by 28 authors from over twenty countries spanning six continents and covers both formal education and continuing education of catalog librarians in these countries. The countries covered in this volume are: Botswana, Nigeria, and South Africa in Africa; China, India, Japan, and Korea in Asia; Australia representing the Oceanic region; Austria, Germany, Poland, Slovenia, Spain, and the countries of the British Isles (England, Ireland, Scotland, and Wales) in Europe; Argentina, Mexico, and Peru in Latin America; and Egypt, Iran, Israel, and Saudi Arabia in the Middle East. The United States is not included here because U.S. ed-

[Haworth co-indexing entry note]: "Introduction." Sun, Dajin D., and Ruth C. Carter. Co-published simultaneously in *Cataloging & Classification Quarterly* (The Haworth Information Press, an imprint of The Haworth Press, Inc.) Vol. 41, No. 2, 2005, pp.1-3; and: *Education for Library Cataloging: International Perspectives* (ed: Dajin D. Sun, and Ruth C. Carter) The Haworth Information Press, an imprint of The Haworth Press, Inc., 2006, pp. 1-3. Single or multiple copies of this article are available for a fee from The Haworth Document Delivery Service [1-800-HAWORTH, 9:00 a.m. - 5:00 p.m. (EST). E-mail address: docdelivery@haworthpress.com].

Available online at http://www.haworthpress.com/web/CCQ
doi:10.1300/J104v41n02_01

ucation for cataloging and classification was already well covered by Janet Swan Hill in *Education for Cataloging and the Organization of Information* (The Haworth Press, Inc., 2002).

Although there are different ways to organize these articles, it seems natural to arrange the contents according to the geographic locations they cover. Some political, historical, cultural, religious, and linguistic factors are also considered in the geographic organization.

Region by region and country by country, the reader will see a kaleidoscope of educational efforts and programs to cultivate cataloging professionals all over the world. From Africa, Kgosiemang depicts the education and training development for librarians in the University of Botswana Library, Iwe shares her study of cataloging in the library science school curricula in the Cross River State of Nigeria, and Cloete discusses the training of students in cataloging via distant education in South Africa. In Asia, Ma and Si describe the education programs in China from different perspectives. Ma introduces the various educational programs at different levels, whereas Si analyzes the varied cataloging instruction and courses by examining the web sites of library and information science programs in mainland China and Taiwan. Raghavan gives an account of the education for knowledge organization (including cataloging and classification) in India, Taniguchi provides a thorough depiction of the current status of cataloging education in Japan, and Kwak presents the result of his survey on the job training of academic catalog librarians in South Korea. There are three authors introducing the education for cataloging in Australia: Hallam describes an independent module in descriptive cataloging that was a pilot project at Queensland University of Technology; Harvey and Reynolds reflect the current status of education for cataloging and classification in Australia by studying the course handbooks and web sites of Australian library and information science programs. In Europe, Münnich, Zotter-Straka, and Hauke join forces to present how catalog librarians are trained in Germany and Austria, and Sitarska describes the library education system in Poland and its recent changes. Saye and Šauperl report the library science programs in Slovenia with emphasis on cataloging and classification courses. Ruiz-Perez and López-Cózar present a critical study of cataloging instruction within the library and information science programs in Spain, and Bowman describes the results of a recent survey of graduate education and training for cataloging and classification in the United Kingdom. In Latin America, Barber and Pisano study the current curriculum in information processing including cataloging and classification at the University of Buenos Aires in Argentina. Martínez gives an overview of the education for cataloging and classification in Mexico, and Talavera explains the development of library education programs in Peru over the last decades of the 20th century. In the Middle East, Abdel Hady and Shaker introduce the current status of cataloging and classification education in Egypt; Kokabi provides a brief account of cataloging and classification education in Iran; Shoham describes cataloging teaching in Israel and the recent changes to it; and Khurshid reports the continuing education for catalogers in Saudi Arabia and explains why it is necessary. It is noteworthy that some of these pieces have been the first effort ever to introduce the education for cataloging in the countries (e.g., Egypt and Japan) which they cover.

For all of our diligent efforts to invite as many contributors and cover more geographic areas, it is to our regret that many countries, including some with long traditions of education for cataloging, are not represented in this volume. Countries that we intended to cover, but from whom we were unable to locate an author, include several each in Africa, Asia, and Europe. Others missing are from the Americas and the Pacific. This by no means indicates our negligence or bias toward these countries, but rather is due to limited time and resources to undertake such a large-scale project within a reasonable time period. We hope that a future volume will cover many more countries, both those with active formal library education programs and those without. Any suggestions or recommendations on possible authors in those countries not included here are exceedingly welcome and can be e-mailed to Dajin Sun (dajin.sun@yale.edu).

It is our sincere hope that readers will find papers in this special issue as interesting and educational as we have, and that our effort, limited as it is, will inspire further research and publication on this important international education topic. Finally, we feel obliged to acknowledge our immense gratitude to all of those who helped us identify and locate authors in different countries.

Dajin D. Sun
Ruth C. Carter

Education and Training for Cataloguing at the University of Botswana Library: An Overview

Rose Tiny Kgosiemang

SUMMARY. This paper discusses the education and training of both junior and professional staff for cataloguing at the University of Botswana Library and examines the formal library school education at the University of Botswana offered by the Department of Library and Information Studies (LIS). It focuses on education for cataloguing and classification with emphasis on descriptive cataloguing; subject access; classification; and bibliographic control for books and other library materials. The paper also discusses on-the-job training and continuing education for librarians and junior library staff. This paper shows the relationship that existed between the Cataloguing Unit and Subject Librarians before the restructuring of the Cataloguing and Ac-

Rose Tiny Kgosiemang, MLS, is Senior Librarian, University of Botswana Library, P/BA 900399, Gaborone, Botswana (E-mail: Kgosiert@mopipi.ub.bw).

[Haworth co-indexing entry note]: "Education and Training for Cataloguing at the University of Botswana Library: An Overview." Kgosiemang, Rose Tiny. Co-published simultaneously in *Cataloging & Classification Quarterly* (The Haworth Information Press, an imprint of The Haworth Press, Inc.) Vol. 41, No. 2, 2005, pp. 5-25; and: *Education for Library Cataloging: International Perspectives* (ed: Dajin D. Sun, and Ruth C. Carter) The Haworth Information Press, an imprint of The Haworth Press, Inc., 2006, pp. 5-25. Single or multiple copies of this article are available for a fee from The Haworth Document Delivery Service [1-800-HAWORTH, 9:00 a.m. - 5:00 p.m. (EST). E-mail address: docdelivery@haworthpress.com].

quisitions units in the late 1990s. That restructuring changed the relationship that existed between the Cataloguing Unit and Subject Librarians regarding the cataloguing and classification of materials and the training activities organized by the Cataloguing Unit for Subject Librarians in an attempt to ensure quality records. It touches on training conducted outside the country. The paper draws information from official documents and the author's long experience in various levels and units of the University of Botswana Library, starting in 1982. *[Article copies available for a fee from The Haworth Document Delivery Service: 1-800-HAWORTH. E-mail address: <docdelivery@haworthpress.com> Website: <http://www.HaworthPress.com> © 2005 by The Haworth Press, Inc. All rights reserved.]*

KEYWORDS. Cataloguing and classification, cataloguing education, continuing education, education and training, formal training, in-service training, quality control, library and information studies, University of Botswana, Botswana

METHODOLOGY: This paper is based on my personal experience as a staff member in the Technical Service unit as well as a Subject Librarian in the University of Botswana Library. In addition, it reflects experience gained as a student in the Department of Library and Information Studies at the University of Botswana. A lot of information is also drawn from official documents generated in the cataloguing division meant for junior staff and Subject Librarians.

While working on this paper, I had discussions with colleagues who had recently completed their Diploma and Master's Degree studies in Library and Information Studies and had done cataloguing-related courses as well as the practicum. I also talked to some lecturers in the Department of Library and Information Studies. The paper cites a few documents which discuss education for cataloguing and in-service training in other countries.

INTRODUCTION

Before the advent of restructuring at the University of Botswana, library professional staff were categorized as academic staff while junior staff were considered para-professional or non-academic staff. In the year 2000, the university restructured staff into academic and support. That restructuring affected all library staff. In view of these changes in the current status of library staff, this paper uses the terms 'professional' for senior staff and 'junior' for para-professional staff.

FORMAL TRAINING

The University of Botswana library provides both formal and informal types of training to its staff members. The type of training offered to an individual depends upon the individual's qualifications at the point of entry into the establishment. Staff who joined the library after three years secondary education (Junior Certificate) or five years secondary education, but got a lower grade than third class (General Education Certificate) Cambridge Overseas Secondary Certificate or Botswana Government Secondary Education, served the library for two to three years after which they were sent to study a one-year Certificate in Library Studies course. Staff who joined the library after completing the five years Cambridge Overseas School Certificate (COSC) or Botswana Government Secondary Education certificate (BGSE), or staff with a Certificate in Library Studies served the library for two to three years before they were sent to study the two-year Diploma in Library Studies. Before 1987, staff who joined the library establishment after completing their general Bachelor's Degrees were required to serve the library for a year before they were admitted into a Postgraduate Diploma in Library Studies. Also, staff who completed their Diploma in Library Studies were allowed to study for a general Bachelor's Degree after five years post-diploma service. After their Bachelor's Degrees they served the library for a year before proceeding into a postgraduate Diploma in Library and Information Studies. It was only in 1987 that the Department of Library and Information Studies (DLIS) introduced a Post-Graduate Diploma in Library and Information Studies which was replaced by a Master's Degree programme in 1996. Therefore, staff who studied for a Master's Degree before the programme was introduced locally by the DLIS applied to universities abroad to do their Master's Degree in Library and Information Studies.

CATALOGUING PROGRAMMES OFFERED
BY THE DEPARTMENT OF LIBRARY STUDIES

The Department of Library and Information Studies has been offering courses in cataloguing and classification since the 1979/80 academic year. The first two programmes that were offered were the Certificate and Diploma course in Library Studies. As time went by, the Department grew in terms of size, programmes, and reputation. It then started offering both undergraduate and postgraduate programmes.

The following are some of the programmes and courses offered by the Department of Library and Information Studies:

Certificate in Library Studies

1979/1980–Library Catalogue and Classification Scheme and the cataloguing-related topics covered in this course were: Introduction to classification: theory and practice; Features of a classification scheme; The Dewey Decimal Classification Scheme; Introduction to cataloguing: theory and practice; Elements of a catalogue entry; and Introduction to indexes.[1]

During the 1980/1981 academic year the name of the Certificate course changed from Library Catalogue and Classification Scheme to Organization and Arrangement of Stock. Topics covered included: Introduction to classification; Dewey Decimal Classification; Introduction to cataloguing; Production and duplication of cards; Practical filing of cards in dictionary and classified order; Logical arrangement of print and non-print materials; Shelf guides; and Manuals.[2] Between 1982 and 2001 the Certificate course remained the same. Then, from 2002 to date, the Certificate course name became Introduction to Organising Information. This course introduces students to the need for organising information in order to facilitate its retrieval. It also introduces them to the principles of classification in both manual and computerized environments.[3]

Diploma in Library Studies

1979/1980–Diploma I–Organisation of Stock

The name of the cataloguing-related course was Organisation of stock. The topics offered in this course were: Theory and practice; The reasons for classification; Author, Title; Subject approaches; Features of classification; Dewey Decimal Classification; Other classification schemes; Special classification problems; Cataloguing: dictionary and classified catalogues; Anglo-American Rules; Elements of the catalogue entry; Physical form of the catalogue.[4]

1980/1981–Diploma II–Cataloguing and Classification

The name of the course for the second-year Diploma was Cataloguing and Classification. Topics covered in this course were Practical cataloguing and Classification of simple library materials including non-book materials.[5]

1981/1982 Diploma I–Classification and Cataloguing

The cataloguing-related topics offered this academic year were: Theory; Library classification; Major classification schemes of the twentieth century in outline; Dewey Decimal Classification; Cataloguing theory and practice; Cataloguing rules and codes.[6] From 1982/1983 on, the cataloguing course for the first-year Diploma remained the same, until 1989/1990 when it incorporated Indexing and Principles of archival classification and description.[7] From 1990/1991-2001/2002 the cataloguing course remained the same.

1981/1982–Diploma II–Practical Classification, Cataloguing and Indexing.

During this academic year, the name of the course changed and so did the course outline. The course outline included the following topics: Books: monographs; Non-book materials; Serials; Audio-Visuals; and Thesauri construction.[8]

1989/1990–Indexing, Classification and Cataloguing

During the 1989/1990 academic year the name of the cataloguing-related course for the second-year Diploma became Indexing, Classification and Cataloguing, and the course outline covered the practical applications in developing manual information retrieval systems for a variety of library and information services; Practical classification, cataloguing, indexing, abstracting, creating and utilisation of thesauri; and The application of indexing to archival collections.[9] From 1990/1991-2001/2002 the course remained the same. The other change that was effected on the curriculum at the Diploma level took place in the 2002/2003 academic year when the course name changed to Organising Information. The course outline covered topics such as Information carriers; Principles of cataloguing; Choice of access points; Fundamentals of classification; Dewey Decimal Classification scheme; Library of Congress Classification scheme.[10]

1986/1987–Postgraduate Diploma in Library and Information Studies

In August 1986 the Department of Library and Information Studies introduced a Postgraduate Diploma programme in Library and Information Studies. Like other programmes at other levels, this new programme offered the cataloguing-related courses as well. The name of the course was Information Organisation and Retrieval. The topics offered by this programme were: Foundations and theory of information retrieval; Bibliography and bibliographic control; Classification, cataloguing and indexing; Finding information–defining needs, search procedures, choosing search terms and reference sources; Basic keys to information retrieval through classification, cataloguing, indexing, abstracting and bibliography; African bibliography; The oral tradition, organisation and access to Africa's written and unwritten record; Developing and using advanced retrieval tools; Using post-coordinate indexing systems and languages and mechanical and computerised information systems and networks.[11]

In the 1989/1990 academic year the course outline was adjusted to accommodate computerised databases, computerisation of library processes, including classification and cataloguing; Automated information from computerised databases; and UNESCO, PADIS, and AGRIS methodologies.[12] The course outline remained the same until the introduction of the Master's Degree programme that replaced the Postgraduate Diploma programme.

1994/1995–Master's Degree in Library and Information Studies

The two-year or four-semester programme was introduced in 1994 but replaced the Postgraduate programme in 1996. At its inception, it offered a cataloguing-related course under the name Information Storage to first year Master's students. The course content included: Introduction to information retrieval; Procedures facilitating information storage retrieval–cataloguing and classification: and Indexing, abstracting, and thesaurus construction. The course also offered both manual-based and computer-based information retrieval systems; Computerised union catalogues; Electronic mail and computerised bibliographic networks such as SABINET; Major search systems and online databases.[13] During the second year the course, renamed Indexing, Classification and Cataloguing, included the following topics in its course content: Introduction to the organisation and retrieval of information; Theory and practice of cataloguing and classification; Use of cataloguing codes and general classification schemes; UDC, BLISS, LC, etc.; Management of cataloguing and classification; Principles of indexing and abstracting; and Vocabulary control and indexing techniques. The course also covered indexing languages, thesaurus construction, computerised databases and other cataloguing related subjects.[14] The cataloguing-related course did not end here. The Department continues to offer these courses under a more improved curriculum.

While working on this paper, I talked to some of our staff members who completed their Diploma and Master's courses a few years ago, including those who returned to work in July 2003. Those who completed their Diploma course in 1999 and 2003 indicated that they were only taught cataloguing theory. However, those who completed their Master's in Library Studies indicated that the course included a practical component. There were times when they were sent to the library for their practical exercise using the DDC schedules and the Library of Congress Subject Headings. This was further confirmed by a staff member in the Department of LIS that, indeed, cataloguing is a core course for Library Science in the Department at Certificate, Diploma and Master's levels. However, the teaching of the course remains largely theoretical. It is expected that when students go for practicum, they are introduced to various practices of cataloguing including the cataloguing of electronic resources.

NUMBER OF FACULTY TEACHING IN THE AREA OF BIBLIOGRAPHIC CONTROL

From staff interviewed in the Department of Library and Information Studies, it seems that the Department does not have the practice of pigeon-holing staff into specialisations as such. However, in the past about three staff have taught the area of bibliographic control. As indicated in the paper, the Department does offer cataloguing, classification and indexing courses to its students.

NUMBER OF STUDENTS
TAKING CATALOGUING-RELATED COURSEWORK
FOR A YEAR OR SEMESTER

The cataloguing course offered by the Department of Library and Information Studies (DLIS) is a compulsory course for all students taking Certificate, Diploma and Master's Degree programmes. Table 1 below indicates the number of students who graduated in DLIS since the 1979/1980 academic year. The figures do not reflect the total enrolment, which would include students who failed or those who did not complete their courses for one reason or another. All of the students

TABLE 1. Number of UB Students Taking Cataloguing-Related Courses Offered by the Department of Library and Information Studies

Course	Certificate		Diploma		Post-Graduate Diploma		Master's	
Academic Year	Total	From UB	Total	From UB	Total	From UB	Total	From UB
1980	9	1						
1981	15	2	7					
1982	16		17	1				
1983	13		17	2				
1984	9	3	12	1				
1985	5		22	1				
1986	13	4	15	3				
1987	6		48		7			
1988	15		19	2	5			
1989	17	2	26	3	5	2		
1990	14	5	18	3	6			
1991	12		21		6			
1992	15	2	20		9			
1993	16		21	2	6			
1994	17	2	17		5			
1995	16	8	25	4	7			
1996	23	4	26	1			6	
1997	16	1	39	2			18	9
1998	18	2	32	6			2	
1999	14		32	2			9	
2000	27		49	4			3	
2001	33	4	39	8			13	
2002	28		56	5			13	2
Total	**367**	**40**	**578**	**50**	**56**	**2**	**64**	**11**

University of Botswana calendars, 1980-2002

who graduated in any particular year took cataloguing and classification courses.

PRACTICUM OF STUDENTS IN LIBRARY CATALOGUING AND/OR A CATALOGUING-RELATED DEPARTMENT

Upon completion, Diploma students are sent to various institutions for practicum in library practices. While on attachment, students are offered only what is available where they are attached. This may include the clearing of backlogs and handling of projects that have been pending over a long period of time. A number of reasons exist for the assignment of projects of all types to students. One of the reasons could be lack of a formalised arrangement between the DILS and the institutions to which students are assigned. It could also be that their attachment objectives do not clearly state the kind of training desired for these students. The University of Botswana Library receives students on attachment after they have completed their examination in May. Since most of the librarians are involved at that time in the teaching of a credit-based Information Literacy Skills programme, they are usually very busy with their core activities. It might not be a convenient time for them to take up extra projects that may require the close supervision of students. That might explain why students are given some of the long-pending projects to work on. Therefore, whatever is stated there may be interpreted to mean any project that is available.

Whatever the case might be, there are several views regarding the importance of cataloguing worldwide. There are librarians who still feel strongly about training on cataloguing whereas there are others who do not feel so strongly about its importance. For example, as Grieg described, on 26 August 1992, members of the Australian Library Association Cataloguers' Section (New South Wales Group) agreed at a meeting on issues in education for cataloguing that education for cataloguing is one of the most significant areas for the development of librarians and library technicians, and that formal education is the beginning of cataloguing development.[15]

However, research suggests that in other libraries, librarians disregard the importance of cataloguing and the organization of information in general, as essential parts of the process of making information available to the communities they are supposed to serve.[16] Solis Valdespino argues that failure to teach the importance of cataloguing, its history and evolution, as well as the technical process involved, has led to a decline in the quality of library services and urges a corresponding alteration of the curriculum to produce librarians who understand their social role and are capable of performing as true professionals.[17] At the University of Pretoria, DeBoer sees a change in the information profession, as well as in the core requirements for information workers, only because the workplace needs specific qualities and skills.[18] DeBoer further says that the necessity of teaching cataloguing and classification is questioned, and many library schools have discontinued teaching these subjects.[19] It is, however, noted that many experts believe that cataloguing and classification are still among the basics of information work.[20]

COOPERATION BETWEEN LIBRARIES AND LIBRARY SCHOOLS

The primary cooperation that exists between the Department of Library and Information Studies and libraries in Botswana is in terms of placements for students doing practical work. On completion of the formal theoretical training, Diploma students from the library school are sent to libraries in Botswana to gain on the job practical experience. Also, there are other forms of cooperation between the Department of Library and Information Studies and the University of Botswana Library. Each Subject Librarian in the library represents a department within a faculty. So, the Subject Librarian responsible for Library and Information Studies liaises with staff of DILS on all matters relating to collection development, subject content analysis, bibliographic instruction, and user education. In that way, if there is a need for students taking cataloguing and classification to be assisted in any way, the lecturer teaching can make appropriate arrangements with the librarian.

ON THE JOB EDUCATION

The University of Botswana Library's current structure has three divisions: the Information and Research Services Division (IRS), responsible for specialized collections, research support, archival management and faculty liaison; Customer and Extension Services Division, responsible for interlibrary relations, user support, customer relations, collection security, access control, etc.; and the Resource Management Division, responsible for information technology, acquisitions, cataloguing, indexing, security, etc. The last two divisions are made up of both professional and junior staff. Although staff in all three divisions sometimes participate in on-the-job training, this paper deals with staff in the Resource Management Division where most technical service activities take place. The Botswana Documentation and Special Collection Unit which falls under IRS also carries out some technical service activities. Also, Subject Librarians who are part of IRS perform subject cataloguing and indexing on materials which require original cataloguing and cannot be handled by professional staff at Technical Services. But when it comes to cataloguing-related training, only Resource Management staff will be discussed.

According to Carson, Carson, and Phillips, one of the reasons why library staff fail to perform effectively is that they do not know how or when to perform, and only training can resolve this problem.[21] I believe that all libraries are aware of the role that on-the-job training plays in effective performance.

Job-related professional development can take many forms. It may involve classroom activities, a seminar, workshop, in-service, induction, short course, or a structured mentoring program. The result of all of these activities should be an increased knowledge, improved performance, skill, or attitude which will enhance the professional value. Literature shows that some form of professional development or in-service training does take place in libraries all over the world. In Germany, in-service training is offered by several library organizations and institutions. The Association of Libraries in Public Libraries (VBB) organises between 60 and 70 events every year.[22] In the Netherlands, on the other hand, the Nederlands Bibliotheek en Lektuur Centrum (Dutch Centre for Libraries and Literature (NBLC)) in 1977 created a department to promote the acquisition of professional expertise by practising librarians.[23] The Department offers courses on subjects such as "Handling of audiovisual materials," "Automation in public libraries," "Children's story hours," and "Cataloguing."[24] As far as training is concerned, NBLC staff, with the help of practicing librarians and library school lecturers, provide the training which runs for 5 to 10 days.[25]

At the University of Botswana Library, on-the-job training takes many formats as well. These formats include workshops/seminars, meetings, internal correspondences addressing cataloguing issues, and supervisory instruction in which the Coordinator or the supervisor teaches a staff member.[26] The following are some of the cataloguing related training activities which took place at the University of Botswana library:

Training in the Form of Workshops/Seminars

Workshop on On-Line Cataloguing at UB Library:
Policies, Challenges and Prospects for the 21st Century

The 3-day workshop, which started on Friday, January 26th and ended on Tuesday, January 30th, 1996, was organized by the Cataloguing Unit of the library. It arose out of the need for clear policies and practices in on-line cataloguing in the UB Library. The workshop aimed to achieve the following objectives:

1. to help clean up the database by identifying various sources of errors which might be human or software- and hardware-related
2. to help initiate an ongoing staff training programme to help with positive reinforcement of staff performance
3. to help update the UB Library cataloguing manual
4. to help evaluate current practices in on-line cataloguing, and serve as a revision study of AACR2R as applied in the UB Library.

The workshop was attended by cataloguing professionals including junior staff, who served as demonstrators during practical sessions, automation staff and Subject Librarians.

Papers presented at the workshop included the following:

1. Introduction to the structure of the database at UB Library, by K. N. Rao, Acting Systems Librarian
2. Common errors to look out for and avoid in on-line cataloguing at UB Library, by J. W. Formson (Jr.), Acting Cataloguing Coordinator
3. The importance of basic training for the retro-conversion team at UB Library, by R. T. Kgosiemang, Retro-conversion manager
4. Use of the validation facility in TinLib: a demonstration by Ms O. Rakgamanyane, an Assistant in the Cataloguing section
5. Serials cataloguing, by R. T. Chiware, Periodicals Librarian
6. In-house cataloguing policies at UB Library, presentations done by Subject Librarians. Subject Librarians were asked to present topics relevant to their sections and subject specializations that they believed had an effect on the levels of accuracy and consis-

tency. For example, the Humanities Subject Librarian presented a paper on Humanities policies outlining particular problems and practices in the Humanities and how they related to overall policy. The paper also looked at various options provided by the Dewey Decimal Classification (DDC), to show how the options affected number-building and other options implemented by the library which were developed with earlier editions by the Johannesburg Public Library because DDC did not adequately satisfy local requirements.[27]

7. A draft on an updated cataloguing manual at UB Library by J. W. Formson (Jr.), Acting Cataloguing Coordinator.

Training of Library Assistants in Dealing with Humanities Books

The training took place on March 28th, 1996, and covered a selection of subjects for which the Humanities Subject Librarian had determined a need.

Training Through Internal Correspondence (Memoranda)

1. A memorandum came from the Cataloguing Coordinator, addressed to Subject Librarians, dated 2nd August, 1993. The subject of the memorandum was: Subject Cataloguing: subject headings, subject cataloguing practices and preferences in the UB Library.

   The memo discussed policy issues on subject cataloguing tools. It was felt that the policy issues provided for various options which resulted in practices and preferences in the library. The Cataloguing Coordinator cautioned Subject Librarians that, although some of the preferences and practices were documented, others were not. He informed them that such failure to document all practices and preferences could lead to inconsistencies, especially when new staff joined the establishment and had no proper documentation to fall back on.[28] The intention of that memo was for Subject Librarians to work jointly with the Cataloguing Coordinator to produce a cataloguing manual which would then be used in the training of new staff and would be consulted by new Subject Librarians joining the establishment.

2. A memorandum from the Acting Cataloguing Coordinator dated 29th August, 1996, was addressed to Subject Librarians. It dealt with Subject Librarians' role in the processing of books for cataloguing. In that memo, the Cataloguing Coordinator expressed

concern at the Subject Librarians' reluctance to perform subject cataloguing. He drew their attention to the fact that the Cataloguing Section alone could not perform all of the activities starting from ordering of books, processing of new books, as well as database management, without Subject Librarians' input. He drew their attention to the fact that their input was the basic step in the line of authority control.[29]

Training in the Form of Meetings

Minutes of the Subject Librarians' meeting held on the 29th of April, 1992, to discuss call number truncation and the DDC 20th edition. The meeting was arranged by the Cataloguing Coordinator and attended by Subject Librarians and the Deputy Librarian. The meeting's purpose was to discuss a library policy which stipulated the number of digits a call number should have. According to that policy, any call number assigned to a book was not supposed to exceed ten digits. However, it was observed that, in some cases, call number truncation was impossible. Although reasons for call number truncation were given, it was conceded that a rigid requirement to limit the call number to ten or fewer digits was not possible.

CATALOGUING ACTIVITIES BEFORE TSS

The discussions and details of correspondence between the Cataloguing Coordinator and Subject Librarians above indicate the relationship that existed between the two units before the Cataloguing Unit became the Technical Services Section (TSS), and also before Cataloguing Assistants were transferred permanently to TSS in 1994. It is also clear that before 1999, the time when Technical Services staff started doing on-line cataloguing, all subject cataloguing activities were the sole responsibility of Subject Librarians. Those activities included classification and indexing. Subject Librarians for each faculty were assigned assistants whose task was to perform descriptive cataloguing on all of the materials in the faculty offices. After descriptive cataloguing was done, Subject Librarians would classify the materials and assign subject headings. Catalogued materials would then be taken to the Cataloguing Unit where the Cataloguing Coordinator would proofread the materials before they were input into the database. The material would then be labelled on the book card, book pocket, and on the spine by Assistants. In addition to proofreading, the Cataloguing Coordinator was responsible for database management to ensure quality. This role of Subject Librarians changed when the Library changed its TINlib system and began using Innopac in 2000.[30]

A number of discussions on cataloguing policy issues at meetings or in the form of correspondences have clearly shown that the Cataloguing Coordinator was not only responsible for the editing of records and database management. He was also responsible for the planning and coordination of all training activities for both the cataloguing staff and Subject Librarians.

CATALOGUING EDUCATION AT TECHNICAL SERVICES

Training at Technical Services for both junior and professional staff is a continuous activity, not limited to new staff joining Technical Services. All Technical Services staff undergo training on software upgrades or any additional information required for their work. Table 2 contains information on some previous training activities within Technical Services.

As already indicated above, both junior and professional staff at TSS undergo training for cataloguing. Staff who are already in the section and have already been trained in Innopac, SABINET, OCLC, and MARC format receive training when the software is upgraded. New staff who join the section receive training during induction.

TRAINING CONDUCTED OUTSIDE THE COUNTRY

Most of the training for cataloguing takes place locally, with trainers being brought in from outside Botswana to train professional staff who, in turn, relay the skills learned to junior staff. There are also cases where staff have been taken outside Botswana for training in the form of seminars/workshops or short visits. These seminars take short periods of time ranging from a few days to a week. In 1996 I attended a seminar on Bibliographic Standards for Promotion of Co-operation at the University of Pretoria, South Africa. The aim of the workshop was the promotion of the uniform application of bibliographic standards, codes, and systems in order to improve the quality of records in databases. At that time, librarians in South Africa and in other parts of the world felt that there were serious problems encountered in all co-operative projects

TABLE 2. Training Activities at TSS

Type of Training	Date of Training	Training Description
Copy cataloguing	8-11 June, 1998	Copy cataloguing from SABINET using both SACat and LC Bibliographic. Training focussed on the editing of existing records. Training of trainers.
Copy cataloguing	16-25 June, 1998	Training organized for both Technical Services and Circulation staff. In Technical Services, all cataloguing assistants working on newly received books and those doing retrospective conversion were trained on copy cataloguing from SABINET using both SACat and LC MARC bibliographic.
USMARC, OCLC and SABINET	21st -30th July, 1999	Introduction to OCLC, USMARC, SABINET cataloguing. Included bibliographic input standards; copy cataloguing; original cataloguing; and quality control.
CatME training	26th August, 1999	Training included searching, original cataloguing, copy cataloguing, and completing transactions.
Innopac training	22-26 November, 1999	Training was conducted by Innopac staff. It covered WebOPAC searches and administration, cataloguing, and authority control.
Innopac (Cataloguing module)	15-17 December, 1999	Introduction to Innopac, the new library system. Staff were introduced to Innopac cataloguing. Training involved cataloguing of new materials and steps to take when searching the materials in Innopac, SACat, OCLC.
SABICAT cataloguing training	22nd -23rd May, 2000	Searching WorldCat for bibliographic records using CatME; searching WorldCat for authority records using CatME as well as subject authority records (LCSH) using CatME; downloading records from WorldCat to SACat and consequently to Innopac.
SABICAT cataloguing	8-9 May, 2001	Arranged for Senior Staff.
SABICAT cataloguing	27-28 June, 2002	Included exporting of records from WorldCat to SACat using CatME software.
Authority control	5-9 May, 2003	Trained on how to assign headings and the use of cross-references.
UB Authority control training	21-23 May, 2003	Introduction to authority control, principles, procedures, and functions; advantages of authority control. Training of some Diploma holders conducted by library Senior Staff.
MARC structure	23-31 July, 2003	Training of new Technical Services Assistants who were transferring from other sections and branches of the library. These were trained on MARC structure (the use of tags for bibliographic fields), the whole cataloguing procedure using Innopac, and downloading of records from SABINET (SACat) and OCLC, as well as editing those records in Innopac.[1] Training was conducted by library Senior Staff.

[1] In-service training activities scheduled for 1st April 1997-31st March 1998. p.1.

where bibliographic records were used, because no general consensus existed on the applications of standards. Among a list of topics that were presented, "The Role of Tertiary Education in the Promotion of Bibliographic Standards" presented by Helena Coetzee, interested me. Some of the issues covered in her paper were:

- causes of poor quality bibliographic records in cooperative databases
- reasons for the shortage of competent cataloguers
- whether or not it was still necessary to teach students how to catalogue, classify, and provide subject access.[31]

Some of the cataloguing-related issues that came up during discussions included the fact that:

- library schools do not prepare students adequately for the work they have to do when they qualify, which includes teaching them cataloguing in the context of bibliographic control
- students find the contents of cataloguing courses strange and often regard it as unnecessarily complicated
- knowledge of cataloguing is not seen as part of the work of a so-called information specialist
- students prefer rendering service to users
- the way in which cataloguing is taught does not correspond to the way it is done in practice
- cataloguing has become a very complex process, requiring knowledge different codes, formats, and systems
- lecturers in cataloguing do not know enough, especially about new developments, and seldom have the experience of cataloguing as it is actually done in libraries
- theory of cataloguing is not inspiring
- students should be involved in practical cataloguing so that they gain knowledge and integrate theory with practice.[32]

Most of the issues raised by this paper are pertinent and they reflect the general feelings of students who complete their studies here at the University of Botswana. Cataloguing and classification courses are practical courses and most of the lecturers who teach those courses lack practice. This lack of practice has a negative effect on students taking cataloguing and classification courses, especially Certificate and Diploma holders. These are some of the people responsible for doing cataloguing, and they need to be conversant with cataloguing rules in order to do original cataloguing of all kinds of materials. They also need to recognise an incorrect class number when they see it, either in the CIP or in any downloaded record. But often they are not able to do so.

CONCLUSION

There is no denying that the University of Botswana Library Management is playing a good role in the provision of basic training for its staff. The figures showing the number of staff sent for Certificate and Diploma courses since 1980 speak for themselves. The figures also show that training is not limited to Certificate and Diploma levels only. There are also staff members who are trained at the Master's level, whereas there are others who completed their Master's Degree programmes abroad. In addition to these training programmes the number of in-house training activities and workshops arranged for staff are impressive. The amount of teamwork between the Cataloguing Coordinator and Subject Librarians and the spirit in which cataloguing-related policy issues were discussed by both parties show a lot of commitment to cataloguing activities. Based on the analysis here, one can safely say that the University of Botswana Library Management and Technical Services Unit staff are doing their level best to sustain the cataloguing and classification activities. The Department of Library and Information Studies faculty also need to be commended for their efforts to sustain cataloguing-related activities in libraries in the region through the programmes they are offering to their students. As indicated in this paper, the Department of Library and Information Studies has never stopped offering the cataloguing-related courses ever since its inception in 1979. Although the course took off as a purely traditional cataloguing and classification course, as time went by, the curriculum changed to reflect changes in information technology. However, students have always been introduced to the basic principles of cataloguing, classification, and indexing.

It is, therefore, appropriate to say that even though we live in the era of modern technology with shared information and records, cataloguers will not become obsolete in the near future. However, many problems exist that require attention regarding the training of cataloguers in the workplace. Some of these are as follows:

1. The compartmentalisation of duties is one of the major problems since it denies staff opportunities to learn new operations and skills. This used to be prevalent among senior staff at the University of Botswana Library where certain tasks, such as classification and subject cataloguing, were considered professional tasks. It is not that junior staff are incapable of performing these skills. With proper training, supervision, and mentoring these people can perform these tasks effectively. As we are all aware, roles change and tasks formerly considered professional tasks are now often the responsibility of junior staff.

2. Lack of attachments for junior staff. Attachments for a period of three to six months in areas where similar tasks are performed using the same system would be a good source of motivation for these staff. They would begin to appreciate what they do and the challenges they face when cataloguing better than they do now. Perhaps that would create more of a sense of ownership in the database and greater commitment to the quality of the database than exists now. Individuals would begin to worry about errors found in the database by users and by staff in other sections, and would not wait for their supervisors to discover such errors. But as it is now, these people cannot wait to be transferred to other sections after working at Technical Services for two years because they do not enjoy what they do.

NOTES

1. University of Botswana and Swaziland. University College of Botswana calendar, 1979/1980. p.127.

2. Ibid., 1980/1981. p.128.

3. *Department of Library and Information Studies Handbook 2002/2003.* p.24.

4. Op. cit., 1979/1980. p.128.

5. University of Botswana and Swaziland. University College of Botswana calendar, 1979/1980. p.129.

6. University of Botswana and Swaziland. University College of Botswana calendar, 1981/1982. p.176.

7. Ibid.

8. Ibid., p.177.

9. University of Botswana calendar,1989/1990. p.227.

10. *Department of Library and Information Studies Handbook.* p.28.

11. Op. cit., 1986/1987. p.213.

12. Ibid., 1989/1990. p.231.

13. Department of Library and Information Studies. Departmental regulations, [2000?]. pp.21-22.

14. Ibid., p.25.

15. E. Greig. "Issues in education for cataloguing: from a manager's point of view." *Cataloguing Australia.* 19(2) 1993, pp.59-93.

16. O. Solis Valdespino. "The history of cataloguing and its importance in training of the Mexican Librarian" = "La historia de la catalocion y su importanicia en la formacion del bibliotecario Mexicano." *Revista Espanola de Documentacion Centifica.* 8(1) 1985, pp.95-115.

17. Ibid.

18. A. L. DeBoer, H. S. Coetzee, H. Coetzee. "Teaching cataloguing and classification of the University of Pretoria: thinking preferences of second year students." *Libri.* 51(2) 2001, pp.14-23.

19. Ibid.

20. Ibid.

21. Paula Phillips Carson, Kerry David Carson and Joyce Schouest Phillips. The Library manager's deskbook: 102 solutions to 101 common dilemmas. Chicago: American Library Association, 1995. p.111.

22. Gabrielle Harms. "On in-service training for librarians in public libraries" = "Zur Fortbildung der Bibliothekare/innen an Offentlichen Bibliotheka." *Buch und Bibliothek.* 38(3) 1986, pp.224-227.

23. Evert Slot. "Promoting in-service training in public libraries" = "Deskundigheidsbevordering in het openbare bibliotheekwerk." *Open.* 14(1) 1982, pp.11-19.

24. Ibid.

25. Ibid.

26. Paula Phillips Carson, op. cit., p.111.

27. Fran Lamusse. In-house cataloguing policies at U.B.: Humanities Policies. Paper presented at the On-line Cataloguing Workshop at U.B. Library: policies, challenges and prospects for the 21st century. January 1996. p.2.

28. Memorandum from Cataloguing Coordinator addressed to Subject Librarians, on Subject Cataloguing: subject headings, subject cataloguing practices and preferences in U.B. Library, dated 8/02/93. p.1.

29. Memorandum from Cataloguing Coordinator addressed to Subject Librarians, addressing the issue of processing of books for cataloguing, dated 29th August 1996. p.1.

30. Minutes of the Library Management Team meeting held on the 10th December 1999 at 10:30 in the office of the Director, Library Services. p.3.

31. P. J. Lor. Bibliographic standards in context: current challenges in bibliographic control. In: H. S. Coetzee, ed. Seminar on Bibliographic Standards for Promotion of Co-operation, Pretoria, 1-2 February, jointly organized by University of Pretoria, SABINET, SAILIS Sub-Committee for Bibliographic Standards. Pretoria: University of Pretoria, 1996. pp.1-2.

32. Ibid.

REFERENCES

Carson, Paula Phillips, Kerry David Carson, and Joyce Schouest Phillips. *The Library manager's desk book: 102 expert solutions to 101 common dilemmas.* Chicago: American Library Association, 1995.

DeBoer, A.L., H. S. Coetzee, and H. Coetzee, "Teaching cataloguing and classification at the University of Pretoria: thinking preferences of second year students." *Libri*, 51(2) 2001.

Department of Library and Information studies. Departmental regulations. [2000?]. *Department of Library and Information Studies Handbook.*

Greig, E. "Issues in education for cataloguing: from a manager's viewpoint." *Cataloguing Australia*. 19(2) 1993.

Harms, Gabriele. "Zur Fortbildung der Bibliothekare/innen an Offentlichen Bibliotheka" = "On in-service training for Librarians in public libraries." *Buch und Bibliothek*. 38(3) 1986.

In-service training activities scheduled for 1st April-31st March 1998.

Lamusse, Fran. In-house cataloguing policies at U.B.: Humanities Policies. Paper presented at the On-line Cataloguing Workshop at U.B. Library: policies, challenges and prospects for the 21st century. January 1996.

Lor, P. J. Bibliographic standards in context: current challenges in bibliographic control. In: H. S. Coetzee, ed. Seminar on Bibliographic Standards for Promotion of Co-operation, Pretoria, 1-2 February, jointly organized by University of Pretoria, SABINET, SAILIS Sub-Committee for Bibliographic Standards. Pretoria: University of Pretoria, 1996.

Memorandum from Acting Coordinator addressed to Subject Librarians, dated 29th August 1996 addressing the issue of processing of books for cataloguing. 1996.

Memorandum from Cataloguing Coordinator, addressed to Subject Librarians, dated 8/02/93, on Subject Cataloguing: subject headings, subject cataloguing practices and preferences in U.B. Library. 1993.

Minutes of the 20th Library Management Team (LMT) held on the 10th December 1999 at 10:30 in the office of the Director, Library Services.

Slot, Evert. "Deskundigheidsbevordering in het openbare bibliotheekwerk" = "Promoting in-service training in public libraries." *Open* 14(1) 1982.

University of Botswana and Swaziland. University College of Botswana calendar. *University of Botswana calendar.*

Valdespino, O. Solis. "La historia de la calogacion y su importanicia en la formacion del bibliotecario Mexicano" = "The history of cataloguing and its importance in training of the Mexican Librarian." *Revista Espanola de Documentacion Centifica*. 8(1) 1985.

The Relevance of Cataloguing in a Library Science Curriculum in Cross River State of Nigeria in This Technological Age

J. I. Iwe

SUMMARY. Since library science education started in Nigeria about half a century ago, cataloguing has been regarded as a core subject in the curriculum. With the diversification of subjects, some core subjects were made electives. This did not affect cataloguing. Nigerian libraries have not gone far in electronic data processing for the storage of data and information and, as a result, libraries are still manual-oriented. Even though some libraries in Cross River State of Nigeria have taken their first steps toward automation, the library schools still find it necessary to continue drilling students in traditional cataloguing. The question of the relevance of cataloguing in an automated library system arises and, using the descriptive survey methodology, this researcher investigates the hypothesis that cataloguing is still relevant in the library school curriculum. The finding is that the manual system will continue to be used for a long time and, thus, cataloguing will continue to be relevant, even with the computer-produced catalogue. *[Article copies available for a fee from The Haworth Document Delivery Service: 1-800-HAWORTH. E-mail address: <docdelivery@haworthpress.com> Website: <http://www.HaworthPress.com> © 2005 by The Haworth Press, Inc. All rights reserved.]*

J. I. Iwe is affiliated with the University Library, University of Calabar, Calabar, Nigeria.

[Haworth co-indexing entry note]: "The Relevance of Cataloguing in a Library Science Curriculum in Cross River State of Nigeria in This Technological Age." Iwe, J. I. Co-published simultaneously in *Cataloging & Classification Quarterly* (The Haworth Information Press, an imprint of The Haworth Press, Inc.) Vol. 41, No. 2, 2005, pp. 27-51; and: *Education for Library Cataloging: International Perspectives* (ed: Dajin D. Sun, and Ruth C. Carter) The Haworth Information Press, an imprint of The Haworth Press, Inc., 2006, pp. 27-51. Single or multiple copies of this article are available for a fee from The Haworth Document Delivery Service [1-800-HAWORTH, 9:00 a.m. - 5:00 p.m. (EST). E-mail address: docdelivery@haworthpress.com].

doi:10.1300/J104v41n02_03

KEYWORDS. Relevance, cataloguing, education for cataloguing, library science curriculum, Cross River State of Nigeria, Nigeria, technological age

INTRODUCTION

Cooper (1971) aptly defines relevance as the property of a text's being potentially helpful to a user in the resolution of a need. So, when we talk about a relevant document, text, or information, we mean that it may potentially help a user with his need. This is the reason why relevance is a very fundamental issue of information science and a most central concern of information retrieval systems. However, differences of opinion exist as to how the word is to be understood theoretically or measured operationally. There seems to be some sort of confusion in the use of the term both as an ideal for a system's goal and as an operational term in systems design. The goal of the ideal document retrieval system is to retrieve a document or text which may potentially help a user with his need (or which is relevant to his need). This is what we mean when we say that a text is relevant to some need. Sometimes when a document is on the same topic, we still say that it is relevant, but the level of its relevance depends largely on other issues.

Green (1995b) asserts that relevance, which is the relationship of a text to a user need that it helps to resolve, is multi-faceted and that prominent among these facets is topicality. There is a commonly held assumption that the determining factor in relevance relationship is topicality, often referred to as "topic matching," that is, where the topic or subject of the document matches the topic of a user need exactly. But experience has shown that documents on the same topic may or may not be relevant to what is needed. And so, whereas topicality is a major factor in relevance relationship, there are still other pertinent factors such as content of document. In this paper, the focus is not on texts and their relevance to user needs, but on the relevance of cataloguing as a core subject in library schools in a technological age such as ours, as it affects libraries in Cross River State of Nigeria.

When library education started in Nigeria about half a century ago, there had been a consensus as to what subjects should be taught. These included: Library in Society; Bibliography; Cataloguing and Classification; Reference and Reader Services; Acquisition; Library Management; and Introduction to the Library. But as time went on, the emphasis on specialization gave rise to elective courses which eventually divided the curriculum into two segments, namely, compulsory or core courses and elective or optional courses. With the introduction of computer-related studies, these compulsory subjects have become greatly diversified and de-emphasized in such a way that only very few courses can be said to be strictly compulsory. This trend was not applicable only to Nigeria but also to other parts of the world.

The IFLA Standards for Library Schools of 1976 declared that, within the professional curriculum, there should be a division between fundamental "core" subjects and specialized subjects. Fundamental subjects should be mastered first by all students. These core subjects were listed and they numbered twelve, and Cataloguing and Classification was subject number three on the list.

The whole system of library practice involves Information Storage and Retrieval. Materials are selected and when they come into the library, they are catalogued and classified among other processes. They are then stored and when the information in them is needed, they are retrieved and used. Cataloguing, as an aspect of this system, obviates the handling of unwanted materials as well as ensuring that the wanted items are found and utilized. The process of "finding" these needed materials is what cataloguing facilitates. A library's catalogue is the record of all bibliographic items in the library's collection. Creating these records is not an easy task, especially where the library is as large as University libraries, and where there is a constant inflow of materials.

Students have been found to be overwhelmed at their first introduction to the long Course Outline and Reading List in Cataloguing, but they feel great relief at the progression of the lectures when they discover that the whole spectrum of the outline consists basically of learning to identify and record the three essential parts of an entry, namely, headings under which library materials can be filed or arranged in the catalogue; the descriptions which identify the documents and show the user whether such document will satisfy his needs or not; and the location of the documents in their respective subject areas and on the shelves.

The relevance of cataloguing as a component of the curriculum of any library school needs no over-emphasis because it is a major aspect of professional training. When we talk about library skills in the library school, we are basically referring to the organisation and management of library materials as is done in the technical services section, and especially, in the processing division. We recognise here that, apart from cataloguing and classification, there are other "housekeeping chores" in the processing division, which include filing of cards; review and revision of the catalogue; and the physical preparation of materials for the shelves. But these are less intellectually demanding than cataloguing and classification and, as a result, they play a supporting role to the major assignments in the section.

Cataloguing has to do with the organisation of library materials. For these book and non-book materials to be used appropriately, the librarian must organise them in a way that makes it possible to find on demand any individual item in the collection. Organisation of library materials could be said to refer, firstly, to the creation of records that will make it possible for clientele to locate and retrieve any of the items in the library, and secondly, to the orderly arrangement of the library's materials on book shelves, in filing cabinets, periodical binders, map cases, or any other facility suitable to the type of material.

The course content of cataloguing as a subject in the curriculum concentrates on an overview of the cataloguing of both book and non-book materials according to the rules in the latest edition of the *Anglo-American Cataloguing Rules (AACR)*. This comprises three basic elements, namely, the selection of the main entry heading; the description of the material; and the tracings. The first element has to do with the selection of the field on the catalogue card by which the card is filed in the catalogue or listed in the bibliography. The second element concerns the description of the material, both physically and otherwise, to enable it to be located and retrieved easily from the collection. The third element has to do with the identification of the subject areas of the material, and providing its classification number and the other added entries as access points.

Librarianship and Internationalism

Librarianship is strictly an international profession and library education has turned out to be one of the beneficiaries of the internationalism of librarianship. The need to provide such national and international services which will enable users to access the widest possible field of information gave impetus to such internationally acclaimed programmes as the Universal Bibliographic Control (UBC) and Universal Availability of Publications (UAP). This standardization of the format of catalogue entries and the rules guiding their creation has tremendously curtailed differences and problems associated with cataloguing. Whether it is the North American or the British or even the Canadian text of the *Anglo-American Cataloguing Rules*, or even the African, or more specifically, the Nigerian modifications, the basics are the same and the student of Librarianship should be made to see himself as part of this worldwide project aimed at universalizing information retrieval in such a way that anybody anywhere can have easy access to information. The objectives of the Internet and Virtual Library Schemes all point to the achievement of more effective access to information. Many Nigerian students go further in education within the profession, and some of them prefer to study abroad. While receiving further education in foreign countries, they should be able to fit into the systems there, having been conversant with the standardized principles and practice of cataloguing back home.

Cataloguing, Creativity and Art

The importance of cataloguing lies not only in its professional attributes but also in its artistic and creative nature, which makes it a factor to be reckoned with in the development of individuals' potential. One of the objectives of cultural and creative art is to promote, foster, develop, and preserve individual potential for the benefit of mankind. Art means different things to different people but it is both a process and a product. One unique thing about art is that you can create new things and solve artistic problems in an individual way. Cataloguing is an art (it is believed to be, first and foremost, a science), because it sometimes demands some amount of creativity, skill, and ability to seek ways and means of assisting the reader, through catalogue entries, to get to his information needs.

Unlike the creative artist, the cataloguer does not use paint, clay, wood, stone, crayon, etc., but like him, he uses paper (catalogue cards), pencil, and ruler. The cataloguer, like the artist, requires good powers of observation and imagination to be able to succeed in individual growth as a librarian. He discovers in the process of his job that, in spite of the existence of the *Anglo-American Cataloguing Rules (AACR)*, the *International Standard Book Description (ISBD)*, Subject Headings lists, etc., as guides, he may sometimes make some decisions on his own as a professional librarian. Multi-disciplinary works must be placed in the subject area where they are needed most and where they will not get lost. The cataloguer should consider such materials critically in relation to the needs of the users, and decide where to place them to the users' benefit. This means that he must have the ability to see and appreciate the needs of his clientele, as well as distinguish between what is standard and what is partisan.

Art is a language of communication and, in cataloguing, the librarian communicates with the readers on what materials exist in the library and how best the reader can get at them. He uses his catalogue entries to make this communication possible. Like the artist, he delves back into history as he considers each catalogue entry to see whether there is any relationship, and he makes this known to the reader. The cataloguer must be versatile in all subjects, since his materials deal with all possible subjects, to be able to discuss intelligently with his readers in their different disciplines, represent his materials in the best possible terms, and give maximum assistance to readers in their different fields of learning. A communication that is blurred, unclear, or uncommunicative is not worthwhile. A cataloguer must be prepared to make the impact expected of him by his clientele. Practice makes perfect, they say, and cataloguing being essentially a practical subject, demands a high level of flexibility and practical work. The conscientious cataloguer discovers that, through practice, his potential can be developed, his skills fostered, and his artistic ability improved. There may be rules underlining the choice of main entry heading, but what does a cataloguer do when author or title is inappropriate for the identification of a material? He provides the appropriate data. What does he do when he meets rare materials, perhaps with peculiar or indigenous features which do not fall within the stipulated guidelines in the *AACR*? He creates their data. These are some of the challenges which face the African cataloguer, more still, the Nigerian cataloguer, and he is required to exercise his specialized knowledge in solving the problems. According to Bloomberg and Evans (1981), all library staff, not just those in the cataloguing department, need a basic knowledge of cataloguing. No wonder cataloguing has remained a core subject all these years.

Cataloguing rules are not static. They can be adjusted and readjusted to suit the needs of the reading public. In "Notes," the cataloguer has many decisions to make on his own, depending on his investigations. Tracings and call numbers are also the personal decisions of the cataloguer, depending on his findings in the Subject Headings List and the Schedules. He decides whether he requires two or more subject headings and what should be chosen as added entries.

Right through the processes of cataloguing, the cataloguer exercises his initiative in deciding what should appear on the entry card, thereby training and developing his potential to the benefit of all readers. His skills are constantly put to the test and, as an artist, he creates and recreates where necessary. The challenges of cataloguing have prompted some libraries in Nigeria to work out modifications on existing international standardized schemes to incorporate areas where the guidelines are either insufficient or inappropriate. In the University of Calabar, Nigeria, the Law Schedule has been modified under KJ to accommodate African primary materials, with special interest in the Nigerian Law Reports which emanate from the existing thirty six (36) states of the country. Given all of the above, one can conveniently assert that cataloguing, if properly articulated and implemented, can help to develop the various potentials of the individual cataloguer, and this is one of the objectives to be achieved with students, both in the classrooms and in the workrooms.

This Technological Age

This technological age, often referred to as the Information Age, dawned on the world during the second part of the last century. Nigeria, being an underdeveloped country like the rest of the continent of Africa, has not yet embraced technology in its full force because of some obvious reasons: an underdeveloped telecommunication infrastructure; poverty, and as a result, lack of capital and investment resources for network development; the high cost of computer and IT components and materials; inadequate training of personnel and lack of facilities, etc. Nonetheless, the Federal Government of Nigeria has initiated a National University Information Agenda in which all of the Federal Universities, Colleges of Education and Polytechniques would be interconnected and hooked to the Internet to access information in its widest possible sense. The Nigeria Universities Network (NUNet) scheme of the Nigerian government is aimed at providing essential electronic infrastructure and training for the development of a University-linked network for academic and research collaboration. With time the network may spread to other sectors including the rural areas. The University of Calabar has benefited from this NUNet scheme as one of the institutions earmarked for the VSAT network for distance education, academic networking, and research collaboration by the National University's Commission. On the state government level, the public library system has started building up its database with the intention of automating the libraries in the very near future. Already the State Library Building Complex in Calabar is being used as a computer training centre for all Civil Servants in the state. This means that the Cross River State of Nigeria, as well as the University of Calabar, is gradually moving towards technological advancements. In spite of this, the card catalogue is still being used in all libraries, including the University of Calabar library where the only library school in the state exists. Cataloguing is still a core subject in the library school at the first-degree level and is compulsory for all students.

In the developed parts of the world where computer-produced catalogues are now being used, IT has drastically transformed information management. Since the libraries in Cross River State are now building up their databases as a step towards computer-produced catalogues, the librarians need a re-orientation in cataloguing to be able to cope with the challenges of the transformation from a manual to an electronic system.

The information processing and management that was known and practiced in libraries has automatically been compounded into the provision of the expected organisation of the resources of the library and the needed access to information. IT has changed the very substance of libraries as the custodian of information and has transformed simple library operations to comprehensive information systems, thereby drastically changing the role of the librarian. The online public access catalogue (OPAC), which makes it possible for multiple access to be obtained online, completely negates the production of such access points on catalogue cards, with all of the time and energy that entails.

In the automated system, the access variables tagged searchable fields play the same role as main entry headings in the manual system. However, sometimes the rules differ. For example, in the manual system, a book that has more than three authors is entered under title and added entry made for the first named author. In the automated system, all of the names of such authors are made access points or created into searchable fields on the computer.

The impact of Information Technology has had more tremendous effect on cataloguing and classification than on other aspects of librarianship, because classification schemes and other cataloguing tools are now on compact disc and can be accessed online. With the introduction of Cataloguers' Desktop, the strain and stresses of cataloguing are reduced while the problem of searching through bibliographic and cataloguing tools have been removed.

According to Kenneth Furuta (1990), the future of cataloguers lies not only in the management of automated systems but also in meeting users' needs. They should provide appropriate access points which will lead the user to the satisfaction of his or her information needs.

PURPOSE

The purpose of this research is to highlight the relevance of cataloguing in the library school curriculum especially in the Cross River State of Nigeria in a technological age such as ours when most libraries of the developed world have embraced the automated system, and the manual system is gradually being phased out. Many libraries in the state have accumulated computers and have started building up their databases with the aim of automating their library systems. In spite of this, cataloguing is still a core subject in the library school curriculum.

SCOPE

The scope of this research is narrowed down to Cross River State of Nigeria, one of the thirty-six states of the country. The state has four tertiary institutional libraries of which the largest is the University of Calabar library. Others are: one very active public library with branches in some of the divisional headquarters; a few school libraries; one branch of the National library; and three special libraries. There is only one library school in the state, situated in the University of Calabar, and it is interesting to note that a significant number of the librarians in the state attended this library school. With the advent of online information storage and retrieval in the country, the question arises as to whether cataloguing should continue to be taught in the library school or not. Some people actually thought that that was the end of cataloguing as a subject in the curriculum. Well, this was not the first time such fears had been entertained about cataloguing by librarians: Svenonius (1981) reports that about a century ago, Cutter lamented that the golden age of cataloguing was over. He made this lament when the Library of Congress initiated its printed card distribution service. According to the report, Cutter was lamenting that cataloguing had become a lost art because it would be performed centrally. After a century, these same fears are becoming more real than ever before, with librarians of the 21st century fearing that cataloguing might be dropped from the curriculum as a result of technological advancements and online catalogue systems.

This researcher watched the very slow pace at which libraries in Cross River State are doing their conversion processes, as well as the online cataloguing, and concluded that manual cataloguing will continue to be taught in library schools as a core subject for a long time to come.

HYPOTHESIS

The hypothesis of this research is that cataloguing, as a core subject, is relevant in the library school curriculum in Cross River State in spite of the move towards automation of libraries. To test this hypothesis, an investigation is conducted into the state of affairs in these libraries to discover how far these libraries have gone in their automation processes, and what the librarians feel about the relevance of cataloguing at this present time as a core subject in library schools. The research questions which will guide the researcher in these investigations include: Is cataloguing an important subject in the curriculum? Does cataloguing equip students for work in the different divisions of the library? Can cataloguing equip the individual for life even outside the library? Does the knowledge of cataloguing enhance the processes of the computer-produced catalogue? Is cataloguing still relevant in library practice in spite of automation of libraries?

THEORETICAL FRAMEWORK

Toward the end of the 20th century, scholars (Barry 1994; Froelic 1991; Harter 1992; Green 1995) put forward two principal theories of relevance, namely, a systems theory and a user-centered theory. The systems theory is based on matching documents with search requests, whereas the user-centered theory is based on the user's perception of the satisfaction of his research needs. The systems theory is believed to be multifaceted and the most popular of its facets is topicality–the idea of seeing relevance through matching topics or subjects. This theory has been seen to be unsatisfactory because many matching topics have turned out to have non-relevant issues as contents. The user-centered theory, which is more convincing, is achieved not only by retaining topicality as an important factor in identifying materials relevant to a user's needs, but also by recognizing that other factors such as recency, personal availability, content, and source quality contribute to this satisfaction.

In their exploration into the relevance theory relationship, Green and Beans (1995) tried to prove that only careful analysis of empirical data can determine which particular relationships account for topical relevance. They did this by conducting an investigation into topical relevance relationships. This paper, like its predecessor, is tailored towards conducting an investigation into the relevance of cataloguing in the curriculum of Library Science in Cross River State in this technological age.

LITERATURE REVIEW

Since the inception of libraries and information centers as manpower development centers in library and information science, a lot has been written on cataloguing, its significance in information storage and retrieval, its core position in the curriculum, its artistic content, and its endowments in creativity. In the review of such literature, the following are identified: Marco (1994) asserts that as far back as 1901, and even up to the present age of computerization in libraries, Cataloguing and Classification has remained a core subject in the United States of America. This shows that the diversification and de-emphasis on compulsory subjects in the library curriculum is a trend not only in Nigerian Library Schools, but also in other parts of the world. Marco, in this same article, opines that a study of the core requirements in accredited programmes of the United States shows that only two subjects–Cataloguing and Reference–are required in more than half the schools. This means that in spite of the de-emphasis over compulsory subjects in library schools, cataloguing is still seen by many of the schools as a necessary requirement in the curriculum.

In the curriculum guidelines for information studies issued by UNESCO (1978), W. L. Saunders offered a programme that will provide the essential generalist basis from which future specialization of all sorts will be developed. In this programme, he listed such courses as: Human communication; User studies; Sources of information; Information/data storage and retrieval, organisational aspects; and Electives. Saunders included Cataloguing and Classification within Information/data storage and retrieval, which means that he regards cataloguing and classification as a very essential basic course that could guide students in their choice of special subjects.

Martell (1981) asserts that since library catalogues hold a central place in the structure of the library as an institution, they are the products of the library's technology. He adds that with the advent of the computer and its free-word association in the development of the online catalogue, the catalogue has the potential for automatic updating that eases maintenance problems and the inflexibility of the current manual catalogues. This researcher agrees with Martell that the library catalogue occupies a central position in the structure of the library and this is essentially the reason why cataloguing has always been regarded as a core subject in the library school curriculum.

While seeing cataloguing as a relevant subject in the curriculum, Derr (1983) seriously advocates for the integration of theory and practice in library education. The reason behind this proposal is that he sees both theory and practice as two sides of the same coin, with one enhancing the other. However, this type of integration can succeed only with a constant focus on the overall aims and objectives of the course during the period of implementation. In the University of Calabar, Processing Division, integration of theory and practice is enhanced by allowing students and their teachers full responsibility and the autonomy necessary for professional practice, and by encouraging free association and the exchange of ideas between students and staff on duty.

Monroe (1981) believes that fieldwork satisfies two major needs, namely, social integration and competence in skill performance. These are not isolated needs but are part and parcel of the overall objectives of library education. Schamber et al. (1990) asserts that relevance, the relation between a document and a search question, is a multi-dimensional and dynamic concept extending beyond traditional definition. He adds that even though topic-matching is closely associated with relevance, other issues such as subject content and related qualities are important in real search situations. According to Cool (1993) different meanings of relevance occur throughout an information search as a result of their encounters with people, things, and ideas. Anderson (1998) believes that studies of user-centered relevance that address evaluation criteria only after a particular information retrieval system has been selected do not adequately address the concept of relevance because many decisions about relevance are made even before the search begins.

METHODOLOGY

The methodology used for this research is the descriptive survey methodology. In conducting the investigation, 50 librarians were selected randomly from eight different libraries in Cross River State of Nigeria. These librarians have gone through some library school professional training ranging from diploma to first degree, to Master's, to Ph.D. degrees. The instrument used was a questionnaire developed by the researcher. This questionnaire has two sections, section A and section B. Section A sought information on the personal data of the librarians, such as age, sex, professional qualification, Library school attended, etc. Section B sought information based on experience in relation to: Cataloguing and library education; Cataloguing in a manual and a computer-produced catalogue; and Cataloguing as applicable in present-day Cross River State libraries. This section also sought to find out whether cataloguing was compulsory in their library school at their time of study, and from their experience, whether they think that cataloguing should continue to be taught in library schools as a core subject, since many libraries in Cross River State are already moving toward automating their libraries.

Section A had 7 questions while Section B had 17 questions. The questions were administered to individual professional librarians who read through them and ticked the ones appropriate to their belief, observation, experience, and conviction. Out of the six different types of libraries that exist in Nigeria, five are represented in this investigation, namely, the academic library, school library, national library, public library, and special library. When the questionnaires were returned, the responses were analysed through profiles based on percentages. Below are the findings of the investigation as analysed in the data provided.

DATA PRESENTATION AND ANALYSIS

Out of the 50 questionnaires administered to respondents, 45 were returned and well-attended to. Section A, which had 7 questions, gave information on the personal data of respondents as shown in Table 1 and Table 2.

Table 1 shows that only about 4.4% of the respondents have the Ph.D. degree while 35.4% have a Master's degree in Library Science. These data show that approximately 40% of the respondents have post-graduate educational qualification in Library Science. Table 2 also shows that, whereas 35.4% of the respondents have had more than 20 years of working experience in library service, 22.2% have had over 15 years of experience and 20% have had over 10 years of working experience. These data depict that a total of 77.6% of the respondents have had at least 15 years of working experience in libraries. One can then assert that the majority of the respondents are quite experienced library staff who have not only undergone some level of educational attainment in librarianship, but have also had considerable years of work experience in different sections of the library and, as a result, are well-equipped to give personal opinions on the relevance of cataloguing in the library education curriculum.

TABLE 1. Educational Qualification of Respondents

Qualification of Respondents	Ph.D.		MLS		PGDL		B.LS		DIP		Total	
	F	%	F	%	F	%	F	%	F	%	F	%
	2	4.4	16	35.4	1	2.4	22	38.9	4	8.9	45	100

F = Frequency
% = Percentage

TABLE 2. Years of Working Experience of Respondents

Experience	21 yrs. & above		16-20 yrs.		11-15 yrs.		6-10 yrs.		0-5 yrs.	
	F	%	F	%	F	%	F	%	F	%
	16	35.4	10	22.2	9	20	6	13.3	5	11.1

RESPONSES TO RESEARCH QUESTIONS

The data from the responses to the research questions are tabulated in Tables 3 and 4.

Table 3 shows that every single respondent sees cataloguing as a very important subject in the Library Science curriculum. It is significant to note that 100% of the respondents "strongly agreed" to the importance of cataloguing as a core subject in Library Science. They have no doubt in their minds that it should be so. It is interesting, too, to add here that the respondents, who graduated from eleven (11) different library schools, had cataloguing as a compulsory subject during their first-degree library school experience. This must have considerably influenced their decisions in responding to the questionnaire.

Table 4 shows that respondents believe that cataloguing has a high potential for equipping students for work in the different divisions of the library. The questionnaire focused attention on six different library divisions, namely, the Processing Unit; the Acquisitions Unit; the Research Division; the Reader Services Division; the Library Automation Division; and the Printing and Bindery Division. Table 5 shows the distribution of responses toward these respective divisions. It is interesting to note that whereas there was a general consensus that cataloguing equips students for the processing of library materials with 100% positive response, Reader Services records 88.9%; Acquisition records 57.8%; Research Library and Automation divisions record 73.3% each; and the Printing and Bindery Division records only 26.7%. The data show that

TABLE 3. The Importance of Cataloguing in the Library Science Curriculum

Is cataloguing an important subject in the curriculum?	Agree		Disagree		Total	
	F	%	F	%	F	%
	45	100	-	-	45	100

TABLE 4. High Potential of Cataloguing in Equipping Students for Work in the Different Divisions of the Library

Does cataloguing equip students for work in the different divisions of the library?	Agree		Disagree		Total	
	F	%	F	%	F	%
	32	70.4	13	28.9	45	100

the majority of the respondents disagree with the view that cataloguing equips students for work in the bindery.

Furthermore, Table 6 shows the responses to the assertion concerning the high potential of cataloguing in equipping individuals for life. Earlier in this paper, the researcher said that cataloguing is an art and highlighted the creativity it can develop in individual librarians. This researcher, who strongly believes in these assertions, decided to seek the opinions of fellow libraries and library staff on this, and the positive response is overwhelmingly 95.6%, whereas only 4.4% disagree on the issue.

There is a strong belief among librarians that a knowledge of cataloguing enhances the processes of the computer-produced catalogue which, in many ways, identifies and describes library materials almost completely in the same way that the manual catalogue does. For example, each identifies the author, the title, the imprint, access points, etc. Table 7 depicts the responses on this issue. Overwhelmingly, 97.8% agree to this assertion while only 2.2% disagree. It is interesting to note that a few of these libraries have already started building up their databases with the objective of automating their libraries, so they have a good idea of what a computer-produced catalogue would look like, and they can compare and contrast this with the manual catalogue.

Before analysing this data, this researcher would like to address the questionnaire where information is sought on the percentage of resources in libraries in Cross River State of Nigeria which have already been converted into machine-readable format. Of the respondents, 73.3% report

TABLE 5. Distribution According to Sections of the Library

Divisions	Agree		Disagree		Total	
	F	%	F	%	F	%
Processing	45	100	-	-	45	100
Acquisition	26	57.8	15	33.3	41	91.1
Reader Service	40	88.7	5	11.1	45	100
Research Library	33	73.3	10	22.2	43	95.6
Automation Division	32	73.3	10	22.2	42	93.1
Bindery	12	26.7	31	68.9	43	95.6

TABLE 6. High Potential of Cataloguing in Equipping Individuals for Life

Has cataloguing high potential in equipping individuals for life?	Agree		Disagree		Total	
	F	%	F	%	F	%
	43	95.6	2	4.4	45	100

TABLE 7. The Enhancement of the Computer-Produced Catalogue by the Knowledge of Cataloguing

Does knowledge of cataloguing enhance the processes of the computer-produced catalogue?	Agree		Disagree		Total	
	F	%	F	%	F	%
	44	97.8	1	2.2	45	100

that about 20% of their resources have been converted; 4.4% report that theirs is 40%; and 6.7% of the respondents report 60%. The truth in these figures is that conversion of the catalogue into machine-readable format has begun in libraries in Cross River State and so respondents are fully aware of the demands in the questionnaire and have been honest in their responses. Incidentally, 100% of the respondents agree that cataloguing is still relevant in the library school curriculum in spite of the automation of libraries, as can be seen in Table 8. As a matter of fact, 75.6% "strongly agreed" to the assertion, while 24.4% agreed to it. There was no disagreement in any form.

TABLE 8. The Relevance of Cataloguing in the Curriculum

Is cataloguing still relevant in the curriculum in spite of the automation of libraries?	Agree		Disagree		Total	
	F	%	F	%	F	%
	45	100	-	-	45	100

DISCUSSION OF FINDINGS

From the data presented, it is apparent that librarians in Cross River State of Nigeria see cataloguing as a very important subject in the Library Science curriculum, not only because it is very relevant to professional practice in this present technological age, but also because it has high value in the development of the individual. It equips the student-librarian and prepares him for library professional practice in different sections of the library. Even in the present age of information technology and the online catalogue, the knowledge of cataloguing enhances and facilitates the production of the online catalogue. In spite of the fact that some libraries in Cross River State have begun to automate their libraries by building up their databases, the librarians believe that the knowledge of cataloguing is still very necessary in Library Science school and that cataloguing should neither be dropped from the curriculum nor relegated to the background. It should be seen as a core subject and treated as such.

Perhaps of great interest is the response to an item in the questionnaire which tries to find out when the libraries in Cross River State might be fully automated. Eleven respondents believe that it will take about 15 years to have their libraries fully automated; 14 respondents think that their libraries will take about 5 years; while another 11 project 8 years. It is significant to note that only 2 respondents project 2 years, while 4 project 11 years. This confirms the fact that the rate of automation in these libraries is quite slow for obvious reasons. The libraries in Nigeria are facing many problems in their march toward automation. Apart from the very common and general problems of lack of funds, poor technological know-how, lack of equipment and facilities, unskilled personnel, etc., there is also the problem of inexperience in the use of application packages.

The University of Calabar library, which can be seen as the model library in Cross River State not only because it has one of the largest library buildings and collections in West Africa, but also because it has the largest number of academic and professional staff within the state, had to halt its automating processes when it discovered that the TINLIB application software it was using was grossly inadequate. Moreover, the capacity of the single computer being used was found to be too small, and there was no fund to meet up with the challenges of the occasion. Therefore, the scheme that took off the previous year was dropped and has not been resuscitated since. However, it is interesting that the automation of academic libraries in Nigeria has become a national issue which is being addressed by the Federal Government of Nigeria.

CONCLUSION

The fear sometimes expressed by librarians that cataloguing may no longer be relevant in Library Science and, as a result, should be dropped from the curriculum has been quashed by many scholars. According to Ola and Adeyemi (1998), IT has not eroded cataloguing and classification practices but has brought about a finesse that has caused cataloguers all over the world to reshape their roles in the information society. Perhaps, such things as punctuation, capitalization, transcription, etc., which have been pertinent in manual cataloguing, are no longer necessary and, as a result, have been dropped, but the primary role of providing access points which lead users to the materials is still a very necessary and important work of the cataloguer. IT has succeeded in making this processing of information less strenuous and cumbersome for the cataloguer. Many librarians who have been involved in both manual and online cataloguing feel that there is no substantial change in the cataloguing in either system, and they also acknowledge that online cataloguing is a lot easier, faster, and appropriate. With the cataloguers' Desktop and CD-MARC provided online, the jobs of cataloguers are enhanced.

Cataloguing is still relevant as a core subject in the Library Science curriculum in Cross River State of Nigeria in spite of the move toward library automation. This paper recommends that this transformation from the manual to an online system be taken more seriously by the governments concerned, so that the automated system of library practice be fully embraced as quickly as possible, as were our counterparts in the developed parts of the world. This will facilitate the interconnectivity of these libraries to libraries outside the state and to international networking systems. It is very interesting to note in this conclusion that 100% of the respondents declared a liking for cataloguing in the question that asked: Do you like cataloguing? Perhaps it is a feeling of nostalgia that is making students fear for cataloguing, which is not yet dead and buried. Cataloguing is still alive and relevant and will continue to be taught in Library Science, online catalogues notwithstanding.

BIBLIOGRAPHY

Barry, C. L. (1994) User-defined Relevance Criteria; An Exploratory Study. *Journal of the American Society for Information Science 45* 149-159.

Bloomberg, Marty and G. Edward Evans. (1981) *Introduction to Technical Services for Library Technicians.* 4th ed. Littleton, Colorado. Libraries Unlimited.

Cool, C. (1993) Information Retrieval as Symbolic Interaction. Examples from Humanities Scholars 56th *ASIS Annual Meeting*; 274-277.

Cooper, W. S. (1971) A Definition of Relevance for Information Retrieval. *Information Storage and Retrieval 7* 19-37.

Derr, Richard I. (1983) The Integration of Theory and Practice in Professional Programmes. *Journal of Education for Librarianship 23* (3) 193-206.

Froelich, T. J. (1991) Towards a Better Conceptual Framework for Understanding Relevance for Information Science Research. *Proceedings of the 54th Annual Meeting of the American Society for Information Science 28* 118-125.

Furuta, Kenneth. "The Impact of Automation on Professional Cataloguers. *Information Technology and Libraries 9* (3) Sept. 1990.

Green, Rebecca. (1995) Topical Relevance Relationships I: Why Topical Matching Fails. *Journal of the American Society for Information Science 46* (9): 646-653.

Green, Rebecca and Bean, Carol A. (1995) Topical Relevance Relationships II: An Exploratory Study and Preliminary Typology. *Journal of the American Society for Information Science (JASIS) 46* (9): 654-662.

Harter, S. P. (1992) Psychological Relevance and Information Science. *Journal of the American Society for Information Science 43* 602-615.

Marco, Guy A. (1994) An International Structure for Library Education. *International Library Review 13* 357-363.

Martell, Charles. (1981) The War of AACR2: Victors or Victims. *Journal of Academic Librarianship 7* (1) 4-8.

Monroe, Margaret E. (1981) Issues in Field Experience as an Element in Library School Curriculum. *Journal of Education for Librarianship 22* (1 & 2) 57-73.

Ola, C. O. and Adeyemi, B. M. (1998) Information Technology: An Erosion of Cataloguing and Classification Practices. A paper delivered during the Business Session of the Cataloguing and Classification Section of the Nigerian Library Association's 36th Annual Conference and General Meeting at the National Universities Commission, Abuja, from 4th-8th May, 1998.

Schamber, L. Eisenberg, M. B.; Nilan, M. S. (1990) A Re-Examination of Relevance: Toward a Dynamic, Situational Definition. *Information Processing and Management 26* 755-776.

Svenonius, Elaine. (1981) "Directions for Research in Indexing, Classification and Cataloguing" *Library Resources and Technical Services 25* (1): 88-103.

APPENDIX

QUESTIONNAIRE

THE RELEVANCE OF CATALOGUING IN PRESENT-DAY LIBRARY SCIENCE EDUCATION IN CROSS RIVER STATE.

SECTION A

INSTRUCTION: Please tick ( ) against the responses as they correspond to each item.

PERSONAL DATA

1. Name of your library...

2. Gender of respondent: F ( )   M ( )

3. What is your highest qualification in Library Science?

     (i)   Diploma ( )

     (ii)   B.A./B.Sc./B.L.S Library Science ( )

     (iii) PGD ( )

     (iv)   MLS ( )

     (v)   Ph.D. ( )

4. Years of Service

     (i)   0-5 yrs. ( )

     (ii)   6-10 yrs. ( )

     (iii) 11-15 yrs. ( )

     (iv)   16-20 yrs. ( )

     (v)   21 yrs. and above ( )

5. In what Section of the Library are you working?

    (i)   Acquisition division   ( )

    (ii)   Processing division   ( )

    (iii) Reader Services division ( )

    (iv) Research Library   ( )

    (v)   Systems Development division (computerization section)/Bindery ( )

6. In what Sections of the Library have you worked before now?

    (i)   Acquisition division   ( )

    (ii)   Processing division   ( )

    (iii) Reader Services division ( )

    (iv) Research Library division ( )

    (v)   Systems Development division (computerization section)/Bindery ( )

7. I did my first Library Science Education in this Library School:

    (i)   University of Ibadan Library School ( )

    (ii)   ABU Zaria Library School   ( )

    (iii) UNN Nsukka Library School   ( )

    (iv) UNICAL Library School   ( )

    (v)   UNIUYO Library School   ( )

    (vi) Imo University Library School   ( )

    (vii) Any other (please mention)   ( )

APPENDIX (continued)

SECTION B

INSTRUCTION: Tick against the options that correspond to your opinion or observation.

NOTE: **SA**   =   **Strongly Agree**

   A   =   **Agree**

   N   =   **Neutral**

   D   =   **Disagree**

   SD   =   **Strongly Disagree**

8. Cataloguing was a compulsory subject in my first Library Science School.

   (a) Strongly Agree ( )   (b) Agree ( )   (c) Neutral ( )

   (d) Disagree ( )   (e) Strongly Disagree ( )

9. Cataloguing should remain compulsory in Library Schools because it equips students for the work in the Processing Division of the Library when they become employed.

   (a) Strongly Agree ( )   (b) Agree ( )   (c) Neutral ( )

   (d) Disagree ( )   (e) Strongly Disagree ( )

10. It equips students for the work in the Acquisition Division of the Library.

   (a) Strongly Agree ( )   (b) Agree ( )   (c) Neutral ( )

   (d) Disagree ( )   (e) Strongly Disagree ( )

11. It equips students for the work in the Reader Services Section of the Library.

   (a) Strongly Agree ( )   (b) Agree ( )   (c) Neutral ( )

   (d) Disagree ( )   (e) Strongly Disagree ( )

12. It equips students for the work in the Research Library Division.

    (a) Strongly Agree ( )   (b) Agree ( )   (c) Neutral ( )

    (d) Disagree ( )   (e) Strongly Disagree ( )

13. It equips students for the work in the Systems Development (Automating) Division of the Library.

    (a) Strongly Agree ( )   (b) Agree ( )   (c) Neutral ( )

    (d) Disagree ( )   (e) Strongly Disagree ( )

14. It equips students for the work in the Bindery.

    (a) Strongly Agree ( )   (b) Agree ( )   (c) Neutral ( )

    (d) Disagree ( )   (e) Strongly Disagree ( )

15. It equips students for life as Librarians even outside the Library.

    (a) Strongly Agree ( )   (b) Agree ( )   (c) Neutral ( )

    (d) Disagree ( )   (e) Strongly Disagree ( )

16. If properly articulated, practised and applied cataloguing can help to develop the various potentials of an individual.

    (a) Strongly Agree ( )   (b) Agree ( )   (c) Neutral ( )

    (d) Disagree ( )   (e) Strongly Disagree ( )

17. Cataloguing is an important part of the curriculum in Library Education whether manual or electronic.

    (a) Strongly Agree ( )   (b) Agree ( )   (c) Neutral ( )

    (d) Disagree ( )   (e) Strongly Disagree ( )

18. Even though most libraries in Cross River State have started building up their databases as a first step towards automation, it is still necessary to continue teaching cataloguing in Library Schools.

    (a) Strongly Agree ( )   (b) Agree ( )   (c) Neutral ( )

    (d) Disagree ( )   (e) Strongly Disagree ( )

APPENDIX (continued)

19. The knowledge of cataloguing enhances the processes of computer-pro-
    duced catalogues.

    (a) Strongly Agree ( )   (b) Agree ( )   (c) Neutral ( )

    (d) Disagree ( )   (e) Strongly Disagree ( )

20. In cataloguing, the Librarian communicates with the readers on what ma-
    terials exist in the Library and how to locate them.

    (a) Strongly Agree ( )   (b) Agree ( )   (c) Neutral ( )

    (d) Disagree ( )   (e) Strongly Disagree ( )

21. We have gone far in the march of our library towards library automation.

    (a) Strongly Agree ( )   (b) Agree ( )   (c) Neutral ( )

    (d) Disagree ( )   (e) Strongly Disagree ( )

22. The percentage of the resources in my Library already converted to ma-
    chine-readable format in the database is:

    (a) 0-20 ( )   (b) 21-40 ( )   (c) 41-60 ( )

    (d) 61-80 ( )   (e) 81-100 ( )

23. Cataloguing is still relevant to our library practice because we still use the
    manual (card catalogue) system.

    (a) Strongly Agree ( )   (b) Agree ( )   (c) Neutral ( )

    (d) Disagree ( )   (e) Strongly Disagree ( )

24. It is my belief that in the next few years, my library would become fully
    automated having tackled the problems of funding, staff training, clientele
    training, computer equipment (hardware and software) provision and fa-
    cilities.

    (a) 0-2 yrs. ( )   (b) 3-5 yrs. ( )   (c) 6-8 yrs. ( )

    (d) 9-11 yrs. ( )   (e) 12-15 yrs. ( )

25. I like cataloguing in spite of its rigorous and highly demanding disposition.

    (a) Strongly Agree ( )   (b) Agree ( )   (c) Neutral ( )

    (d) Disagree ( )   (e) Strongly Disagree ( )

The Education and Training of Cataloguing Students in South Africa Through Distance Education

Linda M. Cloete

SUMMARY. This paper discusses the education and training of cataloguing students in South Africa at a distance education institution where the focus is on career-specific training. The position of the cataloguing course in the curriculum and the content of the course are explained. The utilization of media and technologies in offering the course, and anticipated changes and possible future developments are discussed. *[Article copies available for a fee from The Haworth Document Delivery Service: 1-800-HAWORTH. E-mail address: <docdelivery@haworthpress.com> Website: <http://www.HaworthPress.com> © 2005 by The Haworth Press, Inc. All rights reserved.]*

KEYWORDS. Cataloguing training, computer-based learning, cataloguing education, co-operative education, distance learning, South Africa, training resource program, virtual cataloguing classroom

Linda M. Cloete is Senior Lecturer, Department of Information Science, Unisa, Private Bag X6, Florida, South Africa, 1710 (E-mail: lcloete@iafrica.com).

[Haworth co-indexing entry note]: "The Education and Training of Cataloguing Students in South Africa Through Distance Education." Cloete, Linda M. Co-published simultaneously in *Cataloging & Classification Quarterly* (The Haworth Information Press, an imprint of The Haworth Press, Inc.) Vol. 41, No. 2, 2005, pp. 53-69; and: *Education for Library Cataloging: International Perspectives* (ed: Dajin D. Sun, and Ruth C. Carter) The Haworth Information Press, an imprint of The Haworth Press, Inc., 2006, pp. 53-69. Single or multiple copies of this article are available for a fee from The Haworth Document Delivery Service [1-800-HAWORTH, 9:00 a.m. - 5:00 p.m. (EST). E-mail address: docdelivery@haworthpress.com].

Available online at http://www.haworthpress.com/web/CCQ
© 2005 by The Haworth Press, Inc. All rights reserved.
doi:10.1300/J104v41n02_04

INTRODUCTION

The training of cataloguers forms an important part of the education and training of librarians since cataloguing is still considered one of the most important skills for organizing information. Cataloguing and reference work are still considered the core of Library and Information Science courses (Smith 1985, 35; Stieg 1992, 109; Clack 1993, 27; Holley 2002, 45). Bender (cited in Bearman 1987, 29) mentions that "traditional skills associated with acquiring, organizing, and disseminating information will still be needed by tomorrow's information professional at the entry level." In their perspective on cataloguing and classification in Africa, Mutula and Tsvakai (2002, 62) also emphasize the importance of cataloguing as the core area of professional librarianship in the African information environment.

One of the most important skills for organizing information is cataloguing. The automation of libraries has also changed the nature of the work in cataloguing departments. The functions and tasks of librarians in cataloguing departments have changed. However, bibliographic work can never be completely computerized. Human input, especially with regard to authority control, is very important (Snyman 1998). Co-operative cataloguing has become an important function amongst libraries. Copy cataloguing is now one of the most important tasks of cataloguers. To adapt and utilize a copy record for a library's own purposes, it is very important that the cataloguer have a sound knowledge of cataloguing principles. This can only be achieved through proper education and training in cataloguing. Zyroff (1996, 47) mentions a number of valid reasons why training in cataloguing should now, even in the age of automation, co-operative cataloguing, and shared cataloguing, still be considered a core competency. Her statement that "[t]hose who have not spent time applying and creating subject and name headings, authority records, descriptive cataloguing and classification codes, and indexing norms don't have in-depth perspective on the structure of information" captures the essence of organizing information. Cataloguing skills also play an important role in the organizational aspects of knowledge management (Hill & Intner 1999, 7-8). It has therefore become more important than ever that cataloguers receive appropriate education and training through all possible modes.

Cataloguing training is usually conducted by the following means:

- Contact training
- Distance training
- In-service training

The education and training of Library and Information Science students through distance education is becoming more popular, since an increasing number of students are unable to afford the luxury of full-time studies at a contact class institution.

CATALOGUING TRAINING IN SOUTH AFRICA THROUGH DISTANCE EDUCATION

Until 2003, education and training of library and information students through distance education were offered by two institutions, namely the University of South Africa (UNISA), Department of Information Science, and Technikon Southern Africa (Technikon SA), Department of Library and Information Studies. Traditionally, universities in South Africa offer the academic-orientated programs and technikons offer more technical, career-specific training programs. As from 2004 the two institutions merged to become the University of South Africa (UNISA). UNISA is now Africa's first comprehensive distance higher education institution offering academic-orientated programs as well as career-focused programs. Within this institution it is possible to align programs in order to meet the academic and technical needs of business and industry. The focus in this paper is on the career-specific training program for library and information professionals as offered by the institution previously known as Technikon SA's Department of Library and Information Studies. The program is continued within the new UNISA.

LIBRARY AND INFORMATION STUDIES STUDENTS

The Department of Library and Information Studies offers training in library and information studies through distance learning to students who already work in libraries and information services as administrative assistants and who wish to become fully qualified librarians and information workers. Students work in a wide range of environments: community libraries in rural areas, public libraries in urban areas, academic libraries at universities and technikons, and specialized information centers.

The majority of students resides and works in South Africa, but we also have students in neighboring countries such as Namibia, Zimbabwe, Swaziland, and Lesotho. The Department also collaborates with the Kenya School of Professional Studies (KSPS) through an official agreement. Students in Kenya complete the first part (equivalent to two years at our Department) of their studies at KSPS. They may then enroll at our Department for a B Tech degree. They have to complete the third-year subjects before they may continue with the fourth-year subjects for the degree.

THE PROVISION OF CO-OPERATIVE EDUCATION WITHIN A FLEXIBLE HIGHER LEARNING SYSTEM

Staff members regularly visit libraries and related establishments to inform themselves of current practices and to identify and discuss changes in the labor market. They regularly review the value and relevance of program curricula and syllabi with the aid of the Advisory Committee on Library and Information Studies.

The Department focuses on providing hands-on training for the library practitioner in all sectors of libraries and information services. Within the flexible higher educational system and based on the principles of cooperative education, the Department has been able to establish and maintain an effective experiential learning system.

EXPERIENTIAL LEARNING

"Experiential learning is a way of learning which is facilitated by a philosophy of co-operative education traditionally practiced by technikons in South Africa" (Lazenby 1998, 20). Stanford (1997,181) found that there was general agreement that experiential learning enhances part-time studies in Library and Information Science. Experiential learning is considered an effective part of cataloguing training and is usually included in cataloguing instruction (Garrett 1997, 129). The experiential training of cataloguers is addressed mostly through internships and field experiences (Saye 1993, 129).

Internship, as a form of experiential learning, requires a student to gain practical, supervised experience in a cataloguing department under the guidance of a practitioner (Evans 1993, 56-57). Internship is considered a valuable learning experience for the student. It does, however, take up the practitioner's time, who has to carefully plan the internship program, select applicable examples for the student to work with, and evaluate the student's work.

The education philosophy of the university is that, through co-operative education, students should be prepared for their prospective occupations. Co-operative education is a teaching or training method that combines studying at the university with experiential training and, therefore, presupposes co-operation between the university and the industry or profession concerned. It is thus important to obtain the input of practicing professional librarians in the training of students in library and information studies. To facilitate this close co-operation between the university and the community of practicing library and information professionals, and to enable students to be trained in the relevant practical skills, students are required to complete experiential training in libraries and/or information services.

The establishment where experiential training is conducted, consequently serves as the "practical class" or "laboratory" where the various practical assignments are carried out and the relevant skills practiced and mastered. Because students will need guidance, advice, and support in carrying out the practical assignments, a system has been developed whereby students work under the supervision and guidance of a mentor. The mentor has to be an experienced, suitably trained person with whom the student has regular contact.

QUALIFICATIONS, KNOWLEDGE, AND SKILLS REQUIRED FROM CATALOGUERS

The contents of job advertisements for cataloguers were analyzed during 2003. Analysis was done with regard to knowledge and skills required, and the duties and responsibilities for the cataloguer.

From the analysis it was clear that cataloguing skills still play an important role. Apart from the required relevant degree (B Bibl, B Tech, B Inf) of 3-4 years, the requirements as well as responsibilities could be summarized in Table 1. The outcomes of the cataloguing courses need to meet, as far as possible, the requirements shown in the table.

OUTCOMES-BASED EDUCATION AND TRAINING

The Department of Education of South Africa adopted an outcomes-based approach to education in 1997 (South Africa, 1997).

TABLE 1. Requirements and Responsibilities Expected of Catalogers in South Africa

Requirements	Responsibilities
Knowledge and understanding of AACR2R, DDC, UDC, LC, LCSH, NLM classification, Mesh and indexing	Cataloguing, classification, and subject analysis of: monographs, audio-visual material, periodicals, and in-house reports
Proven expertise in online cataloguing	Maintaining authority catalogue files
Automated cataloguing on USMARC/ MARC 21-based system	Original and copy cataloguing
Knowledge of the URICA, INNOPAC, CPALS and OCLC systems	
Online cataloguing on SABINET, SACat, WorldCat and SABICAT	

Outcomes-based education and training focuses on learner-centered education, which is aligned with the constructivist principle that the learner has to construct meaning. Critical cross-field outcomes and specific learning outcomes underlie the outcomes-based education and training approach. Critical cross-field outcomes and specific learning outcomes for existing library and information qualifications and exit levels have been registered (for the interim period) with the South African Qualifications Authority (SAQA).

Critical cross-field outcomes promote communication skills, critical thinking, problem solving, and teamwork skills—all vital skills for the successful cataloguer.

Specific learning outcomes are context-specific and describe the competence which learners should be able to demonstrate in particular areas of learning at certain levels. Learners are measured against pre-stated criteria. The learning outcomes are set for each specific exit level. At technikons in South Africa the exit levels are determined by the different qualifications that a student can obtain, namely National Certificate: Library and Information Studies, National Higher Certificate: Library and Information Studies, National Diploma: Library and Information Studies, Baccalaureus Technologia (BTech): Library and Information Studies, and Magister Technologia (MTech): Library and Information Studies.

QUALIFICATIONS OFFERED

The Department offers undergraduate as well as postgraduate training in Library and Information Studies since 1993. The following national instructional programs are offered:

- National Certificate: Library and Information Studies (first-year subjects)
- National Higher Certificate: Library and Information Studies (first- and second-year subjects)
- National Diploma: Library and Information Studies (first-, second-, and third-year subjects)
- B Tech: Library and Information Studies (five fourth-year subjects)
- M Tech: Library and Information Studies (Coursework and research paper or Dissertation)

Offerings in the Department are developed in conjunction with advisory committees comprised of lecturers, representatives of professional bodies, major employer organizations, and student representatives. Study assignments are related to the world of work, encouraging students to integrate theory with practice.

Curriculum design and course planning does not begin with the content anymore, but with the intended outcome (Day 1997, 32). The following qualifications are offered by the Department in order to meet the competencies and outcomes set for library and information professionals. These competencies have been established internationally (Crosby 2000, 3-8; Nofsinger 1999, 11; Rehman 2000, 57-58; Robbins 1998, 26) and the outcomes are also included in the library and information studies qualifications currently registered with SAQA. The core modules of the library and information studies curriculum are: library and information practice, information retrieval (including cataloguing training), library and information technology, and user studies.

The learning outcomes per exit level for Information Retrieval are shown in Table 2.

There are four exit levels for students in Library and Information Studies, namely:

- National Certificate for students who have successfully completed all first-year-level subjects and cannot, or do not, wish to continue further with their studies

- National Higher Certificate for students who have successfully completed all second-year-level subjects and cannot, or do not, wish to continue further with their studies
- National Diploma for students who have successfully completed all third-year-level subjects
- B Tech degree for students who have successfully completed all fourth-year-level subjects

The majority of students enroll for the National Diploma followed by the B Tech degree. The National Certificate and National Higher Certif-

TABLE 2. Learning Outcomes per Exit Level

Exit level	Subject name and description	Learning outcomes
National Certificate: Library and Information Studies	Information Retrieval I Introduction to: information storage and retrieval, the theory and practice of cataloguing (AACR2R), the theory and practice of classification (DDC21), the theory and practice of subject headings (*Sears*), and introduction to reference work	Catalogue monographs on AACR2R level 1, do limited copy cataloguing, link copies of a bibliographic record to the record.
National Higher Certificate: Library and Information Studies	Information Retrieval II An advanced study of: information retrieval, the theory and practice of cataloguing (AACR2R), the theory and practice of classification (DDC21), theory and practice of subject headings (*Sears*), and reference work	Catalogue monographs on AACR2R levels 1 and 2, assign DDC21 classification numbers, assign subject headings (using *Sears List of Subject Headings*), do copy cataloguing, link copies of a bibliographic record to the record.
National Diploma: Library and Information Studies	Information Retrieval III Machine readable cataloguing (MARC 21), authority control, co-operative cataloguing, organisation of cataloguing routines and the management of the cataloguing department, reference work in the electronic environment, bibliographic networks, organisation and the management of the reference department	Catalogue monographs on AACR2R levels 1, 2 and 3, assign DDC21 classification numbers, assign subject headings, catalogue in computerized format (MARC 21) and conduct authority work and control on a bibliographic database.
BTech: Library and Information Studies	Information Retrieval IV Bibliographic description of non-book material, analytical bibliographical description, advanced techniques of indexing, abstracting, and thesaurus construction	Catalogue monographs and non-book materials on AACR2R levels 1, 2 and 3, assign DDC21 classification numbers, assign subject headings, catalogue in computerized format, and conduct authority work and control on a bibliographic database. Conduct indexing, abstracting, and thesaurus construction.

icate are available as exit levels for students who cannot complete their studies at the National Diploma level.

The cataloguing component of the program forms part of the subject Information Retrieval. A progressive approach is followed in the subject. On the first-year level, students do basic cataloguing and classification. On the second-year level, the more in-depth and advanced cataloguing and classification is taught. On third-year level, the emphasis is on cataloguing in the electronic environment, including MARC 21, cooperative cataloguing, copy cataloguing, and the utilization of cataloguing networks. On the fourth-year level, advanced cataloguing of non-book materials, indexing, abstracting, and thesaurus construction are taught.

By incorporating the cataloguing and classification component in all four years, students are exposed to these aspects throughout their studies. Cataloguing and classification training is, therefore, not a number of modules addressed in only one or two particular years. We believe that the continuous exposure is important so that students who enter employment at a library and information service center do not have to undergo refresher courses in cataloguing or lengthy on-the-job training.

Educating and training students over a period of four years also gives us the opportunity to address some of the issues mentioned by Holley (2002, 47-51). Issues such as the goals of cataloguing, simulating real world situations, and the application of technology can be addressed over a longer period of training time.

Students who wish to exit their studies at any level can also do so with at least some basic understanding of cataloguing.

In order to prepare students for the third-year-level work of cataloguing and information retrieval in the electronic environment, two subjects from the curriculum are prerequisites. Those subjects are End-user Computing (first-year subject), where students are taught computer literacy, and Library and Information Technology II (second-year subject), where students are introduced to automation, networks, basic HTML, and metadata.

From the learning outcomes in Table 2, it is clear that the emphasis is on training in the use of cataloguing tools such as AACR2R, DDC and *Sears List of Subject Headings*. The *Sears List of Subject Headings* is used since it is more readily available to students. As indicated by Mutula & Tsvakai (2002, 65), most African countries use the AACR2R, DDC, LC, and UDC.

EDUCATION AND TRAINING METHODS

Distance education has traditionally been provided through paper-based correspondence, and the written word is the main medium of instruction. Interaction between the lecturer and student is limited to course material and books, completed assignments from the students, and projects related to their work experience. This low level of interaction between lecturer and student has led to a number of problems in the education and training of cataloguers. Students often need an immediate answer to a question or problem in a practical exercise for them to continue to the next step. With paper-based distance education they usually have to wait weeks to receive an answer to problems encountered during the study of a particular skill. Other delivery modes such as audio, video, and computer technologies are also utilized in distance education (Steiner, 1998), but the time delay in interaction between the student and lecturer still exists. This asynchronous instruction has the advantage that students may choose their own instructional time, but there is no real-time interaction and immediate feedback from the lecturer.

Henderson (1987, 20) suggests that cataloguing students should be presented with sound educational experiences and that enthusiasm for the subject should be fostered. Hill (1985, 730) states that too few students are exposed to the fun of cataloguing and do not appreciate the intellectual exercise. A training resource that includes interactive instruction with the utilization of multimedia could provide this meaningful learning opportunity.

According to Clack (1993, 35), cataloguing teachers and trainers "must be innovative in their teaching strategies and methodologies." Training should not only be done for present practice, but also for the future.

UTILIZATION OF AN INTEGRATED TRAINING RESOURCE PROGRAM

The Department utilizes an integrated training resource program consisting of a mix of media and technologies for the education and training of cataloguing students. The program is described in more detail by Cloete, Snyman, and Cronjé (2003) and is only briefly discussed here.

The training resource consists of:

- print material (study guides, tutorial letters, and prescribed books)
- practical exercises (drill exercises in print format)
- contact classes
- communication channels
- mentor system
- TSA COOL (virtual campus)
- computer program

The printed materials consist of study guides and tutorial letters. The study guide consists of printed study text as well as drill exercises that form an integral part of a training resource. All of the students receive study guides, and printed material is considered the main medium for training. The printed materials must be designed very carefully with clear learning objectives to be met by the contents and evaluation methods applied in the training resource.

Contact classes involve group discussion opportunities conducted in the regions where the largest student numbers are concentrated. They provide an opportunity for face-to-face contact with the lecturer and fellow students. Students can discuss content problems and clarify issues. Classes should revolve around students' needs and not become merely formal lectures.

Communication channels include telephone, fax, and electronic mail and discussion group facilities. These channels can be used to communicate with the lecturer and fellow students to clarify course content problems or just to exchange ideas and comments. Students must be reminded of these opportunities and the responsible use of them should be explained.

The mentor system is a form of experiential learning conducted in libraries where students conduct practical projects under the guidance of a mentor. Students are advised (and encouraged) by duly qualified and experienced practitioners (or mentors). Students conduct work-related projects (cataloguing) under the supervision of a mentor. Clear guidelines of what is expected from them should be provided to the students and mentors.

TSA COOL is combined with the traditional print-based distance education media and could therefore be referred to as a hybrid campus. TSA COOL partially supports a constructivist paradigm in that it encourages collaborative learning. This takes the form of group activities, a discussion group facility, links to sites with related topics, an e-mail facility to the authors of the site, and contact with live subject matter experts. TSA COOL promotes discovery learning in that it has links to other organizations' web sites.

The computer program provides additional practice for cataloguing students and involves the incorporation of problem-solving situations. The program includes true and false questions, multiple-choice questions, completing diagrams and flow charts, and placing books in their correct positions on shelves by first determining the correct classification number. The incorporation of multimedia provides an element of reality. Graphics, sound, and text attract attention.

The following advantages and disadvantages have been experienced with the utilization of a mix of media and technologies in the education and training of cataloguing students:

Advantages

- Students find it more interesting to work with different media and technologies.
- The limitations of one medium such as print can be overcome by the variety of other media and technology.
- Students can work on the course whenever it suits them.
- Neither the distance that geographically separates students, nor the time of day when it suits them to study, places limitations on their progress.
- A degree of individualized instruction is possible.
- A variety of information and additional exercises can be provided by the different media and technologies.
- The electronic media make it possible to train students in specific skills of the cataloguing course which are not possible through the print media.
- The electronic media make it possible to create simulations of cataloguing situations.
- Immediate feedback is possible through the facilities on the virtual campus and the computer program.
- Testing and retesting is possible with a computer.
- The variety of computer-based training stimulates students and promotes positive attitudes to learning.
- It is possible for the student to navigate the content.
- Connectivity makes belonging to discussion groups possible so that students have the opportunity to give and share their opinions.

- The computer program and TSA COOL encourage group work and collaborative learning. This helps students to get to know each other better, and reduces the social isolation associated with distance learning.
- Students can reflect and learn from other students when they participate in the discussion group facility on TSA COOL.

Disadvantages

- The electronic media are still very new to the students and they are therefore reluctant to use them.
- Students have difficulty in obtaining access to the Internet.
- Students do not all have adequate hardware or appropriate software to access the multimedia and interactive capabilities of the virtual campus.
- It takes time and technical support to become a competent user of the virtual campus.
- Students consider the use of the electronic media and technology as extra work in an already demanding course.
- Lack of computer skills creates problems for certain students to adjust to the electronic media.

Important Considerations When Using a Training Resource

The following considerations influence the application of a training resource program and should be carefully considered:

- Students use media and technologies to meet their needs and not necessarily in ways expected by the lecturer.
- Students with little understanding of or familiarity with computers will find the use of media and technology difficult at first, and will have to spend more time on the media and technology than on the contents of the course.
- Frequent communication with students is essential.
- No assumptions should be made about students' abilities, experience, etc. A student profile should be compiled first.
- Students should be told exactly what they can and should do with each component of the training resource program, for example, what each function of TSA COOL is for and how to use it.
- Merely placing course material on the virtual campus, i.e., using it as just another delivery mode, should be avoided.

- Students do not use all of their study material, but only what they consider essential for passing the course.
- The utilization of a mix of media and technologies allows interaction between students, lecturers, and sources of information.
- Many frustrations can be related to technical problems, e.g., Internet connections and download time. Technical problems diminish as students progress with the course.
- Students tend to forget that a variety of communication channels to the lecturer and fellow students are available. They often complain that geographical distance makes it impossible to benefit from the training. They need to be reminded of all possible channels, such as e-mail, fax, and discussion groups.
- There is no definite preference for using the computer program in a group or individually. Students who worked on it during observations preferred to work in groups.
- The immediate feedback provided by the program, which includes correct answers as well as explanations, was highly appreciated.
- Students start to use one component of the program, such as the group discussion facility on TSA COOL, to organize another component, namely, additional contact classes amongst themselves.

DEVELOPMENTS TOWARD
A VIRTUAL CATALOGUING TRAINING CLASSROOM

The ultimate goal of the training resource program is to develop an online, fully interactive course: an online virtual cataloguing classroom. This means that technology is incorporated as a substitute for the classroom and traditional distance training methods. The students may never meet the lecturer in person. The virtual cataloguing classroom incorporates all of the technologies already used and discussed. Yontz (2002, 307-308) has also made some valuable suggestions that could be incorporated. The course is then only offered over the Internet. Weaknesses of this approach lie in the fact that students may become disassociated with the course since they do not feel involved. Lack of personal interaction will also contribute to this.

Since students are familiar with the traditional classroom setup, the classroom metaphor could be kept. The classroom serves as the interface in which students present their own work and view their fellow students' work. Students can thus enter into the spirit of a physical classroom. Training of librarians in the virtual environment is further motivated by the move towards the virtual library or "library without walls." Soon more and more librarians will work in such an environment and, therefore, similar training is considered appropriate.

CHALLENGES FOR THE FUTURE

In their discussion, Mutula and Tsvakai (2002) explain the challenges of the cataloguing and classification of Africana materials and how the utilization of Western cataloguing and classification practices and tools do not adequately meet the needs for cataloguing these materials. A consideration that will have to be investigated is whether more emphasis should not be placed on the training of cataloguers in Africa for these challenges. For example, on fourth-year level in the subject Information Retrieval IV, students could be introduced to the cataloguing and classification of Africana materials.

Another important aspect of cataloguing training that should be addressed is the organization of digital resources and metadata training. Presently the subjects Library and Information Technology III and Library and Information Technology IV offer students the opportunity to study the management of digital libraries. These subjects are web-based and are offered only online. Since many of our students work in traditional libraries, these subjects are electives. However, in the traditional libraries, digital resources are also becoming more and more a part of the collections. The detailed aspects of organizing and cataloguing digital resources should be addressed in Information Retrieval.

CONCLUSION

The Department of Library and Information Studies strives to offer library and information students the opportunity to equip themselves for the challenges in most of the library and information sectors. They are, therefore, trained in the core aspects of library and information work applicable to the more traditional libraries, as well as for the requirements and challenges set in a technological, advanced information world.

Many of the requirements of trained cataloguers cannot be met in the traditional contact class or through the traditional distance training methods. The opportunities provided by the training resource program will contribute to improved knowledge and interaction. It offers the student many more possibilities of interacting and being active in mastering the cataloguing course.

Multimedia capabilities of the virtual campus and computer program mean that learners can access a variety of means of representing information. They can also be afforded opportunities to engage in active learning, working both alone and in group situations with others.

REFERENCES

Bearman, T.C. (ed.) 1987. Educating the Future Information Professional, *Library Hi Tech*, 5(2):27-40.

Clack, D.H. 1993. Education for Cataloging: A Symposium Paper. *Cataloging & Classification Quarterly*, 16(3):27-37.

Cloete, L.M., Snyman, R. & Cronjé, J.C. 2003. Training Cataloguing Students Using a Mix of Media and Technologies. *Aslib Proceedings*, 55(4):223-233.

Crosby, O. 2000. Librarians: Information Experts in the Information Age. *Occupational Outlook Quarterly*, Winter 2000-01:3-15.

Day, J. 1997. Curriculum Change and Development. In: Elkin, J. & Wilson, T. (eds.) 1997. *The Education of Library and Information Professionals in the United Kingdom*. London: Mansell.

Evans, A.F. 1993. The Education of Catalogers: The View of the Practitioner/Educator. *Cataloging & Classification Quarterly*, 16(3):49-57.

Garrett, L. 1997. Dewey, Dale, and Bruner: Educational Philosophy, Experiential Learning, and Library School Cataloging Instruction. *Journal of Education for Library and Information Science*, 38(2):128-136.

Henderson, K.L. 1987. Some Persistent Issues in the Education of Catalogers and Classifiers. *Cataloging & Classification Quarterly*, 7(4):5-25.

Hill, J.S. 1985. Wanted: Good Catalogers. *American Libraries*, November:728-730.

Hill, J.S. & Intner, S.S. 1999. Preparing for a Cataloguing Career: From Cataloguing to Knowledge Management. [cited 6 December 2003]. Available at: http://www.ala.org/congress/hill-intner_print.html.

Holley, R.P. 2002. Cataloging: An Exciting Subject For Exciting Times. *Cataloging & Classification Quarterly*, 34(1/2):43-52.

Lazenby, K. 1998. *Constructivism and the Creation of Virtual Campuses in Higher Education*. MEd in Computer-Assisted Education mini-dissertation, University of Pretoria, Pretoria.

Mutula, S.M. & Tsvakai, M. 2002. Historical Perspectives of Cataloguing and Classification in Africa. *Cataloging & Classification Quarterly*, 35(1/2):61-77.

Nofsinger, M.M. 1999. Training and Retraining Reference Professionals: Core Competencies for the 21st Century. *The Reference Librarian*, 64(1999):9-19.

Rehman, S. 2000. *Preparing the Information Professional: An Agenda for the Future*. Westport, Conn.: Greenwood Press.

Robbins, J.B. 1998. Curriculum Reform in Library and Information Science Education. In: Roy, L. & Sheldon, B.E. (eds.) 1998. *Library and Information Studies Education in the United States*. London: Mansell.

Saye, J.D. 1993. Education for Technical Services: A Summary of the Symposium. *Cataloging & Classification Quarterly*, 16(3):125-141.

Smith, L.E. 1985. Where Are the Entry Level Catalogers? *Journal of Library Administration*, 6(2):33-35.

Snyman, M.M.M. 1998. The Standardisation of Names and the Provision of Information. Provision of Information in Southern Africa Conference (20 August 1998: Pretoria).

South Africa. Department of Higher Education. 1997. *White Paper on Higher Education*. [Cited 7 December 2003]. Available: http://www.polity.org.za/govdocs/white_papers/hihied.html.

Stanford, S.W. 1997. Evaluating ATM Technology for Distance Education in Library and Information Science. *Journal of Education for Library and Information Science*, 38(3): 180-190.

Steiner, V. 1998. What Is Distance Education? [Cited 6 December 2002]. Available: http://www.fwl.org/edtech/distance.html.

Stieg, M.F. 1992. *Change and Challenge in Library and Information Science Education*. Chicago: American Library Association.

Yontz, E. 2002. When Donkeys Fly: Distance Education for Cataloging. *Cataloging & Classification Quarterly*, 34(3):299-310.

Zyroff, E. 1996. Cataloging Is a Prime Number. *American Libraries*, 27(May):47-50.

ASIA

Education
for Cataloging and Classification
in China

Zhanghua Ma

SUMMARY. Education for cataloging and classification in China includes university education, continuing education, and professional training, and is provided at the basic training, junior college, undergraduate, and graduate levels. Cataloging, classification, and subject analysis are generally the core courses in the university curricula and are offered with other required courses. Recent changes in the curricula have been the adjustment and integration of courses, the application of computer technology, the increase of practice, the update of course contents, and the improvement of teaching methods. The future trends of cataloging and classification education in China may include: constant improvement of the teaching system, standardization of library science programs, intro-

Zhanghua Ma is Professor, Information Management Department, Peking University, Beijing, China (E-mail: mzhua@pku.edu.cn).

[Haworth co-indexing entry note]: "Education for Cataloging and Classification in China." Ma, Zhanghua. Co-published simultaneously in *Cataloging & Classification Quarterly* (The Haworth Information Press, an imprint of The Haworth Press, Inc.) Vol. 41, No. 2, 2005, pp. 71-83; and: *Education for Library Cataloging: International Perspectives* (ed: Dajin D. Sun, and Ruth C. Carter) The Haworth Information Press, an imprint of The Haworth Press, Inc., 2006, pp. 71-83. Single or multiple copies of this article are available for a fee from The Haworth Document Delivery Service [1-800-HAWORTH, 9:00 a.m. - 5:00 p.m. (EST). E-mail address: docdelivery@haworthpress.com].

duction to new topics, promotion of graduate education, enhancement of continuing education and training, and development of online courses. *[Article copies available for a fee from The Haworth Document Delivery Service: 1-800-HAWORTH. E-mail address: <docdelivery@haworthpress.com> Website: <http://www.HaworthPress.com> © 2005 by The Haworth Press, Inc. All rights reserved.]*

KEYWORDS. Cataloging, cataloging education, classification, subject analysis, professional education, China

Cataloging, classification, and subject analysis, as the basis of all kinds of library work, are always emphasized in Chinese librarianship. Therefore, cataloging, classification, and subject analysis have always been considered to be the core courses of library science in China. These courses are normally taught through university education, continuing education, and vocational training, and they have shaped the teaching system of library science. This article tries to give an overview of the types, levels, contents, recent changes, and trends of Chinese cataloging and classification education. The following descriptions and examples refer solely to library science education in Mainland China.

TYPES AND LEVELS
OF CATALOGUING AND CLASSIFICATION EDUCATION
IN CHINA

Since the number and type of libraries are so large in China, there is a great demand for professional education in cataloging and classification at different levels and in different forms. In order to meet the national need for professional cataloging and classification skills, the teaching of cataloging, classification, and subject analysis takes three major forms.[1,2]

The first is university education, the most important way of training library professionals in China. Such educational programs are provided by library science or information management schools, and are offered at both undergraduate and graduate levels. At present, there are more than fifty universities or colleges that have library science programs in China. The library science programs at Peking University and Wuhan University are designated as the key programs by the Education Ministry of China. The undergraduate programs usually require four years of study and include a full range of cataloging, classification, and subject analysis courses. The undergraduate student will receive a bachelor's degree upon graduation. In graduate programs, cataloging and classification courses are offered at more advanced, research levels.

The second is continuing education, including correspondence courses, TV courses, and part-time graduate courses. Of these courses, the correspondence courses have the longest history and the biggest influence on professional training. As early as the 1950s, the Library Science Department of Peking University began its correspondence courses to teach students in many provinces, and many library professionals were trained this way. Peking University's correspondence program was interrupted during the Great Culture Revolution (1966-1976) and resumed in 1980. Since then, Wuhan University and Northeast Normal University have also provided correspondence courses in library science. Most students of the correspondence courses are library employees, and the courses are conducted through a combination of self-study, face-to-face teaching on campus, practical work, and homework assignments–a teaching system for library science which includes cataloging, classification, and subject analysis as its core courses. The correspondence programs are offered at preliminary (junior college) and undergraduate (college) levels. The preliminary program requires three years of study and the undergraduate program takes five years to complete. These programs have played an important role in training library professionals. For the past decades, students of the correspondence courses have been all over the country, except for Shanghai, Tibet, Hong Kong, and Taiwan. Students graduating from the correspondence programs receive a certificate for their study in either the preliminary or the undergraduate program. Some students with excellent grades from the undergraduate program can also receive a bachelor's degree upon completion of their senior thesis. Up to 2003, more than 16,000 correspondence students had graduated from the Library Science Department of Peking University–far more than the number of regular undergraduate students in the same department.[3] In addition, the Central TV University began to enroll students for its TV courses in the 1980s, which included cataloging, classification, and indexing language as the key subjects of study. The part-time graduate classes have appeared a new model in recent years and offer special topic courses related to cataloging and information retrieval languages.

The third is on-the-job training, including the various training workshops or special classes. Such training usually aims to meet the special job requirements of some libraries. Library employees who do not have a library science degree are normally required to attend such training activities before undertaking their library work. Cataloging, classification, and subject analysis are normally the basic content of these training workshops. Certificates are issued for these courses and are recognized by the libraries that send their employees to these training courses. Other relevant workshops may also be organized when new editions of subject thesauri and/or new cataloging rules are implemented in order to promote the application of these new subject terms and cataloging rules. Libraries or library associations usually sponsor and organize such training workshops.

Based on the current development of cataloging and classification education in China, the teaching of cataloging and classification takes place at four levels: (1) basic professional training, (2) junior college training, (3) undergraduate training, and (4) graduate training (toward a Master's or higher degree). The basic professional training provides the students with basic knowledge and operational skills, and enables them to apply their skills to their work in libraries. A wide array of professional workshops provide training at this level, including the courses offered by technical or vocational schools in the past, which have been gradually replaced by junior college courses. Junior college training focuses on the development of practical skills, while briefly introducing some theories and principles, in order for the students to build the skills for cataloguing and indexing and become capable of resolving problems in their work. Through undergraduate education, students develop a better understanding of the essential theories and principles, as well as mastering the basic operational skills. The students not only can solve cataloging problems, but also can revise and compile the thesauri, classification schedules, and cataloging rules. Many undergraduate programs and correspondence courses in universities usually offer training at this level. Through graduate education programs, the students build up a thorough understanding of cataloging theories, trends of development, and hot issues in cataloging and classification. They can analyze and resolve a variety of practical problems by applying the theories and knowledge they have learned. The graduate programs at universities offer courses at this level.

DESIGN AND INSTRUCTION
OF CATALOGING AND CLASSIFICATION COURSES

As early as the 1930s and 1940s, when the teaching of cataloging began in China, cataloging was one of the fundamental courses. Since then, the instruction of cataloging, classification, and subject analysis has gone through many changes. Take the library science programs, for example. Over the past years, different universities have developed their own system of courses for cataloging and classification under different names, although the contents of these courses are more or less the same. These courses include general cataloging, cataloging for Chinese language materials, cataloging for Western language materials, library classification, classification and subject analysis, subject indexing, classification language and subject language, information retrieval languages, and so on. Some library schools also offer such courses as indexing, natural language indexing and retrieval, and current development in information retrieval languages. Each school designs and selects different curricula according to their programs. To standardize the teaching of cataloging, the Chinese Ministry of Education invited faculty members from over ten colleges and universities to develop a national syllabus for the core courses of library science programs, which includes courses in cataloging and classification, and subject analysis. This development not only reaffirmed the vital status of cataloging and classification courses, but also greatly impacted the design and development of these courses.[4,5]

Table 1 provides information about the curricula of cataloging, classification, and subject analysis for the library science programs in eleven Chinese universities that were surveyed in 2002. The curricula design for library science programs, according to this survey, can be stated as follows:

First, cataloging, classification, and subject analysis are regarded as the required courses in most library science programs.

Second, most of the cataloging curricula are designed along the lines of cataloging, and classification and subject analysis (or retrieval language), but a few programs still follow the traditional curriculum design of classification, subject analysis, Chinese language materials cataloging, and Western language materials cataloging.

Third, there is a wide variation in the time allocation for the cataloging courses in these curricula. This reflects the impact of different social and teaching environments on the curriculum design.

Based on the curricula of the Library Science Program at Peking University, the essential contents of the two popular courses–cataloging, and classification and subject analysis–are described.[6,7,8]

The cataloging courses of Peking University usually include: cataloging theories, introduction to cataloging practices, structure and usage of CNMARC, comparison of CNMARC with USMARC, and cataloging

TABLE 1

Program and University	Curricula and Credit Hours
Library Science Program, Information Management Department, Peking University	Cataloging (60 hours), Classification and Subject Analysis (100 hours)
Library Science Department, Information Management School, Wuhan University	Cataloging (60 hours), Classification and Subject Analysis (120 hours)
Library Science Department, International Business School, Nankai University	Cataloging (60 hours), Classification Science (60 hours) Subject Analysis Methods (60 hours)
Library Science Program, Information Communication and Management School, Northeast Normal University	Cataloging I and II (120 hours), Classification and Subject Analysis (120 hours)
Library Science Department, Information Management School, Heilongjiang University	Cataloging (60 hours), Classification and Subject Analysis (60 hours)
Library Science Program, Library Science and Archives Science Department, Northwest University	Cataloging, Classification and Subject Analysis
Library Science Program, Economics and Management School, Shanxi University	Information Organization, Reference, Information Retrieval (120 hours in total)
Library Science Department, Management School, Xiangtan University	Cataloging (80 hours), Classification and Subject Analysis (80 hours)
Library Science Program, Information Management Department, School of Computer and Information Science, Southwest Normal University	Library Classification (80 hours), Subject Retrieval Language (40 hours), Cataloging (80 hours)
Library Science Program, Information Management School, Yunnan University	Cataloging for Chinese Language Materials (60 hours), Cataloging for Western Language Materials (60 hours), Library Classification (60 hours), Subject Analysis (60 hours)
Library Science Program, Information Management Department, Nanjing Political Science College Shanghai Campus	Cataloging (80 hours), Information Retrieval Language (80 hours)

for different formats. These courses combine the cataloging for Chinese language materials with the cataloging for Western language materials, and the card catalog rules with the online catalog principles. And the teaching of cataloging rules focuses on the rules developed for Chinese libraries, including the China MARC Format, Chinese Cataloging Rules, General Bibliographic Description, and Bibliographic Description for Monographs. USMARC is also introduced through these courses. The cataloging practice emphasizes hands-on experience with online cataloging systems.

The contents of classification and subject analysis courses cover theories of classification and subject analysis, classification schedules, subject thesauri, controlled language indexing, and natural language indexing and retrieval. Usually classification and subject analysis are taught separately but the connections between these two courses are also properly addressed. For classification, the primary teaching tool and the basis for practical training is Chinese Library Classification, which is compiled collectively by thirty-six large libraries and used by more than 95% of the libraries and archives in China. For subject analysis, various thesauri are taught, and the practical training is based on the Chinese Classified Thesaurus, which incorporates the terminology of the Chinese Thesaurus and corresponds to the structure of Chinese Library Classification. Foreign classification schedules and subject headings such as DDC, UDC, LCC, CC, and LCSH are also introduced in these courses. Other topics for these courses include: the trends in classification, Web resources classification, natural language indexing and retrieval, and automated indexing.

At the undergraduate level, information retrieval language is offered as a selective course in addition to cataloging and classification. The courses for graduate students also cover special topics on information retrieval language, Web resources organization, research on post-coordinated thesaurus, and the study of Chinese and foreign classification systems. These graduate courses emphasize the discussion and exploration of the principles of knowledge organization as well as the leading issues in the field of cataloging and classification.

Based on the above description and analysis, almost all library science programs in Chinese universities offer similar cataloging and classification courses despite the slight differences in their schedules and curricula.

RECENT DEVELOPMENT AND CHANGES IN CATALOGING AND CLASSIFICATION EDUCATION

Influenced by the popularity of the Internet and the use of automated library systems, education for cataloging and classification has undergone many changes in China since 1997. Of these changes, the change in undergraduate teaching has been the most typical.[9] To a certain extent, the cataloging and classification courses described above resulted from the changes in recent years. Notable changes in the courses of cataloging, classification, and subject analysis can be summarized as follows:[10,11,12]

1. Most courses have been adjusted and integrated while new, more effective curricula have been established. Of these changes, the adjust-

ment of cataloging courses is the greatest. Because of the differences between Western language cataloging and Chinese language cataloging in both theory and practice, separate cataloging courses have been developed for Western language materials and Chinese language materials in China's library science programs for a long time. At Peking University, for example: six years ago, a schedule of three hours a week was set for the course Cataloging for Chinese Language Materials, which concentrated on the principles and skills for cataloging Chinese printed materials; whereas, a schedule of four hours a week was established for the course Cataloging for Western Language Materials, which focused on the cataloging of Western printed materials. As a result, the contents of these two courses often overlapped each other, and at the same time, weakened the teaching of cataloging principles and theories as a whole. After much discussion on the hot issues, most universities have already integrated these two courses and teach cataloging in one course. Meanwhile, online cataloging was also included in the new course, and traditional card catalog theory and techniques were combined with computer technology. The new combined course provides a good foundation of cataloging knowledge and expertise and enhances the integrity of cataloging courses. At the same time, many universities have also combined both classification and subject analysis into one single course, so as to strengthen the connection between the two courses and treat both aspects of subject cataloging in a more integrated way.

2. Computer technology has been applied to the teaching of cataloging and classification. With the advent of online catalogs and the institutional use of cataloging software, technology has greatly benefited teaching. In the Information Management Department of Peking University, professors teach cataloging courses by using the two integrated library systems provided by Beijing Dancheng Software Co. and Beijing Chuanji Co. At the same time, electronic classifications and thesauri are used for the course on classification and subject analysis, which helps students understand the characteristics of these electronic tools. In order for the students to better understand trends and new developments in cataloging, classification, and subject headings, professors also introduce the application of cataloging to Web resources organization, subject and keyword directories, and search engines on the Internet.

3. Indexing tools have been improved and practical training enhanced. Since both cataloging, and classification and subject analysis require much practice, emphasis has been placed on providing opportu-

nities for practical training with the teaching equipment. For example, at Peking University, students in the Library Science program arrange to participate in a systematic, step-by-step training in cataloging, classification, and subject analysis. Relevant lab facilities have been established for learning and practice. To facilitate the instruction of cataloging and classification, an experimental system consisting of an exercise database, a help database, and an answer database has been developed. Students can use it to practice selecting access points and assigning main entries from the following four groups of entries: personal names, corporate names, conference names, and titles. Teachers of the classification and subject analysis course have also revised the subject indexing exercises to meet the curricular requirements, and have developed an electronic thesaurus based on the Chinese Thesaurus and the Chinese Classified Thesaurus so that students can learn how to catalog and index in the online environment.

4. The contents of most courses have been updated to reflect new developments in the field, and new technologies and practices have been added to the curricula as they became well developed. For instance, metadata standards, such as the Dublin Core Element Set, are now included in the cataloging course, and the results of recent research in cataloging by both Chinese and foreign scholars are fully covered in the course materials. To enhance the classification and subject analysis course, the subject guide is now added as part of teaching classification, and the teaching of controlled language and natural language indexing now includes: the application and display of subject headings for electronic resources, the features and methods of free-term indexing, post-coordinated headings, and automated indexing, as well as the current development of subject indexing in the electronic environment. These course enhancements will enable students to develop a thorough understanding of the application, future development, and current issues in classification and subject analysis.

5. Teaching methodology has been improved and more attention is paid to the interaction between professors and students, in an attempt to encourage students to participate and take initiatives for their professional education. In accordance with the principle of putting theories to practice, students are given small projects to complete outside of the classroom and in addition to their required practical work. For example, the homework assignments for the classification and subject analysis course include: compiling a specialized classification scheme and a subject thesaurus, investigating the use of subject guides to Internet resources and comparing them with the classification schemes for

printed materials, and investigating the developments of automated indexing at home and abroad. These efforts deepen the students' professional knowledge and skills by honing their analytical and problem-solving skills. In some library science programs, experiments have been made on the administration of different examinations for students who take the classification course.[13]

PROSPECTS OF CATALOGUING AND CLASSIFICATION EDUCATION IN CHINA

In general, Chinese cataloguing and classification education will continue to develop following its current basic patterns. However, possible changes in the next few years may include:

- The adjustment and integration of the current cataloging, classification, and subject analysis courses will continue to develop and optimize. The mainstream of curriculum design for cataloging, classification and subject analysis will remain the provision of the two major courses: (1) cataloging, and (2) classification and subject analysis, or information retrieval language. For those library programs that still offer separate courses in cataloging for Chinese language materials, cataloging for Western language materials, classification, and subject thesauri, attempts at integration will be further accelerated, especially the integration of different cataloging courses.
- New topics and contents will be introduced continuously in cataloging and classification courses. Along with the development of information technology, the focus of cataloging and classification courses will shift gradually from traditional print materials to the emerging digital resources. Corresponding changes may take place with this shift. For example, metadata schemas and theories of Web resources organization will be absorbed into the cataloguing and classification courses. Experimental courses will also be designed on such special topics as metadata development and Web resources organization, to catch up with the development of information technology and to accommodate current Internet developments into the teaching syllabi so that professional teaching can grow in sync with new developments in this field.
- Cataloging and classification courses will be further developed at graduate levels. Peking University, Wuhan University, and other

universities will take the lead in promoting their graduate programs in library science and attract students from other fields of
study in response to the growing need of Chinese libraries for
highly trained professionals. To this end, courses at a higher level
must be developed for the teaching of cataloging and classification.

- Continuing education and training will be further developed. Although there are about fifty library and information science programs offered by the universities and colleges in China, a large
number of non-library science major graduates are hired by libraries every year. Therefore, continuing education and on-the-job
training will continue to be an important means of developing
qualified library staff. For this type of teaching and training, cataloging and classification courses will continue to constitute the core
courses. Furthermore, because information management at business
enterprises and corporations also requires knowledge of cataloging
and classification, professional training classes or workshops will
be developed accordingly. Of course, the teaching of such training
programs will have to meet different practical needs and requirements, and is likely to go beyond the scope of regular cataloging
and classification courses.

- When a national accreditation system is established for the library
science programs in China, the professional teaching of cataloging
and classification will become more standardized. At present, the
lack of a national accreditation policy has hindered the further development of library science programs. The Library Division of
the Culture Ministry of China is considering drafting guidelines
for library science program accreditation, which will have a positive impact on the standardization of professional teaching, including teaching for cataloging, classification, and subject analysis.

- With regard to the form of teaching, online courses will find a wide
application and be developed for teaching cataloging and classification. As China covers vast geographic regions, there remains a
wide variety of needs and requirements for cataloging and classification courses in China. Since online courses are more accessible
and efficient, they will enable the current library science programs
to expand their teaching resources to meet broad social needs and to
effectively improve continuing education for library professionals.

NOTES

1. Department of Information Management, Peking University, *Tushuguanxue zhuanye fazhan dongxiang yanjiu baogao, fen baogao 1: Tushuguanxue benke jiaoyu qingkuang diaoyan baogao* 图书馆学专业发展动向研究报告, 分报告1: 图书馆学本科教育情况调研报告 [Project Report on the Development Trend of Library Science Specialty, Part One: Investigation Report on Undergraduate Education of Library Science in China] by Liu Jia and Zheng Qingwen 刘嘉、郑清文, October, 2002.

2. Department of Information Management, Peking University, *Tushuguanxue zhuanye fazhan dongxiang yanjiu baogao, fen baogao 2: Geleixing tushuguan dui tushuguanxue rencai xuqiu qingkuang de diaocha baogao* 图书馆学专业发展动向研究报告, 分报告2: 各类型图书馆对图书馆学人才需求情况的调查报告 [Project Report on the Development Trend of Library Science Specialty, Part Two: Investigation Report on Personnel Demand from Various Kind Library in China] by Zhang Guangqing 张广钦, October, 2002.

3. Lai Maosheng 赖茂生,"Zongjie jingyan, shenhua gaige, jinyibu banhao hanshou jiaoyu" 总结经验, 深化改革, 进一步办好函授教育 [General Information-Based LIS Education Reformation], *Beijing Daxue xuebao (xinxi guanli zhuankan)* 北京大学学报 (信息管理专刊) 1997.

4. Ke Ping 柯平, "Guanyu tushuguan zhuanye de kecheng gaige yu zhuganke sheji" 关于图书馆专业的课程改革与主干课设计 [On Teaching Reform and A Design of Core Curriculum in Library Science Education], *Jin tu xuekan* 晋图学刊 4 (Dec. 2001).

5. Hou Hanqing 侯汉清, "Qingbao jiansuo yuyan kecheng gaige" 情报检索语言课程改革 [Rethinking the Document Classification and Subject Heading Curriculum], *Daxue tushuguan xuebao* 大学图书馆学报 14, no.5 (Sept. 21, 1996).

6. Duan Minglian 段明莲, *Wenxian xinxi ziyuan bianmu* 文献信息资源编目 [Documental Resources Catalogue] (Beijing 北京: Beijing Daxue chubanshe 北京大学出版社, 2000).

7. Ma Zhanghua 马张华, *Xinxi zuzhi* 信息组织 [Information Organization] (Beijing 北京: Qinghua Daxue chubanshe 清华大学出版社, 2003).

8. Ma Zhanghua and Hou Hanqing 马张华、侯汉清, *Wenxian fenleifa zhutifa daolun* 文献分类法主题法导论 [Introduction to Document Classification and Subject Approach] (Beijing 北京: Beijing Daxue chubanshe 北京大学出版社, 1999).

9. Li Xiaoxin and Yang Yuling 李晓新、杨玉林, "Guanyu gaige 'Tushuguan mulu kecheng de chubu shexiang'" 关于改革 "图书馆目录课程的初步设想" [Preliminary Plan to Innovate the Course of Library Cataloging], *Daxue tushuguan tongxun* 大学图书馆通讯 6, no.2 (April. 15, 1988): 48-53, 64.

10. Department of Information Management, Peking University, *Tushuguanxue zhuanye fazhan dongxiang yanjiu baogao, fen baogao 3: "Wenxian Bianmu" kecheng jiaoxue gaige baogao* 图书馆学专业发展动向研究报告, 分报告3:《文献编目》课程教学改革报告 [Project Report on Development Trend of Library Science Specialty, Part Three: Reform on Document Catalogue Education] by Duan Minglian 段明莲, October, 2002.

11. Department of Information Management, Peking University, *Tushuguanxue zhuanye fazhan dongxiang yanjiu baogao, fen baogao 4: Wenxian fenleifa zhutifa kecheng gaige baogao* 图书馆学专业发展动向研究报告, 分报告4: 文献分类法主题法课程改革报告 [Project Report on Development Trend of Library Science Specialty, Part Four: Reform on Document Classification and Subject Approach Education] by Ma Zhanghua 马张华, October, 2002.

12. Wang Guoqiang and Li Yanbo 王国强、李岩波, "Manxiang 21shiji de tushuguan zhuanye jiaoxue fangfa he jiaoxue shouduan de gaige" 面向21世纪的图书馆学专业教学方法和教学手段的改革 [Facing the 21st Century: Reform of Methods and Ways of Professional Education of Library Science], *Henan tushuguan xuekan* 河南图书馆学刊 2 (2001).

13. Yu Junli, "Two Experiments on Reform of the Examination of Specialized Courses," *Library and Information Service* (in Chinese) 11 (2001).

The Status Quo and Future Development of Cataloging and Classification Education in China

Li Si

SUMMARY. This article depicts the status quo of cataloging and classification education in China, including the library science programs, their curricula, the degrees offered, the contents of courses, and the selection of textbooks. It also analyzes the current problems in library science programs and projects possible improvements and progress in the teaching of cataloging and classification in the next five to ten years. *[Article copies available for a fee from The Haworth Document Delivery Service: 1-800-HAWORTH. E-mail address: <docdelivery@haworthpress.com> Website: <http://www.HaworthPress.com> © 2005 by The Haworth Press, Inc. All rights reserved.]*

KEYWORDS. Classification, cataloging, cataloging education, subject analysis, library science education, China

The earliest history of cataloging and classification education in China traces back to 1920, when the Wenhua Library Science School was founded jointly by the American scholar Mary Elizabeth Wood and

Li Si, DMS, is Associate Professor, School of Information Management, Wuhan University, Hubei, China (E-mail: sunnylily66@hotmail.com).

[Haworth co-indexing entry note]: "The Status Quo and Future Development of Cataloging and Classification Education in China." Si, Li. Co-published simultaneously in *Cataloging & Classification Quarterly* (The Haworth Information Press, an imprint of The Haworth Press, Inc.) Vol. 41, No. 2, 2005, pp. 85-103; and: *Education for Library Cataloging: International Perspectives* (ed: Dajin D. Sun, and Ruth C. Carter) The Haworth Information Press, an imprint of The Haworth Press, Inc., 2006, pp. 85-103. Single or multiple copies of this article are available for a fee from The Haworth Document Delivery Service [1-800-HAWORTH, 9:00 a.m. - 5:00 p.m. (EST). E-mail address: docdelivery@haworthpress.com].

a few Chinese scholars including Shen Zurong and Hu Qingsheng. The Wenhua Library Science School was the first educational institution for library science in China, and since then, cataloging and classification education has grown significantly.

Wenhua Library School was modeled after the New York Public Library Science School, but in its curriculum design, it offered separate courses on Chinese book cataloging, Western book cataloging, Chinese book classification and Western book classification, and paid close attention to the practice of students. This curriculum has greatly influenced modern Chinese cataloging and classification education. This article describes the current status of Chinese cataloging and classification education, based on the universities that offer cataloging and classification courses and degrees. It also analyzes the problems in current course design and teaching material preparation, and shares the author's thoughts on the further enhancement and development of the teaching for cataloging and classification.

INVESTIGATION AND ANALYSIS OF THE UNIVERSITIES OFFERING CATALOGING AND CLASSIFICATION COURSES

The following Chinese universities were investigated with regard to their cataloging and classification curriculum via their Web sites on the Internet (the ending date of the investigation was November 26, 2003). The results are sorted by undergraduate and Master's programs and are presented in Tables 1 and 2, respectively.

Table 1 shows that 34 universities offer cataloging and classification courses for undergraduate programs. It also lists the number of course offerings by each university. An analysis of these basic statistical data indicates: 4 universities offer 4 correlated courses (11.8%); 8 universities offer 3 correlated courses (23.5%); 15 universities offer 2 correlated courses (44.1%); and 8 universities offer one course (23.5%). In addition, 20 universities offer cataloging, classification, and subject analysis courses synchronously (58.8%). At the same time, a new course called information organization is emerging and incorporates several cataloging-related courses into one course. The number of universities that offer this new course is 18 (52.9%).

It is obvious that the majority of universities offer cataloging, classification, and subject analysis courses systematically. Courses in information organization and description have become the core courses in

TABLE 1. Universities That Offer Cataloging and Classification Courses in Undergraduate Programs

	University and Department	Course	Total Periods	Classroom Instruction/ Practicum Periods	Total Number of Courses
		Undergraduate Programs			
1	College of Information Administration and Publicity, *Northeast Normal University*	Document classification	60	50/10	2
		Document cataloging	60	50/10	
2	Department of Informatics, *East China Normal University*	Information resources organization and processing			1
3	Department of Information Management, *Nanjing University*	Information storage and organization	72		1
4	Department of Information Management, *Shanxi University*	Classification and subject analysis	72	36/36	2
		Information description	36	20/12	
5	Department of Information Management, *Guizhou University*	Document classification and subject analysis	54	36/18	4
		Modern document cataloging	54	36/18	
		Information retrieval language	54	36/0	
		Computerized information resources organization and management	54	36/18	
6	Department of Information Management, College of Economics & Management, *South China Normal University.*	Information organization	80		2
		Library catalog	80		
7	Department of Information Management, Faculty of Computer & Information Science, *Southwest Normal University*	Document information index (1)	80	60/20	4
		Document information index (2)	86	67/19	
		Document cataloging	86	67/19	
		Information description and organization principles	120	80/40	
8	Department of Information Resources Management, *Sichuan University*	Information retrieval language			2
		Information organization			

Note: One Period is equal to a 45-minute class.

TABLE 1 (continued)

Undergraduate Programs

	University and Department	Course	Total Periods	Classroom Instruction/ Practicum Periods	Total Number of Courses
9	Department of Library & Archives Science, *Northwest University*	Document classification and subject analysis	60	50/10	2
		Document information cataloging	60	50/10	
10	Department of Information Management, *Beijing University*	Information organization	72		3
		Theory and technology of knowledge organization	34		
		Document cataloging	36		
11	Department of Library Science, International Business School, *Nankai University*	Document classification	54	36/18	3
		Document subject analysis	54	36/18	
		Document cataloging	54	36/18	
12	Department of Library Science, *Xiangtan University*	Document classification and subject analysis	64	56/8	2
		Document cataloging	64	56/8	
13	Department of Library Science, College of Management, *Hebei University*	Information description			2
		Information organization			
14	Department of Medical Information, Medical School, *Central South University*	Information organization 1: Document classification and indexing	76	66/10	3
		Information organization 2: Document cataloging	76	66/10	
		Subject indexing	82	70/12	
15	Department of Medical Information, Tongji Medical College, *Huazhong University of Science & Technology*	Retrieval language and subject indexing	80	64/16	2
		Information organization	90	72/18	
16	Department of Information Management, *Nanjing Agricultural University*	Document indexing	36	36/0	2
		Information retrieval language	36	36/0	

#	Institution	Course			
17	Department of Information Management, *Central China Normal University*	Information storage and indexing	90	82/8	1
18	Department of Information Management, *Zhengzhou University*	Information organization	72	54/18	2
		Computerized cataloging	54	36/18	
19	Department of Information Resource Management, *Changchun University*	Document subject analysis, classification, and cataloging			1
20	Humanities College, *Zhejiang University*	Information retrieval language			1
21	Information Management Department, *Sun Yat-sen University*	Classification and subject indexing	80	68/12	3
		Document cataloging	60	48/12	
		Information organization	80	68/12	
22	Information Management & Systems Program, *Medical College of Northern China Coal Industry*	Information organization			1
23	School of Business & Management, *Shandong University*	Document classification and subject analysis			3
		Document cataloging			
		Information description and organization			
24	School of Humanities, *Hebei University of Economics & Business*	Document classification and subject analysis			1
25	School of Information Management, *Wuhan University*	Document classification	54	36/18	4
		Subject analysis	54	36/18	
		Document cataloging	54	36/18	
		Information organization	36		
26	School of Information Management, *Heilongjiang University*	Document classification and subject analysis			3
		Document cataloging			
		Information organization			

TABLE 1 (continued)

Undergraduate Programs

	University and Department	Course	Total Periods	Classroom Instruction/ Practicum Periods	Total Number of Courses
27	School of Management, *Beijing Normal University*	Information organization			1
28	Department of History, *Fujian Normal University*	Document classification			3
		Document cataloging			
		Information organization			
29	Department of Adult & Continuing Education, *NTNU*	Books information organization			2
		Content analysis			
30	Department of Library and Information Science, *Fu Jen Catholic University*	Content analysis			4
		Classification and cataloging problems research			
		Bibliographic database producing			
		Information organization			
31	Department of Library and Information Science, *Hsuan Chuang University*	Chinese document classification and cataloging			2
		Western document classification and cataloging			
32	Department of Library and Information Science, *NTU*	Classification and cataloging science (1,2)			2
		Automatic classification and indexing			
33	Department of Information & Communication Studies, *Shih Hsin University*	Classification and cataloging			2
		Content analysis			
34	Department of Library and Information Science, *Tamkang University*	Classification and cataloging (1,2)			2
		Library of Congress Classification			

library and information science programs. Currently, the teaching of networked information organization and information retrieval language has received much attention, since these courses meet the demand of information institutions and reflect the developing trends in the field.

Table 2 shows that 21 universities offer cataloging-related courses for Master's degree programs. It also includes the number of course offerings of each university. Two universities offer 4 correlated courses (9.5%), 3 universities offer 3 correlated courses (14.3%), 4 universities offer 2 correlated courses (19%), and 12 universities offer 1 course (57.1%). Furthermore, 12 universities (57.1%) offer "information organization" in place of a cataloging and classification course. Graduate education should pay attention to the leading edge research in the field. For this reason, some educational institutions provide courses in metadata, electronic resources cataloging, networked information organization and use, and automated classification and indexing, which cover the cutting-edge research topics in the field and are demanded by information organizations.

In addition, the Document and Information Center of the Chinese Academy of Sciences has added metadata and digital information organization to its curriculum for its doctoral programs, and the Department of Library and Information Science, NTU (Taiwan) has offered two doctoral level courses in classification theory research and cataloging problems research. Therefore, it is obvious that a quite complete teaching system has been developed for the undergraduate, Master's, and doctoral programs.

CONTENT OF CATALOGING
AND CLASSIFICATION COURSES

About the Classification Courses

From the 1980s to the 1990s, the content of classification courses had four components: theories of classification, main classification schemes in China and foreign countries, classification for different subject disciplines and types of documents, and classification for the same types of books. These topics have been the basic content of classification courses for a long time. Generally speaking, the theory component includes classification standards, classification structure, notation, and subdivision tables. As far as classification schemes are concerned, three Chinese classification systems are studied: *Chinese Library Classifica-*

TABLE 2. Universities That Offer Cataloging and Classification Courses in Master's Programs

University (or School)	Master's Programs		
	Course	Total Periods	Number of Courses
College of Information Administration and Publicity, *Northeast Normal University*	Information knowledge organization	60	1
Department of Information Management, College of Economics & Management, *South China Normal University*	Information organization and retrieval		1
Department of Information Resources Management, *Sichuan University*	Information retrieval language research	36	1
Department of Information Management, *Beijing University*	Information organization research Metadata research		2
Department of Medical information, *Central South University*	Knowledge organization research	54	1
Department of Information Management, *Zhengzhou University*	Information retrieval language	54	1
Department of Information Management, *Central China Normal University*	Information organization and retrieval research	72	1
Department of Information Management, *Nanjing Agricultural University*	Information organization research		1
Information Management Department, *Sun Yat-sen University*	Information retrieval and retrieval language Study of Anglo-American bibliography Organization and use of networked information	60 40 60	3
Document and Information Center, *Chinese Academy of Sciences*	Information resources organization and construction		1
School of Archives, *People's University of China*	Networked information resources organization and use Information retrieval language		2

Institution	Topics		Count
School of Information Management, *Wuhan University*	Document classification research Subject analysis research Document cataloging research	54 54 54	3
School of Management, *Beijing Normal University*	Information retrieval language Information indexing and organization Document processing Information processing research		4
Department of Library and Information Science, *NTU*	Information organization research Classification problems research Cataloging problems research Automated classification and indexing		4
Department of Library and Information Science, *Tamkang University*	Electronic resources cataloging		1
Department of Library and Information Science, *Fu Jen Catholic University*	Introduction to metadata Knowledge organization Metadata system design		3
Department of Adult & Continuing Education, *NTNU*	Books information organization		1
Department of Information & Communication Studies, *Shih Hsin University*	Content analysis Information language Information organization		3
Research Institute of Library & Information Science, *NCCU*	Information organization and content analysis		1
Research Institute of Library & Information Science, *NCHU*	Automated classification and indexing		1
Education Information Institute, *Fo Guang University*	Information organization Content analysis		2

tion, *Classification of the Chinese Academy of Sciences Library,* and *Classification of the Library of the People's University of China.* Four classification schemes in foreign countries are also introduced, namely *Dewey Decimal Classification, Universal Decimal Classification, Library of Congress Classification,* and *Colon Classification.* The students are required to do a practicum with the *Chinese Library Classification.*

In the early 1990s, theory and method for reclassification of books was introduced systematically. Since the mid-1990s, the study of library classification has developed unprecedentedly, as a result of the application of computer, telecommunication, and network technologies to information management and indexing, as well as the demand for classification development and practice. The content of classification courses has been expanded and deepened gradually, and results of the current research have been accommodated into teaching. In addition, such topics as classification systems for networked information and application of the traditional classification schedules to networked information organization, as well as the electronic edition of the *Chinese Library Classification,* are introduced to reflect current trends of development in the field.

About the Subject Analysis Courses

From the middle of the 1980s to the 1990s, the main content of subject analysis teaching included the history of subject analysis, the system of subject headings, unit-term indexing, and keyword and thematic word approach. Emphasis was placed on the use of the *Chinese Thesaurus,* and the method, process, and rules of subject indexing. The *Chinese Thesaurus* was also used for the practice of subject indexing.

Since the 1990s, such new topics as the principle and use of the *Chinese Classified Thesaurus* (an integration of classification and subject languages), application of natural language in information retrieval, etc., have been incorporated into the course on subject analysis. In addition, a systematic introduction is given to document indexing and the organization of index files in an online information retrieval system. The application of subject headings to networked information resources is another major topic taught in the current courses.

About the Cataloging Courses

Cataloging theories and methods are stressed in cataloging courses. The current content of teaching consists of an introduction to cataloging, description rules, description methods for different types of materials (such as books, monographic sets and series, serials, maps, technical standards, and non-print materials), entry method, filing of card catalogs, and management of the cataloging operation. Main cataloging codes are also introduced, including the *General Bibliographical Description (GB3792.1), Rules for Chinese Description, Rules for Bibliographic Description of Western Language Materials, AACR2R (Anglo-American Cataloging Rules, 2nd rev ed.).*

With the application of computer and network technologies in the field of cataloging, the content of cataloging courses has been expanded to include online cataloging, description of electronic information resources, the structure and use of CNMARC and USMARC, authority control, and the current trends in cataloging. Now that card cataloging has been phased out, training in professional skills is greatly stressed. Because of the immense increase of networked information resources, the description of networked information resources has drawn lots of attention in cataloging course design. Using MARC and metadata (especially Dublin Core) for the description of networked information resources has become the cutting edge practice in the field.

As shown in Tables 1 and 2, some library science programs have integrated cataloging, classification, and subject analysis into one course and named it Information Organization, which includes controlled indexing language (i.e., classification and subject headings), automatic indexing, bibliographical information system and method, MARC, authority control, networked information description and organization, and the like. In terms of credit hours, Tongji Medical College of the Huazhong University of Science & Technology allocates a total of 90 hours to the course, and the Faculty of Computer & Information Science of Southwest Normal University, a total of 120 hours. The programs in other universities tend to give much shorter hours to this course, not enough to assure the quality of teaching.

DEVELOPMENT OF TEACHING MATERIALS

In order to find textbooks that have been published since 1949 and used for the teaching of cataloging and classification courses, the author searched the bibliographical databases of the China National Library and the online catalog of the China Academic Library & Information System (CALIS). The results are presented in Table 3.

TABLE 3. The Cataloging- and Classification-Related Textbooks Published After 1949

Course Name	1950s	1960s	1970s	1980s		1990s			2000~	Total	The Number in last five years (percent of the total)
				'80-'84	'85-'89	'90-'94	'95-'99				
Classification	2			4	2	4	3		5	20	6 (30%)
Cataloging	2	1	1		4	6	2		2	18	2 (11%)
Subject analysis					3	3	3		1	10	3 (30%)
Information organization									7	7	7 (100%)

96

To some extent, the number of publications reflects the status of course teaching. An analysis of the quantity and year of publication in Table 3 shows:

1. Since the 1980s, about 20 textbooks have been published on cataloging and classification. This suggests that classification and cataloging are the basic or core courses in the curricula for library science programs.
2. The information organization course was established to meet the demand for selecting, evaluating, describing, and indexing multimedia materials generated in the networked and digital information environment. All of the course books on this subject were published recently, after 2000. Information organization has been the most published topic among cataloging and classification books during the past five years.
3. Compared with the other courses, publication on subject analysis has been relatively slow and weak. Since Professor Zhang Qiyu published the first textbook for the subject analysis course in 1983, only 10 textbooks have been published on the same topic over the past 20 years, amounting to only the half of the textbooks published for classification courses. This imbalanced publishing is worthy of attention.

SOME EXISTING PROBLEMS

Teaching Faculty

The wide application of computer technology puts a new demand on the teaching of cataloging and classification. Although the majority of teaching faculty members in the library and information science programs have a solid theoretical foundation from their school education and training, they do not normally possess practical work experience in their field of specialty and they are not familiar with the application of technologies in the field. In order to enhance their practical skills, these faculty members should be given the opportunity to work in libraries, where they can perform some hands-on tasks in their fields for a period of time and familiarize themselves with relevant software applications and computer programming. This way, they would be able to put theory into practice and gain rich, practical field experience, thus improving the relevance and quality of their teaching.

Teaching Methodology and Facility

In general, cataloging and classification courses depend on traditional classroom instruction with the addition of some hands-on practice. Most of the teaching facilities are relatively outdated and need to be enhanced with computer and multimedia equipment. The author surveyed a few related multimedia courses on the Internet, in which the courseware was straightforward, simple and lively, and gave plenty of information to the students, who welcomed these courses warmly. Some multimedia instruction material for classification schemes is available on the Web. For example, the tutorial of DDC (http://www.oclc.org/dewey/resources/tour/default.htm) on the OCLC Web site provides a good resource for teaching and learning DDC. Some educational institutions outside of China have set up lab facilities that provide packages of online systems and software applications for training purposes. Some of these training facilities are mounted on the Web so that students can access them easily and study at their own pace. Teaching with multimedia technology is the trend for future instruction in cataloging, classification, and subject analysis.

Allocation of Practicum Hours

Both cataloging and classification courses place great emphasis on practice. It is necessary that every effort be taken to design course contents scientifically, that time be distributed appropriately between classroom instruction and student practicum, and that hands-on practice be increased gradually. Only through repeated practice on cataloging and classification, can students turn the book knowledge that they have learned into practical skills, and meet the requirements of their future employers. Table 4 lists the distribution of course hours between classroom instruction and student practicum based on the five courses offered by 24 library science programs.

Of the 24 allocations of course hours, the total hours for each course vary widely, from 36 to 120 hours. There are 13 courses of which the total hours range between 72 and 90, representing 54.2% of the programs surveyed. As for the practicum hours, courses that devote 30% of their time to students' practicum make up 33.3% of the programs surveyed, but there are 41.6% of programs that allow only 15% of their course time for students' practice. The rest (25%) of the courses surveyed allot 20 to 25% of their course time to students' practice. Overall, about 66.6%

TABLE 4. Distribution of Class Hours for Cataloging and Classification Courses

Course Periods	Classification				Cataloging							Subject Analysis				Classification and Subject Analysis				Information Organization				
Total hours	54	76	86	36	54	60	60	64	76	86	90	54	60	80	82	60	64	72	80	72	80	80	90	120
Classroom Instruction hours	36	66	67	20	36	50	48	56	66	67	60	36	50	60	70	50	56	36	68	54	68	56	72	80
Practicum hours	18	10	19	12	18	10	12	8	10	19	30	18	10	20	12	10	8	36	12	18	12	24	18	40
Percentage of practicum (%)	33.3	13.2	22.1	33.3	33.3	16.7	20	12.5	13.2	22.1	33.3	33.3	16.7	25	14.6	16.7	12.5	50	15	25	15	30	20	33.3

of the programs in question allocate less than 25% of the course to students' practicum.

It is obvious that the practicum times for most of the courses surveyed are too short to attain the goal of improving students' practical skills. It is suggested that the students' practice hours be increased to 40% of the total course hours for cataloging and classification courses. For those library science programs that have combined the two courses in Chinese language material cataloging and Western language material cataloging, and those courses that incorporate the description of networked information in the cataloging instruction, the total course time should be set at 72 hours, at least. For the same reason, a total of 90 hours should be given for the information organization courses that integrate the separate classification and subject analysis courses into one.

IMPROVEMENT AND DEVELOPMENT OF TEACHING IN THE NEXT FIVE YEARS

Establishing a Complete Teaching Assurance System

A self-contained teaching assurance system is the key to the quality of classification teaching. This system consists of a complete practice base and sufficient reference tools for students, including the *Chinese Library Classification*, the *Classification of the Chinese Academy of Sciences Library*, the *Classification of the Library of the People's University of China*, the *Chinese Thesaurus*, and the *Chinese Classified Thesaurus*. In addition, it should supply at least a copy of *Dewey Decimal Classification* and the *Universal Decimal Classification*. There should also be a collection of practice materials in different formats and subjects, and appropriate software applications for cataloging training. In the meantime, multimedia classrooms should be built and regular spaces for students' practice should be established in cooperation with libraries and archives, in order to provide enough opportunities for students to obtain hands-on experience and skills.

Increasing Academic Communication and Cooperation Both at Home and Abroad

Increasing academic communication and cooperation both at home and abroad is vitally important for the further development of cataloging and classification education in China. At present, there are few chances for faculty members to communicate with their counterparts in other countries; nor there are enough opportunities for cooperative teaching and research programs in cataloging and classification between Chinese and foreign scholars. China should select and send some of its library science faculty members abroad for academic and research activities. It should also explore other channels for academic exchange and cooperation by holding international conferences and seminars and sponsoring joint teaching and research programs on cataloging and classification topics, as well as taking full advantage of Web communication and resources, to catch up with the teaching and course developments in the world.

Improving Method of Instruction

The traditional method of instruction should be improved as soon as possible by making the best use of multimedia courseware and providing students with adequate examples and intuitive materials to enhance their perception of theoretic concepts and principles. In addition to basic theories and leading edge topics, the courses should also introduce appropriate teaching software packages, including software applications that facilitate the description and classification of networked information resources and the electronic or Web version of subject thesaurus and classification schedules. At the same time, the students should be given more time and opportunities to practice cataloging and classification in an online library system. Online courses in cataloging and classification should also be developed that will enable the teachers to answer the students' questions online.

It is also important to improve the faculty's teaching ability and research by providing opportunities for continued professional training and growth, as these contribute critically to the quality of teaching. Faculty should be encouraged to explore and experiment with new ways of teaching.

REFERENCES

The following Web sites were last accessed on November 26, 2003.

1. School of Information Management. Wuhan University. http://sim.whu.edu.cn/.
2. Department of Library & Information Science. Beijing University. http://www.im.pku.edu.cn/.

3. Information Management Department. Sun Yat-sen University. http://202.116.76.16/.

4. Department of Information Management. Nanjing Agricultural University. http://202.119.40.20/.

5. Department of Library Science. Xiangtan University. http://glxy.xtu.edu.cn:8000/showart.php?id=20.

6. Department of Information Management. Shanxi University. http://www.sxu.edu.cn/yuanxi/xxx/.

7. Department of Information Management. Nanjing Agricultural University. http://info.njau.edu.cn/college/college_x.asp.

8. Department of Information Management. Central China Normal University. http://imd.ccnu.edu.cn/.

9. Department of Medical Information. Central South University. http://www.xymu.net/info/cmti/jiaoxuegongzuo/benkekecheng.htm.

10. Department of Information Management. College of Economics & Management. South China Normal University. http://www.scnu.edu.cn/~jjx/jj/jj/INDEX.htm.

11. School of Information Management. Heilongjiang University. http://www.hlju.edu.cn/edu/dep/xxglxy/xyjj.htm.

12. College of Information Administration and Publicity. Northeast Normal University. http://vod.nenu.edu.cn/department/xgxy/resume.htm.

13. Department of Informatics. East China Normal University. http://www.51-train.com/hdsfdx/hdsfda-yxjs.htm.

14. School of Management. Beijing Normal University. http://www.manage.bnu.edu.cn/.

15. Department of Library and Information Science. NTU. http://www.lis.ntu.edu.tw/.

16. Department of Library and Information Science. Tamkang University. http://www.emls.tku.edu.tw/.

17. Department of Library and Information Science. Fu Jen Catholic University. http://www.lins.fju.edu.tw/modules/news/.

18. Department of Information Management. Guizhou University. http://www.gzu.edu.cn/otherdep/hum/info/index1.htm.

19. Department of Information Resources Management. Sichuan University. http://www.scu.edu.cn/home/tempsite/benkesheng/xinxiziyuan.htm.

20. Department of Library Science. College of Management. Hebei University. http://hanlin2.hbu.cn/glxy/index.asp.

21. Department of Information Management. Zhengzhou University. http://www2.zzu.edu.cn/xxgl/.

22. Department of Information Management. Faculty of Computer & Information Science. Southwest Normal University. http://cyber.swnu.edu.cn/computer/leader.htm.

23. Department of Medical Information. Tongji Medical College. Huazhong University of Science & Technology. http://ultr.tjmu.edu.cn/index.aspx.

24. Department of Library Science. International Business School. Nankai University. http://ibs.nankai.edu.cn/Site/first.asp.

25. Department of Library & Archives Science. Northwest University. http://www.nwu.edu.cn/page/jigoushezhi/department/gongguoyuan/tdx.htm.

26. School of Sociology & History. Fujian Normal University. http://www.fjnu.edu.cn/lsc/.

27. School of Business & Management. Shandong University. http://www.glxy. sdu.edu.cn/.

28. Humanities College. Zhejiang University. http://www.ch.zju.edu.cn/.

29. School of Humanities. Hebei University of Economics & Business. http:// 202.206.192.67/xwx/.

30. North China Coal Medical College. http://www.ncmc.edu.cn/xbsz/index.htm.

31. Department of Information Resource Management. Changchun University. http://www.ccu-edu.cn/ccuview/yuanxishezhi/xinxiziyuanguanlixi/default.asp.

32. Department of Adult & Continuing Education. NTNU. http://www.ntnu.edu. tw/ace/01.htm.

33. Department Library and Information Science. Hsuan Chuang University. http:// www.hcu.edu.tw/lis/.

34. Department of Information & Communication Studies. Shin Hsin University. http://ic.shu.edu.tw/index2.htm.

35. School of Archives. Renmin University of China. http://www.acruc.net/index_ alternate.html.

36. Library of Chinese Academy of Sciences. http://www.las.ac.cn/jypx/ShuoShiDSh. asp.

APPENDIX

Chinese Classification Standards

Chinese Library Classification Editorial Committee, *Zhongguo tu shu guan fen lei fa* 中国图书馆分类法 [Chinese Library Classification] 4th ed. (Beijing: Beijing Library Press, 1999).

Classification of the Chinese Academy of Sciences Library Revising Committee, *Zhongguo ke xue yuan tu shu guan tu shu fen lei fa* 中国科学院图书馆图书分类法 [Classification of the Chinese Academy of Sciences Library] 3rd ed. (Beijing: Scientific Press, 1994).

Classification of the Library of the People's University of China Revising Committee, *Zhongguo ren min da xue tu shu guan tu shu fen lei fa* 中国人民大学图书馆图书分类法 [Classification of the Library of the People's University of China, 6th edition] (Beijing: Chinese People's University Press, 1996).

Institute of Scientific and Technical Information of China, Beijing Library, *Han yu zhu ti ci biao* 汉语主题词表 [Chinese Subject Thesaurus] (Beijing: Science and Technology Literature Press, 1980).

Liu, Xiangsheng刘湘生. *Zhongguo fen lei zhu ti ci biao* 中国分类主题词表 [Chinese Classified Thesaurus] (Beijing: Hua Yi Press, 1994).

Education for Knowledge Organization: The Indian Scene

K. S. Raghavan

SUMMARY. This paper briefly traces the history of library education in India and examines the status of bibliographic organization and control in the country as a major factor influencing the nature and content of courses in knowledge organization. The two basic documents from the University Grants Commission–the first one issued in 1965 and the recent one in 2001–that have influenced university-level course contents are examined. Finally, the nature of changes that are being brought about in recent years in some universities are highlighted. *[Article copies available for a fee from The Haworth Document Delivery Service: 1-800-HAWORTH. E-mail address: <docdelivery@haworthpress.com> Website: <http://www.HaworthPress.com> © 2005 by The Haworth Press, Inc. All rights reserved.]*

KEYWORDS. Knowledge organization–education, cataloguing education, library education, information studies–education, bibliographic organization–education, India

K. S. Raghavan is Professor, DRTC, Indian Statistical Institute, Bangalore, India (E-mail: ksragav@hotmail.com; raghavan@drtc.isiabng.ac.in).

[Haworth co-indexing entry note]: "Education for Knowledge Organization: The Indian Scene." Raghavan, K. S. Co-published simultaneously in *Cataloging & Classification Quarterly* (The Haworth Information Press, an imprint of The Haworth Press, Inc.) Vol. 41, No. 2, 2005, pp. 105-119; and: *Education for Library Cataloging: International Perspectives* (ed: Dajin D. Sun, and Ruth C. Carter) The Haworth Information Press, an imprint of The Haworth Press, Inc., 2006, pp. 105-119. Single or multiple copies of this article are available for a fee from The Haworth Document Delivery Service [1-800-HAWORTH, 9:00 a.m. - 5:00 p.m. (EST). E-mail address: docdelivery@haworthpress.com].

BACKGROUND

India attained political independence in 1947. Modern western-type university education may be said to have begun in the country with the establishment of the three premier Universities of Bombay, Calcutta and Madras in 1857. Formal training programs for library personnel, however, date back only to 1911 and are closely linked to the introduction of free public library service in the country. William Borden, an American librarian, was invited by the then Maharaja of Baroda in 1911 to organize public library service in the princely state of Baroda. Borden started a training program to train the required personnel. In 1915, the Punjab University, Lahore (now in Pakistan), started a training program in librarianship. It was, however, S. R. Ranganathan's appointment in 1924, as librarian of the University of Madras, that triggered far-reaching developments and changes in training for library professionals in the country. Ranganathan founded the Madras Library Association in 1928 and, under its auspices, started a summer training program. This program was taken over by the University of Madras in 1931 and was upgraded into a full-time post-graduate (Graduate) Diploma program in 1937–indeed, the first such program on the Indian subcontinent! Five other universities introduced similar programs during the pre-independence period, viz., Andhra University (1935), Banaras Hindu University (1941), University of Bombay (1943), University of Calcutta (1945) and University of Delhi (1947). S. R. Ranganathan was directly associated with the programs at Banaras and Delhi. It was also during this period that some of the seminal works of Ranganathan–including those expounding his new theories in classification and cataloguing–appeared. These two factors–the direct association of S. R. Ranganathan, and the publication of some of his seminal works that earned 'Library Science' the status of an academic discipline–have both influenced and shaped the content and emphasis of educational programs in the country. The creation of the University Grants Commission (U.G.C.) in 1953 by an act of Parliament provided fillip to higher education in general. The U.G.C., in its schema of things, attached considerable importance to the role of university libraries in higher education and research and, as a necessary consequence of this, sought to improve university education and training for library professionals. The U.G.C. constituted a committee under the chairmanship of S. R. Ranganathan and the 1965 report of the committee, *Library Science in Indian Universities*, has had a significant impact on course contents in practically all of the universities in India (University Grants Commission, 1965).

BIBLIOGRAPHIC ORGANIZATION

The situation which exists in a country with respect to bibliographic organization and control will necessarily have a bearing and impact on the educational programs in the area. In examining the educational programs and course contents for bibliographic organization in India, therefore, it is important to keep in mind the several factors that have possibly had a bearing on these:

- Unlike the more developed countries, India has not seen the emergence of any major centralized cataloguing service at the national level, even to this day. This has meant that libraries have always been and continue to be expected to do original cataloguing of almost their entire acquisitions. Of course, to a significant extent, this has been influenced by the fact that a large proportion of the acquisition of university and research libraries is of foreign origin. These factors have resulted in a situation in which there has not been much uniformity in classification and cataloguing practices among even the major libraries. Even the creation of bibliographic records in the languages and scripts of the item being catalogued is also, comparatively, a recent phenomenon. In a way, all of these have prevented the development and acceptance of national standards in the form of cataloguing codes, lists of subject headings, schemes of classification, etc. A variety of standards and tools with varying degrees of local modifications are, therefore, found to be in use in libraries in the country.
- Efforts at developing machine-readable bibliographies and OPACs are a comparatively recent phenomenon. It is only in recent months that the *Indian National Bibliography* has begun to be made available in machine-readable form also. The emergence of library networks in metropolitan cities began in the 1990s and probably the most successful of these has been the DELNET (The Delhi Library Network, now called Developing Library Network). Many other projects aimed at networking libraries or at creating machine-readable bibliographies are in various stages of development. Very recently a project aimed at retro-con-

version of bibliographic records in the *Indian National Bibliography* has been initiated.

UNIVERSITY LIBRARY SCHOOLS

Educational programs at the Master's level began with the establishment of the Department of Library Science in the University of Delhi as an associated project of UNESCO in 1947. In an indirect way, the course contents of this program became a model for the whole country. S. R. Ranganathan was invited by Sir Maurice Gwyer, then the Vice-Chancellor of the University of Delhi, to be a professor in the University, and Ranganathan was responsible for starting the Master's program in the University of Delhi. When, more than a decade later, Ranganathan established the Documentation Research & Training Centre (DRTC) in 1962, under the auspices of the Indian Statistical Institute, the same set of courses that were approved for the Master's program in the University of Delhi was adopted with some minor modifications. Subsequently, when the U.G.C. invited Ranganathan to head a committee to prepare a report on *Library Science in Indian Universities*, the committee's recommendations insofar as course contents at the Master's level were concerned, more or less reflected the courses that had been in force in the University of Delhi and at the DRTC. Most universities which introduced Master's programs in the 1960s and 1970s adopted the recommendations made in this report with only, if any, minor modifications. The universities of Bombay and Mysore were probably the only two notable exceptions to this general trend. The course contents recommended by S. R. Ranganathan, as is to be expected, laid considerable emphasis on classification and cataloguing. It should be both interesting and relevant here to have an overview of the course contents as they were at that point of time. Such an overview will also facilitate an assessment of the nature of changes that have since been introduced in the course contents of formal university programs at the Master's level. Table 1 presents an overview of the courses and an outline of their contents as recommended by the U.G.C. Review Committee.

The table clearly indicates the heavy emphasis on classification and cataloguing in the course contents–the two areas accounting for over 50% of the courses. However, in the actual implementation of these courses, there were certain imbalances in that certain aspects of bibliographic organization and control received greater attention and certain

TABLE 1. Courses Recommended by the U.G.C. Review Committee (1965)

Course Title	Broad Course Contents	Weight*
Universe of Knowledge	• Mapping of knowledge in philosophical classifications • Modes of thinking and modes of formation of subjects • Research methods	4 Credits
Depth Classification (Theory)	• General Theory of Classification of S. R. Ranganathan and others; Contributions of C.R.G. and other schools of thought • Comparative study of major schemes of classification	4 Credits
Depth Classification (Practice)	• Classification of micro-subjects using *Colon Classification* and *Universal Decimal Classification* including use of depth schedules/fascicules	4 Credits
Advanced Cataloguing (Theory)	• Theory of cataloguing; Normative principles of S. R. Ranganathan • Comparative study of *Classified Catalogue Code* of S. R. Ranganathan and *ALA Rules/AACR* (choice and form of headings) • Descriptive cataloguing • Subject cataloguing • Rules for filing and alphabetization	4 Credits
Advanced Cataloguing (Practice)	• Cataloguing of books, complex serials (and non-book materials) using *Classified Catalogue Code* supplemented by chain indexing and *ALA Rules/Anglo-American Cataloguing Rules* supplemented by *Sears List of Subject Headings* (preparation of main and added entries as for a dictionary catalogue and for a classified catalogue and filing of these entries)	4 Credits
Bibliography and Literature (Elective)**		4 Credits
Academic/Special Libraries (Elective)**		4 Credits
Projects (Literature Survey, Field Survey, Guided Project)**		4 Credits

*Credit system in university courses was not prevalent at that time; the figures in this column have been arrived at on the basis of the approximate number of hours of contact (lectures/seminars, etc., per week) (1 Credit = 1 hour of teaching per week over a semester spread over roughly 16 weeks or half-hour of teaching per week spread over an entire academic year).
**These courses are not directly relevant to Bibliographic Organization and Control; however, students could, if they so desired, choose a theme from the area for their project work.

other aspects received less than the required emphasis. For example, in the courses on classification, there was greater emphasis on teaching/learning notational devices and the desired level of emphasis on vocabulary (the Verbal Plane) was missing. This certainly was the case at least until the 1970s. Similarly, the courses on cataloguing laid great emphasis on choice and form of headings, resolution of conflict in the choice of the main entry, etc., rather than on descriptive cataloguing. The lack of emphasis on descriptive cataloguing probably had to do with the fact that, in the scheme of Ranganathan, detailed and elaborate description of bibliographic entities had no place. Even the rules for national bibliographies in his *Classified Catalogue Code* (which certainly require a higher level of description than catalogues of open access libraries) prescribed only a minimal level of description (Ranganathan, 1964).

Winds of Change

Beginning with the mid-1960s, there were major changes and developments in bibliographic organization and control the world over. In cataloguing, the period marked the beginning of the era of MARC, *AACR*, the ISBDs, a revival of the Cataloguing-at-source (under the label, *Cataloging-in-Publication*), and IFLA's Universal Bibliographic Control program. In the area of subject access, the ASLIB-Cranfield studies and other evaluation studies provided a better understanding of the nature of subject indexing languages. There was increasing discussion on enhancing subject access in online catalogues. In India, the period was marked by certain significant developments:

- S. R. Ranganathan published a paper in 1964 on facet analysis, in the *Journal of Documentation*, which marked the beginning of a major shift in the emphasis from notation to using facet analysis as the basis for structuring subject headings. The research triggered by this led to the development, eventually, of Postulate-based Permuted Subject Indexing (POPSI) in India and the Preserved Context Index System (PRECIS) in the U.K.
- Special libraries in India began looking at thesauri as an effective device for providing subject access; it is not without significance that the first national-level seminar on thesauri in India was held only in 1976, more than two decades after the idea was promoted in the U.S.A. Several in-house thesauri in such areas as Energy, Leather Technology, etc., were developed using semi-automatic methods of generating thesauri.

It was also during the 1970s that the University Grants Commission suggested to universities in the country that there be a change from 'library science' to 'library and information science' in the nomenclature of their departments and educational programs. Courses in computers, systems analysis, etc., were introduced as a part of library school curricula, and there were attempts to introduce aspects dealing with the impact and implications of computers in the core areas of library and information science, including cataloguing and information retrieval. However, it was the arrival of the microcomputer in the 1980s and the free distribution, by UNESCO, of CDS/ISIS (software for the creation and management of textual databases) that really made a big difference. Since the advent of microcomputers, commercial library application software packages have also been developed within the country and have become widely available. More recently major library automation funding agencies such as INFLIBNET[1] have made library automation software packages available to institutions coming under their umbrella. All of this is in sharp contrast to the situation that existed in the 1970s and 1980s when the few libraries that chose to automate some of their operations had to develop software in-house. Today a large number of libraries–academic and special libraries–are in varying stages of automating their operations, and almost all of them use commercially available software or software made available by the funding agencies. Compliance with such standards as, e.g., ISO 2709, is now generally taken for granted, which certainly was not the case in early library automation projects implemented during the 1970s and even early 1980s.

The Revised Programs

Considering the major changes taking place in the universe of information and information technology, the University Grants Commission realized the need for taking a fresh look at course contents and also the structure of the program at the Master's level. A Curriculum Development Committee was set up.[2] The report of the CDC in Library & Information Science, however, turned out to be a disappointment and, soon enough, the U.G.C. suggested that this be reviewed. Another committee went into this and, after a series of consultations and workshops, came out with a document entitled *UGC Model Curriculum: Library and Information Science*, which was published by the U.G.C. in 2001 (University Grants Commission, 2001). The U.G.C. even suggested that all universities should update their own course contents to conform to the suggestions made in this document. This document recommended a substantial revision of course contents. Table 2 presents an overview of the recommended courses and contents relevant to bibliographic organization and control.

TABLE 2. Revised Courses Recommended by the U.G.C.

Course Title	Broad Course Contents	Recommended no. of hours of instruction/ study	Overall weight (against a total of 64 credits)
Knowledge Organization, Information Processing and Retrieval (Theory)	1. Universe of Knowledge 2. Bibliographic Description 3. Methods of Knowledge Organization 4. Subject Cataloguing	120	4
Knowledge Organization, Information Processing and Retrieval (Practice)	1. Classification of Documents (usually using *Dewey, UDC,* and *Colon*) 2. Book Numbering 3. Cataloguing of simple and complex documents (using a standard cataloguing code– usually *AACR2* and Ranganathan's *C.C.C.*) 4. Subject Cataloguing (using a standard tool–usually *Sears List* or *LCSH* and chain indexing)	120	4
Information Retrieval	1. Subject Indexing: Principles and Practices 2. Indexing Languages and Vocabulary Control 3. Information Retrieval	120	4

THE PRESENT SITUATION

University programs in Library & Information Science are being offered in the country in over 75 universities and other institutions of higher learning. It is difficult, in a review such as this, to examine in detail the course contents of all or even a majority of the schools. What has therefore been attempted in the following paragraphs is to provide an overview of the course contents and to illustrate the nature of changes that are taking place with some examples. At present, there are two distinct models of formal university education for library and information professionals in India and both are graduate programs (post-graduate level).[3] The first model represents a continuation of the scheme that was introduced by S. R. Ranganathan in the University of Delhi in 1948. This model consists of two separate graduate programs:

- A one-year Bachelor's degree program (B. Lib. Sc./B.L.I.Sc.) (intended to train middle-level professionals)

- A one-year Master's degree program after B.L.I.Sc. (M. Lib. Sc./M.L.I.Sc.) (intended to train supervisory and higher-level professionals)

This scheme still remains in operation in several universities although, in recent years, many universities have switched over to an integrated two-year (four semesters) Master's degree program in place of two independent programs. Irrespective of the model any particular university school has adopted, courses on knowledge organization–classification, cataloguing, and subject indexing–form a major component of the core curriculum in all universities without exception. Traditionally Indian universities have divided the courses in this area into "Theory" and "Practice," following the recommendations in the U.G.C. Review Committee report. The contents, almost without exception, include:

- Normative principles and postulates forming the theoretical basis of knowledge organization
- Practical training in the use of select schemes of classification, codes of cataloguing, subject heading lists, and subject indexing procedures
  - The classification schemes taught in detail include: *Colon Classification* and the *Dewey Decimal Classification* (at the Bachelor's degree level), and advanced classification using *Colon Classification* and *Universal Decimal Classification* (at the Master's level). One or two schools had the practice of teaching *L.C. Classification* as well; it is not certain whether the practice is still being continued.
  - Cataloguing codes taught include the *Anglo-American Cataloging Rules* and the *Classified Catalogue Code* (*CCC*) of S. R. Ranganathan. The convention in most schools is to teach the use of *AACR* for the preparation of a dictionary catalogue, and invariably, the *Sears List of Subject Headings* is used as the tool for formulating subject headings. The use of *CCC* in the preparation of a classified catalogue is practiced, with chain indexing as the principal tool for preparing the subject index to the classified catalogue. Even at the Master's level, generally the same two codes are taught with emphasis on cataloguing complex serials, non-book materials, etc. In recent years, some schools have begun offering electives in the cataloguing of non-book materials, and the core courses are restricted to the application of cataloguing codes and other tools for the cataloguing of books and periodicals.

- There are wide variations in the teaching of applications of other tools and techniques such as thesauri, subject-indexing techniques, authority files, etc. However, almost without exception, the application of such techniques as PRECIS and POPSI, and post-coordinate indexing are included in the course contents of most schools. Some schools, especially in the 1960s (e.g., DRTC and the library school at the Banaras Hindu University), would insist on students at the Master's level designing a depth version of *Colon Classification* for a micro-subject as a mandatory requirement. This no longer forms a part of the core curriculum today. Design of micro-thesaurus/classaurus are, however, chosen by some students for their project work, which is a mandatory requirement at the Master's level in many schools.

- There are also variations in the teaching of cataloguing for the machine environment. Almost without exception, MARC formats form a part of the core curriculum. A significant development during the past decade and more is the effort in practically every university school to integrate information technology components into the core courses in knowledge organization. For example, in many universities cataloguing is no longer being taught merely to train students to work in a manual environment (say, for a card catalogue). Course contents have been revised to train students in the use of MARC formats such as CCF, US MARC, etc., along with a standard catalogue code. However, most library schools cannot afford commercially available software that can fully support the MARC family of formats. Given this, most schools train students in the use of software packages in the public domain, such as WINISIS. Following INFLIBNET's initiatives, many universities have adopted the SOUL software (Software for University Libraries), the US MARC format, the *Anglo-American Cataloging Rules2*, and the *LCSH* in their plans to computerize their catalogues and other operations. A demo version of this software has been made available to many library schools.

- Digital library research and development in India is a very recent development. However, in the last few years there have been some major initiatives in this area. Following these developments, elective courses in the area of digital libraries, e-publishing, etc., have been introduced in some universities. Course contents have been expanded to include aspects of metadata, and such standards as Dublin Core now form a part of the course contents in some schools. The recently revised course contents of the M. Sc. program of the University of Madras reflect the nature of changes that are taking place:

- Knowledge Organization and Metadata (4 credits)
  - Information Entities and Organization of Information
  - Tools for Knowledge Organization
  - Standards for Bibliographic Databases
  - Organization of Digital Resources, Metadata
- Classification Practicum using recent editions of *Colon, Dewey,* and *UDC* (3 credits)
- Cataloguing and Document Description (3 credits)
  - Elements of Description–ISBD (G) Practicum using *AACR2, Sears List*, and US MARC format/CCF
- Information Storage and Retrieval (3 credits)
  - Subject Indexing Models; Vocabulary; Search Process
- Information Systems Design (3 credits)
  - Practicum in the use of WINISIS (or some other software) along with US MARC or CCF to create (bibliographic and other textual) databases; search and retrieval
  - Practicum in the use of select retrieval packages such as ProQuest, WINSPIRS, etc.

These courses account for 16 credits out of a total of 54 credits in the core curriculum.[4] Besides these courses, an elective course on Cataloguing of Special Materials (3 credits) and elective courses on E-Publishing and on Digital Libraries (each one of which includes a unit on metadata) are also being offered. Many other schools, notably the DRTC (DRTC and NISCAIRS offer an Associateship in Information Science), the University of Mysore (the University of Mysore offers a Master of Information Management Program in addition to the Master's degree programme in Library & Information Science), the National Centre for Science Information (the NCSI offers an advanced post-Master's program in information and knowledge management), Karnataka University, the North-Eastern Hill University (NEHU), and the University of Delhi have carried out substantial revisions of their course contents in recent years.

The School Faculty

The library school faculty in India probably represents the weakest link in the chain of formal and continuing education programs. Faculty strength in many schools is certainly not adequate to meet specialized training requirements in the area of knowledge organization. The result is that probably no school has any faculty member who specializes exclusively in knowledge organization. This has meant that members of the faculty necessarily have to specialize and teach courses in two or more areas. Those who are engaged in teaching courses in knowledge organization are not necessarily those who have earned their doctorates in the same area. However, every school has one or two faculty members who are equipped to teach courses in knowledge organization.

CONTINUING EDUCATION

It is a truism that only a negligible proportion of the total expenditure on education is spent on continuing education. Universities and institutions of higher education in India do not generally have any statutory responsibility for providing continuing education programs. In recent years, however, with rapid all-around developments and the consequent rapid rate of obsolescence of the skills and knowledge of professionals, there is increasing recognition of the need for and importance of continuing education programs. A large number of organizations are now, as a part of their regular activities, engaged in the conduct of training programs aimed at improving and enhancing the skills of professionals. The principal categories of institutions that have engaged in the conduct of such continuing education programs in recent years include:

- Universities and institutions of higher learning:
  - The University Grants Commission has funded the establishment of a centre known as Academic Staff College (in several universities) charged with the responsibility of conducting continuing education programs for faculty in universities and colleges.[5]
  - Several university departments of library & information science, NISCAIRS (formerly, INSDOC), and the Documentation Research & Training Centre have also conducted short-duration training programs in areas including knowledge organization.
- Professional bodies and associations (e.g., The Indian Library Association, Indian Association of Special Libraries and Information Centres, the Society for Information Science, and even professional associations at the state level). In recent years the annual conventions of some of the major professional bodies, and also in-

ternational conferences held in the country, have included tutorials by experts on emerging areas:

- The ICDL (International Conference on Digital Libraries, New Delhi: February 2004) and ICADL (International Conference of Asian Digital Libraries, Bangalore: December 2001) included tutorials on metadata
- The Sarada Ranganathan Endowment for Library Science (founded by S. R. Ranganathan) has been regularly organising short-term training programs in several areas of relevance to the profession including knowledge organization. The emphasis has been on the use of WINISIS/CDS-ISIS for database creation using appropriate standards such as CCF/US MARC, *AACR2*, etc. The Endowment also conducted national level seminars on
  - Classification in the Digital Environment (2001)
  - Cataloguing of Digital Resources (2002)
- National level agencies such as INFLIBNET and the National Centre for Science Information, Bangalore (INFLIBNET, besides conducting tutorials and open training programs for professionals from universities during its annual convention–CALIBER–also conducts on-the-job training for staff working on its project to put into machine-readable form the catalogues of major university libraries). The contents of these programs include relevant areas of *AACR2* and US MARC format, besides the use of SOUL software for creating machine-readable bibliographic records.
- Library networks (The DELNET, especially, has not only been conducting training programs for project staff of its ongoing projects but has regularly been conducting tutorials as part of its annual national level conventions–the NACLIN. Since 1998 every NACLIN has included tutorials on MARC; many have included tutorials on *AACR2* and *LCSH*, and the creation of bibliographic databases in Indian languages and scripts.)
- At the state level also, besides university schools, some other organizations are engaged in continuing education programs. For example, for the Science City–an organization of the government of the State of Tamilnadu as part of its project to network the 30-odd libraries in the Science City area of the city of Chennai–the University of Madras was asked to conduct a series of training programs for librarians in the creation of machine-readable catalogue records. The course contents included *AACR2*, MARC format, *LCSH*, and training in the use of appropriate software.

- The Central Reference Library which is responsible for the *Indian National Bibliography* has instituted a training program for newly graduated library school students in all aspects in the production of the national bibliography
- Large libraries send some of their senior professional staff to attend conferences and seminars

However, a considerable amount of the training that is conducted for library professionals is on-the-job training in the use of specific tools and packages. Such training is generally arranged by the funding agencies that support implementation of automation projects (e.g., INFLIBNET, DELNET, etc.) or by commercial agencies that supply required hardware and/or software.

THE FUTURE

Given the present scenario, what will be the future of education for knowledge organization in India? This is indeed a difficult question to answer. The major factors that will probably shape and influence education in the area will be:

- The standards and tools that are accepted at the national level for creation of bibliographic databases
- The speed with which the national bibliographic agency, other national agencies (especially INFLIBNET), and large research libraries implement automation of catalogs.

Perhaps some of the developments that are taking place elsewhere suggest that there will be a revival of interest in some of the principles, powerful tools, and techniques in knowledge organization that originated in India. For example, the research that has been going on in the application of facet analysis in the Web environment, the interest shown in a re-examination of the fundamental principles and objectives of cataloguing (IFLA's FRBR, and the suggestion that an ICCP (1961)-type conference should be organized which aims at a re-examination of the basic principles in light of the changed circumstances, etc.), the recognition of the need for metadata embedded in digital resources, and the emphasis on adopting standard cataloguing tools for this purpose are all indicators of the emerging trends. It is highly probable that knowledge organization as a discipline will receive the same level of emphasis that it enjoyed in the early years after the introduction of university-level programs in library science in the country. Only the courses and contents will be packaged differently to suit the emerging digital environment.

NOTES

1. INFLIBNET is an Inter-University Centre of the University Grants Commission set up with the objective of automating and networking libraries in institutions of higher education and research.

2. In fact, the U.G.C. initiated the exercise of reviewing course contents in every discipline including Library & Information Science and, for this purpose, constituted curriculum development committees (CDC) in practically every discipline.

3. Para-professionals are, with a few exceptions, trained via programs conducted at the post-higher secondary school level by polytechnics and some library associations.

4. A student has to complete all of the core courses and obtain a minimum of 72 credits to become eligible for the award of the Master's degree.

5. College librarians and professionals working in university libraries at the level of Assistant Librarian and above are generally given parity with faculty.

REFERENCES

Ranganathan, S. R., 1964. *Classified Catalogue Code with Additional Rules for Dictionary Catalogue Code*. 5th ed. Assisted by A. Neelameghan. Bombay: Asia Publishing House.

University Grants Commission (India). *Review Committee*, 1965. *Library Science in Indian Universities*. New Delhi: U.G.C.

University Grants Commission (India), 2001. *UGC Model Curriculum: Library and Information Science*. New Delhi: U.G.C.

Current Status
of Cataloging and Classification Education
in Japan

Shoichi Taniguchi

SUMMARY. This paper provides an overview of the current status of cataloging and classification (C&C) education in Japan and looks forward to developments in the near future. First, the current status of library and information science (LIS) education and its major issues are briefly reviewed. Second, the situation of C&C practice in Japanese libraries is briefly reviewed, since it affects C&C education. Third, the present situation and issues in C&C education are examined and described under two categories: education in LIS schools and education in LIS programs offered by other colleges and universities. Finally, on-the-job training and continuing education in the C&C domain are discussed. *[Article copies available for a fee from The Haworth Document Delivery Service: 1-800-HAWORTH. E-mail address: <docdelivery@haworthpress.com> Website: <http://www.HaworthPress.com> © 2005 by The Haworth Press, Inc. All rights reserved.]*

KEYWORDS. Cataloging education, classification education, LIS education, Japan

Shoichi Taniguchi is Associate Professor, Institute of Library and Information Science, University of Tsukuba, 1-2 Kasuga, Tsukuba-shi, Ibaraki-ken 305-8550, Japan (E-mail: taniguch@slis.tsukuba.ac.jp).

[Haworth co-indexing entry note]: "Current Status of Cataloging and Classification Education in Japan." Taniguchi, Shoichi. Co-published simultaneously in *Cataloging & Classification Quarterly* (The Haworth Information Press, an imprint of The Haworth Press, Inc.) Vol. 41, No. 2, 2005, pp. 121-133; and: *Education for Library Cataloging: International Perspectives* (ed: Dajin D. Sun, and Ruth C. Carter) The Haworth Information Press, an imprint of The Haworth Press, Inc., 2006, pp. 121-133. Single or multiple copies of this article are available for a fee from The Haworth Document Delivery Service [1-800-HAWORTH, 9:00 a.m. - 5:00 p.m. (EST). E-mail address: docdelivery@haworthpress.com].

INTRODUCTION

In this paper I provide an overview of the current status of cataloging and classification (C&C) education in Japan and take a look at its development in the near future. The C&C education in this country is given within the framework of library and information science (LIS) education. Therefore, the current status of the whole LIS education system in Japan and the major issues involved need to be examined first to facilitate an understanding of the background and limitations of the C&C education in Japan. Next, the C&C practice in Japanese libraries is briefly reviewed since it affects C&C education. Finally, an overview of the current situation and issues in C&C education is provided for: (a) education in LIS schools and departments, (b) LIS programs offered by colleges and universities without an LIS school or department, and (c) on-the-job training and continuing education.

Previous articles[1] have described LIS education in Japan, but no article until now has focused on the C&C education.

CURRENT STATUS OF LIS EDUCATION

The LIS profession is not fully developed in Japan, and librarianship is not well-recognized as a profession in our society. This can be stated from several viewpoints–quality of education, employment system, and career development of librarians. Kim[2] and Takeuchi and Kim[3] have provided a good overview of the current status of LIS education and pointed out its major issues. I will briefly describe the current status and issues as follows:

Quality of Education

The legal qualifications of librarians are stipulated by the Library Law, which was enacted in 1950 and revised in 1985 and 1996. The Law covers only public libraries and each member of the professional staff is called a "librarian" (or "qualified librarian"). Training courses given by colleges and universities are designated by the Ministry of Education, Science, Sports and Culture under the Law. The curriculum and credits of the courses are specified by the ordinance of the Ministry. The current ordinance, issued in 1996, specifies a minimum of 20 credits for a qualified librarian. However, more credits are desirable, because the minimum is not sufficient for professional education.

Fewer than 10 universities offer comprehensive programs in LIS education.[4] These universities have a school or department specialized in LIS for undergraduate, master's, and/or doctoral students. In the undergraduate program, students are required to complete no less than 124 credits over four years and submit a thesis for a bachelor's degree. Students in a master's program should complete 30 credits and submit a thesis.

In contrast, more than 150 other colleges and universities, including junior (2-year) colleges, offer extra-curricular programs in LIS education. However, most such programs barely meet the minimum requirements leading to a librarianship certificate, providing 20 to 30 credits. Moreover, several universities offer annual short-term courses (i.e., 20-credit courses) for unqualified library workers. These short-term courses are also recognized as qualifying education under the Law.

Employment System

There is an imbalance between the demand for and the supply of librarians. More than 10,000 students acquire a librarian's certificate every year. However, only 3 to 4 percent of these graduates, and about 10 to 20 percent of the graduates of the LIS schools and departments, are eventually employed as librarians.

This imbalance is caused by the employment system for library staff. For example, many local authorities responsible for public libraries tend to hire library workers as general administration staff and then assign them to library work. Such a tendency has increased under the recent economic slowdown. In fact, they are not required to hire people with the certificate by the Law and are required only to hire people who have passed civil service examinations for public official status. The reality of qualifying librarians through short-term courses further promotes such an employment situation.

As a result, most graduates of the LIS schools and departments who want to work in libraries have to find jobs in other fields.

Under these circumstances, there is no incentive for colleges and universities that offer the minimum courses prescribed by the Law to develop more advanced LIS courses.

Career Development

The low rate of professional employment also indicates that the mobility of librarians is very low. It is rare to move from one library to another in order to develop professional skills and knowledge or to obtain a better position. If a librarian gets a position in a public library run by a local government, in most cases he or she will work for that same library until his or her retirement, or else move out of the library service to another department in the organization.

In contrast, librarians working in a national university library have the opportunities to move to other national university libraries.

The net result is that there is almost no job market in which librarians can find new positions and libraries can hire more skilled or well-trained professionals.

Under such circumstances, a career development path is not clear, and there is no incentive to develop professional skills and knowledge. Continuing education in LIS is, therefore, not regarded as a necessity by employers. Most libraries provide no support for their librarians' professional development via either on-the-job training or continuing education.

C&C PRACTICE IN JAPANESE LIBRARIES

C&C education must reflect the current situation of C&C practice in Japanese libraries, in particular, the use of standards and tools such as cataloging rules. I will briefly describe the situation in this section.

In Japanese libraries, the Nippon Cataloging Rules (NCR)[5] is widely used in addition to the Anglo-American Cataloguing Rules, 2nd ed. (AACR2), according to a survey by the Japan Library Association (JLA).[6] NCR is prepared by the Committee of Cataloging of JLA. The latest version is the 2001 revision of the 1987 edition. NCR is based on ISBDs of IFLA, and hence compatibility between NCR and AACR2 is assured at that level. At the same time, NCR has some special features intended to deal with Japanese publications and to fit with the Japanese language.[7] NCR is widely used in more than 90 percent of Japanese libraries, including the National Diet Library (NDL) and NACSIS-CAT, which is a shared online cataloging system operated by the National Institute of Informatics (NII) as a bibliographic utility.

NCR can handle foreign language materials, but libraries receiving many such materials tend to use AACR2 to catalog them, except for Chinese and Korean works. The reason why AACR2 is used in those libraries is that we can obtain bibliographic records created under AACR2 and MARC 21 records, and it is cost-effective to perform copy-cataloging with those records. Another reason is that NCR does not contain sufficient rules for foreign language materials. AACR2 is used in the NDL, university libraries, and NACSIS-CAT, in addition to NCR.

Classification schedules and subject heading lists commonly used in Japanese libraries are the Nippon Decimal Classification (NDC)[8] and the Basic Subject Headings (BSH),[9] which are compiled by the Committee of Classification and the Committee of Subject Headings of JLA, respectively. NDC has a similar structure to the Dewey Decimal Classification (DDC) but is designed for Japanese publications and libraries. This schedule is widely used in more than 80 percent of libraries. Other schedules currently used in university libraries are DDC and the Library of Congress Classification (LCC).

Japanese libraries traditionally have relied on classification systems to represent subject but have less emphasis on subject headings. Many libraries do not assign subject headings. BSH, Library of Congress Subject Headings (LCSH), or NDL Subject Headings (NDLSH)[10] are used in a small number of libraries.

Public libraries rely heavily on private companies that provide MARC records to libraries. Most libraries use those records as they are, although they must assign their own call numbers according to classification codes. In university libraries, NACSIS-CAT is widely used, and only a small number of these libraries have introduced OCLC WorldCat in addition to NACSIS-CAT. Through NACSIS-CAT, university libraries establish a national union catalog, and at the same time, they obtain records made by other libraries, the NDL, private companies, and several foreign national libraries.

Organizing electronic resources–for example, metadata creation for Web resources, digitization of analog resources, management of electronic journals, and preservation of electronic resources–is a big emerging issue in Japanese libraries. Libraries there have been trying to tackle this issue; it is still at the stage of trial and error.

C&C EDUCATION AT LIS SCHOOLS

There are a few four-year universities with schools or departments specializing in LIS education and offering undergraduate, master's, and doctoral programs in Japan. The undergraduate LIS programs of these universities include courses beyond the 20 credits prescribed by the Library Law and develop their own curricula depending on their objectives and strategies. Of course, their curricula cover the scope of the

20-credit courses which help the students get a librarian's certificate upon graduation.

In contrast, the master's and doctoral programs usually do not cover the scope of the 20-credit courses. The graduate programs have been established not to provide that certificate, but rather to provide the students with advanced knowledge and research skills.

Therefore, LIS education in Japan has been carried out principally at the undergraduate level. Graduate programs have not, so far, taken the major position in that education. Furthermore, graduates from the master's programs can hardly find employment in libraries; the difficulty of employment is the same as that for graduates from the undergraduate programs.

Let me review some LIS schools and focus on their C&C education.

University of Tsukuba
School of Library and Information Science

The University of Library and Information Science (ULIS) was established in 1979 through the reform of the National Junior College for Librarianship, and provided the most comprehensive program covering LIS in Japan. In October 2002, ULIS was incorporated into the University of Tsukuba. ULIS was reconfigured into one undergraduate school and one graduate school.

Each year the school for undergraduates accepts 150 freshman and 30 third-year students transferred from other colleges and universities. Its curriculum covers the LIS field comprehensively and includes a wide variety of courses in information processing. In total, there were about 150 courses in LIS and information processing offered in the 2003 academic year. Students must select one of the two elective modules: Information Management, which is oriented toward the library field, and Information Processing, which concentrates on information and computer science. But students can take any course, regardless of which module they have selected, within the limits of the specified credits.

The courses that are closely related to C&C are:

- Introduction to Information Organization (basic level)
- Classification (basic)
- Cataloging and Cataloging Systems (basic)
- Cataloging and Classification: Practice (basic)
- Library Database Systems (semi-advanced)
- Library Database Systems: Practice (semi-advanced).

Each of these courses is worth 2 credits and is optional, but students who want to get a librarian's certificate must take at least the minimum credits specified in the curriculum. In fact, most of the students (usually, more than 100) take all of these courses.

Other related courses include: Bibliographic Databases, Indexing and Abstracting, Cataloging and Classification of Pre-Modern Documents, Information Retrieval, Information Retrieval: Practice, and Library Management Systems. Most of these courses come under the Information Management module. The Information Processing module incorporates such courses as Library Network Systems and Digital Documents.

As an example, the contents of the course Cataloging and Cataloging Systems include: (1) objectives and functions of catalogs, (2) types of catalogs (e.g., OPACs) and features of each type, (3) history of cataloging, involving standardization activities, (4) principles and manners of description, (5) bibliographic hierarchy and other relationships, (6) headings and access points, (7) MARC formats, (8) national bibliographic agencies and other bibliographic records providers, (9) centralized cataloging and shared cataloging, (10) bibliographic utilities and their cataloging systems, and (11) framework of bibliographic control. The cataloging rules taught in this course and its Practice are NCR and AACR2.

Similarly, the Classification course explains classification schedules and subject heading lists, such as NDC, DDC, LCC, Colon Classification (CC), and BSH, and studies the basic theory of subject analysis and classification. In the practical training, NDC and BSH are mainly used, which reflects the current practices in Japanese libraries. In Library Database Systems and its Practice, some online cataloging systems are taught, including the shared cataloging system NACSIS-CAT.

The school plans to revise the curriculum for the 2004 academic year so as to give more weight to basic courses and slim down the curriculum.

Keio University
School of Library and Information Science

The School of Library and Information Science at Keio University was founded by the Faculty of Letters. The school originated as the Japan Library School, which offered the first formal and professional education of librarians in 1951 under the auspices of the American Library Association.

The school accepts more than 60 undergraduate students every year. They select one of the three major tracks (i.e., modules): Library, Information Media, and Information Retrieval. The school offers more than 40 courses in LIS.

The C&C topic is taught in some of the courses. The most closely related is Organization of Recorded Materials (2 credits) in the Library track. The basic C&C topics taught in this course are: framework of bibliographic control, objectives of catalogs and principles of cataloging, user behavior in using catalogs, standards such as cataloging rules, classification schedules and subject heading lists, cataloging systems (including MARC and bibliographic utilities), and OPACs. The information organization standards covered in this course include NCR, AACR2, NDC, and NDLSH. About 40 to 50 students who want to get a librarian's certificate are enrolled in this course each year.

Subject analysis, indexing, and metadata are dealt with in the courses Structure and Analysis of Information Media (2 credits) and Information Retrieval (2 credits).

Aichi Shukutoku University
Department of Library and Information Science

The Aichi Shukutoku University established the Department of Library and Information Science within the Faculty of Letters in 1985. Currently, about 120 to 150 students are enrolled in the department every year. Nearly 60 courses are provided. The courses dealing chiefly with C&C are Library Materials Organization (2 credits, basic level) and its Practice (2 credits). Both courses are optional, but most students select them to get a librarian's certificate.

The Library Materials Organization covers catalogs and materials organization, bibliographic control, cataloging rules, bibliographic description, headings and authority control, classification, subject headings, and MARC and online cataloging systems. NCR and AACR2 are followed as cataloging rules. The subject heading lists taught in this course include BSH, NDLSH, LCSH, and Sears' List of Subject Headings. The following classification schedules are also taught: NDC, UDC (Universal Decimal Classification), DDC, NDLC (NDL Classification),[11] and CC.

The Library Materials Organization Practice teaches cataloging and classification practice with AACR2, BSH, NDC, and UDC. Part of the practice is done through online cataloging systems.

In addition to these courses, the course Structure and Analysis of Information Media also deals with subject analysis, indexing, and abstracting of some types of materials. Metadata is partly covered in other courses.

Changes to C&C Education in LIS Schools

LIS schools, including the above three, can afford to incorporate new topics or create new courses to reflect the social and technological changes surrounding the LIS field. Such changes are constantly made in order to attract more students and to strengthen their competencies. Knowledge and skills in information technology and in management and leadership are needed to cope with the emerging issues in libraries, such as organizing electronic resources.

In the domain of C&C teaching, metadata is a highly anticipated topic, but the framework and contents of metadata instruction are not clear yet. Each school has been trying to teach metadata standards in its own way.

Master's and Doctoral Programs

There are fewer than 10 master's and doctoral LIS programs in Japan. Graduate programs have been established with the main purpose of not providing graduates with a certificate, but rather providing them with advanced knowledge and research skills. Therefore, each program formulates its own curriculum in accordance with the school's objectives and strategies, and the curricula of these programs are different from each other. The level of the courses in any curriculum for a master's program is rather advanced, and a thesis is required and heavily weighted.

Although the decision on C&C courses varies from individual programs, most graduate programs normally include courses in C&C. The graduate school at the University of Tsukuba offers such courses as Organization of Information and Media, Information Analysis, and Information Resource Management. Likewise, the master's and doctoral programs at Keio University and Aichi Shukutoku University also incorporate courses related to C&C. Metadata management is one of the evolving topics incorporated into C&C courses.

Meanwhile, there is a sign of change in these graduate programs: the librarians' enrollment as a part-time student has increased, indicating that they are seeking continuing education in order to improve their professional competencies. Regrettably, graduation from these programs does not lead directly to career development, i.e., it does not prompt a job promotion. At the current stage, such enrolment of librarians is a personal initiative; usually they receive no support from their libraries.

C&C EDUCATION IN LIS PROGRAMS
BY OTHER COLLEGES AND UNIVERSITIES

More than 150 colleges and universities, including junior colleges, offer extra-curricular programs leading to a librarian's certificate. Most of the programs are based on the minimum requirements determined by the Ministry. The curriculum and credits determined by the Ministry consist of 12 compulsory subjects (18 credits in total) and 6 elective subjects (at least 2 subjects at 1 credit each). Individual colleges and universities can adopt the curriculum and credits specified by the Ministry as is (i.e., 12 compulsory and 2 elective subjects), or they can offer more comprehensive courses beyond that curriculum. However, most of them provide only the required courses.

The C&C subjects are taught in the courses: Introduction to Materials Organization (2 credits, required) and Materials Organization Practice (2 credits, required). Subject analysis and metadata might be taught in the course Information Retrieval Practice (1 credit, required) or Information Technology (1 credit, optional).

The objective and scope of these two required courses are specified in the guidelines by the Ministry as follows:

Title of the subject: Introduction to Materials Organization.

Objective: Learning materials organization and principal methods used in libraries, including methods by use of computer.

Scope: (1) Significance of bibliographic control and materials organization; materials organization and users (2) Functions and types of catalogs; outline and usage of cataloging rules (3) Features of classification; outline and usage of NDC (4) Outline and usage of subject heading lists (5) Outline and characteristics of online catalogs, including OPACs; management and running of online catalogs (including the use of a bibliographic utility) (6) Information processing in cataloging and other library systems.

Title of the subject: Materials Organization Practice.

Objective: Learning practical knowledge and skills through practices of materials organization.

Scope: (1) Practices of creating bibliographic records, including assignment of classification numbers and subject headings (2) Practice of using a bibliographic utility (3) Collecting, editing, and other process-ing of bibliographic and other types of data with a computer.

Cataloging rules, subject heading lists, and classification schedules dealt with in these courses are respectively NCR and AACR2, BSH, and NDC. These reflect the current practice in Japanese libraries and determine the length of time for these courses. Most colleges and uni-versities provide opportunities for students to practice using online cataloging systems and/or bibliographic utilities like NACSIS-CAT, according to the guidelines of the Ministry. The textbooks used in these courses have been published by the JLA and other publishers.

The current curriculum and credits started in 1997 in accordance with the revision of the Library Law ordinance. From 1968 to 1997, a differ-ent curriculum and credits system had been authorized; that is, 19 cred-its were required to get a certificate of "qualified librarian." Within that curriculum, subjects related to C&C were Cataloging (2 credits, re-quired), Cataloging Practice (1 credit, required), Classification (2 cred-its, required), Classification Practice (1 credit, required), and Special Topic on Organization of Materials (1 credit, optional). In comparison, it seems that the total credits in the C&C instruction have decreased in the current curriculum. However, some topics related to C&C are taught in other related courses, such as Information Retrieval Practice and In-formation Technology, which are established in the current curriculum. Thus, the contents taught in C&C-related courses have not decreased, but are reformulated in line with the changes in the current practices of the Japanese libraries.

On the other hand, some anticipated big changes in those programs over the next 5 to 10 years, in my opinion, should not be expected in non-LIS schools. The reason is that most colleges and universities do not have any motivation to expand their curricula greatly beyond the curriculum specified by the Ministry, since the imbalanced demand and supply for librarians will not be resolved in the near future. Also, they will continue to provide their current programs because there are still many students who want to get a librarian's certificate in spite of the im-balance between education and employment.

Within the current framework of the curriculum, a big change in the contents of the current C&C instruction should not also be expected. The limit of time to the courses is the most severe difficulty. Another reason is that the current framework of C&C practice will remain un-changed over the next several years. Additionally, metadata or other topics that attract a broad interest still need to have more standard con-tents to warrant their teaching.

C&C ON-THE-JOB TRAINING
AND CONTINUING EDUCATION

The LIS profession is not fully developed in Japan and is still weak, as mentioned at the beginning of this paper. As a result, on-the-job training and continuing education are neither encouraged nor promoted. Most libraries do not provide support for librarians' professional development.

Nevertheless, there have been many seminars, workshops, and conferences on C&C topics in the profession. Some are held regularly, others are ad hoc. In recent years, organizing electronic resources seems to be a main theme at those meetings. That theme includes metadata creation for Web resources, digitization of analog resources, management of electronic journals, and preservation of electronic resources. At some meetings, XML and other advanced, emerging technologies are discussed.

For librarians in university libraries, NII offers several training courses related to its systems and services. Training for NACSIS-CAT is a three-day workshop. The graduates from a three-week train-the-trainer program become the NACSIS-CAT instructors in regional training courses. These courses are important for university libraries, since NACSIS-CAT is widely used in these libraries and there is a constant need for training as the staff can be reassigned at any time. NII also operates a mailing list for its cataloging system and a Q&A database for Web correspondence between NII and the participating libraries.

Recently, NII has started a new service called Academic Information Resources in Universities, which helps participating libraries create metadata for Web resources and provides users with those metadata through a retrieval system. It has attracted a wide attention from librarians and has spawned workshops on metadata.

Some universities regularly provide special training seminars, such as seminars on cataloging Chinese materials and seminars on cataloging older Western monographs.

CONCLUSION

C&C education as part of LIS education is required in Japan in order to train librarians to cope effectively with the emerging digital world. Information and communication technologies, including networking, have had a big impact on C&C education, as well as on libraries themselves. These emerging trends have forged the reform of the LIS and C&C education. On the other hand, obstacles that prevent further reform are still to be removed in Japan. There is no sign of change in the employment of librarians or in the overproduction of "qualified librarians" here.

The LIS schools should try to improve their students' competencies by equipping them with more knowledge and skills in information technology and in management and leadership as well. It will be easier for these LIS schools, than for those extra-curricular LIS programs in other colleges and universities, to improve their curricula or their individual courses to meet the challenges.

At the same time, a framework of systematic continuing education for librarians should be created so that they can improve their knowledge and skills in keeping up with the rapid changes in libraries. The JLA and other professional societies in the field must collaborate with the LIS schools and take collective actions toward this end.

NOTES

1. Yong Won Kim, "Library and Information Science Education in Japan," *World Libraries* 8 (1998): 39-49; Hiroya Takeuchi and Yong Won Kim, "Current Issues in Library and Information Science Profession and Its Education in Japan" (paper presented at 65th IFLA Council and General Conference, Bangkok, Thailand, August 20-28, 1999). (http://www.ifla.org/IV/ifla65/papers/151-115e.htm); Theodore F. Welch, *Libraries and Librarianship in Japan* (Westport, Conn.: Greenwood Press, 1997).

2. Kim, "Library and Information Science Education."

3. Takeuchi and Kim, "Current Issues in Library."

4. Japan Library Association, *Education of Library and Information Science in Japan, 2000* (in Japanese) (Tokyo: JLA, 2001).

5. Japan Library Association, Committee of Cataloging, *Nippon Cataloging Rules*, 1987 edition, 2001 revision (Tokyo: JLA, 2001).

6. Japan Library Association, Committee of Cataloging, *Survey of Cataloging and OPACs in Japan* (in Japanese) (Tokyo: JLA, 1998).

7. Tadayoshi Takawashi, "Cataloging in Japan: Relationship Between Japanese and Western Cataloging Rules," *Cataloging & Classification Quarterly* 35 (2002): 209-225.

8. Japan Library Association, Committee of Classification, *Nippon Decimal Classification*, 9th ed. (Tokyo: JLA, 1995).

9. Japan Library Association, Committee of Subject Headings, *Basic Subject Headings*, 4th ed. (Tokyo: JLA, 1999).

10. National Diet Library, *National Diet Library List of Subject Headings*, 5th ed. (Tokyo: NDL, 1991).

11. National Diet Library, *National Diet Library Classification*, Rev. ed. (Tokyo: NDL, 1987).

A Study on the Job Training
and Self-Training of the Cataloging
and Classification Librarians
Working in South Korean Academic Libraries

Chul-Wan Kwak

SUMMARY. This study surveys the current status of job training and self-training provided for the cataloging and classification librarians in Korean academic libraries to actively deal with the rapidly changing library environment. Cataloging librarians from 98 universities in South Korea responded to the survey. As a result, 64.3% of the librarians reported that they were trained, and about 43% of them indicated that they had a short training of less than a week. However, all of them emphasized the necessity of job training. The materials used for training were mainly in print. Only 10% of the academic libraries subscribed to journals relating to library work. An overwhelming majority of the academic libraries surveyed provided financial support for staff training. The use of foreign languages and metadata, and job-related library school courses were preferred by the cataloging librarians. In academic

Chul-Wan Kwak, PhD, MLS, is Associate Professor, Department of Library and Information Science, Kangnam University, San 6-2 Gugal-ri, Giheung-eup, Yongin-si, Gyonggi-do, 449-702, Republic of Korea (E-mail: ckwak@kangnam.ac.kr).

[Haworth co-indexing entry note]: "A Study on the Job Training and Self-Training of the Cataloging and Classification Librarians Working in South Korean Academic Libraries." Kwak, Chul-Wan. Co-published simultaneously in *Cataloging & Classification Quarterly* (The Haworth Information Press, an imprint of The Haworth Press, Inc.) Vol. 41, No. 2, 2005, pp. 135-147; and: *Education for Library Cataloging: International Perspectives* (ed: Dajin D. Sun, and Ruth C. Carter) The Haworth Information Press, an imprint of The Haworth Press, Inc., 2006, pp. 135-147. Single or multiple copies of this article are available for a fee from The Haworth Document Delivery Service [1-800-HAWORTH, 9:00 a.m. - 5:00 p.m. (EST). E-mail address: docdelivery@haworthpress.com].

Available online at http://www.haworthpress.com/web/CCQ
doi:10.1300/J104v41n02_09

libraries, more organized job-training programs and more support for librarians' self-training were needed. *[Article copies available for a fee from The Haworth Document Delivery Service: 1-800-HAWORTH. E-mail address: <docdelivery@haworthpress.com> Website: <http://www.HaworthPress.com>*

KEYWORDS. Academic libraries, library schools, cataloging survey, cataloging librarians, job training, cataloging education, continuing education, South Korea

Since the 1990s, as the OPAC was implemented in academic libraries, cataloging and classification librarians have felt the need for job-related training and, as digital libraries have been developed, the demand for job training has increased. In the constantly changing environment, how have the librarians who took initiatives to introduce the OPAC and digital libraries dealt with such changes? This study intends to examine what job training the cataloging and classification staff has had in order to deal with their current, changing environment and whether they have performed self-training.

LIBRARY SCHOOLS AND ACADEMIC LIBRARIES

Library Schools in Korea

As of late 2004, 32 universities in South Korea had undergraduate programs in the department of library and information science, and 25 of these universities also had masters' programs in library and information science (see Table 1). Of the 25 universities that had graduate programs, five offered a doctoral degree in library and information science. The enrollment of the undergraduate programs ranges from about 30 to 60 students, but usually 40 students are enrolled each academic year. When the students complete a minimum of 12 courses (36 credits) or a maximum of 19 courses (57 credits) in the library and information department, the Librarian 2 Certificate is issued. When students graduate from a two-year college program, they get the Librarian Technician Certificate. Most curricula of the library schools include two courses (6 credits) in classification and cataloging, but each university arbitrarily provides from 3 to 5 courses. However, topics of indexing,

TABLE 1. Current Status of Library Schools (2004)

	National	Private	Faculty Members	Enrollment of Students
Undergraduate (2 yrs.)	0	8	29	860
Undergraduate (4 yrs.)	6	26	136	1288
Master's Program	6	19	N/A	-
School Librarian Master's Program	4	13	N/A	-
Doctoral Program	5	9	N/A	-
Special Program (1 yr.)	0	2	N/A	430

OPAC, and metadata are included in information storage and retrieval courses. In 2004, 1,420 Librarian 2 Certificates were issued, and 1,030 Librarian Technician Certificates were issued.[1]

Current Status of Academic Libraries

Since the economic crisis of South Korea in 1998, the number of librarians in academic libraries has remarkably decreased. As of late 2003, South Korea had 169 universities and 258 academic libraries. The number of the librarians went as follows: 403 Librarian 1s, 1,612 of Librarian 2s, and 313 library technicians. The certificate of Librarian 1 is given to the person who has the Librarian 2 Certificate and nine years of job experience with completion of retraining, or who has six years of work experience and has obtained a masters' degree. The Librarian 2 Certificate is given to the person who has graduated from a four-year university majoring in library and information science. The Library Technician Certificate is given to the person who has graduated from a two-year college majoring in library and information science. In the libraries of national and public universities, the average number of Librarian 1s is 2.29, the number of Librarian 2s is 7.17, and the number of Library Technicians, 2.39. In the libraries of private universities, the average number of Librarian 1s is 1.35, the average number of Librarian 2s is 5.97, and the average number of Library Technicians, 0.86. In general, the average number of librarians in the national and public universities is more than that of the private ones. This is because private universities have cut the number of librarians to overcome a financial crisis. The number of cataloging and classification librarians range from one to fourteen in academic libraries.

In terms of collections, the libraries of national and public universities collected 19,743,010 monographs and the average was 334,627, while the libraries of private universities collected 57,344,358 and the average was 288,162. For non-print materials, the national and public university libraries collected 871,994 and the average was 14,779, while the private ones collected 3,108,686 and the average was 15,621. For periodicals, the national and public university libraries collected 90,079 items and the average was 1,526, whereas the private university libraries collected 269,894 and the average was 1,356 (see Table 2).

Following are the results of the analysis based on a questionnaire containing 13 questions. It targeted librarians responsible for classification and indexing in the university libraries, and it identified education status involved in their jobs. The questionnaire is categorized into three sections: (1) personal background of the subjects; (2) education and self-training for job performance; and (3) knowledge required for their jobs.

PARTICIPANTS OF THE QUESTIONNAIRE

Participants

The questionnaire was distributed to the academic librarians who participated in the cataloging and classification track of a symposium held by the Korea Education & Research Information Service on November 18, 2003. One hundred librarians responded. Except for the two respondents who were not responsible for cataloging and classification, the responses of 98 librarians were analyzed. All academic libraries in South Korea except small-scale libraries were included in this analysis.

Fields and Period of Work

Eighty-eight of the 98 librarians (89.8%) were responsible for cataloging and classification, and the ones who were responsible for classification or cataloging alone were 3.1% and 7.1%, respectively. For work experience, 29 librarians said they worked for one to three years, which took up 29.6% of the total participants. Twenty-seven reported that they worked for five to ten years, representing 27.6% of the respondents. The numbers of participants who worked for under one year, three to five years, and more than ten years happened to the same or almost the same (see Table 3).

TABLE 2. Current Status of Academic Libraries

		National and Public	Private	Total
No. of Universities		26	143	169
No. of Libraries		59	199	258
Staff	Librarian 1	135	268	403
	Librarian 2	423	1,189	1,612
	Library Technician	141	172	313
Collection	Monographs	19,743,010	57,344,358	77,087,368
	Non-Print	871,994	3,108,686	3,980,680
	Periodicals	90,079	269,894	359,973

Adapted from: Korean Library Association, *Statistics on Libraries in Korea, 2003* (Seoul: Korean Library Association, 2003), p. 106-125.

TABLE 3. Work Fields and Experience

Work Area	Work Experience					
	Under 1 yr.	1-3 yrs.	3-5 yrs.	5-10 yrs.	More than 10 yrs.	Total
Cataloging	2	3	0	1	1	7 (7.1%)
Classification	0	0	2	1	0	3 (3.1%)
Both	12	26	12	25	13	88 (89.8%)
Total	14 (14%)	29 (29.6%)	14 (14.3%)	27 (27.6%)	14 (14.3%)	98 (100%)

Previous Work Experience

Only 20 participants (20.4%) answered that they had previous experience working in other libraries before they worked in their present library. Of the 20 participants, 90% of them said that they had worked in other libraries for less than five years. Forty-five percent of these 20 respondents had three years of previous work experience; 30% had under one year; 15% had three to five years; and 10% had more than ten years of previous work experience (see Table 4). This result showed that librarians tend to change their jobs within the first five years of work, but if they have worked beyond five years in one job, they tend to stay in the same job.

TABLE 4. Work Experience in Previous Libraries

	Previous Work Experience					
	Under 1 yr.	1-3 yrs.	3-5 yrs.	5-10 yrs.	More than 10 yrs.	Total
Frequency	6	9	3	0	2	20
Percentages	30	45	15	0	10	100

IN-SERVICE TRAINING

Job Training

Sixty-three of the respondents (64.3%) answered that they had job training when they took their new jobs. Of the 63 participants, 34 said that they were instructed by their supervisors in their new tasks and represented 54% of this group of participants. Twenty-five reported that they received job training from their colleagues and represented 39.7% of this group of participants. And 4 participants (6.3% of this group) indicated being trained by others. The period of job training varied: 27 participants (42.9%) had job training for under one week; 18 participants (28.6%) had job training for more than four weeks; 12 participants (19%) had job training for one to two weeks; and 6 participants (9.5%) had job training between two to four weeks (see Table 5). It was reported that when supervisors gave job training to new librarians, it lasted from under one week to more than four weeks. When the training was given by colleagues, it lasted under one week for the majority of the participants. Based on this result, it is assumed that the training by colleagues covered only the basic outline of tasks, not the detailed work procedures.

Thirty-five respondents reported that they received no training at all when they took their new jobs. The reasons were thought to be: first, there were no organized programs for new librarians in these libraries. Because the number of the librarians was small and there were no supervisors in each division, training was not available when the work was assigned to each librarian. Second, due to the different concept of job training, the respondents may think that only organized training should be called job training. Therefore, most of them did not think they were trained when they received only instructions regarding the basic tasks of their new jobs.

TABLE 5. Training Instructors and Period

Instructor	Period of Training				
	Under One Week	1-2 Weeks	2-4 Weeks	More than 4 Weeks	Total
Supervisor	11	8	4	11	34 (54%)
Colleague	14	3	1	7	25 (39.7%)
Other	2	1	1	0	4 (6.3%)
Total	27 (42.9%)	12 (19%)	6 (9.5%)	18 (28.6%)	63 (100%)

Necessity of Job Training

Most of the participants agreed on the necessity of training when they were going to take on a new task. They indicated that the librarians who received training were more capable of doing the new jobs than the librarians who did not. However, there is no statistically significant difference between the two groups (see Table 6). It indicates that training is necessary in various fields to deal effectively with the given tasks.

When the necessity of job training was compared with work experience, the more years of work the respondents had, the more the necessity of training increased (see Table 7). This was because new library systems were introduced and the development of digital libraries continued in their libraries after these librarians graduated from library school a long time ago, and the necessity of training increased as a result. On the other hand, the librarians who graduated from library school most recently were educated with respect to the changing conditions of libraries, and they did not feel much training was necessary. However, the difference between the groups was not statistically significant.

Training After the Introduction of New Automated Systems

When asked about the new automated system in their libraries, 54 (55.1%) of the total participants said that they were trained to use the new system, and 42 (42.9%) said they did not have any training. And two gave no reply. Of the 54 respondents, 23 (42.6%) indicated that they learned from colleagues about how to use the new system. Seventeen (31.5%) reported that they had training from the manager of the library system; 5 (9.3%) reported training by others; and 9 did not reply

TABLE 6. Necessity of Training in New Tasks (Min = 1, Max = 5)

Job Training	N	Mean	Std. Deviation
Received Training	62	4.42	.69
No Training	36	4.22	.54

t = 1.470, df = 96, p > 0.05

TABLE 7. Necessity of Training According to Work Experience (Min = 1, Max = 5)

	Work Experience					
	Under 1 yr.	1-3 yrs.	3-5 yrs.	5-10 yrs.	More than 10 yrs.	Total
N	14	29	14	27	14	98
Mean	4.21	4.24	4.36	4.41	4.57	4.35
Std. Deviation	.58	.83	.50	.57	.51	.64

(see Table 8). It is assumed that the participants who did not respond learned how to use the system themselves.

When a new automated system was introduced to libraries, the relationship between training on the system and job training for new librarians was examined. From the results, it was difficult to find connections between them. Even in libraries where job training for new librarians was provided, when a new system was introduced, there was no training given at all. It was reported that even libraries that did not provide job training for new librarians sometimes provided training when a new system was introduced. Specifically, 35 (36.5%) participants said that they received training both when they took a new job and when a new system was introduced. However, 17 (17.7%) participants reported that they did not receive any training in either of the cases (see Table 9). Only a third of the total participants received training when recruited as new librarians and after the introduction of a new system. It is assumed that the above result is closely related to the size of the libraries.

SELF-TRAINING

Self-Training Materials

Eighty-two (83.7%) participants indicated that they had materials for self-training relating to their work; 15 (15.3%) responded that they had

TABLE 8. Training of Staff After the Introduction of a New Automated System

	Library System Manager	Colleagues	Others	No Reply	Total
Frequency	17	23	5	9	54
Percentages	31.5	42.6	9.3	16.6	100

TABLE 9. Relationship Between Job Training for New Librarians and Training After the Introduction of a New System

Training for New Employees	Training After the Introduction of a New Automated System		Total
	Yes	No	
Yes	35 (36.5%)	25 (26%)	60 (62.5%)
No	19 (19.8%)	17 (17.7%)	36 (37.5%)
Total	54 (56.3%)	42 (43.8%)	96 (100%)

no training materials; and one gave no answer. Of the 82 participants, 72 (87.8%) indicated that the materials for self-training were in print; 3 (3.6%) said they obtained training materials from the Web; 2 (2.4%) said they had training materials on CD-ROMs, 2 (2.4%) reported using other kinds of materials; and 3 (3.8%) provided no response (see Table 10).

When the relations between job training and self-training were examined, it seemed that there were no significant relations between the two kinds of training (see Table 11). However, it is noteworthy that about 7 (7.3%) of the participants worked in libraries which provided neither job training nor any materials for self-training. In examining the necessity of training indicated by the seven participants, the average was 4.57, which was higher than the average of the total groups. These few participants did not have very good work conditions although they had an urgent need for training.

Subscriptions to Work-Related Journals

Most of the libraries did not subscribe to job-related journals and magazines. Ten participants (10.2%) said that their libraries subscribed journals and magazines relating to their work; 85 participants (86.7%) said that their libraries did not subscribe to journals or magazines at all; and three participants (3.1%) gave no answer. As for the number of

TABLE 10. Kinds of Self-Training Materials for Work Performance

	Web	CD-ROM	Printed Materials	Others	No Response	Total
Frequency	3	2	72	2	3	82
Percentages	3.6	2.4	87.8	2.4	3.8	100

TABLE 11. Training for New Librarians and Provision of Self-Training Materials

Training for New Librarians	Self-Training Materials		Total
	Yes	No	
Yes	53 (54.6%)	8 (8.2%)	61 (62.8%)
No	29 (29.9%)	7 (7.3%)	36 (37.2%)
Total	82 (84.5%)	15 (15.5%)	97 (100%)

the subscribed journals, three of the reported 10 libraries subscribed to one title; two libraries subscribed to two titles; two libraries subscribed to three titles; one library subscribed to four titles; and two libraries subscribed to five titles (see Table 12). The reasons that the number of libraries that purchased journals and magazines relating to library work was small are roughly categorized as follows: first, there is a budget limit to the library's purchase of such materials and most of the libraries do not have subscriptions to job-related journals and magazines due to their limited budgets; second, when the universities have a department of library and information science, the libraries of these universities tend to think that library-related journals and magazines should be provided by the department, not by the libraries.

Educational Support

As for educational support for librarians to increase the efficiency of their work performance, 53 participants (54.1%) reported that they had financial support from their libraries; 44 participants (44.9%) said that they received no educational support from their libraries; and one gave no answer. In respect to the kinds of supportive programs, 43 participants (81.1%) indicated that they received support for participation in various educational programs; 8 participants (15.1%) said that they were supported financially for their graduate studies; and 2 participants (3.8%) said they had support when they presented their theses at seminars (see Table 13).

TABLE 12. Subscriptions to Job-Related Journals and Magazines

Subscription		Libraries reported		Percentages
	No. of Titles			
Yes	1	3	10	10.2
	2	2		
	3	2		
	4	1		
	5	2		
No		85		86.7
No Response		3		3.1
Total		98		100

TABLE 13. Kinds of Educational Support Programs

	Tuition for Graduate Schools	Participation in Seminars	Others	Total
Frequency	8	43	2	53
Percentages	15.1	81.1	3.8	100

Contents of Continuing Education

When the participants were asked what continuing education they needed, the use of foreign languages was the highest. The participants were also interested in the use of metadata and computer applications. However, they were not very interested in taking the cataloging and classification courses provided by the department of library and information science (see Table 14). This indicates that, as international academic exchanges are actively pursued and a variety of foreign language materials are collected in libraries, cataloging librarians desperately feel the need to understand foreign languages. Also, due to the implementation of digital libraries, an awareness of metadata is growing. However, the reason that the preference for taking courses in universities was low is that the courses provided by the universities do not provide the practical skills and experience needed to deal with real library tasks. As cataloging and classification courses in many library schools emphasize the theories of library work, the participants do not think that these courses provide much help in resolving actual problems in libraries.

TABLE 14. Kinds of Continuing Education Programs (Min = 1, Max = 5)

	Kinds of Continuing Education Programs			
	Use of Foreign Languages	Library School Courses	Computers	Metadata
N	98	98	98	97
Mean	4.24	4.07	4.06	4.13
Std. Deviation	.59	.84	.61	.59

Project Cooperation with the Department of Library and Information Science

It was reported that cooperation in research projects between the library and the department of library and information science was very poor. Only 8 participants (8.2%) indicated that they participated in cooperative projects with the department of library and information science; 89 participants (90.8%) reported that they did not participate at all; and one gave no answer (see Table 15). This indicates that librarians in academic libraries have not actively participated in research activities, but for further development of libraries, a close cooperation between academic libraries and the departments of library and information science is needed.

CONCLUSION AND SUGGESTIONS

When the cataloging and classification librarians of academic libraries begin their work, many libraries provide job training, but the training varies with individual libraries. Depending on the condition of the libraries, some do not provide job training at all, and others provide only a brief job introduction, not an organized training for cataloging librarians starting in a new job. On the other hand, it is evident that many librarians have a desperate need for job training. When a new automated system is introduced, a similar situation is observed.

Most academic libraries have materials needed for self-training, and the materials they use are mostly in print. Only a few libraries have subscribed to journals and magazines relating to library work. However, a majority of academic libraries provide support for the continuing education of librarians. As for the content of continuing education, the cataloging librarians consider learning foreign languages to be the most

TABLE 15. Project Cooperation with the Department of Library and Information Science

	Project Cooperation with Department of Library and Information Science			
	Yes	No	No Response	Total
Frequency	8	89	1	98
Percentages	8.2	90.8	1	100

important. Next, they are interested in learning metadata standards and computer applications, as well as taking job-related library school courses. The survey results show that the cataloging and classification staff are motivated to actively deal with the rapidly changing environment, but the current conditions in academic libraries make it difficult for such an effort to be rewarded. And the situation varies from one academic library to another.

The above description and analysis are the basis for three suggestions. First, in order to apply the library school education to practical library work, organized job training should be prepared and provided in academic libraries. In particular, overall training programs regarding cataloging and classification should be presented to new librarians with the support of the library administration. Second, for cataloging and classification librarians to actively deal with the changing environment, academic libraries should subscribe to a number of professional library journals. Finally, working in the age of globalization, cataloging librarians should be given more opportunities to learn foreign languages, so as to understand and process foreign information and publications.

NOTE

1. In a telephone conversation with a staff of the Korean Library Association, December 15, 2004.

AUSTRALIA

Beyond Our Expectations: A Review of an Independent Learning Module in Descriptive Cataloguing at the Queensland University of Technology

Gillian Hallam

SUMMARY. This paper discusses an innovative approach to teaching cataloguing. At Queensland University of Technology (QUT), students enrolled in the Graduate Diploma of Library and Information Studies were involved in an independent learning activity which aimed to develop LIS students' foundation knowledge of descriptive cataloguing, while simultaneously encouraging students to think critically about broader issues that would inevitably impact on their role as information

Gillian Hallam, PhD, is Senior Lecturer, School of Information Studies, Queensland University of Technology, Brisbane, Australia (E-mail: g.hallam@qut.edu.au).

Acknowledgement is made to the students in the *Information Organisation* unit, Semester 1, 2003 for their enthusiasm for and engagement in learning about cataloguing.

[Haworth co-indexing entry note]: "Beyond Our Expectations: A Review of an Independent Learning Module in Descriptive Cataloguing at the Queensland University of Technology." Hallam, Gillian. Co-published simultaneously in *Cataloging & Classification Quarterly* (The Haworth Information Press, an imprint of The Haworth Press, Inc.) Vol. 41, No. 3/4, 2006, pp. 149-171; and: *Education for Library Cataloging: International Perspectives* (ed: Dajin D. Sun, and Ruth C. Carter) The Haworth Information Press, an imprint of The Haworth Press, Inc., 2006, pp. 149-171. Single or multiple copies of this article are available for a fee from The Haworth Document Delivery Service [1-800-HAWORTH, 9:00 a.m. - 5:00 p.m. (EST). E-mail address: docdelivery@haworthpress.com].

professionals. In the self-study program, learning activities included an interactive multimedia CD-ROM and a printed workbook with exercises, augmented by the opportunity for group discussion in weekly tutorials to enable students to share key aspects of their independent learning. Students were asked to critically evaluate the CD-ROM and the workbook and also to develop their own professional views about the arguments for and against the inclusion of cataloguing in the LIS curriculum. The paper presents the outcomes of this pilot project. *[Article copies available for a fee from The Haworth Document Delivery Service: 1-800-HAWORTH. E-mail address: <docdelivery@haworthpress.com> Website: <http://www.HaworthPress.com> © 2006 by The Haworth Press, Inc. All rights reserved.]*

KEYWORDS. Cataloguing education, library education, library schools, teaching and learning, Australia

INTRODUCTION

Over the past ten to fifteen years, library schools across the world have been criticised for their lack of commitment to the development of cataloguing skills, with Hill accusing library schools of "abrogating their responsibility to educate catalogers and technical services managers."[1] One of the major arguments against including cataloguing as a subject in tertiary library and information studies (LIS) courses has been founded on the idea that, in major libraries, the work primarily involves the task of copy cataloguing, i.e., retrieving records from a supplier of bibliographic records and modifying these records for the local catalogue. This work is generally undertaken by paraprofessional staff. Also, online library management systems that integrate ordering, cataloguing, public display and circulation systems have further shifted the responsibilities between librarians and technicians. Some library schools have followed the treatise of supply and demand: "if there are fewer openings for catalogers, then by golly, fewer people needed to be trained in cataloging."[2]

Many writers have been vocal in their claims that knowledge of the principles of cataloguing remains critical for library and information professionals.[3,4,5,6,7,8,9,10] At the pragmatic level, Gorman stresses the fact that collaborative cataloguing systems, such as OCLC, RLIN, WLN or Kinetica in Australia, depend just as much on the contribution of bibliographic records by their members as on the sale of records.[11] In a special library or information centre, LIS professionals regularly need to do their own original cataloguing, as they may not be in a position to download records from an external supplier, or, if the collection includes a considerable amount of grey literature, the records themselves may not be available for the resources held. The ability to create good quality bibliographic records remains an imperative for the delivery of good quality information retrieval services. On a higher level, Gorman contends that the structures and thought patterns that need to be applied to bibliographic control reflect "literally, the way in which we, as librarians, think and should think."[12] Both Gorman and Zyroff highlight the interdependency of high quality reference and cataloguing skills: "the intellectual framework of reference is based on the intellectual framework of cataloging."[13]

In response to the ongoing criticism about the reduced interest in library schools in running cataloguing courses, i.e., what is not happening, recent literature provides considerable discussion about the curriculum of cataloguing courses,[14,15,16,17,18,19] but comparatively little about effective teaching and learning strategies. Changes in the information environment, however, are prompting a number of educators to highlight their efforts to redefine the teaching of information organisation and to discuss some of their approaches.[20,21,22,23]

Hill recognises some of the challenges faced by library schools today, indicating that "catalogers and cataloging managers must realize that a library school education is insufficient to everybody's needs, not just catalogers'."[24] Snyman validly indicates that the time limitations in LIS courses make it "impossible to master anything more than the basic principles and activities of bibliographic control," meaning educators should endeavour to become more innovative in order to "teach students thinking and decision making skills and not merely tools and techniques."[25] This paper discusses one example of an innovative approach to teaching cataloguing: a pilot project run at Queensland University of Technology (QUT) which aimed to develop LIS students' foundation knowledge of descriptive cataloguing, while simultaneously encouraging students to think critically about broader issues that would inevitably impact on their role as information professionals. The paper briefly outlines the professional context of LIS education in Australia and an overview of the academic context of the Graduate Diploma of Library and Information Studies (GDLIS) at QUT before reviewing the teaching and learning project.

PROFESSIONAL CONTEXT

In Australia, education for the library and information profession is viewed as the collaborative effort of the universities and colleges, training providers, employers and the professional association, with emphasis placed on the need to remain responsive to change through career-long continuing professional development. The standards for education for the library and information profession are maintained by the Australian Library & Information Association (ALIA) through their course recognition process for entry-level courses. Entry-level courses are offered at both the undergraduate and postgraduate levels.

ALIA states that "entry level courses should provide an examination and analysis of all core knowledge areas and, within this context, develop generic knowledge, skills and attitudes."[26] In terms of defining 'core knowledge areas', reference is made to providing "library and information services by analysing, evaluating, organising and synthesising information to meet client needs."[27] Courses should also "contribute to the development of students' critical, analytical and creative thinking."[28] ALIA's policy document *The Library and information sector: core knowledge, skills and attributes*[29] is presented as a guiding statement to provide a foundation for the development of policies on the knowledge and skills required by library and information professionals. The document consequently delineates the high-level principles, acknowledging that the specific level of skills and knowledge will depend on the formal qualifications, work experience, professional development and the role individual library and information professionals perform.

ACADEMIC CONTEXT

The course offered by the Faculty of Information Technology at QUT is a Graduate Diploma of Library and Information Studies (GDLIS), one year full-time or two years part-time program, comprising eight units of study, with seven core units and one elective. The course is only offered in the face-to-face mode. In 2003, the core units covered the areas of reference and information work, collection and access management, information organisation, library management, principles of information management, and systems analysis and design. The capstone unit is *Professional Practice*, which provides students with the opportunity to consider topical issues impacting on the LIS profession and to undertake two fifteen-day fieldwork placements.

The core unit *Information Organisation* is a one semester (13 week) unit, with 3 contact hours per week (1 hour lecture, 2 hours computer laboratory/tutorial). In Semester 1, 2003, there were 45 students enrolled in the unit. Only three students had any prior experience of cataloguing. The unit outline presents the learning objectives which cover the desired learning outcomes in terms of theory, practice, and generic capabilities. Upon completion of the unit, students should demonstrate theoretical knowledge of the nature of information; the principles of bibliographic database construction, including basic strategies of information organisation: description, indexing, and classification; the major forms of bibliographic databases, including library catalogues, indexing and abstracting services, and fulltext resources; the importance of a client-oriented approach to knowledge organisation. Practical skills should include the ability to construct a bibliographic database using appropriate software; critically evaluate bibliographic databases; ensure that bibliographic records conform to standards in relation to description, indexing, and classification; and independently identify and research contemporary issues in the organisation of knowledge. Generic attributes to be developed include information literacy competencies; critical, reflective, and creative thinking and evaluation; a high level of proficiency in written communication; and working productively both independently and in a team environment.

Strategies for teaching and learning in this unit reflect the view that the appropriate design of assessment is crucial for effective learning. Bowden and Marton believe that a holistic, or "integrative" approach to assessment can drive the teaching and learning process.[30] There needs to be clear articulation of teaching and learning objectives, not only at the individual unit level, but also in terms of the relationship between the unit objectives and the overall course objectives. The correlation between assessment and student learning outcomes is therefore critical. Ramsden discusses the importance of "more developed models of assessment."[31] Simple models of assessment can be regarded "as an addition to teaching, rather than an essential part of it,"[32] that is, "something done *to* students,"[33] which inevitably results in a surface approach to learning. On the other hand, "assessment which is the servant rather than the master of the educational process will necessarily be viewed as an integral part of teaching and the practice of improving teaching,"[34] resulting in deeper learning outcomes.

As technological, social, and economic changes rapidly modify modern day library and information work, LIS educators need to consider how best to assess the ability and knowledge of future information professionals–even when the future itself is still being defined. The design and development of the assessment tasks in the GDLIS at QUT are focused by the question: "How can we assess students in a way that addresses their capacity to handle situations in the future that they have not previously encountered?"[35] Teachers are advised to "assess the capabilities which . . . have been shown . . . to be central to dealing with the unknown future, viz. discernment and simultaneity,"[36] so that the "assessment tasks [students] are faced with must require them to discern what is relevant and deal with the situation accordingly."[37] The ability to distil the critical aspects of any given situation is a vital factor to help students learn to deal with the uncertainty of future events.

Reflective practice has an important role to play in the students' own active process of learning to learn, enabling them to establish the links or connections between their prior experience, their personal lives, and their coursework. Herman discusses the meaning of "good assessment," drawing on the findings of cognitive research which indicate that "meaningful learning is reflective, constructive and self-regulated."[38] He goes on to state that "to know something is not just to have received information but to have interpreted it and related it to other knowledge one already has."[39]

Over the past few years, the assessment activities in the unit had concentrated on the analysis of bibliographic databases as an individual task, and the construction of a database using DB/TextWorks undertaken as a group assignment. In constructing their database, comprising 50 records describing a range of items in different media, students were expected to make decisions about whether they would apply or reject specific bibliographic standards, e.g., the use of AACR2 in the record structure, authority control for authors, subjects, etc. Topics such as AACR2, Dewey Classification, Library of Congress Classification, and Library of Congress Subject Headings were all touched upon in class, but there was little opportunity to develop a strong practical understanding of these bibliographic tools.

Needless to say, the major criticism of QUT students by industry practitioners when they went to complete the practicum component of the course was the lack of sound knowledge of the principles and practice of cataloguing. A number of students also returned from fieldwork having engaged in discussions about the 'death of cataloguing skills' and were eager to know more about the detail of bibliographic description "even if they had to do it on their own." As a response to this student and industry feedback, teaching staff believed that, as a pilot in Semester 1, 2003, there was scope to shift the emphasis in the learning activities to incorporate an independent learning module that would offer the opportunity for students to develop more practical skills in cataloguing.

PILOT PROJECT

Clack stresses the need for cataloguing teachers to be innovative in their teaching strategies and methodologies to support active learning strategies,[40] with a "mix" of pedagogical approaches to foster student involvement in their learning.[41,42] The QUT pilot project endeavoured to be innovative, utilising a range of different approaches and media for the teaching and learning activities. Independent learning was balanced by group discussion and the main resources were a printed workbook and a CD-ROM training program, supported by reflective practice and collaborative learning. The CD-ROM tool was an example of "a training resource that included interactive instruction with the utilisation of multimedia . . . to provide a meaningful learning experience."[43]

The learning objectives for this new activity were outlined to students:

- To develop a general understanding of the principles of cataloguing
- To be able to apply the rules of AACR2 to create library catalogue records
- To understand the issues associated with subject indexing and classification
- To develop skills in working independently
- To feel confident about reflecting on your learning
- To become aware of the process of learning to learn.

Hill has indicated that "the most practical skill of all for both catalogers and those who manage cataloging operations is knowing how to learn."[44] The last two learning objectives also relate to one of the course-wide objectives for the GDLIS, which encourages the development of skills in critical evaluation of a wide range of information and instructional resources, supporting ALIA's desire to see LIS professionals develop skills in "critical, analytical and creative thinking." In addition, LIS education in Australia has seen a growing focus on the importance of information literacy skills in the community, and on the role of library and information professionals to support the development of these skills amongst their clients. In Australia, there is a push for knowledge and skills in the area of information literacy and cognitive processes to be included as a core subject in LIS courses.

At the beginning of the semester, students were invited to begin to think about some of the differing views in the profession about the curriculum of library courses. They were made aware of arguments for and against the inclusion of cataloguing in an LIS program and they were advised that one of the primary goals of the learning activity was to help them, as individuals, develop their own professional views about this issue. The experimental nature of the project was highlighted, encouraging students to contribute to and provide evaluative comment on curriculum issues and approaches to teaching and learning in a professional course. Not unsurprisingly, there was a mixed response from the students about this initiative. Some students had their own assumptions about university education and expected that there would be a given body of knowledge to be learned, with tried and true 'traditional' pedagogical strategies in place. Other students were excited at being participants in an action research project.

For their independent learning activity, students were introduced to Mary Mortimer's text *Learn descriptive cataloguing*, which aims to "cover the skills necessary for a cataloguer in a library or other information agency, at a professional or paraprofessional level."[45] This text has been designed "for use on its own, in a formal course of study, or in conjunction with the interactive multimedia training package *CatSkill*."[46] The flexibility offered by the workbook, plus the Australian focus of the exercises, made it a valuable resource to use in the learning activities. The use of MARC coding for bibliographic description and headings is optional for users of the workbook.

Originally it was hoped that the students would be able to pilot the web version of *CatSkill*, but due to developmental problems with the online format of the resource, these plans were thwarted. Students could only use the CD-ROM version of the multimedia instructional tool, which could be accessed either in the networked faculty computer laboratories or loaded for direct access on their home computers. *CatSkill* is described as a self-paced interactive learning tool which enables students to work at their own pace through a series of modules, culminating in a test to monitor progress. The program provides a certificate of successful completion when all tests have been passed.

Students were provided with a range of resources to support them in their independent learning: copies of *AACR2* were available to students in both hardcopy and electronic formats (via a subscription to *Cataloger's Desktop*). Scanned copies (pdf files) of key chapters of *AACR2* could be accessed through the university's electronic document distribution service, the Course Materials Database (CMD). Students could print out these chapters, download the files onto their computers, or copy them to CD-ROM. Additional readings were made available via the university's online teaching and learning environment (OLT).

Students were given a recommended schedule of activities for the semester to help them schedule their progress through both the workbook and *CatSkill*, which would hopefully encourage them stay on track with the learning activities. The weekly self-study topics were aligned to the theoretical content presented in the lectures. While the program was to be undertaken primarily in a self-study mode, a group learning dimension was planned by allocating time in the tutorials to discuss what students had covered during the week, what issues arose for them, and how they went about resolving any problems. An electronic discussion forum was also available on the OLT. These strategies meant that students could contribute to a collaborative learning environment.

One of the major issues to consider was how to best assess the independent learning activity. The *CatSkill* exercises had to be completed correctly before the student could move on to the next module, and the workbook provided model answers, so the teaching staff decided there would be little value in asking students to submit the actual exercises for marking. Nevertheless, it was felt that some aspect of assessment should be factored into the program, if only to motivate students to complete the course of study. In the past, the teaching staff had been altruistic and encouraged students to undertake certain learning tasks without any formal assessment attached to them. All too often, however, the result was zero motivation and, consequently, zero learning. Sadly there had to be some method of assessment if students were to fulfil the desired learning tasks.

It was decided that students would be asked to maintain a learning journal. Learning journals are used in a number of disciplines, e.g., education, psychology, and law, to support the development of critical thinking skills, to deepen the understanding of the learning process, and to facilitate reflective practice.[47,48,49] The learning framework of constructivism argues that human learning is not achieved through the passive transmission of information from teacher to learner, but through building new knowledge upon the foundation of previous knowledge, thus students *construct their learning.* Reflective practice is used in the GDLIS to support the concepts of adult learning and to encourage students, as adult learners, to take control of and responsibility for their own learning.

In *Information Organisation,* the learning journal was introduced to help students become aware of the ways they learn and the ways in which they acquire new skills and knowledge as information professionals. One of the primary goals of the learning journal was to encourage students to achieve deep, rather than surface learning outcomes by starting to think about their thinking and to learn about their learning. Personal learning styles were also the topic of discussion in another unit coordinated by the same teaching staff.

Critical reflection has been described as those intellectual and affective activities in which individuals engage to explore their experiences in order to lead to new understandings and appreciations.[50] Boud,[51] drawing on the ideas of Moon,[52] highlights some of the key purposes of learning journals:

- To deepen the quality of learning, in the form of critical thinking or developing a questioning attitude
- To enable learners to understand their own learning process
- To increase active involvement in learning and personal ownership of learning
- To enhance creativity by making better use of intuitive understanding
- To foster reflective practice and creative interaction within a group.

It was acknowledged that there would be variations in terms of student response to the task of reflective practice. For some, it would be the first time they had engaged in the process of critical reflection or, indeed, thought about their own personal learning styles. Others would feel more comfortable about the activity. The overall expectations were therefore discussed by the class: students should aim to complete the independent learning module and they should highlight the approaches they had taken, e.g.: Was it necessary to go beyond *CatSkills* and the *Learn descriptive cataloguing* workbook? Did they utilise other resources to broaden and deepen their understanding? Did they relate the exercises to the recommended reading, or vice versa? Did they work collaboratively with other students?

As part of the learning activity, students were asked to critique the key resources, *CatSkills* and the *Learn descriptive cataloguing*, as two educational tools which had been developed specifically for tertiary students in an LIS program. Students were asked to consider how effective these resources were for them personally, the respective strengths and weaknesses of each resource, and the extent to which they supported their learning. They were invited to evaluate how well the two resources worked as complementary learning tools and to provide any other constructive criticism. As noted, teaching staff wanted to increase the students' awareness of the critical role of information literacy skills in the LIS context and to develop their professional ability to critique learning tools. They were also asked to consider their own personal learning outcomes, in terms of both the technical skills of cataloguing skills and the skills of reflective practice.

Beyond this, students were encouraged to think about the value of learning about cataloguing within the field of information organisation and about the development of cataloguing skills in general–whether they believed that these skills fitted into the domain of professional or paraprofessional work, and whether they should be included as a core skill in an entry-level course or as a specialist skill which could be learnt after university, either through an employer program or through a professional CPD program.

The teaching staff had anticipated that the students' learning of the more technical tasks of understanding bibliographic description and the application of AACR2 to be the primary learning outcomes, so the richness of the reflections in the students' learning journals came as a surprise. The reflections have provided valuable qualitative data about the pilot project and the perceived learning outcomes. A large number of students agreed to the anonymous inclusion of their comments, views, and ideas in this article to present a critical review of the multi-faceted dimensions of the independent learning activity. These students are acknowledged for their openness and their willingness to participate in the dissemination of the preliminary findings from the pilot project.

STUDENT LEARNING OUTCOMES

The learning journals were submitted at the end of the semester. There were a number of immediate learning outcomes that were common to students:

- Recognition of the importance of bibliographic standards and conventions
- Clear understanding of the three aspects of cataloguing: description, subject indexing, and classification
- Identification of the different parts of the bibliographic record (heading, description, tracing notes)
- Basic familiarity with the structure and content of AACR2, as well as the some of the strengths and weaknesses of these
- Awareness of the significance of authority control
- Realisation that effective information organisation is essential for effective information retrieval.

This last point, perhaps facilitated by the fact that the teaching staff coordinated both the *Information Organisation* and the *Information Sources* (reference) units, should help allay Gorman's concerns about the rift between cataloguers and reference librarians and support the need for "mutual respect and mutual recognition of interdependence."[53] Interestingly, recent discussions on bibliographic instruction reflect the dovetailing of information organisation and information retrieval courses in the curriculum.[54,55]

As there were 45 students enrolled in the unit, with no prescriptive approach to the learning activities, it was not surprising that students developed a range of strategies, which could be primarily *CatSkill*, supported by the workbook, or primarily the workbook, supported by *CatSkill*. Some students found, however, that there was a high degree of overlap between the print and the electronic tools, so after a couple of weeks, they decided to focus on one or other of the resources as "the option I found more enjoyable." The ability to attain a certificate at the completion of the *CatSkill* program was considered to be a benefit to many students, as they saw this as a useful way to document their skills, above and beyond the generic statement of academic achievement for the unit as whole.

The software program *CatSkill* attracted high praise from most of the students. It was regarded as "dynamic and interesting in its presentation of ideas," providing an enjoyable teaching framework as, "given the number of rules and complexities of AACR2 and cataloguing in general, there is potential for such a topic to be tedious and difficult to learn." The *CatSkill* graphics were "brilliant, particularly for a visual learner like myself. The incorporation of the 'cataloguer's workroom' was likewise brilliant. It simulated closely a real scenario and made the activity therefore seem less a contrived exercise." Students felt that each module covered the topic thoroughly, including additional elements such as MARC codes and links to a glossary for an "extensive explanation of terms."

One criticism of the tool related to progression through the different modules. There were limited options to move forwards and backwards through the modules, for example, to locate a specific fact that had been read at an earlier date. "The only way to find the information again was to start at the beginning of the module in question, and work through the module as though reading it for the first time. This was found to be frustrating when a quick review of the information was desired."

Some students found the 'exactness' of *CatSkill* frustrating. One student referred to it as a 'self-assessment tool,' rather than a 'self-instruction tool.' It was found that the end of chapter tests often did not allow the student, after making one mistake in the answer, to submit a fully correct answer, even though all aspects of their subsequent responses completely matched the responses required by the program. The exactness of the requirements for punctuation and spacing was highlighted as particularly challenging in the tests, as with just one error, the student failed the test. Students indicated that they had to go back and review the material in the module, then reattempt the test. Having to repeat the test three or four times because of one minor mistake each time was demotivating for students. On the other hand, some felt that "a lot more is remembered through these repetitive practical exercises rather than just answering questions in a workbook. The actual learning is enforced through the computer package which is trying to replace the teacher somehow and forces the user into more reading and more research."

Although *Learning descriptive cataloguing* states that the workbook has been designed for use on its own, there was a feeling that it was superficial in the way it covered the theory. The explanation of terms and the instructions provided in the workbook were not felt to be clear enough. A good proportion of students drew on the recommended readings to develop a deeper understanding of some of the problems they encountered. One student suggested that the workbook specifically should have a section at the end of each chapter with references for further reading.

Some students criticised *CatSkill* for the way in which it failed to provide authentic experience in the practice of descriptive cataloguing, as students were generally asked to complete a section of a description already provided, or to identify fields within completed catalogue records, rather than creating a bibliographic record from scratch. The workbook answers, on the other hand, "took longer to complete and, therefore, longer to think about the answers; I found that this helped the information to stay in my head, and therefore made the information more familiar and easier to review at a later date." Another student noted, "I found that doing a complete record from the ground up is easier than doing bits and pieces." This meant there was a preference amongst these students for "the more traditional nature of a written resource and the convenience of being able to refer to the book at any time or place," and to make written annotations in the workbook.

However, the workbook was found by other students to be "dry and boring," although some indicated that it was "written in simple language and laid out clearly." Some perceptive students found that "while *CatSkill* was very appealing at the beginning of the semester (seeming much more entertaining than a seemingly 'dry' workbook), when I actually began working with both tools, I much preferred the workbook, as I felt it closely mirrored a real cataloguing situation."

It was found that modules in *CatSkill* and chapters in the workbook did not correlate as closely as had been initially hoped, which meant that some students elected to concentrate on just one of the two tools. Others were happy with the way in which learning was consolidated if they used both tools, with additional dimensions provided by the lectures and tutorials: "I prefer this method of learning: print the lecture notes and skim through them, attend lecture, attend tutorial, do workbook and then do *CatSkill*. I found the constant reiteration over the week helped me remember the ideas and the information." There were some who took a more strategic approach "due to time limitations" and used primarily the one resource, e.g., the workbook, and then used *CatSkill* to complete only the non-repeat chapters. Others found it easier to use *CatSkill* "to learn the unfamiliar cataloguing material" and then to practice and apply the knowledge using the workbook.

The teaching staff believe that having the choice of the workbook and *CatSkill* as key learning tools enabled students to develop a more critical perspective on their own learning. The positive and negative attributes of each resource were highlighted through their ability to appraise their experiences with each and to, therefore, avoid a sense of complacency that could accompany accepting a single learning tool at face value. One student noted, however, that he felt this metacognitive awareness was distracting: "I was focused upon aspects of the teaching tools and methods, rather than the subject content, techniques and processes that I was trying to incorporate into my personal state of knowledge."

The exercises in both the workbook and *CatSkill* encouraged students to refer to *AACR2*, so they had the opportunity to become familiar with the structure and the content of the relevant chapters. Students who used *Cataloger's Desktop* online appreciated the way they could easily locate specific *AACR2* rules. Some students found they could complete the *CatSkill* exercises, without actually using *AACR2* at all, acknowledging, however, that this was "an approach which seems limited in utility." Nevertheless, students indicated that "it was often difficult to know how to do the exercise. Therefore I would cheat and look at the answers in the back of the book." (Although it took some students a couple of weeks to discover there were answers at the back of the book!) Some acknowledged that the ability to deconstruct a 'correct' answer and to relate the individual steps back to the individual rules in *AACR2* could be a useful approach to learning.

Mortimer points out that users of the text *Learn descriptive cataloguing* "may not always agree completely with the answers given . . . Despite the best endeavours of the creators of cataloguing rules to standardise all cataloguing procedures, there is often room for more than one approach or application of the rule."[56] One student highlights her own emerging realisation about these issues: "What one has to realise in cataloguing, is that there is often an absence of a 'black or white' rationale behind rules and sometimes there is the presence of a 'grey area,' which requires the cataloguer to make decisions that will result in the best application of a rule so as to suit the particular users of the library. The cataloguer has a lot of complex decisions to make regarding cataloguing options . . . and has to be able to think laterally."

The more enterprising students examined sample catalogue records from different sources, such as the National Bibliographic Database available via the Kinetica service, university library OPACs, or public library catalogues. This comparative approach was found to be very valuable in highlighting the differences (and often inaccuracies) in catalogue records and in fact increased the students' own confidence in their abilities as cataloguers as they realised there was no one absolute and perfect solution.

Some students felt restricted in aspects of their learning as, although relatively up to date (publication dates 2002), neither the workbook nor *CatSkills* adequately addressed more current issues like the problem of electronic resources: "I think this is the future direction of cataloguing, and there is a definite need for cataloguers to be more innovative and open in their methodologies, particularly in the electronic environment where the distinction between surrogate records and the documents themselves blurs."

Beyond developing some basic skills and initial confidence in cataloguing, most students appreciated the opportunity to engage in reflective practice. The learning journal was acknowledged to be a positive and useful tool–"surprisingly useful"–even if the assessment angle meant that "being 'forced' to keep a journal was the best way to ensure that I would actually diligently do so." Some students found that initially the suggested format of reflecting before, during, and after their work on the learning activities to be beneficial in terms of becoming aware of the way they were constructing new knowledge. "I felt that keeping a personalised learning log helped me to make the learning deeper by having to think and re-think throughout the whole learning process. It was not a matter of 'ticking off the modules'; it was a case of questioning the prior knowledge I had, identifying questions I wanted addressed and modifying all of this as I progressed." Concept maps were found to be valuable as a graphical interpretation of their understanding: "I have attempted to draw the interrelated library system to show the connection between major areas. When I was drawing it, I realised how linked everything was and that I couldn't truly show all the links on one piece of paper." Yet, as the semester, and their learning, progressed, further dimensions were added to the concept maps.

Collaboration with other students also helped the reflective process, providing different perspectives on individual learning: "Discussing the program with my peers assisted me to understand the material contained in the self-study program. It was useful to listen to the opinions and ideas of other people, particularly in relation to difficult or confusing material." This learning was especially powerful when aligned with the group work they were doing to construct their own bibliographic database using DB/TextWorks: "The process of cataloguing our own records stimulated discussion of AACR2 rules, as well as their relevance and use." While the journal was primarily focussed on the independent learning activities, some students found that when lecture material was directly related to topics in the module, it was valuable to add notes in at the relevant place in the journal: "This combined reflection with content, and provided an easy way to view the content on which I wished to reflect," thus becoming useful in both "an operational and reflective sense."

The value of reflective practice extended beyond the immediate learning context of *Information Organisation*, flowing into the personal and work domains, as highlighted by one student: "I found that the experience highlighted some factors about which I was not previously aware, such as personality traits and weaknesses in my approach to certain situations and types of work task. It was a learning experience for me in multiple ways." Another was exuberant: "Wow! This is really helpful (reflection, I mean). It really helps getting all the random ideas from my head into some sort of structure so I can understand the overall meaning of something and see its application to the bigger picture."

One significant outcome from the learning activities was the stimulus to think about the "emphasis that should be placed on cataloguing skills in a postgraduate professional librarianship course." Students responded positively to Gorman's views that cataloguing skills are at the "heart of librarianship,"[57] and Thomas' claim that cataloguing should indeed be regarded as the "cornerstone of the librarian's craft."[58] They felt that graduates "absolutely do need quite a good knowledge of these skills."

While students understood from their wider reading and discussions with industry professionals that not many librarians do original cataloguing any more, and that the 'divisionalisation' of library activities had led to reduced integration between cataloguers and non-cataloguing staff,[59] some of them were fearful of a library world with no cataloguing skills: the "loss of professionals with cataloguing skills would represent a serious deficiency in the discipline of librarianship and information management." They therefore appreciated the "need for cataloguing skills in at least a selection of the collective library staff's population." Some went further to query whether a librarian should "know (how to catalogue) just in case or learn it just in time." Students felt the learning activities had been successful in becoming familiar with the process, as opposed to developing a detailed skill set, something that they could potentially build on through their practicum. Beyond this, however, one student believed that "professionals need an historical understanding of how and why things developed and changed and how technological advances have and will continue to impact," and that her work in the independent learning module had helped her to explore this perspective in more detail.

There was a general feeling that it was important for "the basics of cataloguing to be taught at the tertiary level, to provide students of librarianship with a fundamental understanding on which they can build through future courses and practical experience." They noted that the limited role of cataloguing activities in libraries and information agencies meant that there was little scope to teach advanced cataloguing skills in an entry-level course. Students suggested that "these would be better and more meaningfully learnt through workplace instruction, or through professional development courses." One student recommended the latter option, suggesting that "if run through the national association, it would hopefully provide a more consistent skill level than workplace training alone."

Students were aware of the "dangerous baloney"[60] inherent in the idea that computerisation could, in itself, solve bibliographic questions, commenting that: "While a computer program can achieve routine, automated tasks with supreme efficiency, it cannot inject the essential thought processes needed to design a system that serves all intended users. It takes human intellect to produce a human, workable, appealing system. It also takes that intellect to modify the systems when necessary, and improve on them as new understanding comes to light. Information management should be a dynamic field, and the specific area of cataloguing is no exception." Quality and consistency were seen to be key issues in information organisation.

Some students found that one major aspect of their learning focused not on cataloguing skills per se, but on the broader professional and philosophical issues: "I must say now, that even though I was sceptical of the learning journal at the onset, I have enjoyed the moments of reflection. Not only have I developed the technical aspects of cataloguing such as a good knowledge of AACR2 and MARC, but I have also developed a broader 'big picture' perspective of the issues and concerns that surround cataloguing." One student expanded on this: "In constructivist terms, I was making more and more connections with all the concepts, the more I reflected on and explored my questions and feelings about the subject matter. For example, I found the whole issue of whether cataloguing should be taught at all in professional level courses, led me not only to explore the broader issues of the professional/paraprofessional debate, but the very values upon which librarianship is based."

CONCLUSION

The student reflections which were presented in the learning journals indicated their satisfaction with both the content and the pedagogic approach of the independent learning activities. Teaching staff felt it would be important to broaden the stated learning objectives to include the "big picture" perspectives of the issues associated with cataloguing, both in Australia and internationally, to capture the valid views and responses of students, and to encourage further critical, analytical, and creative thinking. It was felt that the activities should be augmented to include a greater emphasis on cataloguing electronic resources and other non-print media, which were not covered in either *Learning descriptive cataloguing* or *CatSkill*.

Improvements to the unit could also ensure more effective consolidation between the formal and informal learning activities, for example, by allocating more tutorial time to discuss the independent study activities: "My recommendation is to insist that the first hour of the tutorials cover these exercises only and that answers are discussed as part of the tutorial process. This structure would enhance student learning outcomes in this area." One student was more ambitious about the potential: "Ideally it would be fantastic if QUT could develop an online version that could be done over the OLT (online teaching site), customised for the Australian context and customised for the QUT course; perhaps even integrated into the SCP (tool to monitor the development of generic capabilities). If there was enough time and money, it could almost happen. . . ."

Students felt they had achieved a great deal during the semester: "I feel pleased with my learning progress in both the field of cataloguing and the skill of reflective practice." One student noted, however, that while he was aware that he "had developed so many skills" and was "incredibly appreciative" of what he had learnt, he didn't think he really enjoyed the process. He found it beneficial, however, to see how these learning activities invited him to think more deeply about how people do learn, and consequently to consider the challenges of developing interesting and challenging teaching and learning activities that are 'enjoyable.' Another student found the project rewarding: "By way of a conclusion to the reflection, I will say that I have enjoyed this independent learning program, and have gained a great deal of satisfaction from it . . . I have enjoyed being able to direct my own learning to a degree, and I have also enjoyed the content, as cataloguing and classification are areas I am enthusiastic about."

In conclusion, it was found that the independent learning module was successful in developing a "strong functional knowledge" of cataloguing. It was positive to learn that students viewed their time not as 'spent on' but 'invested in' the learning activities and that, consequently, the groundwork had been laid for further learning through continuing professional development. "The module revealed the basics of cataloguing, classification and subject indexing, but also served to show how much is left to read, process and discover!"

The outcomes from this pilot project extend beyond the original expectations of both the students and the teaching staff. While the immediate objectives were to help students develop an understanding of the principles of cataloguing, through reflective practice the students have been able to relate their learning in this one unit to their learning in other units, to their learning in other disciplines, and to their values and ethos. They have begun to understand their own learning styles and how different approaches to teaching and learning can influence personal learning outcomes. The positive multidimensional outcomes from this one innovative activity clearly indicate that learning about descriptive cataloguing is highly relevant for future information professionals.

REFERENCES

1. Janet S. Hill, "What Else Do You Need to Know? Practical Skills for Catalogers and Managers," *Cataloging & Classification Quarterly* 34:1/2 (2002): 249.

2. E. Zyroff, "Cataloging Is a Prime Number," *American Libraries* 27 (May 1996): 48.

3. Michael Gorman, "Why Teach Cataloguing and Classification?" *Cataloging & Classification Quarterly* 34:1/2 (2002): 1-13.

4. Michael Gorman, "The Corruption of Cataloguing," *Library Journal,* 120:5 (1995): 32-35. Also available online, retrieved on April 7, 2004 from: http://www.lib.csufresno.edu/libraryinformation/publications/gormanarticle.html.

5. Michael Gorman, "How Cataloging and Classification Should Be Taught," *American Libraries,* 23 (September 1992): 694-697.

6. Janet S. Hill, and Sheila S. Intner, *Preparing for a Cataloging Career: From Cataloging to Knowledge Management* (1999). Retrieved on April 7, 2004 from: http://www.ala.org/congress/hill-intner_print.html.

7. M. El-Sherbin and G. Klim, "Changes in Technical Services and Their Effect on the Role of Catalogers and Staff Education: An Overview." In *Cataloging and Classification: Trends, Transformations, Teaching and Training,* edited by J.R. Shearer and A.R. Thomas (New York: The Haworth Press, Inc., 1997), 23-34.

8. H.A. Olson, "Thinking Professionals: Teaching Critical Cataloguing," *Technical Services Quarterly* 15:1/2 (1997): 51-65.

9. A.R. Thomas, "The Work-Wide Web: A Cataloguing Career for Every Librarian?" In *Cataloging and Classification: Trends, Transformations, Teaching and Training,* edited by J.R. Shearer and A.R. Thomas (New York: The Haworth Press, Inc., 1997), 5-22.

10. Zyroff, "Cataloging Is a Prime Number," 47-50.

11. Gorman, "The Corruption of Cataloguing," 32-35.

12. Gorman, "How Cataloging and Classification Should Be Taught," 694.

13. Zyroff, "Cataloging Is a Prime Number," 48.

14. Ingrid Hsieh-Yee, "Cataloging and Metadata Education: Asserting a Central Role in Information Organization," *Cataloging & Classification Quarterly,* 34:1/2 (2002): 203-222.

15. Sheila S. Intner, "Persistent Issues in Cataloging Education: Considering the Past and Looking Toward the Future," *Cataloging & Classification Quarterly*, 34:1/2 (2002): 15-29.

16. D.N. Joudrey, "A New Look at US Graduate Courses in Bibliographic Control," *Cataloging & Classification Quarterly*, 34:1/2 (2002): 59-101.

17. Arlene G. Taylor and D.N. Joudrey, "On Teaching Subject Cataloging," *Cataloging & Classification Quarterly*, 34:1/2 (2002): 223-232.

18. M.R. Turvey and K.M. Letarte, "Cataloging or Knowledge Management: Perspectives of Library Educators on Cataloging Education for Entry-Level Academic Librarians," *Cataloging & Classification Quarterly*, 34:1/2 (2002): 165-187.

19. S.L. Vellucci, "Cataloging Across the Curriculum: A Syndetic Structure for Teaching Cataloging," *Cataloging & Classification Quarterly*, 34:1/2 (2002): 35-59.

20. L.M. Cloete, R. Snyman, and J.C. Cronjé, "Training Cataloguing Students Using a Mix of Media And Technologies," *Aslib Proceedings*, 55:4 (2003): 223-233.

21. G.S. Koh, "Innovations in Standard Classroom Instruction," *Cataloging & Classification Quarterly*, 34:1/2 (2002): 263-287.

22. P.M. Hider, "Developing Courseware for Cataloging: The Cat with Mouse Project," *Journal of Education for Library and Information Science,* 41:3 (2000): 187-196.

23. Ingrid Hsieh-Yee, "Organizing Internet Resources: Teaching Cataloging Standards and Beyond," *OCLC Systems and Services,* 16:3 (2000): 130-143.

24. Hill, "What Else Do You Need to Know? Practical Skills for Catalogers and Managers," 249.

25. R. Snyman, "Bibliographic Control–Is the Current Training Still Relevant?" *International Cataloguing and Bibliographic Control,* 30:1 (2001): 13-15.

26. Australian Library & Information Association (ALIA), *ALIA Board of Education Policy Statements,* (2003). Retrieved on April 7, 2004 from: http://www.alia. org.au/policies/education/index.html.

27. Australian Library & Information Association (ALIA), *Courses in Library and Information Studies,* (2003). Retrieved on April 7, 2004 from: http://www.alia.org. au/education/courses.

28. Australian Library & Information Association (ALIA), *ALIA Education policy: No 1–Entry level courses,* (2000). Retrieved on April 7, 2004 from: http://www.alia. org.au/policies/education/entry-level.courses.html.

29. Australian Library & Information Association (ALIA), *Library and Information Sector: Core Knowledge, Skills and Attributes,* (2003). Retrieved on April 7, 2004 from: http://www.alia.org.au/policies/core.knowledge.html.

30. John Bowden and Ferens Marton, *The University Of Learning: Beyond Quality and Competence,* (London: Kogan Page, 1998), 162.

31. Paul Ramsden, *Learning to Teach in Higher Education,* (London: Routledge, 1992), 186.

32. Ramsden, *Learning to Teach in Higher Education,* 183.

33. Ramsden, *Learning to Teach in Higher Education,* 183.

34. Ramsden, *Learning to Teach in Higher Education,* 186.

35. Bowden and Marton, *The University of Learning: Beyond Quality and Competence,* 167.

36. Bowden and Marton, *The University of Learning: Beyond Quality and Competence,* 167.

37. Bowden and Marton, *The University of Learning: Beyond Quality and Competence,* 167.

38. J. Herman, "What Research Tells Us about Good Assessment," *Educational Leadership,* 49:8 (1992): 75.

39. Herman, "What Research Tells Us About Good Assessment," 75.

40. D.H. Clack, "Education for Cataloging: A Symposium Paper," *Cataloging & Classification Quarterly,* 16:3 (1993): 27-37.

41. L. Romero, "The Cataloging Laboratory: The Active Learning Theory Applied to the Education of Catalogers," *Cataloging & Classification Quarterly,* 21:1 (1995): 7.

42. Koh, "Innovations in Standard Classroom Instruction," 263.

43. Cloete, Snyman and Cronjé, "Training Cataloguing Students Using a Mix of Media and Technologies," 228.

44. Hill, "What Else Do You Need to Know? Practical Skills for Catalogers and Managers," 258.

45. Mary Mortimer, *Learn Descriptive Cataloguing,* 4th ed., (Canberra: DocMatrix, 2002), 6.

46. Mortimer, *Learn Descriptive Cataloguing,* 6.

47. R. Ballantyne and J. Packer, *Making Connections: Using Student Journals as a Teaching/Learning Aid.* HERDSA Gold Guide, (Canberra: HERDSA, 1995).

48. J. Bain, R. Ballantyne, J. Packer, and C. Mills, "Using Journal Writing to Enhance Student Teachers' Reflectivity during Field Experience Placements." Paper presented at the *Annual Conference of the Australian Association for Research in Education,* Brisbane, November 30-December 4 1997. Retrieved April 7, 2004 from: http://www.aare.edu.au.

49. J. Moon, *Learning Journals: A Handbook for Academics, Students and Professional Development,* (London: Kogan Page, 1999).

50. D. Boud, R. Keogh, and D.Walker (Eds.), *Reflection: Turning Experience into Learning,* (New York: Nichols, 1985).

51. D. Boud, "Using Journal Writing to Enhance Reflective Practice," In *Promoting Journal Writing in Adult Education,* edited by L.M. English and M.A. Gillen. New Directions in Adult and Continuing Education No. 90. (San Fransisco: Jossey Bass, 2001). Retrieved April 7, 2003 from: http://www.education.uts.edu.au/ostaff/staff/publications/db_31_boud_in_english.pdf.

52. Moon, *Learning Journals: A Handbook for Academics, Students and Professional Development.*

53. Gorman, "The Corruption of Cataloguing," 32-35.

54. M. Madsen. "Teaching Bibliography, Bibliographic Control and Bibliographic Competence," *International Cataloguing and Bibliographic Control* 30:1 (2001): 16-17.

55. J. McIlwaine. "Bibliographic Control: Self-Instruction from Individualized Investigations," *International Cataloguing and Bibliographic Control* 30:1 (2001): 17-19.

56. Mortimer, *Learn Descriptive Cataloguing,* 6.

57. Gorman, "The Corruption of Cataloguing," 32-35.

58. Thomas, "The Work-Wide Web: A Cataloguing Career for Every Librarian?" 5-22.

59. Thomas, "The Work-Wide Web: A Cataloguing Career for Every Librarian?" 5-22.

60. Gorman, "The Corruption of Cataloguing," 32-35.

MARCup to Markup:
Education for Cataloguing and Classification in Australia

Ross Harvey
Susan Reynolds

SUMMARY. This article considers the current state in Australia of education for cataloguing and classification (considered broadly and encompassing descriptive cataloguing, subject access, classification, metadata, knowledge organisation, bibliographic control, and other related areas for all formats of library resources). Data comes from subject and course descriptions located in the handbook entries and web sites of Australian programs in library and information studies, and from an informal survey of practising cataloguers and library educators. Conclusions are drawn about the range of subjects taught, their focus, and their levels. *[Article copies available for a fee from The Haworth Document Delivery Service: 1-800-HAWORTH. E-mail address: <docdelivery@haworthpress.com> Website: <http://www.HaworthPress.com> © 2006 by The Haworth Press, Inc. All rights reserved.]*

Ross Harvey, PhD, is Professor of Library and Information Management, Charles Sturt University, P.O. Box 1463, Wagga Wagga, NSW 2650, Australia (E-mail: rossharvey@csu.edu.au). Sue Reynolds, MLS, is an educator in the Information Management Program, RMIT University, Melbourne, Australia, and in the Library and Cultural Studies Unit, Victoria University, Melbourne, P.O. Box 14428, Melbourne City MC, Victoria 8001, Australia (E-mail: Sue.Reynolds@vu.edu.au). She is also a Doctoral Candidate, School of Information Studies, Charles Sturt University.

The assistance of Rachel Salmond is gratefully acknowledged.

[Haworth co-indexing entry note]: "MARCup to Markup: Education for Cataloguing and Classification in Australia." Harvey, Ross, and Susan Reynolds. Co-published simultaneously in *Cataloging & Classification Quarterly* (The Haworth Information Press, an imprint of The Haworth Press, Inc.) Vol. 41, No. 3/4, 2006, pp. 173-192; and: *Education for Library Cataloging: International Perspectives* (ed: Dajin D. Sun, and Ruth C. Carter) The Haworth Information Press, an imprint of The Haworth Press, Inc., 2006, pp. 173-192. Single or multiple copies of this article are available for a fee from The Haworth Document Delivery Service [1-800-HAWORTH, 9:00 a.m. - 5:00 p.m. (EST). E-mail address: docdelivery@haworthpress.com].

doi:10.1300/J104v41n03_02

KEYWORDS. Australia, cataloguing, classification, cataloguing education, education programs, paraprofessional training, professional education, surveys

INTRODUCTION

In an address to the New York State Library School in 1915 . . . William Warner Bishop . . . [declared]: 'Catalogs and catalogers are not in the forefront of library thought. In fact, a certain impatience with them and their wares is to be detected in many quarters. Shallow folk are inclined to belittle the whole cataloging business . . . I think I am safe in saying,' he adds, 'that most students in library schools would rather do anything else than take up cataloging on graduation.'[1]

This description reflects the current situation in Australia.

In order to understand why, it is necessary to be aware of some key influences on education for librarianship in Australia. One is the dominance of a British, rather than American, model of library education. Initially the Library Association of Australia awarded professional qualifications; then, from 1960, the awards were made from library schools based in universities. The graduate diploma, comprising a full year's study of librarianship following a bachelor's level qualification in any discipline, is the professional qualification held by most Australian librarians. Master's degrees were introduced into Australia in the 1970s but have not been of much interest to the profession, although this is changing. The second key influence is the strong role that undergraduate qualifications play. The first bachelor's degrees in librarianship and information studies were introduced in 1971. Adoption has been widespread, and professionally recognised bachelor's qualifications awarded by Australian LIS (Library and Information Studies) schools are now accorded the same professional status as graduate diplomas or master's degrees. A third major influence is the role played by ALIA (the Australian Library and Information Association, formerly the Library Association of Australia). Professional recognition of a program by ALIA is very important because the holder of a recognised qualification can be granted professional membership of ALIA automatically on application. All ALIA-recognised programs must offer subjects that include bibliographic organisation content, covering "Processing of information, demonstrated by the ability to enable information access and use through systematic and user-centred description, categorisation, storage, preservation and retrieval."[2] "Currently a qualified LIS professional can attain professional membership of ALIA (the Australian Library and Information Association) with either a bachelor's degree in LIS, a graduate diploma, or a master's."[3]

A strong paraprofessional group is another factor shaping Australian librarianship and education for it. Library technician qualifications were first offered in 1970 at TAFE (Technical and Further Education) colleges. Australian library technicians are a vocal group who have effectively argued their case, and this is one reason for the continuing popularity of bachelor's degrees, as it is relatively straightforward to upgrade a technician's qualifications to a fully professional university-awarded bachelor's qualification. However, the presence of this strong group creates significant confusion on the part of Australian employers, potential students, and librarians about the distinctions between each level of qualification (technician, bachelor's, graduate diploma, master's).[4,5]

There can be no dispute that libraries have changed significantly in recent years, in response to increasing amounts of information in digital form and the widespread use of networked computing. Bibliographic organisation practice has been significantly affected by these changes. Examples are plentiful, and the language used to describe these activities is also changing, from *cataloguing books* to *developing metadata* for *information resources* (which may be *digital objects*). Education for cataloguing and classification is reflecting these changes, perhaps the most obvious indication being the titles of subjects that cover bibliographic organisation practice, no longer *Cataloguing* and *Classification*, but now *Organising Information*. Changes such as these are the reason for the 2002 ALCTS/ALISE Task Force (Association for Library Collections and Technical Services/Association for Library and Information Science Education) report *Cataloging and Metadata Education: A Proposal for Preparing Cataloging Professionals of the 21st Century*.[6] This report proposes a "model curriculum for cataloging and continuing education"[7] and one section briefly lists some of the bibliographic organisation knowledge that experts and practitioners consider to be required by the new graduate. As well as "a general understanding of AACR2, MARC, Z39.50, name and subject authority, and classification schema," "an overview of 'metadata' and of 'interoperability' is necessary, as well as general understanding of ISBD, APPM, TEI, Dublin Core, GILS, FGDC, VRA, EAD, Metadata crosswalks, HTML, XML, SGML."[8]

We can assume, given that Australia is very firmly part of the Anglo-American tradition of librarianship, that the same is required by Australian LIS graduates. But is it what is currently being taught?

CATALOGUING CONTENT
IN AUSTRALIAN UNIVERSITY-BASED PROGRAMS

One way to answer this question is to analyse the content of cataloguing subjects offered by Australian LIS programs. The twelve university-level schools in 2003 offered 26 ALIA-recognised bachelor's, graduate diploma, and master's programs in library and information studies (see Table 1). Data was taken from subject and course descriptions found in the handbook entries and web sites of Australian university-level programs in library and information studies, located using the web listing of courses recognised by ALIA.[9] The data used was extracted in June 2003, but it should be noted that the information on this site relates to courses offered in 2002, and changes have occurred. Despite these changes, the data provides some indication of what is currently taught. It should also be noted that all subjects are of a standard length of one semester, usually 12 or 13 weeks in duration and two to three hours per week of contact time. There are some variations, such as those subjects taught in the distance education mode where the number of hours of contact time does not apply, but the generalisation is valid.

The bibliographic organisation subjects currently taught in these programs can be loosely characterised as either grounded in traditional library practice, or based in a wider information context. Traditional subjects typically focus on tools such as AACR2, DDC, LCSH, and MARC, and on practices such as copy cataloguing and acquiring records from bibliographic utilities. An example is the subject IMS5017 *Information Organisation* offered at Monash University. Its content covers:

> Standards governing description, distribution and access to information at the local and global levels with respect to AACR2, subject headings lists, indexing and thesaurus construction, classification schemes, the MARC and the Dublin Core metadata. The effects of economic, social and technological factors on the developments of bibliographic networks and cataloguing operations. Major bibliographic tools and utilities for organising bibliographic records on a bibliographic network. (Details were taken from the Monash web site in June 2003.)[10]

TABLE 1. LIS Programs and Subjects Offered by Australian Universities

University of Canberra, Division of Communication and Education, Information Studies Program

- *Bachelor of Communication (Information):* 005821 Information Organisation (required)–Focuses on library practice
- *Graduate Diploma in Library and Information Management:* 005188 Cataloguing G (required)–no information available

Charles Sturt University, School of Information Studies

- *Bachelor of Arts (Library and Information Science):* INF102 Organising Information (required)–Focuses on library practice; INF116 Describing and Analysing Information Resources (optional)–Metadata standards; broader information context; focus on electronic resources
- *Master of Applied Science (Library and Information Management):* INF425 Describing and Analysing Information Resources (required)–Metadata standards; broader information context; focus on electronic resources; INF411 Organising Information (optional)–Focuses on library practice
- *Master of Education (Teacher Librarianship):* ETL505 Organising Knowledge (required)–Focuses on library practice in the school library environment
- *Master of Applied Science (Teacher Librarianship):* ETL505 (required)
- *Graduate Diploma in Applied Science (Teacher Librarianship):* ETL505 (required)

University of New South Wales, School of Information Systems, Technology and Management, Faculty of Commerce and Economics

- *Graduate Diploma in Information Management:* IMGT5120 Organisation of Knowledge (required)–Knowledge representation, metadata
- *Master of Commerce in Information Management:* IMGT5120 (required)

University of Technology, Sydney, Faculty of Humanities and Social Sciences

- *Bachelor of Arts in Communication (Information Management):* 50491 Organising Information for Access (required)–Both library and metadata practice
- *Graduate Diploma in Information Management:* 57099 Enabling Information Access (required)–Metadata focus; 57090 Information Organisation (required)–Metadata focus
- *Graduate Diploma in Knowledge Management:* 57099 (required)
- *Master of Arts in Information Management:* 57099 (required)

Northern Territory University, Faculty of Law, Business and Arts

- *Bachelor of Library and Information Management:* Professional studies are conducted externally by arrangement with Charles Sturt University: see CSU entry above

Queensland University of Technology [Gardens Point], School of Information Systems

- *Bachelor of Information Technology (Information Systems) Library Studies Stream:* ITB337 Information Organisation (required)–Focuses on library practice
- *Graduate Diploma in Library and Information Studies:* ITN337 Information Organisation (required)–Focuses on library practice

Queensland University of Technology [Kelvin Grove], School of Cultural and Language Studies in Education

- *Graduate Diploma in Education (Teacher Librarianship):* CLP Bibliographic Organisation (elective)–Focuses on library practice in the school library environment

University of South Australia, School of Communication Information and New Media

- *Bachelor of Arts (Information Studies):* LIBR 1005 Library Automation (required)–Focuses on library practice
- *Graduate Diploma in Information Studies:* LIBR5012 Organisation of Knowledge (required)–Knowledge management, metadata focus; LIBR5023 Knowledge Representation (elective)–Both metadata and library practice

TABLE 1 (continued)

Monash University, School of Information Management and Systems

- *Graduate Diploma of Information Management and Systems:* IMS5017 Information Organisation (required)–Both metadata and library practice
- *Master of Information Management and Systems:* IMS5017 (required)

Royal Melbourne Institute of Technology, School of Business Information Technology

- *Bachelor of Business in Information Management:* 1 required subject
- *Graduate Diploma in Information Management:* LIBR1018 Information Organisation in Libraries (required)–Library practice

Curtin University of Technology, School of Media and Information

- *Bachelor of Arts (Librarianship and Corporate Information Management):* IS203 Information Design (required)–Metadata focus; IS204 Information Organisation (required)–Library practice focus
- *Graduate Diploma in Information and Library Studies:* IS503 Information Design (required)–Metadata focus; IS504 Information Organisation (required)–Library practice focus

Edith Cowan University, School of Computer and Information Science

- *Graduate Diploma in Science (Information Services):* IST4106 Information organisation (required)–Library practice

Subjects in the second category typically examine topics such as how information objects are structured, metadata, DTDs, and schema. An example is the subject LIBR5012 *Organisation of Knowledge* offered at the University of South Australia. Its content covers:

Theoretical foundations of bibliographic organisation; epistemologies, knowledge structures, ontologies and taxonomies, information mapping and information architecture; basic principles and theoretical foundations of traditional organisation schemes, including materials from traditional librarianship, information science, cognitive science, semiotics, and artificial intelligence that have contributed to an understanding of how people obtain, store, retrieve and use information; study of principles organising various types of documents; representation and organisation of information resources, including organisational structures such as classification schemes, indexes, bibliographies and catalogues which provide access to the document and its intellectual content; national and international standards of bibliographic control; various approaches to organising in different environments; the role of technical standards. (Details come from the University of South Australia web site in June 2003.)[11]

Table 1 lists the twelve Australian universities offering programs in library and information studies recognised by ALIA, the 26 courses offered, the 25 bibliographic organisation subjects offered in each course, and a brief characterisation of the content of each subject.[12]

Eighteen of the 26 courses require one bibliographic organisation subject to be taken in order to complete course requirements. Three courses require two bibliographic organisation subjects. One course required no bibliographic organisation subject to be taken, but offered an elective, and four courses required one bibliographic organisation subject and also offered one elective (see Table 2).

The listing of subjects provided in Table 1 allows a general indication of the nature of the contents of subjects. It is based on the summaries or abstracts of the subjects available on the web sites of the universities that offer them. Considerable caution must be exercised when using these abstracts, as such summaries are by their very nature brief and not always sufficiently informative. Nonetheless, the general trend is clear (see Table 3)–subjects that deal with library practice are still the most heavily represented, although subjects that take significant note of the wider information context, especially metadata concepts, are also well represented.

CATALOGUING CONTENT
IN AUSTRALIAN PARAPROFESSIONAL PROGRAMS

Unlike the university-based LIS programs, Australian library technician programs adhere to a national curriculum. Library technician qualifications are offered by TAFE colleges. The first of these programs was offered in Australia in 1970. Up until 1995 the TAFE colleges in each of the seven states and two territories used different curricula, devised at state or territory level, for educating library technicians. The outcomes of these programs were very similar, but they were delivered in modes that suited the differing requirements of each state. In 1997 a national curriculum was introduced. This incorporated a set of Library Competency Standards whose use was agreed on by all TAFEs that taught library technicians. The individual programs were revised at state level to match the national curriculum for the new Diploma of Library and Information Studies, so that library technicians graduated with a qualification that was intended to be both portable and consistent within Australia.

TABLE 2. Number of Bibliographic Organisation Subjects Offered

Subjects offered	Number of courses (n = 26)	Percentage
No required subjects; one elective offered	1	4
One subject required	18	69
One subject required; one elective offered	4	15
Two subjects required	3	12

TABLE 3. Content of Bibliographic Organisation Subjects

Characterisation of content	Number of subjects (n = 25)	Percentage
Primarily library practice	12	48
Primarily metadata/wider information context	8	32
Both	3	12
Not clear/insufficient information available	2	8

The national curriculum was reviewed within a few years of its introduction, and this process resulted in the introduction of the Museum and Library Information Services Industry Training Package in 1999. Training Packages are intended to result in "one industry-managed process . . . creating a comprehensive tool kit for learning and assessment that leads to nationally recognised qualifications."[13] A Training Package specifies skill and knowledge outcomes to be achieved, and does not provide a curriculum to be delivered. The 1999 Museum and Library Information Services Industry Training Package revised the existing competency standards to a set of standards which "describe the skills, and knowledge used by practitioners . . . [and] also provide guidance on assessment."[14] It specifies several exit levels (qualifications) starting with the basic-level Certificate of Library and Information Services II and leading through Certificates III and IV to a Diploma and an Advanced Diploma of Library and Information Services. Students may exit at any of the levels above, depending on the policy of the particular TAFE. Certificate II holders would be considered a 'library aide,' Certificate III holders a 'library assistant,' and with Certificate IV a 'library technician in training' working towards the Diploma. The Diploma is the full library technician qualification. The Advanced Diploma is not currently offered, but is intended for experienced technicians wishing to upgrade their qualification. The 1999 Training Package is, in turn, being revised, with the revision to be completed by June 2004 and implemented in 2005.

Currently, fifteen TAFEs are listed by ALIA as offering the Diploma of Library and Information Services, usually incorporating some or all of the Certificates (Table 4). In addition, Edith Cowan University in Western Australia offers an Associate Degree and Bachelor of Science (Library Technology) that is recognised by ALIA as a technician-level qualification.

Cataloguing and classification content in the Diploma of Library and Information Services is present in the 'Information Management' modules (as they are termed in the Training Package). With regard to their teaching, not much has changed through the various incarnations of library technician programs. These modules remain soundly based on traditional library practice–that is, focussed on AACR2, DDC, LCSH and MARC–but now, typically, also pay some attention to metadata and management of cataloguing procedures.

The current situation is indicated in Table 5. The table shows which competencies in the Training Package can be offered as Information

TABLE 4. TAFEs Offering LIS Awards*

Canberra Institute of Technology

Hunter Institute (NSW)

Riverina Institute (NSW)

Sydney Institute

Illawarra Institute (NSW)

Western Sydney Institute

Northern Territory University

Southbank Institute of TAFE

Adelaide Institute of TAFE

Tasmania Institute of TAFE

Box Hill Institute (Victoria)

Swinburne University of Technology (Victoria)

University of Ballarat

Victoria University

Central TAFE (Perth)

*Source <http://www.alia.org.au/education/courses/library.technician.html>.

TABLE 5. Information Management Competencies in the Museum and Library Information Services Industry Training Package

COMPETENCY	HOURS*	CORE or OTHER UNIT (ELECTIVE)	2004**
CULLB302A Use bibliographic methods	40	Core–Cert III	Core–Cert III
CULLB412A Undertake cataloguing activities	30	Other–Cert IV	Core–Cert IV
CULLB503A Organise information for client access	100	Core–Diploma	Deleted
CULLB505A Analyse and describe material	50	Other–Diploma	Core–Advanced Diploma
CULLB506A Catalogue and classify material	50	Other–Diploma	Core–Diploma
CULLB701A Analyse and describe specialist and/or complex material		May be used with Advanced Diploma	Core–Advanced Diploma

*Hours are nominal; that is, more or less may be allocated to each Competency, though teaching hours may not be reduced to less than 80%.
** The Training Package is currently under revision with units changing constantly. This is how it stood in April 2004.

Management modules, though not every competency may be offered by individual TAFEs. The content of the competencies may also vary, depending on interpretation and mapping of the earlier national curriculum subjects to the new Training Package modules.

In 2004/2005 the situation will change slightly (see Table 5), with Information Management modules becoming required but reduced in number. The Training Package does not specify hours that should be allocated to each module; these are derived through an implementation process following the publication of the Training Package. The 1999 Implementation Guide was produced by the State of Victoria and then followed by the other States and Territories.[15]

VIEWS OF AUSTRALIAN LIS EDUCATORS

In an attempt to understand better the issues and concerns around education for cataloguing and classification in Australia, an informal survey of practising cataloguers and library educators was carried out in March 2004. This survey did not attempt to be representative; rather, its responses were solicited in order to provide some general evidence about attitudes and concerns. The questionnaire was e-mailed to potential respondents and requested details of cataloguing and classification subjects offered, and information about the number of academics and practitioners involved in teaching these subjects. It also sought comments on seven questions and statements:

- How many other people participate in the delivery of information organisation subjects (e.g., practitioners employed on a casual basis)?
- Are students required to include information organisation as part of their industry placement/practicum?
- What major changes to information organisation education/training have you observed over the past 5-10 years?
- What changes to information organisation education/training do you foresee in the next 5-10 years?
- Please comment on the adequacy or appropriateness of current information organisation education/training (e.g., what is currently included but could be eliminated; what could be included but currently is not).
- Describe any constraints you have on developing information organisation subjects/modules.
- Please comment on the role of employers in the development of information organisation skills (i.e., on-the-job training).

All Australian university and TAFE LIS schools were approached. Specific educators were contacted where they were known, and the Head of School where not. Nine returns were received, six from university educators giving details of ten university-level subjects, and three from TAFE level educators. No attempts were made to improve the response rate.

The responses to the question, "How many other people participate in the delivery of information organisation subject (e.g., practitioners employed on a casual basis)?" indicated that all schools except one involve practitioners in delivery of subjects. No conclusion was possible from the limited data received in answer to the question "Are students required to include information organisation as part of their industry placement/practicum?" although the data suggested that information organisation is not typically required to be part of the students' industry placement.

The major change to information organisation education and training observed over the past five to ten years by almost all of the university-level and TAFE-level educators was the move, as described by one respondent, from "library studies to a broader information and knowledge management context." This is characterised by an increasing emphasis on non-library-specific standards: a respondent described it as "information organisation expressed as information architecture with emphasis on Web front end to databases." This change has resulted in an emphasis on teaching the underlying principles and knowledge: "we now try to teach principles of organisation which the students can then take away and apply using whatever tools are appropriate in the workplace they find themselves in." Library cataloguing and classification practice has become, one respondent suggested, "an exemplary instance of metadata."

The predominant response to the question "What changes to information organisation education/training do you foresee in the next 5-10 years?" was that there would be "a continuation of similar trends" with a need to accommodate "more varied tools, more varied contexts." One respondent noted that information organisation teaching would be about "controlling content of any type of defined markup, not just MARCup." Another predicted that "increasingly intuitive search engines will have a major impact on online information retrieval, possibly outdating present metadata principles and opening up new principles and tools in the area." It was suggested that teaching would "move largely/fully to the online environment." One respondent may perhaps have been feeling his or her age, judging from a comment that new standards involving less human intervention would be rapidly implemented "as all the old cataloguers die!"

The central issue regarding the adequacy or appropriateness of current information organisation education and training was considered overwhelmingly by university-level educators to be the limited room in the curriculum to cover all that should be taught. "At post-graduate level there is not enough room in the curriculum for the development of sound theoretical and practical competency; . . . the widening of information organisation syllabi makes it even more difficult to provide an adequate grounding for graduates." TAFE-level educators were significantly more satisfied with current teaching, which was described as "very relevant" and reflective of "current industry practices."

The major constraint at both university and TAFE levels was "access to tools," although here the increasing availability of these online was appreciated, despite high licensing costs–"the online learning environment and availability of electronic resources means that constraints are a diminishing factor." Another constraint noted by university-level educators was the length of the course at graduate level (i.e., the Graduate

Diploma, one-year, full-time study) that typically allows room for only one bibliographic organisation subject.

Respondents were unanimous in the opinion that employers played a significant role in the development of information organisation skills. It was noted that employers have needed to "supplement information organisation education with on-the-job training" for a long time, but this role has become more critical. "Increasingly there will be a need for employers to take on the specific training for the tools and context that they need, building on the generalist training" provided by the library schools. Consequently, "employers are going to have to either devote greater financial resources to bringing in on-the-job trainers or rely to a greater extent on CPD [Continuing Professional Development] opportunities developed by universities, the professional associations and other bodies."

VIEWS OF THE AUSTRALIAN LIS PROFESSION

An informal survey of practising cataloguers was also carried out in March 2004. The questionnaire was posted on relevant Australian listservs. Twenty-one responses were received, and no attempts were made to improve the response rate. Thirteen of the 21 responses came from practitioners working in school libraries, reflecting the re-posting of the invitation to participate onto an active electronic forum widely read by librarians working in schools.

This survey sought to identify whether practitioners perceived there was any difference in the knowledge and skills of cataloguing and classification required by entry-level professional librarians and newly graduated library technicians. It asked respondents to rank in importance 42 statements about the knowledge and skills required for librarians and technicians. The ranking was 1 = Essential, 2 = Important, 3 = Desirable but not necessary, and 4 = Unimportant. The statements are reproduced in the Appendix. They were loosely based on the list of cataloguing competencies described in Letarte et al.[16] Respondents were invited to suggest additional knowledge and skills not listed in the questionnaire, and were also requested to comment on the role of employers in the development of information organisation skills, and to add any further comments on the adequacy and appropriateness of what is currently taught in information organisation subjects.

The limited number of responses allows only very general conclusions to be drawn. Ranking by respondents allowed for the 42 statements about knowledge and skills required to be grouped into five categories:

- Knowledge and skills required by professional librarians and library technicians–*substantial agreement*
- Required by professional librarians and library technicians–*some agreement*
- Required by professional librarians but not by library technicians–*substantial disagreement*
- Required by professional librarians but not by library technicians–*some disagreement*
- *Not required* for either professional librarians or library technicians.

These categories were determined by totalling the responses for each statement. Where the totals of 1 (Essential) and 2 (Important) were 18 or higher (80% of the total number of responses) in both professional librarian and technician categories, this was considered to be substantial agreement that these skills and knowledge were necessary for both. Where the responses in each category were generally similar (that is, there were approximately similar totals for each of 1, 2, 3, and 4), this was considered as some agreement, rather than substantial agreement. Similarly, substantial disagreement was indicated where there was a difference of 10 or higher between the totals of 1 (Essential) and 2 (Important), and disagreement was indicated where the responses in each category were dissimilar, but not to the significant extent of substantial disagreement. Table 6 lists the statements in each category.

The results from this small and unrepresentative sample can only indicate trends, and even then significant qualifications apply. The data does suggest a high degree of agreement about what should be in the curriculum of both levels of qualification. For instance, a working knowledge of cataloguing tools and of DDC was required at both levels, as was the ability to interpret bibliographic records. The data also suggest a high degree of agreement about what the differences in curriculum content between each level of qualification should be (categorised in Table 6 as Substantial disagreement). For instance, professional librarians should have knowledge of what could be described as conceptual knowledge–interpreting bibliographic records no matter what form they are in, evaluating information retrieval systems in relation to user needs and information-seeking behaviours, understanding how data

TABLE 6. Statements Listed in Categories

Substantial agreement: required by professional librarians and library technicians

Interpret a bibliographic record in an OPAC
Effectively search a wide range of information retrieval systems
Understand information-seeking behaviours of users
Understand how to provide the products and services users need
Understand the relationship between classification and shelf order
Understand the role of bibliographic utilities
Understand how searching techniques affect precision and recall
Basic knowledge of cataloguing tools
Working knowledge of cataloguing tools
Knowledge of Dewey Decimal Classification

Some agreement: required by professional librarians and library technicians

Knowledge of classification methods
Knowledge of indexing theory
Knowledge of thesaurus construction methods
Knowledge of sources of bibliographic records
Knowledge of national and international cataloguing standards
Knowledge of Library of Congress Subject Headings
Knowledge of Anglo-American Cataloguing Rules
Knowledge of Library of Congress Rule Interpretations
Knowledge of MARC format
Knowledge of HTML

Substantial disagreement: required by professional librarians but not by library technicians

Interpret a bibliographic record wherever it is stored (e.g., embedded in web page; in XML file)
Evaluate information retrieval systems in relation to user needs and information-seeking behaviours
Apply syndetic structure and controlled vocabulary in *searching* information retrieval systems
Understand the connection between data structures, database design, and searching techniques
Understand how data structures affect precision and recall

Some disagreement: required by professional librarians but not by library technicians

Ability to develop and apply syndetic structure and controlled vocabulary in *designing* information
    retrieval systems
Knowledge of information organisation and intellectual access theory
Knowledge of indexing methods
Knowledge of subject analysis theory
Knowledge of subject analysis methods
Knowledge of thesaurus construction theory
Knowledge of the theory of describing, identifying, and showing relationships among materials
Knowledge of methods for describing, identifying, and showing relationships among materials
Knowledge of basic database design concepts
Knowledge of principles for designing user-driven information retrieval systems
Knowledge of bibliographic relationships underlying database design
Knowledge of state-of-the-art research and practice in cataloguing and classification
Knowledge of XML
Knowledge of Dublin Core metadata standard

Not required for either professional librarians or library technicians

Knowledge of AGLS [Australian Government Locator Service] metadata standard*
Knowledge of EDNA [Education Network Australia] metadata standard**

*<http://www.naa.gov.au/recordkeeping/gov_online/agls/summary.html>
**<http://www.edna.edu.au/metadata>

structures affect precision and recall—but library technicians were not considered to need this knowledge.

These trends are not surprising. What is of more interest is the suggestion from the data that library technicians do not (or perhaps, may not, as this trend is most apparent in the 'Some disagreement' category) require knowledge of indexing methods, subject analysis methods, methods for describing, identifying, and showing relationships among materials, basic database design concepts, and Dublin Core metadata standards. This supports the trend noted earlier (see Table 3)—that library practice is still largely concerned with the use of traditional tools and techniques, with relatively little note yet being taken of the tools and techniques developed and applied in the wider information context.

Additional skills suggested by respondents were few: principles of filing (alphabetical and numerical), how to evaluate a classification system, and a suggestion that classification schemes other than DDC should be included (UDC was specifically named).

All respondents considered that employers played an 'important' and 'vital' role in the development of information organisation skills (i.e., on-the-job training). "On-the-job training is an essential part of becoming a competent cataloguer," noted one respondent, because "ongoing dialogue with other more experienced staff members gives knowledge that can't be experienced through training." Several respondents noted that this depended on the size of the institution and suggested that even where it was too small to support formal in-house training programs, the employer "must have a role in ensuring that workers have continuing PD . . . (e.g., providing support, funding attendance at PD courses if too small to have trainer/training on staff)."

Many respondents indicated that there was a clear role between the skills and knowledge that new entrants to the profession should have after graduating, and those the employer should provide. "The role of the educational institution is to provide students with the basic skills required," whereas the employer "helps [the new graduates] evolve in their job and understand how things work in the real world." There was, however, a strong suggestion that employers needed to be "clear and confident about the information organisation knowledge and skills they require, document these in relevant position descriptions and recruitment materials, and update these as their requirements change."

Two comments made by respondents who identified themselves as senior practitioners (one indicated that they had 28 years of professional practice) encapsulate most of the comments made in the responses:

An understanding [of information organisation] is a basic competency for library practice. It is a lot more difficult to provide specific training and impart local knowledge of procedures, etc., if they do not have a good understanding of the concepts and how to apply skills. I do not think it is necessary to distinguish too much between professional and paraprofessional approaches with such fundamentals.

Employers must ensure that training opportunities are available, either in-house or externally, for staff to acquire new skills to meet constantly changing job requirements. One cannot rely on the assumption that all professionals they employ will regularly update their knowledge and skills.

Respondents were relatively silent about the adequacy and appropriateness of what is currently taught in information organisation subjects. One respondent suggested that the library technician's curriculum "is still one step behind what is happening in reality. Metadata is not learned–not even the basics. There should be more concentration on . . . copy cataloguing–this is what the industry is asking for." Another suggested that "we are putting too much importance on management subjects and information technology subjects, and losing the skills [e.g., searching] that information organisation gives to a librarian . . . how are you supposed to search for something and find what you are looking for if you do not understand the structure?" Another argued for the inclusion of filing in the curriculum "as it is still required and is an essential consideration in designing indexes, report formats, etc., as well as the physical arrangement of library material (of which loose-leaf and statute filing are good examples)." And again, a comment made by a senior practitioner is worth noting:

What individuals bring out of these courses to the workplace after they have graduated depends on the levels of application and intellect they took into the course of study [and a whole range of other factors]. I have, however, been surprised that many recent graduates, and long-standing practitioners are lacking the basics and look blank when I talk about IR concepts such as precision, recall, relevance, precoordination, postcoordination, authority control . . . Are information organisation subjects not getting the space and focus they need in information studies programs?

CONCLUSION

Australian bibliographic organisation practice is part of the wider Anglo-American tradition and is influenced by the same trends, resulting from the increasing amounts of information in digital form and the widespread use of networked computing. This paper has examined education for this field in Australia, noting some of the key influences, especially the role of the key professional organisation, ALIA, and the effect of a strong paraprofessional group. Its examination of the curricula of the Australian university and TAFE courses, and data from small surveys of educators and librarians has indicated trends, clearly pointed out the Australian profession's perception of the differences between the skills and knowledge about bibliographic organisation required by paraprofessional and professional librarians, and has reiterated that a sound foundation in bibliographic organisation skills and knowledge is still the key to effective professional practice.

NOTES

1. Sarah E. Thomas, "The Catalog as Portal to the Internet," (2000), <http://lcweb.loc.gov/catdir/bibcontrol/thomas_paper.html> (20 April 2004).

2. Australian Library and Information Association. "The Library and Information Sector: Core Knowledge, Skills and Attributes," (2003), <http://www.alia.org.au/policies/core.knowledge.html> (June 2003).

3. Ross Harvey and Susan Higgins, "Defining Fundamentals and Meeting Expectations: Trends in LIS Education in Australia," *Education for Information*, 21 (2003): 150.

4. Ibid., p. 151.

5. Mary Carroll, "The Well-Worn Path," *Australian Library Journal*, 51 (2002): 117-125.

6. Ingrid Hsieh-Yee, "Cataloging and Metadata Education: A Proposal for Preparing Cataloging Professionals of the 21st Century," <http://www.loc.gov/catdir/bibcontrol/CatalogingandMetadataEducation.pdf> (20 April 2004).

7. Ibid., p. I.

8. Ibid., p. 9.

9. Website <http://www.alia.org.au/education/courses/librarianship.html>.

10. <http://www.sims.monash.edu.au/index.html>.

11. <http://www.unisa.edu.au/>.

12. Source <http://www.alia.org.au/education/courses/librarianship.html> and web sites of the universities as at June 2003.

13. *Library and Information Services: Museum and Library/Information Services Industry Training Package: CUL99* (Surry Hills, NSW, CREATE Australia, 1999), p. 2.

14. Ibid., p. 7.

15. Human Services Curriculum Maintenance Manager, Swinburne University of Technology, on behalf of the Office of Post Compulsory Education, Training and Employment, *Victorian Implementation Guide: Museum and Library/Information Services Training Package* ([Melbourne], Department of Education, Victoria, 2000).

16. Karen M. Letarte, Michelle R. Turvey, Dea Borneman & David L. Adams, "Practitioner Perspectives on Cataloging Education for Entry-Level Academic Librarians," *Library Resources & Technical Services,* 46:1 (2002): 11-22.

APPENDIX. Statements Used in the Practitioners' Survey

Interpret a bibliographic record in an OPAC

Interpret a bibliographic record wherever it is stored (e.g., embedded in web page; in XML file)

Evaluate information retrieval systems in relation to user needs and information-seeking behaviours

Apply syndetic structure and controlled vocabulary in *searching* information retrieval systems

Ability to develop and apply syndetic structure and controlled vocabulary in *designing* information retrieval systems

Effectively search a wide range of information retrieval systems

Understand information-seeking behaviours of users

Understand how to provide the products and services users need

Understand the relationship between classification and shelf order

Understand the role of bibliographic utilities

Understand the connection between data structures, database design, and searching techniques

Understand how searching techniques affect precision and recall

Understand how data structures affect precision and recall

Knowledge of information organisation and intellectual access theory

Knowledge of classification theory

Knowledge of classification methods

Knowledge of indexing theory

Knowledge of indexing methods

Knowledge of subject analysis theory

APPENDIX (continued)

Knowledge of subject analysis methods

Knowledge of thesaurus construction theory

Knowledge of thesaurus construction methods

Knowledge of the theory of describing, identifying, and showing relationships among materials

Knowledge of methods for describing, identifying, and showing relationships among materials

Knowledge of basic database design concepts

Knowledge of principles for designing user-driven information retrieval systems

Knowledge of bibliographic relationships underlying database design

Knowledge of sources of bibliographic records

Knowledge of state-of-the-art research and practice in cataloguing and classification

Knowledge of national and international cataloguing standards

Basic knowledge of cataloguing tools

Working knowledge of cataloguing tools

Knowledge of Library of Congress Subject Headings

Knowledge of Dewey Decimal Classification

Knowledge of Anglo-American Cataloguing Rules

Knowledge of Library of Congress Rule Interpretations

Knowledge of MARC format

Knowledge of HTML

Knowledge of XML

Knowledge of Dublin Core metadata standard

Knowledge of AGLS (Australian Government Locator Service) metadata standard

Knowledge of EDNA (Education Network Australia) metadata standard

EUROPE

Education for Cataloging and Classification in Austria and Germany

Monika Münnich
Heidi Zotter-Straka
Petra Hauke

SUMMARY. This article discusses the training of catalog librarians in Germany and Austria. First, the various library careers and degrees are described; then the various types of library schools and the varying educational content of different degree programs are described, along with continuing education programs in both countries. Typical job categories in German and Austrian libraries are described in terms of the qualification levels required in each category. Since the question of whether to retain the current official cataloging code is now a subject of intense

Monika Münnich, DWB, retired, was formerly Associate Librarian, University Library, University of Heidelberg, Plöck 107-109, 69117 Heidelberg, Germany (E-mail: moni@monika-muennich.de). Heidi Zotter-Straka is Head, Division for Descriptive Cataloging, Graz University Library, Univ.-Pl. 3, A-8010 Graz, Austria (E-mail: heidi.zotter@uni-graz). Petra Hauke, MA, is Lecturer, Institute of Library and Information Science, Humboldt University Berlin, Germany (E-mail: petra.hauke@buchprojekte.com).

[Haworth co-indexing entry note]: "Education for Cataloging and Classification in Austria and Germany." Münnich, Monika, Heidi Zotter-Straka, and Petra Hauke. Co-published simultaneously in *Cataloging & Classification Quarterly* (The Haworth Information Press, an imprint of The Haworth Press, Inc.) Vol. 41, No. 3/4, 2006, pp. 193-225; and: *Education for Library Cataloging: International Perspectives* (ed: Dajin D. Sun, and Ruth C. Carter) The Haworth Information Press, an imprint of The Haworth Press, Inc., 2006, pp. 193-225. Single or multiple copies of this article are available for a fee from The Haworth Document Delivery Service [1-800-HAWORTH, 9:00 a.m. - 5:00 p.m. (EST). E-mail address: docdelivery@haworthpress.com].

Available online at http://www.haworthpress.com/web/CCQ
© 2006 by The Haworth Press, Inc. All rights reserved.
doi:10.1300/J104v41n03_03

debate (with a potentially significant impact on library education), the main points of that debate are outlined here. Mention is made of the manuals and textbooks currently used in cataloging courses. *[Article copies available for a fee from The Haworth Document Delivery Service: 1-800-HAWORTH. E-mail address: <docdelivery@haworthpress.com> Website: <http://www.HaworthPress.com> © 2006 by The Haworth Press, Inc. All rights reserved.]*

KEYWORDS. Catalogers, cataloging education, library education, library schools, cataloging codes, Austria, Germany

Part A: Catalog Training in Germany
Prepared and Compiled by Monika Münnich

The compiler wishes to thank the following colleagues for their contributions: Ms. Petra Hauke, M.A., Berlin; Ms. Gabriele Messmer, Bayerische Staatsbibliothek, Munich; Prof. Dr. Klaus-Peter Mieth, Humboldt-Universität, Berlin; Prof. Margarete Payer, Hochschule der Medien, Stuttgart; Mr. Kurt Pages, Fachhochschule Hannover, Mr. Hans Popst, Fachhochschule für Öffentliche Verwaltung und Rechtspflege in Bayern, Munich; Prof. Dr. Kornelia Richter, Hochschule für Technik, Wirtschaft und Kultur (FH), Leipzig; Ms. Ute Schäfer, Hochschulbibliothekszentrum, Cologne; Ms. Susanne Schuster, M.A., Bibliotheksservicezentrum, Constance; Dr. Gerhard Stumpf, Universitätssbibliothek Ausgsburg; Prof. Dr. Konrad Umlauf, Humboldt-Universität, Berlin; and, especially, my American colleague, Professor Charles R. Croissant, Saint Louis University, for assistance with English.

1. INTRODUCTION

The "cataloging landscape" in Germany differs considerably from that in the United States:

- We differentiate three different levels of library careers (see later for an explanation of these levels).
- The separate parts of the cataloging process are performed by different persons:
  - descriptive (formal) cataloging is performed by Diplombibliothekare (certified librarians, i.e., librarians of the upper-level rank) and sometimes by librarians at the mid-level rank;

- subject cataloging is normally performed by librarians belonging to the senior rank (the highest rank).
- We usually have no copy catalogers–upper- and mid-level librarians do original and copy cataloging.
- A further difference is that Germany does not have an institution like OCLC. Most of the academic libraries are organized in library consortia, for example, the Bavarian Library Network (Bibliotheksverbund Bayern, BVB, located in Munich); the Academic Library Center North Rhine-Westphalia (Hochschulbibliothekszentrum, HBZ, in Cologne); the South West German Library Consortium (Südwestverbund, SWB, in Constance); the Common Library Network (Gemeinsamer Bibliotheksverbund, GBV, in Göttingen); the Hessian Library Consortium (Hessisches Bibliotheksinformationssystem, Hebis, in Frankfurt).

There is no open interface between these consortia so far, so it is difficult for us to use each other's records.

On the other hand, most of the library consortia import records for German books from the German National Library (Die Deutsche Bibliothek, DDB) and records for foreign books from a number of sources (Library of Congress for English books, other national bibliographic databases, and files of national and international book dealers (such as Casalini, Erasmus, etc.)).

This article presents a series of examples based on contributions from my colleagues and on my personal inquiries; it does not attempt to achieve a complete description of cataloging education in Germany. The article also focuses more on academic libraries, since cataloging plays a much more significant role in academic libraries than it does in public libraries. Public libraries usually get their bibliographic records from ekz.bibliotheksservice GmbH–a service institution for public libraries–or from the Deutsche Bibliothek.

2. LIBRARY CAREERS AND DEGREES

In Germany, all librarians in public and academic libraries are members of the civil service. Within the civil service, three professional ranks have been established for librarians:

- mittlerer Dienst (mid-level service, also known as Bibliotheksassistenten or library assistants; more recently, the title of Specialist for Media and Information Services ("Fachangestellte für Medien- und Informationsdienste") has come into use;

- gehobener Dienst (upper-level service, also known as Diplom-bibliothekare or certified librarians);
- höherer Dienst (senior-level service, i.e., professional librarians holding the highest available academic degree).

Assignment to one of these three ranks is associated with one's educational background in terms of school and university degrees. In practice, the fields of activity associated with these ranks sometimes overlap. Nevertheless, these main fields of activity have developed:

In general, it can be stated that duties requiring subject expertise (for example, selection/acquisition, subject cataloging and classification in large academic libraries, and researching in subject-specific databases) are performed by the senior-level service (höherer Dienst). Also, management functions in large public and academic libraries along with planning and development duties belong to the activities of the senior-level service.

Typical for the upper-level service are demanding and complex activities that require a higher level of expertise than that expected from library assistants. Activities such as collection development and acquisition, descriptive cataloging of special or difficult literature, complex bibliographic searching, online database reference, data processing maintenance, library instruction, organizing and leading activities within departments and working groups, etc., are performed by the upper-level service. To an increasing degree, the creation of new subject headings now belongs to the duties of an upper-level librarian.

The assistant must have good knowledge in such areas as acquisition, descriptive cataloging, circulation, stacks management, and ready reference.

3. LIBRARY SCHOOLS

The history of library education in Germany goes back more than one hundred years. Most of the present forms of library education are considerably younger, however.

Some twenty years ago, the former Library Schools changed their status and became Universities of Applied Sciences (Fachhochschulen). Shortly afterward, the status of librarians-in-training also changed: they had formerly been interns within the civil service system

("Beamtenanwärter" in the mid-level and upper-level service or "Referendare" in the senior-level service), earning a (modest) salary during their education, but they now became university students. The one exception is Munich, where librarians-in-training are still Beamtenanwärter or Referendare.

According to different professional levels, there are a variety of different training institutions in Germany. Some of these training institutions are Fachhochschulen, or universities of applied sciences; some are full universities, or Universitäten. The difference between education at a full-fledged university (Universität) and education at a university of applied sciences (Fachhochschule) is that education at the Fachhochschule is more practice-oriented. In universities of applied sciences, a large number of adjunct lecturers are engaged–in Bavaria, for example, adjunct lecturers teach about one-third of all classes. Apart from a number of specialized institutions, the main schools for library education are as follows:

Library Schools for Senior-Level Service

Bavarian Library School, Munich; Center for Education of the State Library of Lower Saxony, Hannover; Humboldt University, Berlin; Library School in Frankfurt/Main (closed in late 2003); the Universities of Applied Sciences (Fachhochschulen) with Departments of Library and Information Science, in Hamburg and Cologne. Additionally, the following universities offer "Book Sciences" as a main or secondary subject: Cologne, Erlangen-Nürnberg, Mainz, Munich.

- Prerequisite for this library education is a university degree. The education normally comprises a year-long library internship and one year of library school. The degree is "Höherer Dienst an wissenschaftlichen Bibliotheken"–senior-level service at research libraries.

Library Schools for Upper-Level Service at Academic Libraries

The Universities of Applied Sciences (Fachhochschulen) at: Cologne, Hamburg, Hannover, Leipzig (Hochschule für Technik, Wirtschaft und Kultur), Munich (Fachhochschule für Öffentliche Verwaltung und Rechtspflege in Bayern), Potsdam, Stuttgart (Hochschule der Medien).

- Prerequisite for attending a University of Applied Sciences is the "Abitur" (the highest level of high-school diploma). Some schools now require only one foreign language, usually English; this used to be two languages, and up until the 1970s, as many as three foreign languages were sometimes required. The length of the education is usually between six and eight semesters.
- The degree normally is Diplombibliothekar (Certified Librarian). Some degrees are called Informationswirt (Information Manager), Information Designer, etc.

Library Schools for Mid-Level Service

Bavarian Library School, Munich; Center for Education of the State Library of Lower Saxony, Hannover; Thuringian Library School, Sondershausen; Stauffenbergschule, Frankfurt/M.

- Prerequisite is a tenth-grade high school education (i.e., an intermediate high school certificate from a Realschule or middle-track high school, or a final certificate from a Hauptschule, the lower-track high school), plus knowledge of one foreign language.
- The education lasts between two and three years.
- The degree is Bibliotheksassistent (library assistant) or Fachangestellte für Medien- und Informationsdienste; the latter designation started coming into use just a few years ago.

Library Schools for Librarians in Public Libraries

Most of the universities of applied sciences offer courses for librarians in public libraries. There used to be a seperate school: University of Applied Sciences in Bonn (Fachhochschule für das öffentliche Bibliothekswesen)–but it was closed at the end of 2003.

Centers for Continuing Education

In Germany most of the universities of applied sciences (Fachhochschulen) offer continuing education courses for librarians. Continuing education is also offered by several full universities (Universitäten) that have faculties of library science. Additionally, most of the German Library Consortia offer special courses in cataloging, often together with their format applications.

4. OFFICIAL CATALOGING CODES, MANUALS AND TEXTBOOKS

The current official cataloging rules for *descriptive cataloging* are: Regeln für die Alphabetische Katalogisierung (RAK; Rules for descriptive cataloging), established in 1976/77[1] with the following official editions:

- RAK-WB (RAK for research libraries–wissenschaftliche Bibliotheken)
- RAK-ÖB (RAK for public libraries–öffentliche Bibliotheken) Note: Most of the public libraries in larger cities apply RAK-WB
- RAK-Musik (music)
- RAK-UW (unselbständige Werke–works contained within larger works)
- RAK-Karten (cartographic materials)
- RAK-NBM (non-book materials).

There are further unofficial rule applications, e.g., for art librarians and early printed monographs.

These descriptive cataloging codes are about to change. Germany will either:

- adopt use of a new version of its own code that is more adapted to the online environment and more closely aligned with AACR2 (especially in terminology and in bibliographic description; it will have the chapter structure of AACR2), or
- introduce AACR2 as it is. A project at the Deutsche Bibliothek is studying these options at the moment.

My colleague Petra Hauke led a project at Humboldt University that deals with this subject (see part 9 of this article).

The most widely used textbook for descriptive cataloging is: Klaus Haller, Hans Popst: Katalogisierung nach den RAK-WB. - 6. Aufl. - München : Saur, 2003.

The standard *subject cataloging code* for German-speaking countries is the "Regeln für den Schlagwortkatalog" (RSWK–Subject cataloging code; it was first published in 1986, 2nd edition in 1991, 3rd edition in 1998). It was established to make the assignment of subject headings more efficient by using them in library networks and was adopted by the national authority center, Die Deutsche Bibliothek.

RSWK is suitable for indexing publications of all types, including electronic resources and other non-book materials, music, maps, historical books, teaching and learning material.

RSWK provides guidelines for syntactic indexing, i.e., for arranging the headings in a comprehensible chain. The headings encompass all subject areas and heading categories. Topical, geographical, chronological, and form headings are combined with names of persons or corporate bodies (which are also included in the subject authority file) in a standard order, but the order may be modified according to the logic of the topic. So, it is intended to present to the catalog searcher an extremely concise abstract of the document content which is presented in browsing lists or as content description included in a bibliographic record.

In addition to the RSWK itself, the so-called "Praxisregeln zu den RSWK und der Schlagwortnormdatei" or Guide to the RSWK and Subject Authority File, established by Die Deutsche Bibliothek, Frankfurt, is widely used.

As *classification schemes*, some of the libraries within library consortia use:

- the Regensburg Classification,[2] a home-grown scheme. Like the Library of Congress classification scheme, a Regensburg classification number includes, as its principal elements, a class number (expressing a subject area) and an author number. It differs from LCC in that its first element, referred to as a "Lokalzeichen," corresponds most closely to a location code, i.e., a designation indicating a particular area within a library building. This classification scheme has been widely used in academic libraries for more than thirty years, especially in Eastern and Southern Germany, Austria, Switzerland and Southern Tyrol. More than 140 libraries in a number of library consortia apply this code.
- the Universal Decimal Classification (UDK)–widely used in technical libraries;
- the DDC German: The Deutsche Bibliothek started providing DDC German class numbers last year.

In public libraries, the ASB and KAB are used as shelf classification:

- ASB: Allgemeine Systematik für Bibliotheken (General classification schedule for libraries). It is widely used in Western German public libraries.
- KAB: Klassifikation für Allgemeinbibliotheken (Classification for general libraries). Use of this classification scheme was required in the former German Democratic Republic. Most public libraries in East Germany still use the KAB.

5. NAME AUTHORITIES

One aspect of library education in Germany is becoming familiar with the different authority files in use there.

At the Deutsche Bibliothek, Frankfurt, and the Berlin State Library several distinct authority files have been established:

- Personennamensdatei–PND: Personal Names Authority File
  This file comprises personal names for descriptive and subject cataloging. Under current rules, it sometimes happens that a name heading is set up one way as a descriptive heading and in a different way as a subject heading (this is most often the case for persons entered under their given names, such as kings and rulers). When that is the case, these headings are distinguished from one another by different tag numbers. An expert group is currently working on harmonizing these headings.
- Gemeinsame Körperschaftsdatei–GKD: Corporate Names Authority File
  This file comprises only the names of corporate headings for descriptive cataloging. These differ considerably from the corporate headings used by subject catalogers, which are kept in the
- Schlagwortnormdatei–SWD: Subject Authority File
  This authority file with thesaurus characteristics is constructed according to RSWK. In addition to corporate name headings and references, this file comprises all other subject headings and references: for subjects, geographic names, author/title records (so-called Werktitel), form, and chronological subject headings and references.

6. CATALOGING EDUCATION
FOR THE DIFFERENT LEVELS OF LIBRARIANS

6.1 Education in Cataloging for Upper-Level Librarians

The education for upper-level librarians is mainly provided at the universities for applied sciences, or Fachhochschulen.

Four typical, though different, library degree programs in cataloging for the upper-level degree at academic libraries are described and to some extent evaluated in the following examples.

In sections (a), (b), and (d) the units/week mean units per week per semester. In the Bavarian schools there are no semesters but rather theoretical and practical blocks; the indication of number of hours in the section on Bavarian schools refers to actual hours of time spent within one of these blocks.

(a) Fachhochschule Hannover, Fachbereich Informations- und Kommunikationswesen (University of Applied Sciences and Arts, Hannover, Department for Information and Documentation– http://www.ik.fh-hannover.de/ik/de/)

In Lower Saxony, the library education for upper service librarians was established in the winter semester of 1979/80 as a study course of seven to eight semesters within a university of applied science. The goal of this pilot project was to offer integrated courses for the different information areas for the first time in Germany. The students had a common introduction into the theory of descriptive cataloging and to RAK-WB during the two first semesters. These terms were divided into 2 units/week of lectures and 3 units/week of small-group tutorials.

At the end of the pilot project, it was decided not to continue this integrated model.

The program was fundamentally restructured in 2001. The programs for librarians and general documentation were merged into a single "information management" program. The students can choose their area of concentration with regard to their future occupational fields. The areas of concentration are:

- audiovisual material
- information brokerage
- information institutions with music collections

- internal information institutions and special libraries
- media informatics, and
- academic libraries.

All lectures within the basic course of two semesters are mandatory. At the end of this time, the students have to choose their area of concentration. The main course (semesters 3-8) includes a practicum of six months. The 7th semester can be absolved at a foreign university; alternatively, another practicum of 3 months is possible. The final 8th semester comprises courses that focus on the students' professional embarking; in addition, a thesis (Diplomarbeit) is written.

The basic course (Grundstudium) comprises:

- 1st semester: principles of cataloging (3 units/week as lecture)
  - in descriptive cataloging (bibliographic description, kinds of entries, principles of headings, different filing rules),
  - in indexing using different subject cataloging and classification systems,
- 2nd semester: basics of descriptive cataloging with the aim of terminology knowledge and the creation of simple bibliographic records.

The main course (*Hauptstudium*, semesters 3-6) comprises:

- Advanced courses in descriptive cataloging; students must elect the cataloging course that corresponds to their field of concentration (2 units/week as lecture and 2 units/week as small-group discussion). The result should be the ability to create complex records accordings to RAK-WB and to create headings for persons and corporate bodies independently. This course of study is compulsory for students with the area of concentration "academic library."
- Descriptive cataloging in a library network lecture (3 units/week of seminar). Students are supposed to apply their knowledge to online cataloging. This is also mandatory for students with the area of concentration "academic library."
- Descriptive cataloging of musical works (6th semester–lectures and seminars of 3 units/week). This is compulsory for students with the area of concentration "library with music collection."

My colleague Kurt Pages, who teaches descriptive cataloging, expects that in the future there will be a considerable reduction in the number of cataloging courses offered. See also (d) in this section.

(b) Leipzig–Hochschule für Technik, Wirtschaft und Kultur,
Studiengang Bibliotheks- und Informationswissenschaft
(Leipzig University of Applied Sciences–http://www.htwk-leipzig.de)

In Leipzig the formal program for library education consists of two successive parts:

- the basic course (semesters 1-3), leading to the intermediate examination (Vorprüfung)
- the main course (semesters 4-8). After completing the program, the student receives the degree of Diplombibliothekar (FH); the qualifier "FH" stands for "Fachhochschule.

The students can choose between different pathways in the main course: there are compulsory courses and a range of optional subjects. Optional courses are taken according to the chosen pathway. The fifth semester is taken as a practicum in a library.

Curriculum changes are expected within the next five years, probably resulting in the introduction of new academic degrees (bachelor and master).

The basic course comprises:

- principles of cataloging (4 units/week during the 1st semester)
- cataloging I (4 units/week, 2nd semester)
- cataloging II (2 units/week, 3rd semester).

Completion of the basic course should result in:

- mastery of basic terminology, knowledge of standard methods of cataloging, basic knowledge of descriptive cataloging, knowledge of application of different filing methods (by the end of the first semester)
- good theoretical knowledge of descriptive cataloging, knowledge of cataloging codes and their application, basic knowledge of computer aided descriptive cataloging (by the end of the second semester)
- practical ability in creating bibliographic records in a variety of data formats.

In the main course, there are no mandatory courses in descriptive cataloging, but there are mandatory courses in subject cataloging. The following optional courses are offered during the main course:

- advanced course in RAK and cooperative cataloging (in library consortia)
- selected cataloging rules, e.g., RAK-NBM, RAK-UW, Computer-aided cataloging (4 units/week, 4th semester)
- RAK-Music (1 unit/week, 4th semester)
- RAK-Alte Drucke–Early printed monographs (1 unit/week, 7th semester)
- subject indexing by classification (4 units/week, 6th semester)
- subject cataloging (subject headings).

Completion of the main course should result in:

- good knowledge in cataloging early printed monographs
- ability to use catalogs constructed according to the Prussian Instructions
- basic knowledge of RAK-UW (works contained in larger works), RAK-NBM, and RAK-Karten (cartographic material)
- knowledge of MAB (the German bibliographic data format)
- knowledge of the application of Libero (the local system used in Saxony)
- advanced knowledge of RAK-WB
- practical knowledge of cataloging in PICA (Gemeinsamer Bibliotheksverbund, Göttingen) and BIS (Southwestern German Library Network).

Courses are taught by experienced librarians. Members of the staff also conduct seminars and workshops for library staff.

(c) Munich–Fachhochschule für Öffentliche Verwaltung und Rechtspflege in Bayern, Fachbereich Archiv- und Bibliothekswesen (University of Applied Sciences for Public Administration and Administration of Justice, Faculty of Archival and Library Science–http://www.bib-bvb.de/fachbereich/index.html)

As mentioned before, the librarians-in-training in Munich are still interns. The three-year course begins yearly on October first. The education is structured as follows:

Structure and duration of the whole education	
1st theoretical block	6 months
1st practicum	7 months (including 1 month of vacation)
2nd theoretical block	5 months
intermediate exam	
3rd theoretical block	6 months (including 1 month of vacation)
2nd practicum	6 months
4th theoretical block	6 months (including 1 month of vacation)
final exam	
total	36 months = 3 years

As there is no semester schedule, the following scheme will give an overall view of lessons during the theoretical education:

Class hours (45 minutes) in the theoretical education		
block	all subjects together	hours spent in cataloging courses
1.	715	130
2.	550	105
3.	555	105
4.	455	110
total	2275	450

Examination periods are not part of the schedule. The separate courses during the theory blocks are described in the following overview.

Classes in the area of catalogs and cataloging					
subject	1st block	2nd block	3rd block	4th block	total
1. introduction in cataloging theory	20	--	--	--	20
2. search training in catalogs	30	--	--	--	30
3. descriptive cataloging	--	15	--	20	35
4. subject cataloging	--	25	10	25	60
5. classification	--	--	30	15	45
6. descriptive cataloging according to RAK-WB	40	30	25	20	115
7. discussion of the RAK-WB tutorials	20	15	15	15	65
8. online cataloging	20	15	10	15	60
9. cataloging of special resources and media	--	5	15	--	20
total	130	105	105	110	450

As shown in the schedule, descriptive cataloging accounts for the largest portion within cataloging education. During the first and second theoretical blocks, RAK-WB is taught according to the textbook "Katalogisierung nach den RAK-WB" by Klaus Haller and Hans Popst (see section 4 of this article). The objective is to impart a basic knowledge that enables the interns, during their first practicum, to use bibliographies, catalogs, and databases (filed according to RAK-WB), and to differentiate between types of works.

During the second theoretical block, instruction in RAK-WB focuses on headings and references for personal corporate names, entries under corporate bodies, problems of subseries and supplements, multivolume works with subdivisions, uniform titles, parallel and variant titles, dissertations, laws, and commentaries.

In the third and fourth theoretical blocks, the students learn to work with the code, i.e., to understand the logical structure of the rules and to recognize which subject is dealt with in which section, so that they can use RAK without consulting the index.

Already, after a few lessons, the students have to practice appⁱying RAK using copies of title pages. Cataloging these title pages is done as homework. These records are discussed and analyzed in discussion groups, the solution is shown on a transparency, and the lecturer explains the rule that should be applied.

During the practica, the students spend 10 weeks with acquisition and descriptive cataloging and 5 weeks with subject cataloging.

During the education in subject cataloging, the main focus is on the "Regeln für den Schlagwortkatalog (RSWK)," since these are the rules most commonly used in the libraries where the practica take place. As subject cataloging is taught beginning with the second theoretical block, and classification starting with the third block, practical training in subject cataloging (apart from several exercises accompanying some of the lectures) does not begin until the second practicum.

In classes on classification, the "Regensburger Verbundklassifikation, RVK" (see section 4 of this article) is the main focus, since most of the Bavarian academic libraries apply this classification. But, in addition, the Universal Decimal Classification is introduced and an overview of further classification is given, e.g., Dewey Decimal Classification, Library of Congress Classification, and classification codes for public libraries (see section 4 of this article).

(d) Stuttgart–Hochschule der Medien (University of Applied Sciences– http://www.hdm-stuttgart.de)

In Stuttgart the degree programs are library management (Diplom, FH), information management (Diplom, FH) and library and media management (Master). They comprise 6 to 8 semesters. The following cataloging courses are offered: cataloging and indexing of print media, musical works, non-book material including Internet resources, formats, database usage, automatic indexing and theory of cataloging and indexing.

The following cataloging codes are covered in class:

• RAK-WB, RAK-Musik, Dublin Core, rules for Dokumentare[3] (DIN 1505, part 1)
• RSWK, UDK, Regensburg Classification, Shelf classification for public libraries.

In the basic semesters the following courses are taught: 4 units/week RAK; 2 units/week rules for archival materials; 3 units/week subject cataloging and indexing; 2 units/week training in the Southwestern Network (SWB), 1 unit/week formats (currently, MARC and MAB2), 1 unit/week Dublin Core; 1 unit/week cataloging theory (regarding international codes, network organization, and international associations such as IFLA).

In the advanced semesters the following courses are taught: 2 units/week advanced course in RAK; 4 units/week RAK-Music (Master); 2 units/week automatic indexing (mandatory in the course for information manager).

Mandatory courses are: for librarians: 4 units/week RAK, 1 unit/week formats, 1 unit/week Dublin Core, 3 units/week subject cataloging, 1 unit/week theory of descriptive cataloging; for music librarians in the master course: 4 units/week RAK-Music; for information managers: 2 units/week archival cataloging, 2 units/week automatic indexing.

Optional courses are: for librarians: 2 units/week advanced course in RAK; 2 units/week SWB usage; sometimes 2 units/week non-book materials or other special rules, e.g., applications in art libraries; sometimes AACR2.

Practicum: the students must absolve a mandatory practicum of six months during the fifth semester, along with two additional practica of six weeks each.

Changes in the curriculum over the past 5-10 years: more emphasis on formats, database knowledge, and cataloging of Internet resources; and reduction of RAK lectures from 8 units/week to 4 units/week as mandatory courses.

In the opinion of Margarete Payer, the reduction of RAK courses means that the student will begin her/his professional career without sufficient knowledge in cataloging.

Anticipated changes over the next 5-10 years: beginning with the winter semester 2004/2005 bachelor's and master's degrees must be offered, and the degrees for certified librarians (Diplombibliothekar) will no longer be offered. The basic course RAK is supposed to be increased within the bachelor's education to at least 4 units/week. These proposals are still under discussion. The general tendency is to reduce the bachelor's education to a core course lasting 6 semesters. The names to be used for the new degrees have not yet been decided upon.

6.2 Education in Cataloging for Senior-Level Librarians

In the following, two very different educations for senior-level librarians are described:

(a) Munich–Bavarian Library School (http://www.bib-bvb.de/bib)

Library education for senior-level librarians in Bavaria is in transition. Munich offers the last remaining "classical" library education in the form of a "verwaltungsinterne Ausbildung" (an education administered within the civil service; the person in training is a civil service intern rather than a university student–in German, this is also known as a Referendarausbildung).

This education is described first: as mentioned above, this education is divided into a practicum (which can take place at any university library or state library in Germany) and a theoretical part at library schools; in Bavaria, a two-week introductory theoretical course precedes the practicum. The aim of this introductory course is to give an overview of the organisation of libraries.

A third of this introductory course is devoted to cataloging:

- 4 hours to RAK-WB
- 4 hours to subject cataloging
- 4 hours to classification.

The introductory course finishes with a colloquium on trends, problems, and perspectives of librarianship.

The practicum is a major part of this kind of library education. During the practicum year, the trainees have to serve in each department. The practical education in cataloging is certainly focused on subject cataloging, though 4 weeks are devoted to descriptive cataloging. During their practicum the trainees are introduced to cataloging rules and library formats; they are expected to catalog all kinds of materials including electronic resources; and they are introduced to retrospective conversion.

The theoretical education is based on the knowledge of the practical one. It takes place in the Bavarian Library School at the Bavarian State Library.

The theoretical year in Munich comprises nearly 1,600 hours (including advanced courses, excursions, visits to public libraries, publishers, etc.). A total of 960 hours are dedicated to the theoretical main course (theoretischer Hauptteil).

- 80 hours are devoted to cataloging
- 16 hours to cataloging theory
- 30 hours to RAK-WB (including electronic resources)

- 6 hours to copy cataloging
- 15 hours to subject cataloging (RSWK)
- 13 hours to classification.

The main focus of the cataloging education is:

- to impart an overview of cataloging codes
- to introduce authority files
- to introduce library formats
- to explain the involvement of library catalogs in a worldwide information network.

Descriptive cataloging is taught mainly by librarians of the Bavarian State Library. Since other institutions stopped accepting civil service trainees, the number of trainees at the Bavarian State Library has increased significantly, from 7 to 25. Currently trainees from seven federal states are receiving their theoretical education in Munich.

(b) Humboldt University in Berlin–Institute of Library Science (http://www.ib.hu-berlin.de)

The Institute of Library Science of the Humboldt University in Berlin is the only institution in Germany now offering a library degree at the full university level (the other library education programs are located at the universities of applied sciences, or Fachhochschulen).

The courses of study offered at the Institute of Library Science are:

The regular courses–
    In the near future there will be some changes. The bachelor's and master's degrees already existing in our distance education programs will introduce new contents and methods of teaching and learning, supplementing our existing curriculum leading to the degree of "Magister" and to the doctorate. This is a classical syllabus for students who can choose a combination of library science and many other disciplines offered by universities in Berlin and Potsdam. The combination can be done with one or two other disciplines. Students can choose library and information science as a main or subsidiary subject. More complex combinations such as medicine, legal studies, or architecture can be covered in the post-graduate curriculum. Nine semesters are required, divided into four semesters of basic studies and five semesters of ad-

vanced studies. Students have to take an examination before beginning advanced studies and have to choose either library or information science as the main focus. Training sessions in libraries and other institutions in the field of information and documentation are obligatory. Some 450 students are enrolled in these regular courses and some 50 students are attending the Ph.D. course.

The courses of the distance education program–
    Courses for students of the University of Koblenz-Landau:
    In cooperation with the University of Koblenz-Landau, a distance learning program was created to give students at Koblenz-Landau the possibility of combining regular classes at Koblenz-Landau with classes in library and information science offered by the Humboldt University in Berlin via teleconferencing, e-mail, and distance learning materials on the Internet. Some 40 students are studying in these courses, planning to receive the M.A. or Magister degree. In spite of positive evaluations, the University of Koblenz-Landau foresees difficulty in continuing this program, for financial reasons.

    Post-graduate Master in Library and Information Science (M.A. LIS) in a combined form of distance education and direct studies at the Humboldt University:
    In this curriculum graduates with doctoral or other academic degrees can study in a two-year distance education course for library and information science. Most of them are working in libraries, information services, or other related institutions, and are trying to get a more profound theoretical background and additional practical knowledge, enabling them to qualify for leading jobs in library management. Since 2003 the conventional German training for senior civil servants in libraries (the Referendarausbildung described above) has been integrated into this modernized form of education. All teaching material is made available via the Internet. Ten days of attendance (on Fridays or Saturdays), of eight hours each, are planned per semester. Up to sixty students can be accepted each year. There is a charge of 1,250 Euros per semester for this four-semester course.

Cataloging and classification as an important part of the courses of the Humboldt University–
    The forthcoming introduction of the curriculum for the bachelor's and master's degrees, in which the ECTS-System (European Credit Transfer System) for grading will be applied, gives a welcome opportunity to reconsider the content and the form of our courses. Distance

learning education, which emphasizes the responsibility and motivation of the student, will change the role of the teaching staff from the prevailing trend of lectures and seminars toward a kind of directing, advising, discussing, monitoring, and supervising the student's progress in his studies.

We also have to rethink a lot of divisions existing in the library and information scene in Germany. There are good reasons for some of them, but sometimes they are sheer obstacles to progress. The different library careers with their different areas of responsibility led to a damaging division of descriptive cataloging on one side, and indexing and classification on the other. We don't have a standard textbook like *Wynar's Introduction to Cataloging and Classification.* We have differences within the subject headings for persons, titles, and corporate bodies, and their equivalent descriptive headings, and we are fixing these imperfections retrospectively instead of having avoided them from the beginning. We use many different classifications in the various types of libraries in Germany, making life more complicated for users and librarians alike. Some classifications have a wide distribution, but none of them can claim a real predominance. To make things worse, the unified world of our descriptive catalogs is also in danger. There is a heated discussion going on right now among German librarians about the rules for descriptive cataloging. Should we change completely from RAK to AACR? Would it be better to continue to develop RAK making it more similar and coherent with AACR? A change of rules would mean another division because not all libraries would or could adopt the new rules.

All of these controversial subjects have to appear in our teaching and cannot be discussed without the necessary foundations. In Germany, descriptive cataloging is done mostly by librarians with the upper-level degree and not by the senior-level faculty librarians. It is taught at the universities of applied sciences in an intense manner with which we cannot compete, because our charge is to educate the future senior-level faculty librarians, not the Diplombibliothekare or upper-level certified librarians who include the future descriptive catalogers. At the Institute of Library and Information Science of the Humboldt University there are various professors and lecturers treating different forms and aspects of subject cataloging in the library and information area, but only one concerned–among other subjects–with descriptive cataloging, and that is for all types of materials, from early books to electronic resources. Nevertheless, we must create an awareness in the minds of our students of the importance of good catalogs, appropriate cataloging rules, and a well-founded theory of catalogs and cataloging. What is a good catalog? What are appropriate cataloging rules? Why do we need not only catalogs, but also a theory of cataloging and catalogs? It is not easy to find satisfying answers to these questions. Together with the teachers and students of our institute, we follow old and new paths to find solutions.

The Final Report of the IFLA Study Group on the Functional Requirements for Bibliographic Records, which introduced such concepts as the entities of interest to users of bibliographic records (work, expression, manifestation, item; person, corporate body; concept, object, event, place), the attributes of the entities, and the types of relationships that operate between entities, is a most interesting piece of theory on cataloging and catalogs and is worth studying with care and attention. The basic requirements for national bibliographic records published at the end of the report indicate that theoretical reflections can have practical consequences.

This final report is available on the Internet (URL: http://www. ifla.org/VII/s13/frbr/frbr.pdf). The Internet offers a multitude of possibilities for finding interesting material about cataloging and classification for our students. There are many important texts in different languages about these subjects, and also sound files, for example, the lecture on the revision and future developments of AACR given by Barbara B. Tillett at the annual conference of German librarians in Augsburg in 2002 (URL: http://www.bibliothek.uni-augsburg.de/kfe/mat/bt_staa_ sound.html). The RAK database offered on the Internet by Bernhard Eversberg is also a helpful tool which my students and I appreciate very much and use very often (URL: http://subito.biblio.etc.tu-bs.de/rak/ detail.php). There are OPACs, authority files, lists of subject headings, thesauri, and metadata accessible via the Internet. They offer visual aids to back up the theory of cataloging and classification. We can search, judge the results of the catalogers' efforts, and the form of their presentation on the screen of our computer. This is quite instructive. For the average user the catalog entry is a means to an end. He is looking for a document, and he is interested in the document itself, not in the catalog entry of the document. But our students learn quite a lot by reading and analyzing the catalog entries with attention and care. It hardly ever happens that two catalog entries for the same work are completely identical, even though they were made according to the same rules. Most differences, of course, are minor ones, and don't matter at all. But many of them do. If we look, for example, for a CD-ROM containing a collection of complete monographs on the history of the German book trade

(Geschichte des deutschen Buchwesens), we are really amazed at the differences we find in the OPACs of German and foreign libraries. The good catalog entries not only mention the monographs contained, but there is also a link combining the printed and the electronic versions of each work. The bad entries deliver only the title and some technical specifications of minor importance. What are we to think of a catalog entry that registers, pedantically, the diameter of the CD-ROM (12 cm), but says absolutely nothing about its content?

And the record on the screen leads to topics behind the catalog entry: the indexing methods used in different fields, the authority files, the data formats, the rules for descriptive cataloging, the formation of subject headings, and the use of classifications.

An actual search with subject headings alone does not always produce satisfactory results. If there is a combination of various terms combined in a chain to describe more complex subjects, the number of variations we find for a concrete work in different catalogs is considerable, even exceeding the number of variations we find in the assigned class number when the same classification scheme is used by different libraries analyzing the content of a given work.

What does a particular OPAC offer for performing a subject search? Only subject headings, only notations from a classification scheme, or a combination of both? If different classification schemes are used in one catalog, are there different fields, or is an indicator needed to designate from which classification the notation comes? What possibilities are there to have a look at the classification scheme used by the library? Can I only browse in the classification scheme or start a search immediately? Are there only subject headings indexed as single terms, or is it possible to look in an index, or do a string search for a combination of terms? How does the OPAC display the results of the search? Is there only one form of display, or various possible forms? What assistance does an OPAC give to a user in doing an effective search and processing the data from the catalog entries relevant to his topic?

Sometimes, if our analyses of catalog entries found in all sorts of OPACs turn hypercritical, we change the procedure. We do the cataloging first and afterwards compare our catalog entry with the entries found in other OPACs. It quickly becomes evident that we are not always the best catalogers. When we look at the past history of catalogs and cataloging in our classes, we can come up with practical ideas and conclusions that are still useful today. There is certainly a development and progress to be noted, for example, changing from traditional cataloging habits to fixed rules, or from the conventional card catalog to the OPAC, but this development is not linear. Not only do the technical possibilities for catalogs and cataloging vary in different times, but also the functions of the catalogs and the requirements of the users change. To cope with these changes while keeping the needs of our users in mind is a challenge we have to confront while we teach cataloging and classification, and it's worth the trouble.

6.3 Cataloging Education for Mid-Level Librarians

In the following passage the compiler would like to describe two very typical educational paths:

(a) Bavarian Library School, Munich

The education lasts two years–6 months theoretical education and 18 months practical work:

- theory, part I: introductory course: 2.5 months
- practicum at a public library: 8.5 months
- practicum at an academic library: 3.5 months,
- theory, part II: 2 months
- practicum at a large academic library: 5 months
- theory, part II: final course: 2 months

The theoretical education comprises 660 lectures; 112 lectures are devoted to cataloging. The cataloging courses mainly consist of teaching RAK (over 100 lectures), and another few lectures for catalog theory and fundamentals of RSWK.

(b) Thuringian Library School, Sondershausen
(http://www.bibs.kyf.th.schule.de)

The Thuringian Library School has changed their curriculum for Fachangestellte für Medien- und Informationsdienste (FAMI) according to the new curriculum guidelines of the Kultusministerkonferenz (Conference of the Ministers for Cultural and Educational Affairs).

This education lasts 3 years, consisting of theory for 2 days per week and practicum for 3 days per week. The theoretical education can also be divided up into several blocks (for example, four months per year theoretical education).

The future FAMIs are taught cataloging for five hours per week during their theoretical education. The five hours comprise: 1 hour for fundamentals of cataloging, 3 hours for RAK, and 1 hour for indexing in general.

7. CONTINUING EDUCATION

Continuing education is mainly provided by regional library networks and some universities of applied sciences.

In addition, staff associations (Verein Deutscher Bibliothekare, VDB–Association of German Senior-Level Librarians and Berufsverband Information Bibliothek, BIB–Occupational Union Information Library) offer continuing education, regionally and supraregionally; and last, but not least, the annual "Bibliothekartag–a German Library Congress" has a broad variety of cataloging education possibilities.

Here again the compiler will give some examples supplied by colleagues:

(a) Hochschulbibliothekszentrum des Landes Nordrhein-Westfalen Academic Library Center North Rhine-Westphalia, Cologne (http://www.hbz-nrw.de/)

The Academic Library Center North Rhine-Westphalia in Cologne, Germany (Hochschulbibliothekszentrum, HBZ), serves as a center for library services and development for academic libraries within the federal state of North Rhine Westphalia and beyond. HBZ aims its services and products at the needs of libraries and, in particular, takes on those tasks for which a single library on its own does not have the resources. One of these services is a portfolio of continuing education courses for librarians, a service the Center has offered since 1995. The Center's courses are organized into two semesters each year.

Utilization of the cataloging code (Regeln für die alphabetische Katalogisierung in wissenschaftlichen Bibliotheken–RAK-WB) is an important task in academic libraries. Continuing modifications and upgrades of the code, changes in the allocation of human resources in libraries, and changes of workflow demand a continuous education programme for catalogers. Hence, this is one of the course segments which is in high demand.

As a rule, a three-day course for beginners is offered yearly, complimented by two courses upgrading and enhancing the skills in two subsequent semesters. Cataloging codes for special collections such as non-book-materials and musical publications, or unique problems such as the cataloging of personal names and corporate bodies, are covered by special courses on demand. As an add-on, HBZ conducts information meetings on cataloging to cover the most recent developments and holds discussions on cataloging codes and formats.

All seminars and courses are designed to be practice-oriented; Web-based trainings or other forms of e-learning are not used. The trainers are selected colleagues with a sound reputation in the field who come from large academic libraries. They know the workflows in libraries and are familiar with cataloging modules in local library systems.

The HBZ continuing education programme offers about 8 seminars and courses limited to a maximum of 15 participants.

(b) Bibliotheksservice-Zentrum–BSZ
The Library Service Center Baden-Württemberg in Konstanz
(http://www.bsz-bw.de/)

The BSZ is a state institution providing service for libraries, museums, and archives. The BSZ operates the Cataloging Union in South Western Germany "Südwestdeutscher Bibliotheksverbund" (SWB), local systems, the Regional Union Catalog (ZKBW), and the "Digital Library." Part of the services offered for participating institutions are courses for staff in libraries. These courses take place on demand, and a minimum of five participants are needed. In 2002, 14 courses took place. All courses are open to any interested SWB cataloger. Some courses are designed especially for new staff or those that need to refresh their knowledge after parental leave, etc.

Courses offered are:

- Cataloging course "RAK-WB" (beginning and advanced levels)
- SWB database training (beginners, various advanced levels)
- Indexing courses for various classification systems and databases used in the SWB database (subject cataloging, RSWK, SWD, RVK, etc.)
- Cataloging courses for special collections (e.g., RAK-NBM)
- Cataloging in the ZDB, the German serials database
- Workshops on various topics, e.g., Cataloging with MARC.

Trainers for courses offered by BSZ are either experienced staff from large academic libraries or BSZ staff with special knowledge in the required field. Workshops may be held by outside trainers. Courses take place either in the BSZ training classroom or in one of the University libraries. Staff from larger academic libraries are encouraged to train and/or supervise cataloging staff of small libraries in their vicinity.

All training courses are practice-oriented. As trainers prefer direct contact with the participants, no forms of self-training are provided. Participants, however, often distribute training material in their libraries for the use of colleagues.

An annual colloquium offers information about new developments and discussions, e.g., in the field of formats and codes.

8. QUALIFICATION LEVELS AND TYPICAL JOBS IN GERMAN LIBRARIES

Professional Level	Special Training	Typical Jobs	Percentage of Total Library Staff at Academic Libraries	Percentage of Total Library Staff at Public Libraries
Research Librarians (always in university libraries, not in all libraries of the universities of applied sciences, only in very big public libraries)	University Degree in any subject area + 2-year additional study program in library and information science, mostly as part of a senior civil service training	Collection development, upper management, reference services, subject cataloging and indexing, database searches, public relations and exhibitions	15%	3%
Upper-Level Certified Librarians (Diplom-bibliothekare)	3 1/2-4 year-degree program in library and information science at a university of applied sciences	Descriptive cataloging, middle management, reference services, acquisitions, database searches, interlibrary loan, public relations. Only in public libraries: Collection development, subject cataloging and indexing, upper management	39%	34%
Specialist Staff for Media and Information Services (former professional designation: Library assistant or Assistant at libraries.)	3-year dual training program, i.e., in combination with education at a vocational school	Acquisitions, technical media processing, lower management	44%	63%
Semi-Skilled Staff	None	Media orders, process, technical advisory concerning media, circulation	2%	

9. CURRENT CATALOGING DISCUSSION IN GERMANY BY PETRA HAUKE

As the current discussion surrounding descriptive cataloging[4] may have considerable impact on future cataloging, we decided to add this part of the article in order to give the American and international audience an idea of what may happen in Germany. In addition, it is a very good example of a successfully-conducted group project.

RAK versus AACR–From Idea to Realization

From April to July 2002, the Institute for Library Science at Humboldt University Berlin offered a seminar entitled "Von der Idee zum Buch," meaning the realization of a library science class project with the goal of producing a published monograph.

The seminar was taught by Petra Hauke, M.A., a librarian who has also edited library science publications for many years.

Initially, 35 interested students met to determine the focus of the seminar. These students were studying library science along with some other subject, for example, political science, gender studies, musicology, economics, English and American language and literature, Romance languages and literatures, journalism, etc. They learned very quickly that managing a professional publication is a lot of work! But first of all: How to find the IDEA?

On December 6th, 2001, the Committee on Standardisation (Standardisierungsausschuss), responsible for development and decisions on standardisations in German libraries, decided to strive for a migration away from German cataloging rules (RAK) and formats (MAB) to international rules (AACR) and formats (MARC). The result was mostly protest from all kinds of libraries and library associations: special libraries, public libraries, library cooperatives, current bibliographies, etc.

> The Deutsche Bibliothek, Frankfurt/Main, commissioned a 2-year study of feasibility and costs, financed by the Deutsche Forschungsgemeinschaft (German Research Council). The study was to address only feasibility and costs, not the underlying reasons for such a migration or the interests of catalog users.

There were many discussions about that decision all over Germany, in Switzerland, and in Austria. There was also a website with a great deal of information, with statements and examples comparing the different rules and formats. During the German Library Congress, held in May 2002 in Augsburg, there was a public discussion showing that the official members of the Committee of Standardisation were not really willing to discuss or defend their decision.

Because of this extremely relevant discussion, it was not too difficult for the participants of the seminar "From Idea to Realization" to find an interesting, relevant IDEA for a publication on a library science subject! The group wanted to take part in this discussion–not as experts, because they were not experts, but as editors asking questions, looking for experts who could give answers, and publishing the results in a book that would be effective as publicity and available for all interested librarians, whether they had access to the Internet or not.

The seminar's intent was not to write a book but to manage a publication, i.e., to find out what it means to do "project management." So it was necessary to find authors with different points of views who would write articles for the projected publication. Among the authors found were participants of the professional mailing lists like INETBIB or RAKLIST, authors full of engagement, appreciating the idea, and writing their statements, essays, experiences, and visions.

Every student was responsible for one author, which meant finding, contacting, and convincing an author, correcting and formatting the manuscript, finding abbreviations and putting them into the "List of Abbreviations," getting permission to publish the result, and getting information about the author's biography for the "List of Authors." Some students collected an interesting bibliography on the rather long history of the discussion on "RAK versus AACR" from the 1970s on, including an index of authors.

It was also necessary to learn and to do effective public relations work, to write advertising copy, to write an article about the whole project, and to offer it to one of the main German library journals. At last, the article was published in "BuB."

The group also discussed how to publish the book: as a "Book on Demand," at their own expense, as an electronic publication, or in the classic way, by finding a professional publishing firm specializing in library science. They visited a famous publishing firm in Berlin (de Gruyter) to learn some of the principles of publishing, and then located a firm outside of Berlin that specialized in library science publications: Bock + Herchen, in Bad Honnef, who quickly agreed to work together with the group.

One of the main things was how to finance the project. The group was happy to learn that all of the authors were willing to write their articles for free; instead of royalties, the authors all accepted a contract promising just two free copies of the book.

In the end there were 17 very busy working students, 19 authors and articles, a preface by the president of the German Libraries Association, and the product:

RAK versus AACR : Projekte–Prognosen–Perspektiven ; Beiträge zur aktuellen Regelwerksdiskussion / hrsg. von Petra Hauke. Mit einem Geleitwort von Friedrich Geisselmann.–Bad Honnef : Bock + Herchen, 2002.–208 S. : graph. Darst. -ISBN 3-88347-225-6.

The project was a special way of teaching and learning cataloging issues. The students were extremely motivated to take part in the actual debate and to help the professional public to get more information about the issue, in order to make their own judgments and to decide whether or not to participate in the discussion. The students themselves learned not only how to manage the publishing of a book project, but also how to take a critical look at a discussion on cataloging rules and formats that serves as an important example of library science and practice.

For the "RAK versus AACR" website, see: http://www.ib.hu-berlin. de/buchidee (Project '02).

Part B: Catalog Training in Austria
by Heidi Zotter-Straka

BASIC CONDITIONS

In Austria, training in librarianship was not formalized until 1979; for many years, it took place within the framework of the civil service. This administrative internal training was regulated by directives (which were reformed in 1999 and 2000) within the frame of the official public service employment law. Training courses for three different levels within the civil service–comparable to Germany–have been provided at five so-called training libraries.

The uniform pattern changed when the Academic Study Course for Information Professions (Eisenstadt, 1997) and the University Programme for Library and Information Management (Krems, 1998) were established.

With the passing of the Universities Act 2002 (Universitätsgesetz 2002, or UG 2002) university reform, which had begun in the 1990s, came to a provisional conclusion. As of January 1, 2004, the Austrian universities (of which there are now twenty-one) are "legal entities in public law" and, thus, are no longer directly subject to the federal administration. Although they are independent organizational units, university libraries are not actually mentioned in the UG 2002 at all. Yet, strangely enough, the government's one intervention into the autonomy of the universities is a requirement for library education, in the form of the following clause:

> Provision shall be made for the library staff at all universities to receive a uniform training in librarianship, information science and documentation. (§ 101 Abs.3 UG 2002)

The fundamental changes in the legal situation led to the development of new training offers, i.e., an interuniversity course for the upper-level and senior-level library service, and a standardized education for trainees for the mid-level library service.

By doing so, Austria brought itself very close to the standards established in the Federal Republic of Germany and of Switzerland.

EDUCATION IN CATALOGING

(1) Interuniversity Studies Master of Science (Library and Information Studies) at the Universities of Vienna, Graz, Innsbruck, Salzburg and Klagenfurt and in Cooperation with the Austrian National Library

The studies consist of:

- Basic course (1st and 2nd semester: 15 units/week)
- Professional practical training (20 weeks, in part, subject-specific): between and after the first two semesters
- Advanced training course and Master's thesis (3rd and 4th semester).

Students can graduate after completing two terms along with their subject-specific library training; then they receive the degree known as Academic Library and Information Expert. Alternatively, they can continue to study towards a Master's degree.

The basic studies comprise:

- One course in the theory of cataloging, concepts of information retrieval, and metadata formats: 2 units/week.

During the first part of the practical training two courses are held: one course in descriptive cataloging (2 units/week) including theory of cataloging rules (RAK; AACR) and formats (MAB; MARC), authority files established by the Deutsche Bibliothek, Frankfurt and the State Library in Berlin in connection with practical training in online cataloging with the system of the Austrian Library Consortium (ALEPH).

The other course comprises subject cataloging (2 units/week) including theory and practice of the RSWK–subject cataloging code and the subject authority file in connection with practical training in online subject cataloging of the Austrian Library Consortium.

During the second part of the practical training students have to choose an additional course in either descriptive or subject cataloging (4 units/week).

(2) Academic Study Course for Information Professionals (Fachhochschulstudiengang Informationsberufe) Eisenstadt

The program consists of:

- Basic course (1st to 4th semester)
- Main course (5th and 6th semester): degree courses for Knowledge Management, Library and Information Studies; Web and Mobile Communication Solutions
- Professional practical training (7th semester) and Thesis (8th semester).

The degree is Magister/Magistra (FH).

During the main course, the following classes in cataloging are offered: one course in descriptive cataloging (3 units/week): RAK (theory and practice); one course in subject cataloging (3 units/week): RSWK (theory and practice).

(3) Professional MSc Library and Information Management in Krems

Structure:

- 1st to 4th semester part-time (14-15 modules/5 days each)–offering theoretical approaches to cataloging.

CONTINUING EDUCATION

Special continuing education in cataloging is offered by the Austrian National Library, e.g., for non-book materials, continuing integrated resources, cartographic material, and RAK-Music. Continuing education is also offered within the framework of the Austrian Library Consortium (56 libraries, among them, the Austrian National Library and 20 academic libraries) in special working groups for descriptive and subject cataloging, and in connection with format applications, new releases, etc.

NOTES

1. See *CCQ*, vol. 35 (1/2) "The development of descriptive cataloging in Germany / Hans Popst."

2. See *CCQ*, vol. 25 (1) "The Regensburg Classification / Bernd Lorenz."

3. In Germany we differentiate between Bibliothekar, Dokumentar, and Archivar as information professions. A Dokumentar is concerned with the cataloging and indexing of all types of documents, especially articles in periodicals, research and congress reports, patents, etc. Increasingly a Dokumentar also concerns himself with scientific, medical, legal, or numerical data.

4. See also *CCQ*, vol. 35 (1/2) "RAK or AACR2? The current discussion in Germany on cataloging codes / Charles R. Croissant."

Education and Training on the Nature and Description of Documents: Polish University Studies and Professional Librarianship Schools

Anna Sitarska

SUMMARY. This article describes the education system for librarians and information professionals in Poland and includes a discussion of change agents. The international bibliographic standardization has brought considerable change to this education. Another change factor has been Poland's openness to broader international connections as a result of the country's political and social transformation beginning in 1989. Technological development (computer system applications in libraries and references services) is a third key factor for change in Polish

Anna Sitarska is Professor, Insitute of Librarianship and Information Science, Faculty of Management and Social Communication, Jagiellonian University, Cracow, Poland (E-mail: sitarska@uwb.edu.pl).

Address correspondence to: Anna Sitarska, ul. Zamenhofa 15 m 2, 15-435 Bialystok, Poland.

A special, personal word of thanks is owed to Eva Mahrburg, Head of the Division of Bibliological Documentation at the National Library in Warsaw, for allowing the author access from home in Białystok to copies of component parts from foreign library journals.

[Haworth co-indexing entry note]: "Education and Training on the Nature and Description of Documents: Polish University Studies and Professional Librarianship Schools." Sitarska, Anna. Co-published simultaneously in *Cataloging & Classification Quarterly* (The Haworth Information Press, an imprint of The Haworth Press, Inc.) Vol. 41, No. 3/4, 2006, pp. 227-267; and: *Education for Library Cataloging: International Perspectives* (ed: Dajin D. Sun, and Ruth C. Carter) The Haworth Information Press, an imprint of The Haworth Press, Inc., 2006, pp. 227-267. Single or multiple copies of this article are available for a fee from The Haworth Document Delivery Service [1-800-HAWORTH, 9:00 a.m. - 5:00 p.m. (EST). E-mail address: docdelivery@haworthpress.com].

doi:10.1300/J104v41n03_04

library education. Additionally, the article includes a survey of recent events and the most important institutions. The quality of teaching is examined and suggestions made for future changes. *[Article copies available for a fee from The Haworth Document Delivery Service: 1-800-HAWORTH. E-mail address: <docdelivery@haworthpress.com> Website: <http://www. HaworthPress.com> © 2006 by The Haworth Press, Inc. All rights reserved.]*

KEYWORDS. Poland, library education, information professionals, bibliographic description, cataloging, cataloging education

> *Żeby umieć księgę opisać, potrzeba pewnej nauki . . .*
> *[To describe a book, one needs some knowledge . . .]*
>
> –Joachim Lelewel
> *Przemowa do moich ksiąg bibliograficznych[1]*

INTRODUCTION

The current system of teaching and training librarians and information professionals in Poland has undergone a number of transformations in the last decade. It is important to know that this system stems from an almost 200-year-long tradition in which bibliology, as well as methods and rules of description of documents included therein, take a very special place. This is so because the first matter of library education were university lectures on bibliography and naturally linked teaching on cataloging and classification since the first half of the 19th century.[2]

The contribution of two people was especially important for the Polish tradition of teaching about the description of books for libraries and bibliographies–Joachim Lelewel and Karol Estreicher. The first, an outstanding historian of the 19th century, the creator of taxonomy of historical sources, was also a librarian and the author of works in which the questions of catalog and bibliographic descriptions have a prominent place. His work–*Bibliograficznych ksiąg dwoje* [*Two Bibliographic Tomes*], and especially two component parts there included, on the subject of cataloging and classification, "Przedmowa do mojich Ksiąg bibliograficznych" ["Oration to my Bibliographic Tomes"] and "Bibliotekarstwo czyli Książnictwo" ["Book Lore"] are still in some way present, as is further evidenced by the latest publications.[3]

The latter of the two–Karol Estreicher–the progenitor of the family of creators of the retrospective Polish national bibliography–became known in the history of librarian and bibliographer education as the chair of the first Polish department of bibliography in Szkoła Główna Warszawska (Warsaw Main School–the earlier Warsaw University), as well as the author of lectures there conducted in 1865-1868.

A wide variety of publications exists concerning the basis for the current librarian education, which started in the 19th century and was really developed only after World War II; however, all of them are in Polish. Unfortunately, there are also no works concerning teaching about the description of documents. The ideas of cataloging and classification teachers sometimes appear in the margins of their works concerning the subject matter of teaching. Some of these ideas will be discussed later in this article.

THE SYSTEM OF EDUCATING LIBRARIANS AND INFORMATION SPECIALISTS IN POLAND

Contrary to publications on teaching document description, there are many general works concerning the system of educating librarians and information professionals. Current information–usually up to date–on the didactic offerings of Polish universities and colleges can be found in the Electronic Information Bulletin for Librarians (EBIB).[4] Furthermore, almost all library schools have their own websites. The ones which are the most interesting from the point of view of teaching document description will be presented later. The complete list of Polish institutions educating librarians, as found in EBIB, is presented by level of education and place names in Table 1 in the Appendix.

The data in Table 1 show that, for a medium-sized country, Polish librarian education is quite well developed. Librarians are being trained in 17 cities, in 18 schools, 10 of which are universities. But if one considers the quality of this education, then the evaluation of the current state of affairs is not so positive. That is why, when the Conference of Rectors of Polish Universities[5] assessed the quality of librarianship studies in 2002, only 5 schools were granted a five-year-long accreditation (the universities in Cracow, Warsaw, Wrocław, Toruń and Katowice). The Maria Curie-Skłodowska University in Lublin was granted only two-year accreditation.

Before the accreditation, there was a great debate in scientific circles on the need and direction of change in the structure of the education system, especially concerning the curriculum.[6] Regrettably, the issues of document description did not get in these works, as in the previous ones, the attention they deserve. Even so, from the curricula which emerged from this discussion (which will be further described), it is clear that the authors of those publications, and at the same time, the authors of curriculum changes, are aware of both the multi-functional quality of electronic document descriptions and the necessary changes in teaching methods and to the bibliographic control content taught in cataloging classes. In their general meaning, the quoted publications agree with the arguments of Ingrid Hsieh-Yee[7] supporting the introduction of changes in teaching document description to correspond to changes in the information environment, place of information in the society, and information technologies. For example, two statements by Jadwiga Woźniak (2001) and Anna Sitarska (1994) clearly supported these arguments.[8]

Apart from the aforementioned academic works, there are some noteworthy opinions of practitioners on the necessity of introducing changes in librarian education. In 2003, a forum was opened in the EBIB dedicated to the subject of education.[9] We shall analyze two of the opinions in the discussion of this forum. Both are connected to the subject of document description and, at the same time, are in a way a confrontation of two points of view–that of an academic teacher, Professor Mirosław Górny, Head of the Information Systems Institute in the Faculty of Neophilology, University in Poznań, and that of a practitioner librarian and head of the Information and Subject Experts Department at the University Library in Toruń.

Professor M. Górny deals in his statement with two common assumptions concerning education. First of all, he opposes the concept that "while learning to 'do the job,' it is not worth wondering about the deeper sense of particular library activities–acquisition, cataloging, indexing, making abstracts and so forth." He writes that: "It is not only worth doing, it is necessary. *A student should get used to wondering all the time about what she/he is doing* [italics A. Sit.]. She/he is not a part of the processing line. If she/he is cataloging, she/he should know why she/he is doing it in this particular way and not another. She/he must think about the user and his behavior, about the cohesion of databases, costs, and so on. Otherwise she/he will just keep on thoughtlessly saying 'because that's how it's always been done.'" Secondly, M. Górny does not agree with the quite common idea that "it is not worth teaching all students to be designers and managers." He states that: "Even if they never do this, it is better if they learn to think of their library as designers and managers would. This avoids fossilization. But what is most important is that it is a way to make libraries work better. Because a librarian who has learned to look at a library, a library network, or a central catalog in a way which allows him *to understand the aim of any activity, see the relations between particular elements, and evaluate the effects of his actions will always use a more or less adequate methodology of analyzing the system in which he works* [italics A. Sit.]. It is generally good to make a librarian see the library system as a whole."[10]

Bożena Bednarek-Michalska, when answering the general question of M. Górny, "What do modern libraries need?" [as far as education is concerned], answered: "digitalisation specialists (protecting and scanning documents, making new and storing electronic documents collections, etc.), librarians specializing in various fields of knowledge (managing special collections and information), instructors (planning regular training and professional development of the staff), electronic collections building specialists (making new collections with the use of new technologies)."[11]

It can be seen from these opinions–clearly enough, I suppose–that although the authors of the quoted opinions addressed the questions of educating library staff in general, they mentioned the aspects which were, for the most part, connected with knowledge and skills necessary to describe documents, use those descriptions in various information services, and design changes prompted by the evolution of the needs of users and the transformation of the form of documents and meta-information concerning those documents.

To sum up this discussion, one should underline that the disputants were not aware that, apart from the aforementioned weaknesses of the education system, there are three other facts about its condition: ". . . lack of connection between university didactics and research process, . . . too little effort put into preparing students for team work, . . . too little stress put on knowledge and skills necessary for managing smaller institutions."[12] During the open discussion this last fact was mentioned by only one librarian.[13] Earlier, a distinguished librarian and a professor at the Jagiellonian University, Jacek Wojciechowski, expressed the opinion that he "can see no way for librarians from smaller libraries to specialize, apart from specializing in giving information. . . ."[14]

Important sources of information about the librarian education system are works relating to the past as well as the present state, and the perspectives of prominent libraries, universities, and professional "schools." Anniversary editions are one type of such publications. Some of those publications are listed in the annotation, as they include many important, if rather general, comments on the subject of training librarians in cataloging and classification in the most important Polish educational institutions.[15]

CEBID–the Center for Library, Information and Documentation Education, which is "a nationwide center for professional education concerning books, libraries and related professions, providing various forms of education and professional development, as well as curriculum, editorial and media activity" plays a special role in educating librarians in Poland. "It operates in Warsaw and 17 regional branches set up at Regional Libraries, situated in cities, which are at the same time important cultural and scientific centers"[16] (Figure 1). Since the middle of the '90s, CEBID organizes only post-secondary school extramural colleges which have a 4-semester course (640 hours altogether), and generally organized courses for librarians which will be discussed further in the part of this article devoted to teaching document description.

The highly valued role of CEBID in librarian education originates not only from its 50-year-long traditions (under various names),[17] but also from the fact that it graduates 800 librarians every year from its 17 branches in all parts of the country. The vital features of this education are: (1) the best qualified librarians are the teachers of these courses; (2) the close connection of didactics with the actual workplace of librarians (achieved thanks to the placement of CEBID branches in regional libraries); and (3) the possibility (since 1998) of progressing into further college and university education (gaining the BA and MA title equivalents).

The CEBID curriculum was modified twice in the last decade of the 20th century–in 1993 and 1998–mostly to live up to European standards of education for librarians and related professionals (e.g., archivists).[18] The subject of document description in the extramural CEBID curriculum and the special cataloging and classification courses will be discussed later in this article.

Finally, it is worth noting that in some private colleges new courses have appeared which originate in a way from librarianship and are connected with teaching document description.[19]

FIGURE 1. Librarian Education in Poland

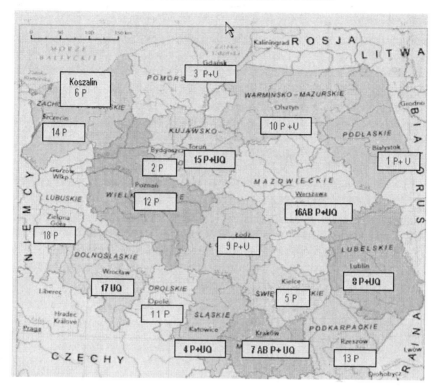

To sum up: we now have in Poland a well-developed librarian education system structure. The profession can be learned on a few levels–from the basics on the post-secondary school level, through college and university studies giving BA and MA degrees, up to obtaining the title of Doctor of Bibliology, equivalent to a PhD (Table 1). In the system, there are differences not only in the quality of education, which seems to be obvious, but also in the contents of the curriculum which is, in many ways, not adjusted to the trends in international librarianship. Interestingly, librarians in the 'worse' schools seem to be better prepared to meet the current needs of small and usually old-fashioned school and public libraries. This will be further discussed in the sections about document description.

THE PLACE OF DOCUMENT DESCRIPTION TOPICS
IN CURRICULA

The appearance of the International Standard Bibliographic Description (ISBD) was a breakthrough in teaching document description in Poland. It coincided with the reform of university librarianship studies, which was being prepared since the '70s (It was a period of relative openness between communist Poland and the West, allowing easier contacts with foreign libraries and international organizations, as well as access to foreign publications.) In the reformed curriculum of university librarianship and information science studies (only 5-year MA courses at that time), two distinct courses were introduced–'humanistic' and 'socio-mathematical' (usually just called the 'mathematical program').

The first aimed at education based on the bibliological paradigm, which took the book and social communication processes connected with it (not only the library!) as the center of its attention. The second was supposed to connect librarianship with information science and included the subjects of information systems and services and using new technologies for data processing in libraries. The mathematical curriculum did not include such traditional subjects as 'cataloging' and 'classification.'[20] Subjects under those names began disappearing 30 years ago–not always rightly, as it seems–especially from the curriculum of colleges. They were usually replaced with "formal document description" and "document content description." This still continues in the curriculum of some universities and colleges (e.g., University in Wrocław–see Table 2 in the Appendix).

These changes did not, however, apply solely to the names of those subjects, but also to the division of curriculum content into so-called librarian and bibliographic subjects, which were up to now concerned with structurally and functionally different document descriptions. The main stimulants for this change were the international rules of bibliographic description, which have very slowly, only in the middle of the '80s, started filtering into Polish library practice. Today it can be definitely stated that, in the professional training process, especially at universities, document description training is based on the latest international standards. It can be seen from the studies' curriculum, the selected subjects of which, chosen from the curricula of the three largest Polish universities, are listed in Table 2. However, before its content can be discussed in detail, the problems between the educational process and the situation in libraries should be mentioned. Librarianship, which, just as many other domains of life in Poland, is still undergoing the process of transformation, creates a very non-uniform field of professional needs, which makes the task of librarian-training institutions considerably complex and difficult.

Two factors are responsible for the strong, not to say, dramatic, differences in the state of Polish libraries, especially away from the main centers of scientific and cultural life:

1. the features of the Polish library management system, including the rules of dividing and restricting resources and the development differences in the provinces (emphatically called Poland B), especially the anachronistic mentality and lack of professionalism of librarians and local authorities in charge of the most numerous libraries in Poland;[21]
2. the negative influence of these factors on the resource structure and the technological level of libraries.

At the same time, it should be stressed that, in the '90s, there was in Polish librarianship, in scientific libraries, and especially in academic librarianship and the largest public libraries, what might be called a civilization leap in technology and organization. This makes a very important, as it would seem, context for discussing the problems of education, including the questions of cataloging and classification. Without the knowledge of this context and of the rate of change, it is hard to understand the amount of effort and courage that was needed to overcome, in but a few years, at least by most academic libraries, an almost 25-year gap separating them from the European standards of Western libraries, which started to build their computer systems in the '60s. It required and still requires making many difficult decisions concerning, among other things, the practice and teaching of cataloging rules.

Among up-to-date works concerning the complicated situation of Polish cataloging practice, we find the especially worthy opinion of Jerzy Franke–an academic teacher,[22] who commented also on the influence of this situation on the difficulties in teaching document description. In his opinion, the first decade of the 21st century is, for Polish libraries, "*a turning point of fundamental change in the practice of formal document description.*"[23] Time has come to abandon the "Grycz rules" (the rules of cataloging named after their creator Józef Grycz,[24] sometimes colloquially called simply "Grycz"). These rules have a long and well-rooted tradition of being used in all types of Polish libraries.

That is why they still have an important place in the teaching of cataloging rules.

In the last decade, new regulations connected, first of all, with adaptation to international standards (ISBD directives and Polish standards (in short form, PN) applying to various types of main entries, authority file records, and bibliographic data formats, etc.) are constantly appearing, and the applicability of the 'old Grycz' is rapidly diminishing or has disappeared completely. But this is true only in the case of academic libraries and most large public libraries, which stopped using traditional (card) catalogs when they introduced integrated computer systems (usually after 1994). It is, however, worth repeating the question of Jerzy Franke: "Are the Grycz rules so irrevocably a thing of the past?"[25] Currently, it is one of the very important dilemmas in Polish cataloging didactics on all levels of librarian education. Graduates work mostly in medium and small public and school libraries where card catalogs remain the standard form of a library catalog, even if the process of computer-aided cataloging has already begun.[26]

The main problems of the Polish standardization process, adapting the rules of document description to international standards, were mostly overcome by 2001. It would therefore seem that librarian schools would cease teaching the old "Grycz" cataloging rules. But one should not forget what the reality is in the significant group of medium and small libraries, which now and–as would seem apparent from their financial conditions–in the nearest future, will not be able to have modern cataloging systems and will, therefore, not abandon old cataloging rules. Curricula should therefore include at least those parts of the old instructions which apply to kinds and forms of main entries and making cross-references, while explaining the differences in relation to the new standards, and the reasons for inability to use them to the fullest in card catalogs.

This is also connected with the coexistence in many libraries of the USMARC/MARC 21 formats (in just a few very large libraries which have integrated library systems) and MARC BN (the old version of the format of the National Library in Warsaw, connected with the MAK program package with no authority files module).[27]

What is more, the MARC BN format is not only the most common format in small and medium Polish libraries, which use the MAK program based on it, but is also used in the current National Bibliography on CD-ROM and on-line. Therefore, many large general and special libraries which transfer data into their own OPACs from the Polish current national bibliography (also from the printed weekly part for books registration named 'Przewodnik Bibliograficzny') convert the data to MARC 21.

In this analysis of the features of library practice, not only from the point of document description, but catalog construction as well, some weaknesses, which are a sort of young-age ailment of the use of computer technology in Polish libraries, cannot be omitted. In practice, the symptoms of this weakness are the imperfections of OPAC catalogs with low-quality and inconsistent data. In teaching cataloging, there seems to be a lack of not only good tools and didactic experience, but also of a deep enough understanding and explanation of the meaning and influence of format structures (e.g., content designators), connections between them and the form of data on the catalog, and the bibliography-making process. This is discussed, unfortunately, only from the library practice not the teaching point of view by Andrzej Padziński and Jerzy Franke.[28] The first author discusses the problem of insufficient use of authority files, and the importance of Z39.50 in searching for and presenting various types of data. He goes on to explain many of the terminological intricacies in the Polish translations of cataloging module topics in integrated library systems documentation and its use. Similarly to library practice in teaching, these new elements of cataloging are not yet fully merged in teachers' and students' awareness. Andrzej Padziński makes a very good point of how the slow creation of new cataloging standards in Poland and the relatively high pace of introducing integrated systems in not many, but the most important, Polish libraries caused a misconception to appear that creating an OPAC consists only of making bibliographic descriptions. Not enough attention is given to the selecting and verifying of entries and the structure of the whole catalog data file. One could assume that teaching cataloging suffers from the same weaknesses, although infrequent and very critical opinions of academic teachers, concerning the new type of information services appearing in new library systems, could be the heralds of a positive turn in teaching.[29] This opinion is supported by the latter of the two authors–Jerzy Franke, in his adamant evaluation of the product of the National Library in Warsaw.[30]

In the context of connections between the services of the National Library in Warsaw and the problems of teaching document description, it is time to consider the questions of document content description and classification. In this area, it seems, there are fewer dramatic dilemmas to be solved by teachers than in the case of formal description teaching. Apart from the aforementioned problems, there are also serious problems caused by limited (due to lack of funding) time for lectures and, most of all, classes, which makes teaching especially difficult because it's necessary to include all of the new data formats and cataloging rules, but also to teach the 'old' rules.

The National Library is also connected with the practice of classification and teaching primarily due to the fact that current Polish national bibliography services, in both printed and electronic form, are naturally, for many libraries, the main source of descriptions of Polish books for their own catalogs. What is more, the subject headings language developed by the National Library (further referred to as JHP BN (from the Polish name *Język Haseł Przedmiotowych Biblioteki Narodowej*, i.e., *Subject Headings Language by the National Library in Warsaw*) is, for public and school libraries and also for some research libraries, the main tool used in creating their own content descriptions of documents, and in catalogs and bibliographic works.

In the early '90s, with the appearance of the VTLS system in the largest Polish university libraries, another language (competitive to JHP BN) was developed–a new generation content description language called KABA (Katalogi Automatyczne Bibliotek Akademickich–Automatic Catalogs of Academic Libraries), based on the methodology of authority files. The harmonious coexistence of both languages in library practice in a way created a methodologically beneficial situation for teaching content description.

During practice time in the libraries, students gained a wider perspective for observation and practice, pointing to the distinct differences between the two generations of content description languages. The starting point and, at the same time, a kind of competition and controversy connected with the need for different tools and mechanisms for libraries to acquire the descriptions in these two languages was formed by the creation in the '90s of the union catalog–NUKat (Narodowy Uniwersalny Katalog Centralny).[31]

The process of creating the KABA language was initiated by the Warsaw University Library and later continued as a common program of the VTLS Libraries' Consortium–Virtua Virtua (see http://konsorcjum. bg.univ.gda.pl/). The many-year-long process of creating the KABA language, teaching activities connected with it, and scientific seminars–with the help of academic teachers from many schools, international cooperation, as well as published coursebooks and methodological elaborations–created an especially beneficial atmosphere in Poland for all forms of librarian education on document content description. Among the publications The FO-KA series (FOrmaty-KArtoteki–Formats and Authority Files), which had 14 issues in recent years (see http://ebib.oss. wroc.pl/sbp/serfoka.htm), among which was the first part of the KABA coursebook *Subject cataloging in the KABA language*,[32] is especially useful in didactics.

Taking into account this situation of library practice, as well as other factors influencing the didactic process, it can be assumed that the most important factors influencing both the quality and range of teaching the rules for content description of documents in Polish schools are:

- firstly–a deep and rich didactic and methodological reflection, often expressed in conferences and published works;
- secondly–better theoretical support of specialist subjects connected with the document content description by general subjects in study curricula (lectures and classes in logics and selected aspects of linguistics);
- thirdly–the fundamental value of intensive research on information-retrieval languages conducted for years in connection with didactics and supporting the practice of document classification.

The research has been conducted in recent years mostly, though not only, thanks to the so-called 'Warsaw School' of information-retrieval languages and system theory.[33] Scientists-academic teachers gathered in this 'school' concentrate on research on the border between linguistics, semiotics, and library and information science.[34] In this research direction, many doctoral thesis were written by teachers of classification and content description. Over the last ten years, only two doctoral theses connected in some way with formal document description were identified.[35]

A distinctive area for didactic reflections connected with document content description can be seen in teaching subject description, which is connected in Polish librarianship both with the long tradition which appeared thanks to Adam Łysakowski–the author of the subject cataloguing theory and the first Polish-content cataloging coursebook.

To finish the analysis of general problems which form the library practice context for teaching document description, it is worth noting two important changes that have undoubtedly influenced the final forming of the knowledge and skills of graduates–the problems of vocational practice required on all levels of education, and international contacts which have, in the last decade, become an inalienable element of the university and professional life of librarians.

Vocational practice is strongly connected with teaching document description and usually, regardless of the particular curriculum of a 5-year master's studies, two out of three required practice periods (21 days each) concern mostly gaining document description and meta-information files management skills. The first period takes place after the first year of studies and the students' main activity is acquiring or forming formal descriptions (formerly descriptions for the alphabetic catalog, now bibliographic descriptions, serving various purposes in the library system). These tasks are connected with getting to know the organizational and task structure of the library. It is supposed to promote understanding of the multi-functionality of the description and practical knowledge on the flow of meta-information connected with the physical form of collected documents on various stages of resource forming and user service.

The second period of professional practice, after the 2nd year of study, concerns content description and in recent years–in accordance with the changes in the structure of library activities–is connected with information service performed by reference librarians–experts in particular fields of knowledge, whose duties combine document classification with reference services.

The third period (after the 3rd or 4th year) serves specialization–the student is sent to a chosen type of library (e.g., school or pedagogical library) or to a chosen department (e.g., Special Collections), depending on the chosen specialization or the subject of the master's thesis. Unfortunately in recent years, when constantly seeking to make savings and reduce costs, we have faced a reduction in the vocational practice span. It is a severe limitation and various attempts are made to compensate for the loss. One way is to organize practice abroad, which in Poland still requires a lot of organizational effort from the teachers, cooperation with Polish centers abroad, or acquiring special grants (e.g., in the TEMPUS or ERASMUS programs). The latter usually have a broader program and do not concentrate on the questions of document description. Cooperation with Polish centers abroad is usually a very good occasion for the students to compare Polish description rules with foreign implementations of international regulations for libraries. For a relatively small part in paying the students' cost of stay, centers gain qualified employees who can perform tasks for which there is no time in the everyday work schedule.

A good example of how fine results can be achieved even when teaching the most difficult problems of cataloging (e.g., old prints or rare book description) can be found in the activities of the Students' Research Club described by Mikołaj Osmański in an anniversary publication of the Warsaw University. For many years, the Students' Research Club has organized Summer Librarianship Schools. During these sessions, students have put in order and cataloged a large part of the antique collections of the Cieszyn Public Library and the Library of the Order of St. Paul in Kraków. It can be definitely stated that those practical "lessons" in cataloging were exciting for the students. At the same time a bond was created between the Warsaw University Institute and libraries in Poland, which still need support, especially in managing special collections.

In the opinions on three sides of the process—students, lecturers, and librarians—these practical lessons in cataloging were not only useful for the libraries, which had their antique collections 'brought back to life,' but were also fascinating for the students. This was due to the fact that they were not based only on getting to know cataloging rules. The whole context of these activities, which showed cataloging as one of the problems of library resources and information sources management, was equally important. Students would start their work by putting neglected books in order and raising them from the 'void devoid of readers.' Then they would catalog the books, get to know them better in seminars devoted to the problems of cultural heritage protection, and finally, would find the antique books that they got to know while cataloging on the Internet, sometimes in digitalized versions of the most precious collections, sometimes in special OPACs for such collections.[36]

It should be stressed that the aforementioned example of cooperation between student research clubs and the library is not a common way of teaching cataloging in Poland. It is, however, not a completely singular case. Similar practical classes took place at the Wrocław and Jagiellonian Universities' student research clubs. The example of cooperation between Warsaw and Cieszyn was evoked under the influence of the thought of Robert Holley, who pointed out in his article the reasons why learning cataloging skills can be interesting, or even fascinating for students—

> ... if it stresses cataloging as one specific answer to the problems of managing information and places cataloging within a larger context that also includes indexing and Internet search engines.

> Students deserve cataloging courses that combine theory and prac-
> tice, avoid memorization, and require them to show a mastery of
> core principles rather than picky details.[37]

International cooperation with librarianship schools and libraries,
which under normal circumstances is a standard element of academic
education, is still often treated as something exceptional in Poland.[38]
Therefore, in educating librarians, only the most renowned universities
now have well-developed international contacts, thanks to which common research programs, conferences, exchanges, etc., are organized.[39]
In the matter of cooperation between scientific libraries, there are numerous questions connected with cataloging (e.g., problems of building
common multilingual subject heading authority files). However, they
mostly concentrate on the functioning of various integrated library systems. So far during these international contacts, there has been little interest in the problems of document description, which have not yet been
granted proper bibliographic control in Poland. It seems, therefore, that
it would be advisable to hasten the practice by proper training of future
librarians.

TEACHING DOCUMENT DESCRIPTION–
CATALOGING AND CLASSIFICATION
IN SELECTED POLISH UNIVERSITY CURRICULA

The list of teaching subjects concerning document description presented in Table 2 seems to require some commentary, both of the criteria of choice and a closer characteristic of connections between these
subjects and the entirety of the curriculum. The standards of university
curricula which are subject to accreditation are set out by two institutions–the Ministry of Education and Sports (further referred to as
MENiS), which forms the so-called program minimum of hour and subject content limit, and the University Accreditation Committee (further
referred to as UKA).

This duality has its sources in the sluggishness of the ministerial authorities in preparing accreditation conditions which would ensure a
European standard of teaching at Polish universities. Independent of
govermental authorities, the rectors of universities who form the Conference of Rectors of Polish Universities created the UKA, as they
could no longer wait for the states' decisions in this respect. The Committee's expert groups worked out the procedures and standards of ac-

creditation for university disciplines of study, and then in 2000-2003, accredited a number of courses including information and library science.

The proportions of time devoted to teaching document description can therefore be formed on the basis of the overall number of class hours, as set out by either the MENiS' 'minimum' or by the UKA standards (Table 3 in the Appendix). Although they are unfortunately not fully comparable, they can be used to form an idea of the proportions between document description and other parts of the curricula, especially the obligatory professional subjects.[40]

Figures and uncountable data in curricula descriptions are compared with the standards in Table 3. Curricula data come from the three highest rated universities in Poland, out of the ten with 'Information and Library Science' studies. Other universities more or less follow the curricula of these three universities, while at the same time making their own, original contributions in their curricula, often marked with a valuable regional mark or a specialization found nowhere else in academic Poland. The curriculum of the Mikołaj Kopernik University in Toruń (UMK) can be an example here.[41] It includes a very interesting profile in the history of books for the region of Pomerania, special knowledge about the printing press (in cooperation with the Faculty of Journalism at Oslo University College), and a bibliotherapy for pathological families and for dependent persons.

Coming back to the data in Table 3, which was first of all supposed to draw attention to the prolific place of document description subjects in Polish librarian education curricula: the middle part of the table is our main concern, where the required hours for subjects of 'document description' are given. In relation to the overall number of class hours of the BA studies curriculum, in which these subjects are concentrated in the Warsaw (UW) and Jagiellonian (UJ) Universities, these subjects take up, respectively, 9.3% in UW and 9.9% in UJ; in relation to the number of hours of professional subjects, in UW–17% and in UJ–15%. In Wrocław University, where there is still only a 5-year MA study, subjects of 'document description' take up almost 8.5% of the total hours limit and 10.5% of classes dedicated to professional subjects. It would be very interesting to compare these numbers with similar data from universities in other countries, especially the UK and USA. Unfortunately the author was unable to acquire such information.

The comparisons with standards seem to have less value for perfecting didactics. It is a bit of a surprise that the proportions in relation to both standards were so alike. Therefore, it must once more be stressed that there is a visible difference between those standards, so that it is not 'drowned' by numbers. The ministry standard applies only to 5-year MA studies, and therefore, can be compared only to the data from the University of Wrocław. In the other two universities where the studies are divided into the BA and MA level, these numbers have less value, though they do not seem to be completely useless. It is worth noting that *the MENiS minimum for professional subjects in the frame for 5-year MA studies is equal the UKA standards* (i.e., European Union standards) *for 3-year BA studies* (825 h).

Apart from the data from Table 3 mentioned earlier, it is also worth noting the set of 'document description' subjects in 3 groups. Group 1–'main subjects'–comprises compulsory subjects and is full. It reflects the accepted division of descriptive skills in curricula. The detailed description of every subject can be found on the respective website of each university.[42] In Illustrations 1a-d some descriptions from the Warsaw University curriculum are shown.

In the second group, 'Other obligatory subjects' in Table 3, there are courses connected with document description and procedures for various document functions in library systems. The third group, 'Other extracurricular subjects,' also contains a number of courses connected with document description but designed as extracurricular or optional subjects, or in the master's paths for students to choose along with diploma seminars.

To sum up comments on Table 3, it is worth noting the data in the upper part of the table, where the relationship between standard requirements and general limits in the actual curricula are shown. It seems that most explicit are the proportions between general requirements for the whole in the two standards, and the hour limits in the curricula of the three universities which have achieved an international standard of education, thanks to their own efforts.

A very important factor which is giving quite satisfactory results in librarian education in Poland is the aforementioned international cooperation of institutes. The three university curricula used as models in Table 3 can take this role, thanks to the fact that they were developed and verified in the context of international cooperation.

Finally, one should mention two major changes which happened in Poland in recent years–first, in the context of access to coursebooks; second, in the educational activity of libraries and some of the committees of the Polish Librarian Association. Each of these subjects, even restricted to the problems of cataloging and classification, deserves closer attention.

ILLUSTRATIONS 1a-b. Two First Professional Subjects on 'Document Matter' in the BA Curriculum at Warsaw University

a)

1105 DOCUMENTS AND DOCUMENT COLLECTIONS	
Lecturers:	Anna Radziejowska-Hilchen, MA Mikołaj Ochmański, MA
Lectures: Classes: Seminars: Labs:	15 h.(1/week) 15 h.(1/week) - -
Basic of evaluation:	Semestral assignment + exam

DESCRIPTION:

Basic terms and definitions connected with the typology and morphology of documents, and document collections stored in libraries and other institutions (archives, information centres, museums) are introduced. The rules of building up and developing of contemporary collections, their specialisation, methods of acquiring, registering, storing and selected problems of preservation are discussed. During trips to chosen institutions the students are acquainted with the variety of collections and the procedures of collecting, registering, keeping and accessing in relation to the type of the host institution.

b)

1108 INFORMATION PROCESSING (I): FORMAL ASPECTS	
Lecturers:	Dr. Jerzy Franke Andrzej Bator, MA Mikołaj Ochmański, MA
Lectures: Classes: Seminars: Labs:	15 h.(1/week) 45 h.(3/week) - -
Basic of evaluation:	Semestral assignment + exam

DESCRIPTION:

This is an introductory course to the formal description of documents according to the ISBD and its Polish version: PN-N-01152. The main goal of this course is to acquaint the students with the principles of the bibliographic description of books, periodicals, sound recordings, cartographic materials, electronic documents and films in accord with the Polish norm and cataloguing instructions. The course encompasses problems concerning description headings (rules governing choice and form), formats (MARC and variants, including USMARC), and usage of authority records. Laboratory classes are devoted to the problems of describing collections in the automated systems.

Level: elementary; no prior requirements are necessary to attend this subject.

Source: http://www.lis.uw.edu.pl/uk/indexe.htm

ILLUSTRATIONS 1c-d. The First and Last Professional Subjects on 'Content of the Document's Matter' in the BA Curriculum at Warsaw University

c)

1109 INFORMATION PROCESSING (II): CONTENTS ANALYSIS	
Lecturers:	Prof. Dr. Barbara Sosińska-Kalata Andrzej Bator, MA
Lectures:	-
Classes:	-
Seminars:	15 h.(1/week)
Labs:	-
Basic of evaluation:	Semestral assignment

DESCRIPTION:

The main themes of the course encompass the principles of analysing the contents and creating of descriptions of contents of texts. The types of content elements reflected in the descriptions, types of characteristics (including content annotation and documentary analyses), models of information structure of scientific texts, and methods of logical and informative analysing of micro- and macrodocuments are discussed. Attention is focused on the two approaches to contents analysis: 1) oriented at the identification of the document□s subject and its distinctive features, 2) oriented at the identification of the contents elements relevant to the specific information needs of a group of users.

Level: elementary; no prior requirements are necessary to attend this subject.

d)

1112 INFORMATION PROCESSING (V): AUTHORITY FILES	
Lecturers:	Dr. Jadwiga Woźniak
Lectures:	-
Classes:	-
Seminars:	15 h.(1/week)
Labs:	-
Basic of evaluation:	test

DESCRIPTION:

The aim of the course is to provide students with the knowledge of:
1) the place, the functions and the role of authority files in automated storing and retrieval systems;
2) currently created Polish authority files of bibliographic description headings.
The main issues discussed during the course are: authority files; international recommendations; USMARC format of the authority files records; authority files created by the VTLS libraries: authority files of name headings, corporate headings, unified titles and serial titles, authority files of the KABA subject headings language; authority files in the process of the central catalogues creation and the retrospective conversion of data.

Level: elementary; required prior completion of the courses: 1108-1111.

Source: http://www.lis.uw.edu.pl/uk/indexe.htm

Let us note, for the sake of order, that after 1989 and the great political changes, great progress was made in the publishing policies of the Polish Librarian Society and the National Library. In these few years, many books have appeared which are useful for teaching document description. Thanks to the tremendous efforts of professor Zbigniew Żmigrodzki of the University of Śląsk, two essential coursebooks have appeared: *Bibliotekarstwo* [Librarianship] and *Bibliografia* [Bibliography], providing important chapters on document description. Their appearance was an important event in librarian circles.[43] The weak point of librarian publishing policy in Poland is, together with a certain internal inability,[44] the lack of translations of foreign coursebooks. During these last years, the foreign coursebook by Alain Jacquesson was the only one published.[45]

There is, in Poland, a clearly visible rise in professional training activities in the libraries, on both the local and nationwide levels. Nationwide trainings are usually initiated either by large libraries, or by some committees of the Librarian Association and CEBID. Large libraries, while working out ambitious training programs for their staff, often turn them into open trainings on the national level. This way, they share their experience with other librarians, while at the same time profiting themselves by teaching partners for future cooperation (e.g., in consortia or data exchange) and by drawing financial benefits from entry fees. A worthy example of such trainings, sporting a masterly constructed program and high level of classes, is the course 'Czasopisma elektroniczne' [i.e., electronic periodicals], already organized since 2000 by the Library of Wrocław Technical University.[46] The course curriculum includes classes on the description of electronic periodicals, shown in a broad context of procedures for manipulating descriptions, e.g., information on collection policies and aquisition procedures, legal questions connected with buying licences for access to on-line sources, consortia, and statistical data analysis connected with circulation and serving a rational financial management.

The second stream of trainings is initiated by the Polish Librarian Association, which–it should be mentioned–does not have as extensive an influence on educational issues as similiar groups in Great Britain, Germany, or the USA. Recently, however, thanks to the activity of some of the commissions of the Main Board (in Polish ZG–Zarząd Główny), we can talk about fast responses to the urgent needs of expanding professional qualifications of librarians. We will mention, only by way of example, the series of workshops organized by the

Committee for Collection Content Description (in Polish–KORZ SBP–Komisja Opracowania Rzeczowego Zbiorów ZG Stowarzyszenia Bibliotekarzy Polskich). We should remember, however, that there are other lasting and valuable initiatives which are organized, for example, by the Team for Regional Bibliography.

The above mentioned KORZ workshops are where librarians, apart from becoming acquainted with the latest advancements in creating content description, receive information about the development of linguistic tools used in description procedures. In May 2004, the second session of Poland-wide workshops, titled *"The Language of Subject Headings of the National Library in Warsaw–new vocabulary, the latest methodological findings and their application in library catalogs. Universal Decimal Classification in bibliographical and catalog databases,"* took place. What is important, the workshops were organized through the common effort of KORZ SBP and the Information Science and Bibliology Institute of Warsaw University. The main strengths of these workshops, apart from smooth institutional cooperation, were the eminent personalities who served as chairpersons for the last two terms. Jadwiga Woźniak is now a professor at Warsaw University and Piotr Bierczyński is the main manager of the Department for Collection Content Description of the Regional and Municipal Public Library in Łódź (the largest Polish city after the capital, Warsaw).

The third and latest training stream, important for document description skills, includes the courses of CEBID which were mentioned when characterizing the main sphere of activity of the Educational Center, i.e., vocational two-year, post-secondary studies. We want to mention here that the sphere of activity of CEBID has been developed in the last two years. These are two-level courses: basic is 20 hours and advanced, 12 hours. In May this year, these courses were on "The Language of Subject Headings KABA." Specific issues connected with document content description from specific branches of knowledge (finances, law and management, issues connected with the European Union, and local policy) were discussed at the advanced level. What is essential, CEBID offered training on new issues of description, such as "Cataloging electronic documents in MARC 21 format to the needs of regional bibliology in the MAK system" (literary, cartographic, and iconographic documents) and "Cataloging of sound documents" (only for teachers-librarians of music schools), which had not been included in courses thus far.[47]

CONCLUSION

The overview of education on cataloging and classification knowledge and skills presented in this article contains fewer details about didactic work but more elements and characteristics of general documents description. It seemed necessary to discuss both the problems of librarian practice, and the institutional and organizational issues of the education and training system, which have the greatest influence on the level of awareness of librarians and workers of information services in Poland. It is difficult to extract from the whole image of librarianship the problems of document description and creating information resources out of them. They are not only "the heart of library education," as Michael Gorman wrote,[48] they are the main matter for all of the most important meta-informational resources and data processing procedures in library and information systems.

That is why it can be predicted that the coming years will bring similar changes in programs of educating and training in describing documents as have occurred in other countries. In the first instance, it can be predicted that new subjects devoted to Functional Requirements for Bibliographic Records (FRBR)[49] will be introduced. It seems that varied functional properties of document description scattered in different areas of the curricula should be gathered into one place as a distinct subject of teaching. Bibliographic and functional relationships, as the attributes of document description data, should constitute one cohesive didactic space to capture problems of description and all of the procedures of its functioning in the information systems about documents. Moreover, it seems that in the Polish environment, with the delay in computer education, program changes such as the general subjects module are needed. Apart from subjects like "Network computer use" (that teach behavior rather than understanding), we need– from the point of view of understanding modern catalog processing–a subject like "Data structures in textual information processing." It would have a similar function in all curricula of general librarian education as those fulfilled by Logic and Elements of Applied Linguistics. Those two subjects are the foundations for teaching information retrieval languages and their application in the description of document content and in searching for information about them.

Many years of the author's didactic experience and observations of librarians' activity show that there are some lacks in common professional knowledge. There is no awareness of how crucial it is, in the successful processing of information about documents, to have both data values and all of the attributes of data names.[50] In the Polish library environment, rather simplified and narrow concepts of "data formats" still exist. It is very often narrowed down to the list of elements marked by codes of fields and subfields in records. It is done both without substantial awareness of the net of relationships between the nature of the names of these elements and their attributes, and without an awareness of functions performed by the retrieval system. So, in the education curricula for librarians for the future, we need deeper understanding of how document descriptions are strongly connected with a net of structural relationships presented in language structure, in the structure of described objects (e.g., documents and texts!), and in the software system, and how, in the most complicated arrangement of human-system-human interaction, they should occupy a wider space.

NOTES

1. J. Lelewel, "Przemowa do moich Ksiąg Bibliograficznych," in: J. Lelewel: *Bibliograficznych ksiąg dwoje [Two Bibliographic Tomes].–T.2.–*(Wilno, 1826), p. 253, [see also chapters: "Librarianship or Book Lore," p. 261-339; "Inventory," p. 278-301].

2. The first university lectures in historical bibliography were conducted by distinguished scholars at the Jagiellonian University in 1811-1834, at the Warsaw University in 1820-1821, and at the Vilna University in 1829-1931. For the sake of order, it should be added here that the first Polish lectures in bibliography were conducted in 1809-1831 by Paweł Jarkowski in the, then famous, Wolyn High School in Krzemieniec. One should not forget that it was the period of the partitions of Poland (1795-1918), when Poland was under the government of three states–Russia, Austria, and Prussia.

3. Stanisława Kurek-Kokocińska, "Lelewelowski obraz usług informacyjnych bibliografa i bibliotekarza z perspektywy formy informacji o dokumentach" [Lelewel's view of the bibliographers and librarians reference services from the perspective of the forms of information about documents], in: *Bibliotekarz w świecie wartości*/ed. Stefan Kubów (Wrocław, 2003), p. 24-34; S. Kurek-Kokocińska, "Joachim Lelewel o działalności informacyjnej bibliografa i bibliotekarza" [Joachim Lelewel on the reference duties of a bibliographer and librarian], *Zagadnienia Informacji Naukowej*, 2003, no 1, p. 3-11.

4. Unfortunately, the part of EBIB concerning education is only available in Polish (last modified–1/01/2004) http://ebib.oss.wroc.pl/edukacja/index.php, although its other parts are available in English: http://ebib.oss.wroc.pl/english/services.php (last modification: 22.10.2002).

5. http://main.amu.edu.pl/~ects/uka/uka.html.

6. Here is a choice of the most important university teachers' publications (starting from the newest):

Barbara Sosińska-Kalata, "Kształcenie bibliotekarzy dla globalnego społeczeństwa informacyjnego" [Training librarians for the global information society], in: *Polskie bibliotekarstwo w perspektywie wejścia do Unii Europejskiej* [*Polish librarianship from a perspective of accessing European Union*] (Warszawa: SBP, 2001), p. 79-89.

Aleksander Radwański, "Potrzeba rewizji podstaw dyscyplin bibliotekoznawczych" [The need to revise the basic librarianship disciplines], *Roczniki Biblioteczne*, 2000, R. 44 p. 207-215, sum.

Janusz Dunin, "Księgoznawstwo przyszłości" [Book science of the future], *Forum Akademickie*, 1998, R. 5, no 2, p. 24-25.

Marcin Drzewiecki, Barbara Sosińska-Kalata, "Europejskie standardy kształcenia a restrukturyzacja polskiego systemu edukacji bibliotekarzy i pracowników informacji, (program TEMPUS–JEP–12165–97)" [European education standards and the transformation of the Polish system of training librarians and information specialists], *Zagadnienia Informacji Naukowej*, 1998, no 2, p. 87-99.

Maria Kocójowa (ed.), *Światowa strategia edukacji bibliotekarzy i specjalistów informacji naukowej = Education of librarians and information professionals: global strategy*, (Kraków, cop. 1998) see component parts: p. 141-146: Wanda Pindlowa, "Unia Europejska a kształcenie wyższe bibliotekarzy i pracowników informacji naukowej w Polsce" [The EU and the university education of librarians and information professionals]; p. 161-164: Małgorzata Komza, "Przyszłość kształcenia bibliotekoznawców i pracowników informacji naukowej w Polsce" [The future of librarians and information professionals training in Poland], also in *Roczniki Biblioteczne*, 1997, R. 41, z. 1/2, p. 240-242.

Peter Muranyi (ed.), *Renewing the Education and Training of Librarians and Information Professionals*, (Szombathely, 1997) see component parts: p. 52-60: Bronisława Woźniczka-Paruzel, Małgorzata Fedorowicz, "On models academic education of librarianship and information science in Poland"; p. 171-179: K. Żurawska, B. Żurawski, "Changes in education of librarianship and information science connected with the development of information technology: the place of the World Wide Web."

Barbara Sosińska-Kalata, "The reform of information and book studies at the University of Warsaw," *Polish Libraries Today*, 1997, p. 27-32; Jan Sójka, "Uwarunkowania projektowania systemu kształcenia bibliotekarzy: o kształceniu bibliotekarzy na poziomie wyższym zawodowym" [The conditions of designing a librarians education system: training librarian on the college level], *Bibliotekarz*, 1997, no 5, p. 7-11; no 9, p. 14-18.

Joan M. Day, Maria Śliwińska, (ed.), *The role and functions of a modern academic library*, (Toruń, 1997), see component parts: p. 181-191: Czesław Jan Grycz, "Educating and managing professionals for the libraries of the 21st Century"; p. 193-197: Maria Śliwińska, "Suggestions for the modernisation of librarians' education."

7. Ingrid Hsieh-Yee, "Cataloging and Metadata Education: Asserting a Central Role in Information Organization," *Cataloging & Classification Quarterly*, 2002, vol. 34 no 1-3, p. 204-206.

8. Jadwiga Woźniak, "Katalogowanie świata: Z Jadwigą Woźniak z Instytutu Informacji Naukowej i Studiów Bibliologicznych Uniwersytetu Warszawskiego / rozmawia Andrzej Gontarz" [Cataloging the World: An Interview with Jadwiga Woźniak from the Warsaw University Scientific Information and Book Studies Institute / by Andrzej Gontarz], *Computerworld Polska*, 2001, nr 1 (2 stycznia), s. 48-49 [electr. doc.] http://www.computerworld.pl/archiwum/.

Anna Sitarska: "'Środowisko' elektronicznych systemów i służb informacyjnych: potrzeby kształcenia profesjonalnej kadry i szkolenia użytkowników" [The electronic systems and information services 'environment': the need for educating professional

staff and user training], in: *EuroInfo '94 Poland: materiały okonferencyjne = Proceedings*, Warsaw, June 1994 (Warszawa, Business Foundation, 1995), p. 147-149.
9. "Forum–Kształcenie bibliotekarzy" [Education for librarians], [electr.doc.], *EBIB Electronic Library Bulletin*, 2002, http://ebib.oss.wroc.pl/forum/ksztalcenie.php (last mod. 4/03/2003).
10. Mirosław Górny, "Kształcenie–głos w dyskusji (1)" [Education–a voice in the discussion], [electr. doc.], *EBIB Electronic Library Bulletin*, 2002, no 8(37) http://ebib.oss.wroc.pl/2002/37/1gorny1.php.
11. Bożena Bednarek-Michalska, "Kształcenie–głos w dyskusji (2)" [Education–a voice in the discussion], [electr. doc.], *EBIB Electronic Library Bulletin*, 2002, no 8(37) http://ebib.oss.wroc.pl/2002/37/12michalska2.php.
12. Anna Sitarska, "Dylematy kształcenia bibliotekarzy i pracowników służb informacyjnych" [The dilemmas of training librarians and information professionals], [electr. doc.], *EBIB Electronic Library Bulletin*, 2002, no 8(37) http://ebib.oss.wroc.pl/2002/37/sitarska.php.
13. Bogumiła Wojciechowska-Marek, "Kształcenie–głos w dyskusji" [Education–a voice in the discussion], [electr. doc.], *EBIB Electronic Library Bulletin*, 2002, no 8(37) http://ebib.oss.wroc.pl/2002/37/10wojciechowska.php.
14. Jacek Wojciechowski, *Bibliotekarstwo: kontynuacje i zmiany [Librarianship: continuation and change]*, (Kraków: Wydaw. Uniw. Jagiellonskiego, 1999), p. 98 (in chapter: "Uroki małych bibliotek" [Fascinations of the small libraries], p. 91-100).
15. (1) Hanna Tadeusiewicz, "Jubileusz najstarszej Katedry Bibliotekoznawstwa" [The anniversary of the oldest Chair of Library Science], *Biuletyn Głównej Biblioteki Lekarskiej*, 1996, 42, no 354, p. 103-105; Joanna Hiller, "Katedra Bibliotekoznawstwa i Informacji Naukowej Uniwersytetu Łódzkiego w opiniach absolwentów z lat 1945-1995" [The Chair of Library Science of the Łódź University in the opinions of graduates 1945-1995], *Acta Universitatis Lodzensis, Folia Librorum*, 1999 z. 9, p. 15-24.
(2) Maria Kocójowa (ed.), *Biblioteka i informacja w komunikowaniu, jubileusz 25-lecia studiów Bibliotekoznawstwa i Informacji Naukowej w Uniwersytecie Jagiellońskim [Library and information in social communication, the 25th anniversary of Library and Information Science studies in the Jagiellonian University]*, (Kraków, Wydaw. Uniwersytetu Jagiellońskiego, 2000), 431 s., (*Prace z Bibliotekoznawstwa i Informacji Naukowej = Jagiellonian University Scholary Fascile;* no 1243).
(3) Elżbieta Barbara Zybert (ed.), *Warszawskie uniwersyteckie studia bibliotekoznawcze i informacyjne (1951-2001), praca zbiorowa = University library and information science studies in Warsaw (1951-2001)*, (Warszawa, Inst. Informacji Naukowej i Studiów Bibliologicznych U.W., 2002), 176 p.; see component parts: p. 15-42: Aleksander Birkenmajer, "Rozwój i stan obecny wyższych studiów bibliotekoznawczych w Polskiej Rzeczypospolitej Ludowej 1957 r." [The development and current state of university library studies in Poland 1957]; p. 43-58: Barbara Sosińska-Kalata, "Programy kształcenia bibliotekoznawczego i informacyjnego w Instytucie Informacji Naukowej i Studiów Bibliologicznych Uniwersytetu Warszawskiego" [The Library and Information Science curriculum in the Scientific Information and Book Studies Institute of the Warsaw University]; p. 129-132: Mikołaj Ochmański, "Koło naukowe Instytutu Informacji Naukowej i Studiów Bibliologicznych Uniwersytetu Warszawskiego w latach 1990-2000" [Library and Information Science Students' Research Club at the Warsaw University in 1990-2000].

16. "CEBID: I[nstitution characteristics], *EBIB Electronic Library Services*, [electr. doc.] http://www.cebid.edu.pl/.

17. Barbara Ciesielska, "Półwiecze Sorbony Jarocińskiej [Państwowy Ośrodek Kształcenia Bibliotekarzy], refleksje i wspomnienia" [50 years of the State Center for Librarian Education, reflections and recollections], *Poradnik Bibliotekarza*, 1998, no 10, p. 7-9 ; Jan Wołosz, "45-lecie Centrum Ustawicznego Kształcenia Bibliotekarzy" [45 years of the Center for Permanent Librarian Education], *Bibliotekarz*, 1998, no 12, p. 23-24.

18. Marcin Drzewiecki, Barbara Sosińska-Kalata, "Europejskie standardy kształcenia a restrukturyzacja polskiego systemu edukacji bibliotekarzy i pracowników informacji, (program TEMPUS–JEP–12165–97)" [European education standards and the re-shaping of the Polish system of librarian and information professional education (TEMPUS–JEP–12165–97 program), *Zagadnienia. Informacji Naukowej*, 1998, no 2, p. 87-99; B. Sosińska-Kalata, "Zagadnienia informacji w programach pomaturalnych szkół bibliotekarskich i dwustopniowych studiów w IINSB UW" [The subject of information in post-secondary library school and library studies of the Warsaw University curricula], in: M. Drzewiecki, J. Puchalski (ed.): *Informacja naukowa a dydaktyka . . .* (Warszawa: CUKB; IINSB UW, 1999), p. 145-153.

19. For example, in the High School of Social Knowledge and Skills in Poznań–the "Journalism and Social Communication" course includes the following subjects: "Methods of Gathering and Processing Information" and "Information Science," as well as "Information Broker" specialty http://www.wsus.poznan.pl/diks.php.

20. An interesting proof of how deeply rooted the two terms are in Polish librarian language can be found in the latest librarianship and bibliography coursebooks, where these traditional words are still used even if with a new meaning. One of the authorities on OPAC design–Andrzej Padziński writes: ". . . In Poland, since the 'shortened rules of alphabetical cataloging' were abandoned . . . there are no cataloging rules . . . cataloging rules are only included in Polish [bibliographical] Standards. . . ." (see A. Padziński, *Stosowanie polskich norm w zautomatyzowanych katalogach bibliotecznych* [Using the Polish Standards in automated library catalogs], (Warszawa, Wydaw. SBP, 2000), p. 7).

21. According to the statistical data for the year 2002, there are about 9,000 public libraries in Poland, 6,000 of which are in rural areas; according to data for the year 2001 there were 1,225 scientific libraries, 1,000 of which are at schools of higher education (academic libraries have the status of research libraries according to Polish statistics, and the school libraries are classed libraries at the elementary, secondary, and post-secondary schools only); unfortunately there is no data about the school libraries–the largest group of Polish libraries–probably because of the dynamic changes in Polish primary and secondary education, which has undergone a radical structural transformation in recent years. In 2002, there were approximately thirty thousand primary schools, junior-high, secondary, and post-secondary schools. According to Polish Library Law, every school should have a library, but when the new level of education was created (junior high, in Polish–gimnazjum), they often had a joint library together with a nearby primary school. This was most common in smaller towns and villages. The number of school libraries in 2003 can be estimated at about twenty thousand, while the overall number of all libraries equals around thirty thousand (source see *EBIB Electronic Services* http://ebib.oss.wroc.pl/raporty/index.php).

22. Prof. J. Franke is an employee of the Scientific Information and Book Studies Institue at the Warsaw University; he has been teaching document description for

many years, and has particularly valuable experience in solving problems connected with processing and storing catalog data in the system with the most commonly used software package in Poland for cataloging purposes–MAK/BN–which is also used in the electronic version of some parts of the Polish current national bibliography (both in the CD-ROM and on-line version–http://mak.bn.org.pl/w1.htm).

23. J. Franke: "Biblioteki wobec zmian w opisie bibliograficznym = Libraries in view of changes in bibliographic descritpion," in: *Ksiłżka i biblioteka w środowisku edukacyjnym = The Book and the Library in Educational Environment*/ed. Elżbieta B. Zybert, (Warsaw, Polish Librarians Association, 2002), p. 218-227.

24. Józef Grycz was an outstanding organizer of Polish librarianship after Poland regained independence in 1919. One of the main fields of his activity was standardization of cataloging rules, which he had been working on since 1924 doing, among other things, a comparative study of the rules used in foreign libraries. In 1934, he published "Przepisy katalogowania w bibliotekach polskich" [The cataloging rules for Polish libraries], which have gained the status of the obligatory instruction for research libraries. During the war, 1939-1945, he continued his work over adapting the rules to the needs of school and public libraries. Thanks to this, as soon as 1946, "Skrócone przepisy katalogowania alfabetycznego" [The short rules for alphabetic cataloging] could be published (co-auth. W. Borkowska). These rules were improved over time (the 6th edition was in 1975) and were the common standard for every type of library until 1983. It means that the "Grycz rules" were used in research libraries for almost 50 years. In other types of libraries they still are. New cataloging rules *Przepisy katalogowania książek* [*Book cataloging rules*]/ed. by Maria Lenartowicz (Warsaw, SBP, 1983) have officially succeeded the "Grycz rules" after the first part of the Polish Standard for bibliography PN-82/N-01152.01, based on the ISBD(M) 2nd ed., had been published, but they also included the older rules of choice and form of main entries, which allowed them to be used without closing the old catalogs based on 'Grycz.' This state of affairs is still common in very numerous medium and small libraries in Poland.

25. J. Franke, op. cit.

26. According to a report for the Commission of Culture and the Media of the Polish Parliament (http://isip.sejm.gov.pl/Biuletyn.nsf), the number of public libraries and their branches reached 8,858 in 2002, out of which 1,336 (15.08%) were undergoing a process of building of computer catalogs; 7.7% had access to the Internet; 4% allowed their users to use on-line resources; and 2.1% were advertising themselves on websites. Only 46 public libraries were attempting to create computer catalogs in 2000, and 141 in 2002. And only 44 libraries were acquiring data from outside databases in 2000, and 117 in 2002; out of 18 regional public libraries, 7 have integrated systems: ALEPH (2 libraries), HORIZON (1 library), PROLIB (3 libraries), and VTLS (1 library). The remaining 11 use, among others, the ISIS program and the Polish programs MAK/BN, SOWA, LIBRA, PATRON. The most popular professional system of cataloging software in Polish libraries (used in 433 public libraries) is MAK/BN created in the National Library in Warsaw. This system was sponsored by the Ministry of Culture and was distributed free of charge to all public libraries which fulfill the conditions necessary for use and installation of this system. What is most important–the MAK/BN is used for creating and distribution of the main parts of the Polish current national bibliography (registration of books and periodicals component parts). The report was prepared at the request of the Computerization Section of the Association of Polish Librarians (see Elżbieta Górska, Katarzyna Winogrodzka, "Stan i plany komputeryzacji bibliotek publicznych (raport dla Sejmu RP, 04/06/2002)," [State and

plans of computerization of public libraries (a report for the Parlaiment, 04/06/2002)], [electr. doc.], *EBIB Electronic Library: Reports & Projects* http://ebib.oss.wroc.pl/raporty/raport_kbp.html).

27. In the latest version of the MAK/BN 4.3 package issued in 2003, modifications in the indexing module were included which add some attributes of authority files to the indexes.

28. Andrzej Padziński, *Stosowanie polskich norm w zautomatyzowanych katalogach bibliotecznych* = Application of Cataloguing Rules in Automated Library Systems, (Warszawa: SBP, 2000), 111, [1] p.; Jerzy Franke, "Przewodnik Bibliograficzny 1983-1996: edycja na CD = 'Bibliographic Guide' 1983-1986 CD-ROM edition," *Zagadnienia Informacji Naukowej*, 1998, no 1, p. 85-92.

29. Maria Janowska, "Normalizacja w zakresie bibliotekarstwa w Polsce po wprowadzeniu nowej Ustawy" [Standardization in Polish librarianship after the execution of the new Polish Standardization Act], *Biuletyn Informacyjny Biblioteki Narodowej*, 1999, [nr] 2, s. 35-36; Natalia Dziosa, "Normalizacja w zakresie informacji naukowej i bibliotekarstwa" [Unification and standarization processes in librarianship and reference services], *Bibliotekarz*, 2000, nr 4, s. 19-21; Marta Grabowska, "Normalizacja w zakresie informacji i dokumentacji w Polsce w latach 1993-2000" [Standardization in Poland in the fields of information and documentation in 1993-2000], *Przegląd Biblioteczny*, 2001, R. 69, z. 1/2, s. 11-38.

30. See the criticism of J. Franke (quoted in ref. no. 28), which analyzes the mistakes, inconsistencies, and even simple sloppiness in the CD-ROM version of the current Polish national bibliography, commonly used in libraries as the most important source of description data. The national bibliography is known as the Bibliographic Guide and is compiled from weekly book registrations. See also, an article by a linguistics professor from the Warsaw University–Bożenna Bojar: "Definicje w dokumentach normalizacyjnych" [Definintions in standards], *Zagadnienia Informacji Naukowej*, 2002, nr 1, s. 34-46.

31. P. Bierczyński, Henryk Hollender, "NUKat i jhp BN," *Bibliotekarz*, 2003, nr 2, s. 2, 31 (see also complete and up-to-date information on NUKAT at http://www.nukat.edu.pl/katalog/ or http://193.0.118.55/).

32. Jadwiga Woźniak (ed.), *Katalogowanie przedmiotowe w języku KABA. [Subject cataloginig in KABA]* Cz.1: T. Głowacka: *Analiza dokumentu i jego opis przedmiotowy,* [Part 1: *Document analysis and subject description*], (Warszawa, SBP, 2004), 96 p. (FO-KA ; 13).

33. The 'Warsaw school' was developed thanks to Prof. Olgierd Adrian Wojtasiewicz, an outstanding linguist from the Warsaw University, and his students, e.g., Bożenna Bojar, "Języki i systemy informacyjno-wyszukiwawcze–refleksje na koniec wieku: od strukturalizmu do kognitywizmu" [Information-retrieval languages and systems–reflections for the end of the century: from structuralism to cognitivism], *Zagadnienia Informacji Naukowej*, 2001, no 1, p. 55-59; Anna Sitarska, "Systemowa problematyka języków informacyjno-wyszukiwawczych: w polu widzenia nauczyciela akademickiego" [The system issues of information-retrieval languages: from the point of view of the academic teacher], *Zagadnienia Informacji Naukowej*, 2000, no 1, p. 60-66, (see also obituaries: Andrzej Bogusławski, Bożenna Bojar, "Olgierd Adrian Wojtasiewicz (1916-1995)" [nekr.], *Rocznik Towarzystwa Naukowego Warszawskiego*, R. 58, 1995, p. 59-61; B. Bojar, "Olgierd Adrian Wojtasiewicz 11 XII 1916–7 IV 1995" [nekr.], *Zagadnienia Informacji Naukowej*, 1995, no 1/2, p. 101-102).

34. After the death of Prof. Wojtasiewicz, the research of the 'Warsaw school' continued under the supervision of Prof. Bożenna Bojar, editor of the periodical *Zagadnienia Informacji Naukowej*, which visibly favors publications on document content characteristics (see, e.g., B. Bojar, "Związki teorii informacyjno-wyszukiwawczych z językoznawstwem" [Connections between information-retrieval theory and linguistics], *Zagadnienia Informacji Naukowej*, 2001, no 2, s. 12-27, in content: p. 22-27: "The Warsaw school . . ."–a list of 80 chosen publications, including many doctoral theses. B. Bojar is also the author of a course book for librarianship students: *Zarys językoznawstwa dla studentów bibliotekoznawstwa i informacji naukowej* [*The basics of linguistics for librarianship and information science students*], (2nd ed., Warszawa, Wydaw. UW, 1991), 338 p.

35. Aleksander Radwański, "Analiza ilościowa danych z 'Przewodnika Bibliograficznego'" [Data quantitative analysis of "Bibliographic Guide"], *Acta Universitatis Wratislaviensis. Bibliotekoznawstwo* 1995, no. 19, p. 101-123; Rafał Lewandowski, *Analiza porównawcza formatów elektronicznych dokumentów tekstowych* [*Comparative analysis of text document electronic formats*], (Wrocław, Politechnika Wrocławska, 2001), 177 p.

36. The website of the Public Library in Cieszyn can serve as an example here (http://www.ata.com.pl/kcc/) and the so-called Cieszyn Virtual Library (http://www.ata.com.pl/kcc/biblioteka/index.html), the existence and form of which is connected with the cooperation between the librarianship students and lecturers of the Warsaw University with the librarians and regional historians from Cieszyn.

37. Robert P. Holley, "Cataloging: An Exciting Subject for Exciting Times," *Cataloging & Classification Quarterly*, vol. 34, 2002, no 1-3.

38. A certain testimony in favor of this opinion can be found in the doctor's thesis of Mirosław Górny *Kształtowanie się współczesnych form współpracy w bibliotekach naukowych*, [*The forming of the modern forms of cooperation in research libraries*] (Poznań, impr. by auth., 1992), 90 p., which shows an almost complete lack of Polish experience!

39. Maria Kocójowa, "Współpraca Krakowa z [University Library] Bochum i inicjatywa marburska [Herder Institute]" [The cooperation between Kraków, Bochum and the Marburg initiative], Przegląd Biblioteczny, R. 65, 1997, z. 1, p. 109-113; M. Kocójowa, (ed.), Światowa strategia edukacji bibliotekarzy i specjalistów informacji naukowej (Kraków, 1998, Wydaw. UJ), (Research Reports of Librarianship and Information Studies of the Jagiellonian University, no 7); J. Woźniak, R. Miller, (ed.), Research libraries–cooperation in automation, November 16-19, 1998, Cracow, (Warszawa, Wydaw. SBP, 1999), 168 p., (Formaty, Kartoteki ; 3), see component parts: R.C. Miler–visiting professor from USA, Dr. Klára Koltay from Hungary, Laura J. Goss from the University of Hertfordshire and the Hertfordshire Colleges, Manfred Walter–Berlin and Brandenburg; from the subject point of view: "VTLS Libraries consortium," "Union Authority File: 1993-1998," "Union Serials Catalog: 1995-1998," "Standardization of the data in the automated catalogs," "KABA subject headings system: an example of the collective effort," "The cooperation of Tinlib libraries," "Patrons of central catalogs," "Cooperation of ALEPH libraries," "PROLIB Libraries Group," "Z39.50 protocol in creation of shared cataloging systems and union catalogs," "HORISON and academic libraries," "VOCAL–a model for a union catalog."

40. The so-called ministry minimum sets out the rules for 5-year MA studies only, while UKA standards include two-part studies: 1st part is 3 years for the BA and the 2nd part is 2 years for the MA degree. One of the reasons for these differences is that the ministry merely repeats the minimal standards set out 15 years ago, while the UKA

bases its standards on the reality and needs of Polish universities which, for the most part, have managed to match western standards. The ministry not only used out-of-date variables, completely inadequate to the needs of current university studies, but also changed the intentions of the expert group which set the minimum standards. They were misunderstood as the core curriculum content on all universities instead of the limits of class hours in the curricula. To this core, every university–according to primary intentions–would be required to add subjects which complete the curriculum, according to staff availability and, what is more important, such as would allow students to get to know the state of the art and directions of development in information and library science. The author, as a member of this group, is convinced that the current MENiS standards are a bureaucratic manipulation, motivated by lack of funding for higher education.

41. See also, description of the LIS curriculum at Toruń University http://www. inibi.uni.torun.pl/studia/dz_um_pr.html; English version http://www.inibi.uni.torun. pl/en/dp.html.

42. The web addresses can be found in Table 1. Unfortunately not all subject descriptions are currently available in English, perhaps because of modification in the curricula before the beginning of term.

43. (1) Z. Żmigrodzki (ed.), *Bibliotekarstwo = [Librarianship]*, (1st ed. 1994, 2nd ed. impr. & abridg. 1998, Warszawa: SBP), p. 370, [1] (*Nauka, Dydaktyka, Praktyka) =* [*Science, Didactics, Practice*], 10); [one needs to underline–the former academic handbook on librarianship was published in Poland in 1956!]; see also, rev.: B. Bojar, "Języki informacyjno-wyszukiwawcze w 'Bibliotekarstwie'" [Information-retrieval languages in the *Librarianship*–evaluation of coursebook ed. by Zbigniew Żmigrodzki, 2nd edition. Warszawa 1998], *Zagadnienia Informacji Naukowej*, 1998, no 2, p. 106-112; (2) Z. Żmigrodzki, (ed.), *Bibliografia, metodyka i organizacja = Bibliography: Methodology and organisation*, (Warszawa, 2000, Wydaw. SBP) 351 p., *(Nauka, Dydaktyka, Praktyka = Science, Didactics, Practice]*, 38); [somewhat better situation was with the handbook on bibliographical methodology–the former publication was in 1963!].

44. The unwillingness to work on academic coursebooks is often justified by the fact that, in formal assessment of one's scientific achievements, coursebooks are not highly valued, even though they require a lot more work experience than a small academic treaty.

45. A. Jacquesson, *Automatyzacja bibliotek [Library Automation]* [*oryg. L' Informatisation des bibliothèques: historique, stratégie et perspectives]*/transl. from Fr. A. Bator et al., (Warszawa, Uniw. Warszawski, 1999), 367, [1] p.

46. See, for details of the curriculum and entry conditions, http://www.bg.pwr. wroc.pl/USLU/kursy/oferta.htm.

47. Look for the remaining topics of similar CEBID courses planned for 2004 and their programs under the heading "training" on web pages http://www.cebid.edu.pl.

48. Michael Gorman, "Why Teach Cataloguing and Classification?" *Cataloging & Classification Quarterly*, 2002, p. 10-11.

49. Barbara B. Tillett, "A taxonomy of bibliographic relationships," *Library Resources & Technical Services*, 1991, no 2, p. 150-158; IFLA Study Group on the Functional Requirements for Bibliographic Records, *Functional Requirements for Bibliographic Records: Final Report* (München: K.G. Saur, 1998).

50. For the sake of precision it should be noted that 'data' in this context is understood according to the definition used in computer studies as a "*name–value pair*"; in other words: data value = information inscribed into the record structure, parts of which are identified by data name.

APPENDIX

TABLE 1. The System of Training Librarians and Information Professionals in Poland

City	Postmatural Courses	University Studies–levels and forms of study			
		BA / BAadd	MA	PGd	PhD
Białystok	Pt	ft + pt + par (1)		/pt	
Bydgoszcz		ft+pt (2)		/pt	
Gdańsk	Pt		/par + pt (3)	/pt	
Katowice	Pt	BA+BAadd/pt (4)	/ft+pt	/pt	
Kielce		ft+pt (5)			
Koszalin	Pt				
Kraków A Kraków B	Pt	BA+BAadd/ ft+pt (6A) BA+BAadd/ ftd+pt (6B)	MA/ft+pt (6A) MA+MA_add/ ft+pt (6B)	PGd x 3/pt (6A) PGd x 2/pt (6B)	(6B) PhD seminars
Lublin	Pt		MA/ft+pt (7)	PGd	
Łódź	Pt		MA/ft+pt (8)	PGd	
Olsztyn	Pt			PGd x 2/pt (9)	
Poznań		/ft+pt (10A)		PGd x 2 (10B)	
Rzeszów	Pt				
Szczecin	Pt				
Toruń	Pt	BA/ft+pt (11)	MA_add/ft+pt	PGd x 3/pt	
Warszawa	Pt (12A)	BA+BAadd/ft+pt (12B)	MA/ft+pt (12)	PGd x 3 (12B)	PhD seminars (12B)
Wrocław			MA/ft+pt (13)	PGd	PhD study
Zielona Góra	Pt				

Source: *EBIB* http://ebib.oss.wroc.pl/edukacja/index.php (available in May 2004)
Abbreviations: (1) Level of Studies : BA–Polish equivalent of the Bachelor of Arts; BAadd–additional studies for graduates of post-secondary schools giving a BA equivalent; MA–Polish equivalent of the Master of Arts; PGd–postgraduate studies; PhD–seminars or studies giving the Polish equivalent of the Doctor of Philosophy title; (2) forms of study: ft–full-time studies; pt–part-time or extramural studies. In the footnotes, names of schools and universities in a particular city were given and, if there were different postgraduate studies, those names as well; if there is no footnote with the name of a postgraduate study, it means that it is a general library and information science course.

Footnotes

(1) University of Białystok, Faculty of Philology, Eastern-Slavonic Philology Institute
(2) Bydgoszcz Academy, Faculty of Humanities
(3) Gdańsk, University of Gdańsk, Faculty of Philology, Polish Philology Institute

(4) Katowice, University of Śląsk, Faculty of Philological, Library and Information Science Institute
(5) Kielce, Świętokrzyska Academy, Faculty of Humanities, Librarianship and Journalism Institute
(6) Kraków A. The KEN, i.e., Pedagogical Academy in Kraków, Faculty of Humanities, Library and Information Science Institute
    Kraków B. Jagiellonian University, Faculty of Management and Social Communication, Library and Information Science Institute
(6A) (1) Postgraduate Marketing Studies, Management of Libraries and Cultural Institutions; (2)Postgraduate Studies of Media, Reader and Library Education in the Reformed School; (3) Postgraduate Information Technology Studies
(6B) (1) Postgraduate Librarianship Studies (2) Postgraduate Information Science Studies
(7) Maria Curie-Skłodowsksa University, Faculty of Humanities, Library and Information Science Institute
(8) Łódź, University of Łódź, Faculty of Philology, Department of Library and Information Science
(9) Olsztyn, University of Warmia and Mazury, Faculty of Humanities, History and International Relations Institute
    (1) Postgraduate Study of Library and Information Science
    (2) Postgraduate Study of Archive Digitalization (see: http://human.uwm.edu.pl/historia/pka.htm)
(10A) Poznań, Higher School of Social Knowledge, Faculty of Journalism and Social Communication with 2 specializations–
    (1) Electronic Reference Services and Librarianship
    (2) Information Broker
(10B) Poznań, Adam Mickiewicz University, Faculty of Neophilology
    (1) Postgraduate Information Electronic and Library Science Studies
    (2) Postgraduate Culture Management Studies
(11) Mikołaj Kopernik University, Historical Faculty, Library and Information Science Institute
    (1) Postgraduate Library and Information Science Studies
    (2) Postgraduate Archivist Studies–basic course
    (3) Postgraduate Archivist Studies on Digitalization
(12A) Warszawa, CEBID–Educational Center on Librarianship Information and Documentation Services–main unit for Postmatural Courses in 13 branches in 2003/2004 ac. year
(12B) Warszawa, Warsaw University, Faculty of History, Institute of Scientific Information and Book Studies
    (1) Postgraduate Library Science Studies
    (2) Postgraduate Information Science Studies
    (3) Postgraduate Publishing Policy and Book Market Studies
(13) Wrocław University, Philological Faculty, Library and Information Science Institute

APPENDIX (continued)

TABLE 2. The Main Subjects Connected with Formal and Content Description of Documents in the Curricula of the Largest Polish Universities

Internet Address Level of education year/semester of study	Name and number of the subject in curricula	Subject content range	Forms of classes and number of hours
Warsaw University (UW) http://www.lis.uw.edu.pl/uk/indexe.htm **Bachelor of Arts studies** I / 1			
I / 1	Documents And Document Collections	Basic terms and definitions connected with the typology and morphology of documents, and document collections . . . (1)	L + Cl Ft–30 h Pt–20h
I / 1	Information sources (general)	The aim of the subject is to present . . . the selected . . . information on old and contemporary documents, both Polish and foreign . . . (2)	L + Cl Ft–30 h Pt–10 h
I / 2	Information Processing (I) Formal aspects	This is an introductory course to the formal description of documents according to the ISBD and its Polish version: PN-N-01152 . . . (3)	Ft–60 h Pt–20
II / 3	Information Processing (II) contents analysis	The main themes of the course encompass the principles of analysing the contents and creating of descriptions of contents of texts . . . (4)	Sem. Ft–15 h Pt–5 h
II / 3	Information Processing (III) Subject cataloging according to subject	The course encompasses problems concerning the presentation of knowledge on the forms of subject cataloguing . . . (5)	L + Cl Ft–30 h Pt–15 h
II / 4	Information Processing (IV) Knowledge organization and classification	The course is concerned with the principles of the logical and semantic organisation of knowledge and the issues of constructing and applying classification information retrieval languages . . . (6)	L + Cl Ft–30 h Pt–15 h
III / 5	Information Processing (V) Authority files	The aim of the course is . . . to provide students with the knowledge of: (1) the place, the functions and the role of the authority files . . . (7)	Sem. Ft–15 h Pt–5 h
III / 6	Library Automation	This course is an introduction to the issues of library automation . . . discussion of topics connected with . . . standards . . . retroconversion of catalogues or access to primary documents.	Sem. Ft–30 h Pt–10 h

University abbreviations: UW–Warsaw University; UJ–Jagiellonian University, Kraków; UWroc.–University of Wrocław; forms of study: Ft–full-time Pt–part-time; forms of teaching: L = lectures; Cl = classes; Lab. = lab. classes; Know. = discussion classes; Sem. = diploma classes

Warsaw University http://www.lis.uw.edu.pl/uk/indexe.htm UW Master studies	Selected from 9 'master paths' for MA degree + obligatory connected lectures and classes		
IV / 7 (optional)	Hypermedia systems	Creating and use of hypermedia systems. A review of selected systems is done. The history and evolution of hypermedia information (definition of hyperinformation, beginnings of hyperinfromation, evolution of hypermedia information); basic components of hypermedia systems; research of hypermedia systems; critical analysis of hypermedia systems; current tendencies in designing hypermedia systems	Lab. 45 h
IV / 8 (optional)	Electronic document	Official and private documents; contents, context, metadata in traditional and electronic documents; document vs. act. Electronic documents–archive experience of other countries; projects of: University of Pittsburgh, University of British Columbia–InterPARES, British EROS project. Legal and technical aspects of handling technical documents; legal regulations concerning electronic documents, especially in Poland; the questions of authenticity, reliability and integrity in long time perspective; EU standards–DLM, American description standard EAD. Information society–e-government; systems; document circulation; electronic signature . . .	Know. 90 h
IV / 8 (optional)	Full text systems	Methods and tools for creating conventional and digital full text systems; similarities and differences between full text system databases and full text presentation systems; problems of group work and transmission of documents in networks; standard Z39.50 (especially in WAIS implementations); organization of electronic full text documents, with special consideration of hypertext techniques; electronic archives and systems of presentation of electronic periodicals.	Lab. 45 h

261

APPENDIX (continued)

TABLE 2 (continued)

Internet Address Level of education year/semester of study	Name and number of the subject in curricula	Subject content range	Forms of classes and number of hours
Uniwersytet Jagielloński http://bilon.miks.uj.edu.pl/eng/index_e.html **UJ Bachelor of Arts studies** I / 1	Documents description	Description of books and periodicals	45 h
I / 1	Information sources	Classification and review of printed and electronic reference works	30 h
I / 1	Managing Library resources		60 h
I / 2	Document Description	Description of audiovisual and electronic documents	15 h
II / 2	Sources of Information		60 h
II / 2	Databases		60 h
II / 2	Audio & Video Collections		30 h
II / 3	Content Characteristic of Documents		45 h
II / 3	Use of Computers in Libraries		30 h
II / 4	Content Characteristic of Document		30 h

Jagiellonian University
http://bilon.miks.uj.edu.pl/eng/index_e.html
UJ Bachelor of Arts studies

II / 4	Authority Files		15 h
II / 4	Information Systems		60 h
III / 5	Document Evaluation		15 h
III / 5	Information Retrieval Languages		60 h
III / 5	Virtual Libraries		60 h
III / 5	International Librarianship		15 h
III / 5	Information and Libraries in the EU		30 h
III / 6	Grey Literature		15 h
III / 6	Information Retrieval in Networks		30 h
III / 6	Information Services in Libraries and Information Centers		60 h
	Selected review		

http://bilon.miks.uj.edu.pl/eng/index_e.html
UJ Master studies

IV / 7	Web Page Development	Obligatory for each master path	30 h
IV / 7	User Interfaces to Databases	OPACs, etc.	30 h
IV / 7	Online periodicals	Licensing, reference for users, archiving, and editing	
IV / 8	Documents Digitization and Archiving	spacialization	225

APPENDIX (continued)

TABLE 2 (continued)

Internet Address Level of education year/semester of study	Name and number of the subject in curricula	Subject content range	Forms of classes and number of hours
University of Wrocław http://www.ibi.uni.wroc.pl/programy/ przed_ob/po_101.htm **UWroc. MA studies** I / 1-2	Formal description of documents	Bibliographic and catalog description. Bibliographic and catalog description standards. Bibliographic and catalog description forming methods. Description of various types of documents. Description of special collections. Organizing a formal catalog. Description in USMARC	Know. 60 h
I / 1-2	Bibliography organization and theory	Among other topics, Problems of bibliographic description	L 30 h
II / 3 -4	Content description of documents	I. documentation analysis and abstracts; II. Frame catalogs–section catalog, systematic catalog, Universal Decimal Classification); III. Content catalogs–subject headings language , vocabularies, exercises in the National Library in Warsaw ; IV. Information retrieval languages, keywords, descriptors languages, retrieval procedures for various systems	Know. I 30 k; II 30 h III 45 h IV 30 h
I / 1-2, II / 3	Information sources	The ability to distinguish, choose and use various types of information sources. Definitions. Information carriers. Classification of information sources. Non-document sources (mass media, informal information channels. Primary documents. Secondary documents–types and forms. Primary reference documents (factual information)–traditional and electronic; construction and use. Secondary reference documents (bibliographic information)–traditional and electronic; classification, construction and use.	Know. 3 x 30 h
II / 1-2	Collection construction and organization	Among other topics, document types, types of records and document information banks	Know. 15 h
II / 3	Library Automation	Among other topics, cataloging modules in chosen systems	Lab. 30 h
II / 4	Bibliography methodology	Among other topics, correct use of description rules in bibliography creation, adjusting the form and content of a description to the abilities of the user, materials arrangement, etc.	Know. 30 h
III / 5 or IV / 7	Cataloging and bibliographic databases on the Internet	In the *Electronic Services* and *Editorial* specialization–practical skills of searching for information.	Lab 30 h

TABLE 3. Time Limits for 'Document Description' Subjects in the Curricula of 'Information and Library Science' Faculties

Level of study, Name of subject modules and separate subjects	Standards		University programs								
	Minima MEN	UKA	UW			UJ			UWroc.		
			Ogółem	% MEN	% UKA	....	% MEN	% UKA	....	% MEN	% UKA
MA studies as a whole	1215	1700	1175 + lic. =	255	182	1005 + lic. =	294	210	2295	183.6	135
general subjects	390	-	**3100**	338		**3575**			450	115.3	-
professional subjects	825	-	420	190		105			1845	223.6	-
librarianship	240	-	745			900					
BA studies	-	1200	1935	-	161	2570	-	214			
General subjects		390	900	-	230	870		223			
Professional subjects		825	1035		125	1700		206			
Main 'document description' subjects	X	X	X	X	X	X	X	X	X	X	X
Documents & document collections			30			X			X		
Information processing I: formal aspects			60			X			X		
a.a. II: contents analysis			15			X			X		
a.a. III: subject cataloging—according to subject			30			X			X		
a.a. IV: knowledge organization a. Classification			30			X			X		
a.a. V: Authority files			15			30			X		

Time limits in standards and university curricula in 2003/2004

265

APPENDIX (continued)

TABLE 3 (continued)

Time limits in standards and university curricula in 2003/2004

Level of study, Name of subject modules and separate subjects	Standards		University programs								
	Minima MEN	UKA	UW			UJ			UWroc.		
			Ogółem	% MEN	% UKA	...	% MEN	% UKA	...	% MEN	% UKA
Document description–books, etc.			X			45			X		
Document description–periodicals			X			15			X		
Audiovisual and electronic documents			X			30			X		
Document content characteristics			X			75			X		
Information retrieval languages			X			60			X		
Formal description of documents			X			X			60		
Content description of documents			X			X			135		

Time limits in standards and university curricula in 2003/2004

Level of study, Name of subject modules and separate subjects	Standards		University programs								
	Minima MEN	UKA	UW			UJ			UWroc.		
			Ogółem	% MEN	% UKA	...	% MEN	% UKA	...	% MEN	% UKA
Number of obligatory class hours for document description	X	x	**180** **9.3%** **total** **of BA** **17%** prof. subjects of BA	14.8% total 21.8% prof. subjects	15% total of BA 9.3% prof. subjects of BA	**255** **9.9%** **total** **of BA** **15%** prof. subjects of BA	20.9% total of BA 30.9% prof. subjects of BA	21.25% total of BA 30.9% prof. subjects of BA	**195** **8.5%** **total** **of MA** **10.5%** prof. subjects of MA	16% total min. of MA 23.6% prof. subjects of MA	16.25% total of BA 23.6% prof. subjects of BA
Other obligatory subjects concerning documents											
Evaluation and selection of documents			30						60		
Automated central catalogs with elements of retroconversion			30								
Other extracurricular subjects concerning documents and cataloging											
Electronic document			90								
Full-text systems			45								
Introduction to bibliographic formats			30								
Electronic document quality evaluation									30		
Preparing office documents						15					
Document evaluation						15					
Grey literature						15					
Grey literature in archives						15					

Cataloging Education
on the Sunny Side of the Alps

Jerry D. Saye
Alenka Šauperl

SUMMARY. This paper describes the status of library and information science education in Slovenia with emphasis on cataloging and classification courses. The program in the Department of Library and Information Science and Book Studies, Faculty of Arts, University of Ljubljana is reported in detail at both the undergraduate and master's level. Also addressed are requirements to be employed as a librarian in Slovenia, and continuing education opportunities for catalogers. *[Article copies available for a fee from The Haworth Document Delivery Service: 1-800-HAWORTH. E-mail address: <docdelivery@haworthpress.com> Website: <http://www.HaworthPress.com> © 2006 by The Haworth Press, Inc. All rights reserved.]*

KEYWORDS. Library and information science education, library schools, cataloging education, classification education, organization of information education, Slovenia

Jerry D. Saye is Professor, School of Information and Library Science, The University of North Carolina at Chapel Hill, Chapel Hill, NC 27599-3360 (E-mail: saye@ils.unc.edu). He was a Fulbright Scholar, Department of Library and Information Science and Book Studies, Faculty of Arts, University of Ljubljana, Ljubljana, Slovenia, 2003. Alenka Šauperl is Assistant Professor, Department of Library and Information Science and Book Studies, Faculty of Arts, University of Ljubljana, Aškerčeva 2, 1000 Ljubljana, Slovenia (E-mail: alenka.sauperl@FF.Uni-Lj.si).

[Haworth co-indexing entry note]: "Cataloging Education on the Sunny Side of the Alps." Saye, Jerry D., and Alenka Šauperl. Co-published simultaneously in *Cataloging & Classification Quarterly* (The Haworth Information Press, an imprint of The Haworth Press, Inc.) Vol. 41, No. 3/4, 2006, pp. 269-289; and: *Education for Library Cataloging: International Perspectives* (ed: Dajin D. Sun, and Ruth C. Carter) The Haworth Information Press, an imprint of The Haworth Press, Inc., 2006, pp. 269-289. Single or multiple copies of this article are available for a fee from The Haworth Document Delivery Service [1-800-HAWORTH, 9:00 a.m. - 5:00 p.m. (EST). E-mail address: docdelivery@haworthpress.com].

Available online at http://www.haworthpress.com/web/CCQ
© 2006 by The Haworth Press, Inc. All rights reserved.
doi:10.1300/J104v41n03_05

It's a tiny place–there's no disputing that fact. . . . But 'good things come in small packages,' and never was that old chestnut more appropriate than in describing Slovenia (Slovenija).

–Steve Fallon, *Slovenia*

Education for library and information science (LIS) in Slovenia, as in other parts of the world, is a reflection of the higher education structure of that country. Higher education in numerous European countries is currently under review. These national reviews are driven by efforts to conform with the principles stated in the *Bologna Declaration* signed by the European Ministers of Education.[1] European Union (EU) members, forthcoming member countries, those hoping to join the EU in the future, and countries who desire to have their educational systems conform to the EU's are engaged in this process. Slovenia, which became a full EU member on May 1, 2004, is actively involved in these reviews. Recognition of the increasing interdependence of EU members underlies the *Bologna Declaration.* EU members, and even those countries which will remain outside of the EU, temporarily if not permanently, seek to have educational structures that are in structural agreement.

A number of elements of the new educational system are new to European higher education, although some are very familiar features of American higher education. One is the availability of easily readable and comparable degrees. Another is a system of two levels of higher education–undergraduate and graduate. Admission to graduate status would be achieved only after completion of the undergraduate level. The graduate-level study would include both master's and doctoral degrees. Another important element of the new system is the association of courses with credits. The introduction of the use of credits is intended to foster the mobility of students and faculty and provide for an equitable way to evaluate the scope of their work.

Before examining the state of library education in Slovenia, and specifically education for work in cataloging, we should address a very basic question. Where is Slovenia? First, there is a very important distinction that must be made. Slovenia is not Slovakia. As a saying on a t-shirt for sale in Europe once read. "It's Slovenia, not Slovakia! There is a difference." Slovakia is one of two countries, the other being the Czech Republic, created from the former Czechoslovakia. Slovenia, on the other hand, was the northernmost republic of the former Yugoslavia. Slovenia is located south of Austria on the southern side of the Alps, north of Croatia, and west of Hungary (Figure 1). Although it is on the

FIGURE 1. Slovenia in Europe

Adriatic Sea, Slovenia has only 29 miles of coastline. Most of the area to the west of Slovenia is the portion of Italy located on the eastern side of the Adriatic.

In 1991, Slovenia was the first of the Yugoslav republics to achieve independence. Its capital, Ljubljana (pronounced Lyee-ub-lyee-ana), is also the country's largest city (pop. 280,000). The tragedy that befell the other republics of Yugoslavia in the 1990s did not occur in Slovenia. Its war for independence lasted but 10 days. Unlike the other former Yugoslav republics, Slovenia's population is very homogeneous–88 percent Slovene with no other ethnic group exceeding two percent of the population.[2] This was a major factor in its ability to remain free from the ethnic violence that ravaged the other republics in the 1990s. The Slovenes are justifiably proud to be, for the first time in their history, an independent country. Prior to becoming part of Yugoslavia, Slovenia had been part of the Austrian Empire since the 14th century.

Slovenia is one of the smallest countries in Europe. It covers 7,768 square miles (compared to 3,696,000 sq. mi. for the U.S.). This makes Slovenia slightly smaller than the state of New Jersey (8,722 sq. mi.). Slovenia has a population of 1,948,250 compared to the population of 262,300,000 for the U.S. Although nearly the size of New Jersey, New Jersey's population (pop. 8,414,350) is four times that of Slovenia.[3]

HIGHER EDUCATION

Now that we know that Slovenia is not Slovakia, where it is, and have a little idea of its size, a quick review of its system of higher education is in order. We have just compared Slovenia to the U.S. and New Jersey in terms of size and population. A similar comparison might be useful in gaining a sense of scale of their higher education structure. The U.S. has 3,658 institutions of higher education and New Jersey has 43.[4] Slovenia, on the other hand, has three universities—the University of Ljubljana, the University of Maribor, and the University of Primorska located in Koper.

Higher education in Slovenia is at both the undergraduate and graduate levels (master's and doctoral). Undergraduate education, as in the U.S., is currently a four-year program, although this possibly may change under ongoing higher education review. Work at the undergraduate level is most often undertaken through coursework and a thesis defense. Medicine and some other professions do not have a thesis defense as a requirement. At the master's and doctoral level, however, independent research and the production of a thesis or dissertation are the elements used to evaluate a student's work. Formal coursework plays little to no role at the graduate level.

FORMAL LIS EDUCATION

Education for many, if not most, professions in Europe, including LIS, takes place at the undergraduate level. This differs greatly from American LIS education where a post-baccalaureate degree has been the norm since the 1920s. Formal LIS education in Slovenia is offered at only one of the three universities—the University of Ljubljana. There, the Department of Library and Information Science and Book Studies (Oddelek za bibliotekarstvo, informacijsko znanost in knjigarstvo),[5] or as it is also known, BINK, is part of the university's Faculty of Arts. Like many European universities, the University of Ljubljana is not situated on a campus. Rather, the faculties—the American equivalent of schools of university colleges—are distributed throughout the city. The Faculty of Arts, located within walking distance of the city center of Ljubljana, is but a few blocks from the National and University Library (Narodna in univerzitetna knjižnica) (NUK)—Slovenia's equivalent of a combined Library of Congress and university library. BINK occupies part of the top floor of the six-story Faculty of Arts building which provides space for classrooms, faculty offices, and its departmental library.

The department admits 50 undergraduate and 15 graduate students each year. Unlike many American LIS programs, the vast majority of its students are full-time. Although there is a part-time student cohort, full-time and part-time students are not co-enrolled in the same courses. The part-time program is treated separately from the full-time program.

The academic year consists of two terms–Winter (October to January) and Summer (February to June). They are roughly comparable to the Fall and Spring terms at most American universities, although the months associated with these terms in America often differ. The department does not offer courses during the summer. Unlike most American colleges and universities, the majority of courses offered within the department extend across both semesters of an academic year, rather than beginning and ending in one semester. Consequently, most courses begin in October and end in May. This is similar to the academic course structure of many American secondary schools. Classes end in May followed by a month of exams in June. Exams for a course are given multiple times in that month. Another opportunity to take exams occurs in September for courses taken the previous academic year.

Undergraduate education in Slovenia is structured very differently from undergraduate education in the U.S. When undergraduates choose a field of specialty their coursework is generally confined to courses in that field and perhaps a few courses from allied or cognate fields. Thus, students do not take the panoply of courses in the liberal arts and sciences that are so common in American undergraduate education. Rather, they are totally focused on their chosen field.

UNDERGRADUATE LIS PROGRAM

Undergraduates in BINK can elect one of two study options. They can take the single-subject program in library and information science or they can elect the two-subject program in which one subject is library science. In the two-subject program students do not take the courses in psychology and information science taken by single-subject students. Rather, they take a second field of study offered by the Faculty of Arts. The distribution of single-subject and two-subject students is 3 to 2, 30 each year in the single-subject and 20 in the double-subject program. Students in both programs earn a B.A. in Library Science.

This virtually exclusive concentration on library and information science for the undergraduate degree is a major change that occurred in the 1996-1997 academic year. Prior to that, students were able to take library science as either a major, or as a minor in combination with programs offered by other departments of the Faculty of Arts. That previous program was similar to the major and minor structure American undergraduates experience today, although seldom in the field of library science. The major difference was that the combination with other majors and minors was limited to other programs in the Faculty of Arts rather than with the offerings of all of the University of Ljubljana's faculties.

Students in both the one- or two-subject programs take a prescribed set of courses. Unlike American higher education, there are no elective courses. The concept of elective courses is a totally alien one. In addition to courses being prescribed, the year of study in which courses are to be taken is also set. Thus, a specific course will have as its students all first-year, or all second-year, etc., students.

Students in the single-subject program take courses in 33 subject areas plus practical work. Table 1 displays the titles of subjects covered by BINK's curriculum. One might notice that some of the titles may not be as current as one might expect. This can be accounted for by academic bureaucracy. The process of changing a course name or adding a new course is very difficult and takes approximately two years. This period is considerably longer than that experienced at most American universities. Accordingly, innovative instructors frequently revise the topics and scope of coverage of courses for currency, rather than initiate the formal course change process.

Table 1 displays the subject title, year(s) in which a course(s) in the subject area is offered, and the number of hours per week the course meets. This grid shows a total of 33 subject areas distributed across four years. When examined in terms of a subject area being offered as separate courses in different years a total of 47 courses are offered across the four years. This ranges from ten courses in Year 1 to thirteen in Year 3. Most courses are offered for a total of 60 hours of instruction for the year, although a few are 30 hours in duration and several are 90 hours. In addition to these formal courses, students take a total of 160 hours of practical work–80 hours during the Winter Break in both Years 2 and 3. A graduation thesis is a requirement for the undergraduate degree in addition to the successful completion of all coursework.

The language of instruction in BINK is Slovene. However, virtually all faculty in the department have an excellent mastery of English, as do

TABLE 1. BA in Library Science

Subjects	Hours/week				Total Hours	Total Courses
	Year I.	Year II.	Year III.	Year IV.		
1. Basics of Librarianship	2				60	1
2. History of Librarianship	2				60	1
3. History of Printing and Books				1	30	1
4. Codicology			2		60	1
5. Protection and Repair of Books				2	60	1
6. Contemporary Organization of Librarianship		2	2	2	180	3
7. Public Libraries		1			30	1
8. School Libraries		1			30	1
9. University Libraries			1		30	1
10. Special Libraries			1		30	1
11. Library User Studies				2	60	1
12. Library Marketing				2	60	1
13. Library Management				2	60	1
14. Publishing and Book Selling	2	2	2	2	240	4
15. Bibliometrics			2		60	1
16. Comparative Librarianship				2	60	1
17. Cataloging	2	2	2	2	240	4
18. Bibliography	2				60	1
19. Classification		2	2		120	2
20. Documentation Systems				2	60	1
21. Comunication with Library Users			2		60	1
22. Cognitive Psychology			2	2	120	2
23. Developmental Psychology		2			60	1
24. Information Technology	3				90	1
25. Library Automation		3			90	1
26. Introduction to Information Science	2				60	1
27. Databases I		2			60	1
28. Databases II			2		60	1
29. Computer Communication				2	60	1
30. Introduction into Scientific Work	2	2			120	2
31. Development and Systematics of Science	2	2			120	2
32. Sociology of Mass Media			2		60	1
33. English Language	2	2			120	2
34. Second foreign language			2		60	1
Practical Work		80	80		160	2
Total hours	**21**	**23**	**24**	**23**	**2,890**	
Total courses	**10**	**13**	**14**	**12**		**49**

Cataloging, classification, and documentation courses

the students. Students in Slovenia take four years of English in both primary and secondary school. An additional two years of English language instruction, in Years 1 and 2, is required for BINK undergraduate students.

The department's instructional staff includes full-time and part-time faculty. Faculty, both full-time and adjunct, are required to hold doctoral degrees. However, this is not always possible. When the department has no one available to teach a course, an exception can be made. This exception must be granted by the University Senate and it allows the non-doctoral degree instructor to teach a course(s) and give exams. Currently this exception applies to two members of the BINK faculty. The shortage of instructors with doctoral degrees is mostly attributable to the number of potential instructors being limited by language. Unlike the U.S. where faculty can be recruited from throughout the 50 states and abroad, Slovene university departments are essentially limited in their selection of faculty to those who speak Slovene. Although some members of the BINK faculty earned their doctoral degrees from universities in the U.S. and Croatia, they were raised in Slovenia. The limited number of persons in the world who speak Slovene (approx. 4 million) greatly limits the pool of doctoral holders. Many of those not living in Slovenia live in adjacent regions in Austria and Italy. Coincidently, following Ljubljana, the city in the world with the largest Slovene population is Cleveland, Ohio.

Students in undergraduate programs, as in most universities in the U.S., are not allowed to teach their peers. Master's students can teach practical exercises but not courses. Thus, for cataloging courses a master's student might supervise practical exercises using cataloging tools.

The size of the BINK faculty has increased significantly over the past decade. Ten years ago BINK had three full-time faculty. Since then, two faculty have retired but seven dynamic new faculty members have been added, bringing the total full-time faculty to eight (an increase of 260 percent). Two of the new faculty now cover the area of cataloging and classification.

The cataloging and classification component of the BINK curriculum consists of three subjects–cataloging, classification, and documentation systems, i.e., abstracting and indexing. The cataloging portion of these subjects consists of four courses, Cataloging I to IV–one offered in each of the four years of study. Classification is offered as two courses, Classification I and II, one each in Years Two and Three. Finally, documentation systems, a single course, is offered to fourth-year students. Together, these seven courses account for 420 hours of instruction or 14 percent of the total course time. If one includes Database I and Database II as part of an organization of information course component, the total number of courses increases to nine, and the total hours to 540. For the purposes of this paper we will concentrate on only the seven cataloging, classification, and documentation systems courses.

The cataloging subject area begins with an introduction to cataloging in the first-year course and progresses to very advanced coverage in the fourth year. The methods of instruction are lecture and practical exercises. The topics covered are:

Year 1: Library materials, e.g., monographs, serials, etc.
Technical services: Acquisitions. Catalogs: union, card, online. Stacks and shelving. Circulation. Weeding.
Cataloging: Authorship, main and other types of entries. Naming authors from antiquity to the present day. Development of cataloging rules. ISBD(G) and (M) to Area 4.

Year 2: Continuation of ISBD(M) areas 5-8, main entry. Headings for corporate and geographical bodies, royalty and church officials. Main entries for non-European authors, corporate bodies, etc. UNIMARC. COMARC. COBISS (Co-operative Online System and Services).

Year 3: Paris Principles. Copenhagen Conference, 1969. ISBN(A), ISBD(CM), ISBN(ER), ISBD(NBM) and ISBD(PM).

Year 4: Cataloging of more complicated documents.

The classification two-course sequence covers the following topics:

Year 2: Catalogs. Principles of classification for libraries. Subject analysis. Universal Decimal Classification (UDC). General Slovene Subject Headings (GSSH).

Year 3: Dewey Decimal Classification (DDC) and Library of Congress Classification (LCC). Overview of Colon Classification and Bliss Bibliographic Classification. Theory of thesaurus construction and maintenance.

Lastly, the one course in documentation covers:

Year 4: History and development of documentation in Slovenia and abroad. Theory of summarization. Abstracting. Indexing (preparing back of the book indexes). ISO Standards for information and documentation. Structure of documents.

In addition to these courses students can obtain experience in cataloging and classification as part of their two 80-hour practical work experiences (in Years 2 and 3). Some libraries also have particular cataloging, classification, or collection organization problems that can be, and are, theoretically addressed in graduation theses.

The difference in cataloging and classification course requirements for single-subject program students and two-subject students is limited to one course. Single-subject students take all seven cataloging and classification courses. Two-subject students take all four courses in cataloging and Classification I (Year 2), but do not take Classification II (Year 3). Both groups also take Documentation Systems (Year 4).

As one would expect, material covered in these courses reflects Slovenia's heritage and its presence in Europe. One noticeable difference in the coverage of cataloging is the seeming lack of cataloging rules. There is no AACR2 or a Slovene single document equivalent of national cataloging rules. Rather, multiple sources are used to provide coverage comparable to AACR2. The ISBDs are used for the principles of description. They are quickly translated into Slovene and re-published in Ljubljana. Still in use are two older works: *Pravilnik i priručnik za izradbu abecednih kataloga. #Dio #2, Kataložni opis. [Catalog rules and handbook for preparing author catalogs. Part 2. Bibliographic description]*[6] and *Abecedni imenski catalog [Author catalog]*.[7] The latter work and *Pravilnik i priručnik za izradbu abecednih kataloga. #Dio #1, Odrednice i redalice [Catalog rules and handbook for preparing author catalogs. Part 1. Headings]*[8] are used for heading work. Although these publications are somewhat dated, a number of their rules remain valid. To assist catalogers, two manuals were published to simplify the use of the rules that are scattered in multiple publications: *Prekat: priročnik za enostavno uporabo katalogizacijskih pravil [Handbook for the simple use of cataloging rules]*[9] and *Značka: priročnik za določanje značnic pri katalogizaciji [Handbook for determining headings for catalogs]*.[10] These manuals provide the rules and the source(s) of the rules.

Clearly, the scope of and depth of coverage in the four cataloging courses far surpasses that encountered by LIS students in the U.S. and Canada. In fact, as of 2001, only 23 of the 56 schools (41 percent) with ALA-accredited master's degree programs in the U.S. and Canada required a cataloging course of their students. Twenty-one schools (38 percent) required a more general organization of information course, while 12 schools (21 percent) required neither.[11] Thus Slovene LIS students are well prepared to assume a cataloging role in whatever institution they may be employed.

The content covered in the four cataloging courses is also far more diverse than that offered in many American schools. In Slovenia the coverage of description includes serials, electronic resources, printed music, and archival, non-book, and cartographic materials. Many American schools, even in advanced cataloging courses, pay minimal attention to varied information carrier formats. While we cannot easily assess Slovene students' overall mastery of this content, the scope of descriptive cataloging coverage is clearly greater than that taken, or even offered, to most American students. Similarly, the exposure to the range of technical services functions presented to all Slovene LIS students surpasses the limited technical services coverage for American LIS students.

American LIS students who take courses in cataloging and classification are most frequently presented with the DDC and LCC. All LIS students in BINK receive instruction in these two classification systems as well as in the classification system most directly relevant to their work in libraries–UDC. Overall, coverage of classification offered to Slovene students exceeds that offered to most American students. Again, for subject heading work, Slovene students concentrate on the controlled vocabulary of most direct concern to them–GSSH, although they do study LCSH and Sears subject headings to a limited degree. Similarly, when American students take a cataloging course, they become familiar with the controlled vocabulary of greatest use in the U.S.–Library of Congress Subject Headings (LCSH).

In terms of the role of cataloging and classification courses in their curriculum, Slovene students clearly have a more extensive coverage of this aspect of librarianship (7 courses) than do their American counterparts. We believe that it is safe to assume that even those American students who take an introductory cataloging course, whether as a requirement or an elective, are unlikely to follow it with an advanced cataloging course. Thus, we are confident in stating that the average Slovene LIS undergraduate has a far greater exposure to cataloging and classification than does an American LIS graduate student. The greater coverage of cataloging and classification is reminiscent of its role in the earlier days of American LIS education.

One element that has become very noticeable in American LIS education is metadata. At BINK, the organization of electronic resources is covered in the cataloging course taken in Year 3. It, however, addresses the organization of these resources from a more traditional cataloging approach as articulated in ISBD(ER). Metadata is covered briefly in the Database I course. At present there is no other coverage of metadata in the curriculum. Although no Slovene libraries are known to be using metadata, this does raise the "chicken or the egg" question of which should come first–instruction in metadata or its use by the profession?

TEXTS

In Slovenia, educators in all areas of LIS face a major problem not shared with their counterparts in the U.S. and many European countries–a lack of textbooks written in the language of instruction. As a country with a population of less than 2 million, there is an insufficient market for commercial publishers to publish texts in Slovene. Consequently, instructors find it necessary to write the texts they need to support instruction in their courses. At BINK, some instructors write their texts, which are then published by the department. Beyond their courses, there is little, if any, additional market in Slovenia or elsewhere for these texts.

The texts and readings used in all seven cataloging and classification courses are listed in the Appendix. When examining these works one sees that some have been translated into Slovene, e.g., ISBDs, others were written in Slovene, and a few were written in English. All four cataloging courses and the two classification courses use texts written by the course instructors–professors Petek and Šauperl. The documentation course uses as one of its texts an English language monograph–Cremmins' *The Art of Abstracting.*

The use of instructor-written texts would be unusual in most American LIS programs. Its occurrence in cataloging and classification courses at BINK exemplifies the difficulty encountered by a small country that has a language which is not widely used. American instructors and students may not realize how fortunate they are to be in schools that use a dominant language which has a large market base. This makes works published in English in the U.S., Great Britain, and other countries available for student use. Imagine the problem that would be faced by American faculty and students if, conversely, American instructors could choose from only texts written in German, or had to write their own texts in English.

MASTER'S PROGRAM

The master's program at BINK was approved in 1996. The program has three specializations: librarianship, informatics, and publishing. Entry into the master's program requires the diploma in LIS, two years of practice, and knowledge of two foreign languages, one of which must be English.[12] These requirements are more demanding than those typically required for American LIS programs in terms of practice, language skills, and even in terms of earned degree. The Slovene diploma in LIS has greater requirements than does the typical American baccalaureate degree. Absent from admission requirements are two frequent requirements for American graduate program admissions–letters of reference, and any equivalent of the American Graduate Record Examination. The Slovene requirement of two years of practice harkens to a requirement of past decades for entry into many LIS doctoral programs in the U.S. That practice requirement began to disappear in the 1970s and no longer exists.

A number of subjects are covered by the master's program including the cataloging of library materials and theory of classification. As is common in European master's programs, few courses are offered for master's students. Rather, the program is primarily research focused, leading to the production of a master's thesis. Given that the undergraduate degree is the terminal degree for most Slovene professional librarians, the attainment of a master's degree is somewhat unusual and, thus, is given special recognition. When one has been awarded the master's, the lowercase abbreviation "mag" (for "magister") is placed before one's name, e.g., mag, Polona Vilar, similar to the use of "dr." before the name of those with doctoral degrees.

NATIONAL INFRASTRUCTURE SYSTEMS SUPPORT FOR CATALOGING

An institution with special importance for cataloging work is the Institute of Information Science (Institut informacijskih znanosti or IZUM). IZUM is located in Maribor, approximately 80 miles northeast of Ljubljana. Among the responsibilities of IZUM, the following have a significant impact on cataloging:

- co-ordination of the development and operation of the shared bibliographic system and services,

- co-ordination of the development and application of standards for computer support to meet the requirements of the shared bibliographic system and services,
- software development and maintenance to meet the requirements of the shared bibliographic system and services,
- determination of the suitability of library staff for shared cataloging purposes, in co-operation with NUK,
- organization of professional training and counseling in the fields covered by the national shared bibliographic system.[13]

Among its varied activities, IZUM provides Slovene librarians with an essential shared cataloging tool. Shared cataloging is part of COBISS: "The Virtual Library of Slovenia." COBISS is the acronym for Co-operative Online Bibliographic Information System & Services (Kooperativni online bibliografski sistem in servisi). For Slovene catalogers, shared cataloging had its birth when the Association of the Yugoslav National Libraries adopted that approach in 1987. IZUM assumed responsibility for its development and operation. In 1991 the name COBISS was adopted. Fifty-five libraries were affiliated with COBISS at the time of Yugoslavia's dissolution. The libraries in the republics outside of Slovenia discontinued their affiliation with COBISS at that time. Most have since resumed collaboration with COBISS as their republics also develop their own information systems based on the COBISS platform.

Catalogers throughout Slovenia use COBISS to input cataloging using COMARC. Catalog records for the holdings of Slovene libraries are available using the COBIB.SI union bibliographic/catalog database (http://cobiss.izum.si/scripts/cobiss?ukaz=getid&lang=win&lani=en). Catalogers must obtain a license in order to be allowed to contribute cataloging records to COBIB. Licenses are granted after the completion of a series of preparatory courses offered by IZUM and NUK and after good quality cataloging is demonstrated in a test environment. This marks a major difference cataloging with COBISS and cataloging using OCLC.

COBISS also provides Slovene libraries with access to OCLC's databases including access to WorldCat's bibliographic data. Currently 272 libraries use the COBISS shared cataloging system. The bibliographic catalog database has 2,400,000 master records and 6,200,000 bibliographic records in local library databases.[14]

OTHER PREPARATION FOR LIBRARY WORK

Persons who possess a secondary school diploma or a two-year university degree can work in libraries but are required to take a professional national examination in order to be considered qualified for such work. Persons who obtain this credential hold paraprofessional positions such as circulation and routine technical services tasks in Slovene libraries.

In addition to formal educational offerings for librarians, new library employees also receive informal on-the-job instruction. All new employees are assigned a supervisor. Those with a high school degree are assigned a supervisor for three months. Those with a two-year university degree have one for six months, while a professional librarian has a supervisor assigned for one year. While at first it might seem odd that those with the least experience are supervised the shortest period of time, the time allocated for supervision is in direct proportion to the level of responsibility of work undertaken, i.e., lowest level paraprofessional, the least time vs. professional librarian, the most time. A major difference from the American experience, which sometimes may involve supervisory assistance, is that this period of supervision in Slovenia is mandated by law. During the period of supervision, additional training outside the library is rare. In order to provide for a more comprehensive overview of library work than they are able to provide, some smaller libraries request that a larger library provide assistance in supervising a new employee for part of the supervisory period.

CONTINUING EDUCATION

There are no continuing education programs designed specifically for catalogers in Slovenia. The conference of the Union of Associations of Slovene Librarians (Zveze bibliotekarskih društev Slovenije, or ZBDS), however, does provide for individual presentations on thematic issues that can, and do, include cataloging topics. No informal lines of communication for catalogers, such as listservers or online discussion groups, exist in Slovenia. Rather, catalogers can communicate by publishing papers in *Knjinžica* [*Library*] (the journal of ZBDS), although this is not a frequent occurrence. However, there exist invisible colleges of catalogers that allow them to assist each other.

BINK does not provide any instructional programs for library support staff. NUK, IZUM, and other non-library institutions offer continuing education programs that can provide useful knowledge and skills for librarians. Topics covered might include, but are not limited to, writing papers for *Knjinžica,* management topics, computer software training, etc. Libraries that place emphasis on personnel development often pay their employees' expenses for one- or two-day courses.

LANGUAGE REQUIREMENTS OF CATALOGERS

One qualification frequently cited when searching for a cataloger is language skills. A normal requirement for all librarians working in bilingual areas (those areas of Slovenia that border another country) is either Italian or Hungarian. This is not as important in the areas that border on Croatia given the strong similarities between the Slovene and Croatian languages. Despite its potential usefulness, knowledge of German is not as essential, given the barrier that the Alps pose between Slovenia and Austria. English, German, and other languages may be required for some positions. If not required, knowledge of these languages will likely give such an applicant a competitive advantage. Recently, when libraries searched for a cataloger, they have often indicated a preference for a person with a four-year university degree. Considering the time and expense associated with taking courses and exams for licensing, trying to find a cataloger with the a higher degree makes very good sense.

DEMAND FOR CATALOGERS

Searching for a licensed cataloger can be challenging for a library. There are both cultural and economic reasons that underlie this difficulty. Slovenes are not noted for changing employers, whether frequently or even a few times, in their careers. This trait is not exclusive to the library profession, but is common throughout Slovene society. An economic consideration is also a factor. There is very little variation in salaries. Accordingly, there is little economic incentive to seek another position. These factors contribute to a lack of turnover in positions and, thus, a lack of applicants for vacant positions.

FINAL THOUGHTS

As we have seen, cataloging and classification education in Slovenia has some common features with American library and information science education. As one might expect, Slovenes share even more common features with European LIS education. The Slovene system additionally has strengths and challenges that are somewhat unique to the Slovene experience. It reflects a small, very independent country with a unique language, and borders shared with other countries, all with yet different languages. Slovenia has a high literacy rate, a solid library infrastructure, and a healthy LIS education program. Technologically the country has not only kept pace with its former fellow republics of Yugoslavia, but has far surpassed them in economic and technological development. All told, in many ways, Slovenia is truly a gem long hidden.

NOTES

1. European Ministers of Education. *The Bologna Declaration of 19 June 1999.* [online]. [cited 3 January 2004]. Available from World Wide Web: (http://www. bologna-berlin2003.de/pdf/bologna_declaration.pdf).
2. Republic of Slovenia. Census ethnic data. [online]. [cited 8 March 2004]. Available from World Wide Web: (http://www.legacyrus.com/library/CensusData_Various/ sloveniaCensusData.htm).
3. *Infopedia.* [CD-ROM]. ver. 2.0. No place: SoftKey International, 1995.
4. U.S. National Center for Education Statistics. 2001. *Digest of Educational Statistics Tables and Figures, 2001.* [online] [cited 3 March 2004]. Available from World Wide Web: (http://nces.ed.gov/pubsearch/pubsinfo.asp?pubid=2002130).
5. Faculty of Arts, University of Ljubljana, Department of Library and Information Science and Book Studies. [online]. [cited 13 January 2004]. Available from World Wide Web: (http://www.ff.uni-lj.si/biblio/anglesko.htm).
6. Eva Verona. *Pravilnik i priručnik za izradbu abecednih kataloga. #Dio #2, Kataložni opis.* Zagreb: Hrvatsko bibliotekarsko društvo, 1983.
7. Pavle, Kalan. *Abecedni imenski catalog.* Nova izd. Ljubljana: Društvo bibliotekarjev Slovenije: Narodna in univerzitetna knjižnica, 1967.
8. Eva Verona. *Pravilnik i priručnik za izradbu abecednih kataloga. #Dio #1, Odrednice i.* 2. izmijenjeno izd. Zagreb: Hrvatsko bibliotekarsko društvo, 1986.
9. Zlata Dimec, Matjaž Hočevar, and Irena Kavčič, eds. *Prekat: priročnik za enostavno uporabo katalogizacijskih pravil.* Ljubljana: Narodna in univerzitetna knjižnica, 2000.
10. Zlata Dimec, Irena Kavčič, eds. *Značka: priročnik za določanje značnic pri katalogizaciji.* Ljubljana: Narodna in univerzitetna knjižnica, 2001.
11. Jerry D. Saye. Where are we and how did we get here? or, The changing place of cataloging in the library and information science curriculum: causes and consequences. *Cataloging & Classification Quarterly,* 34, nos. 1/2 (2002) p. 130.

12. Irena Marinko. Introduction to library and information science in Slovenia. *Journal of Education for Library and Information Science*, 40, no. 4 (1999): 299-305.
13. IZUM. *Institute of Information Science, IZUM.* "About IZUM." [online]. [cited 8 March 2004]. Available from World Wide Web: (http://www.izum.si/en/izum_eng.htm).
14. COBISS. *COBISS: virtual library of Slovenia.* "About COBISS." [online]. [cited 8 March 2004]. Available from World Wide Web: (http://cobiss.izum.si/cobiss_eng.html).

BIBLIOGRAPHY

COBISS. *COBISS: virtual library of Slovenia.* [online]. [cited 8 March 2004]. Available from World Wide Web: (http://cobiss.izum.si/cobiss_eng.html).

Dimec, Zlata, Hočevar, Matjaž, and Kavčič, Irena, eds. *Prekat: priročnik za enostavno uporabo katalogizacijskih pravil.* Ljubljana: Narodna in univerzitetna knjižnica, 2000.

Dimec, Zlata, Kavčič, Irena, eds. *Značka: priročnik za določanje značnic pri katalogizaciji.* Ljubljana: Narodna in univerzitetna knjižnica, 2001.

Faculty of Arts, University of Ljubljana, Department of Library and Information Science and Book Studies. [online]. [cited 13 January 2004]. Available from World Wide Web: (http://www.ff.uni-lj.si/biblio/anglesko.htm).

European Ministers of Education. *The Bologna Declaration of 19 June 1999.* [online]. [cited 3 January 2004]. Available from World Wide Web: (http://www.bologna-berlin2003.de/pdf/bologna_declaration.pdf).

Fallon, Steve. *Slovenia.* 2nd ed. Oakland, Calif.: Lonely Planet, 1998.

Infopedia. [CD-ROM]. ver. 2.0. No place: SoftKey International, 1995.

IZUM. *Institute of Information Science, IZUM.* [online]. [cited 8 March 2004]. Available from World Wide Web: (http://www.izum.si/en/izum_eng.htm).

Kalan, Pavle. *Abecedni imenski catalog.* Nova izd. Ljubljana: Društvo bibliotekarjev Slovenije: Narodna in univerzitetna knjižnica, 1967.

Marinko, Irena. Introduction to library and information science in Slovenia. *Journal of Education for Library and Information Science* 40, no. 4 (1999): 299-305.

Republic of Slovenia. Census ethnic data. [online]. [cited 8 March 2004]. Available from World Wide Web: (http://www.legacyrus.com/library/CensusData_Various/sloveniaCensusData.htm).

Saye, Jerry D. Where are we and how did we get here? or, The changing place of cataloging in the library and information science curriculum: causes and consequences. *Cataloging & Classification Quarterly* 34, nos. 1/2 (2002): 121-143.

U.S. National Center for Education Statistics. *Digest of Educational Statistics Tables and Figures, 2001.* [online]. [cited 3 March 2004]. Available from World Wide Web: (http://nces.ed.gov/pubsearch/pubsinfo.asp?pubid=2002130).

Verona, Eva. *Pravilnik i priručnik za izradbu abecednih kataloga. #Dio #1, Odrednice i.* 2. izmijenjeno izd. Zagreb: Hrvatsko bibliotekarsko društvo, 1986.

Verona, Eva. *Pravilnik i priručnik za izradbu abecednih kataloga. #Dio #2, Kataložni opis.* Zagreb: Hrvatsko bibliotekarsko društvo, 1983.

APPENDIX

Course texts and readings

[Texts are listed in the order in which they appear in the course syllabus]

[Commentary in brackets by the authors]

Cataloging–Year 1

Osnove knjižničarstva. Ljubljana, 1987. [an old textbook on librarianship, quite outdated]

Poličnik-Čermelj, Tereza. *Pridobivanje gradiva in inventarizacija.* Ljubljana, 1994. [a new source on acquisitions, well written]

Korže-Strajnar, Ančka. Delovni pripomočki za organizacijo poslovanja knjižnic. *Obvestila republiške matične službe.* 1988, št.1. [a paper on organizing library services]

Sporazum za medbibliotečno izposojo. Obvestila republiške matične službe. 1988, št.2, str. 25-34. [an agreement for inter-library loan among Slovene libraries]

Petek, Marija. Nekaj najpomembnejših pravilnikov za katalogizacijo. *Zbornik razprav:* 10 let Oddelka za bibliotekarstvo. Ljubljana, 1998. [an overview of cataloging rules]

Abecedni imenski katalog. Nova izd. Ljubljana, 1967. [cataloging rules]

Verona, Eva. Pravilnik I priručnik za izradbu abecednih kataloga. Zagreb, 1983-1986. 1-2. [cataloging rules]

Verona, Eva: Pravilnik i priručnik za izradbu abecednih kataloga. Razlage strokovnih izrazov in stvarni kazali. Ljubljana, 1998. [a Slovenian index to the rules above which was written in Croatian]

ISBD(G). Predelana izd. Ljubljana, 1997. [cataloging rules]

ISBD(M). Predelana izd. Ljubljana, 1997. [cataloging rules]

Cataloging–Year 2

Same texts as Year 1

Cataloging–Year 3

Petek, Marija. Nekaj najpomembnejših pravilnikov za katalogizacijo. *Zbornik razprav:* 10 let Oddelka za bibliotekarstvo. Ljubljana, 1998. [an overview of cataloging rules]

Abecedni imenski katalog. Nova izd. Ljubljana, 1967. [cataloging rules]

APPENDIX (continued)

Verona, Eva. Pravilnik I priručnik za izradbu abecednih kataloga. Zagreb, 1983-1986. 1-2. [cataloging rules]
Verona, Eva. Pravilnik i priručnik za izradbu abecednih kataloga. Razlage strokovnih izrazov in stvarni kazali. Ljubljana, 1998 ISBD(G). Predelana izd. Ljubljana, 1997. [cataloging rules]
ISBD(M). Predelana izd. Ljubljana, 1997 Oblika in struktura korporativnih značnic. Ljubljana, 1998. [cataloging rules]
ISBD(NBM). Predelava izd. Ljubljana, 1997. [cataloging rules]
ISBD(CM). Predelana izd. Ljubljana, 1999. [cataloging rules]
ISBD(PM). 2. predelana izd. Ljubljana, 1998. [cataloging rules]
ISBD(A). 2. predelana izd. Ljubljana, 1997. [cataloging rules]
ISBD(ER). Predelana izd. Ljubljana, 1999 (v tisku). [cataloging rules]
Načela, sprejeta na mednarodni konferenci o katalogizacijskih načelih v Parizu, oktobra 1961. V: Knjižnica. Letn.5 (1961) št 1/4, str. 110-117. [The *Paris Principles* in Slovene]
Dimec, Zlata. Normativna kontrola iz preteklosti v prihodnost. V: Zbornik razprav: 10 let Oddelka za bibliotekarstvo. Ljubljana, 1998. [A paper on authority control]
Names of Persons: national usages for entry in catalogues / [International Federation of Library Associations and Institutions, IFLA Universal Bibliographic Control and International MARC Programme, deutsche Bibliothek, Frankfurt am Main]. 4th, rev. and enl. ed. München [etc.]: Saur, 1996. (UBCIM publications; N. S., Vol. 16). [cataloging rules]
Načela, sprejeta na mednarodni konferenci o katalogizacijskih načelih v Parizu, oktobra 1961. V: Knjižnica. Letn. 5 (1961) št. 1/4, str. 110-117. [A paper on the *Paris Principles*]

Cataloging–Year 4

No texts

Classification I–Year 2

UDC tables
Šauperl, A. *Klasifikacija knjižničnega gradiva*. Ljubljana: Filozofska fakulteta. Oddelek za bibliotekarstvo, 2000. [text]
Splošni slovenski geslovnik. Ljubljana: NUK, 2002. [GSSH Slovene subject headings]

Classification II–Year 3

Šauperl, A. *Klasifikacija knjižničnega gradiva*. Ljubljana: Filozofska fakulteta. Oddelek za bibliotekarstvo, 2000. [text]
Classification schedules and tools

Documentation–Year 4

Cremmins, E.T. *The Art of Abstracting*. ISI Press Philadelphia 1996. [text]
Standardi SIST–ISO za področje dokumentacije. Standards ISO. [standards]
Članki iz revij *Knjižnica* in *Obvestila a COBISS* (npr. Kabaj M., Spanring J.). [selected papers from *Knjižnica* and *Obvestila a COBISS*]
Zbrani prispevki iz revije *Informatologija*. Zagreb (npr. Milas-Bracović M. Topolovec itd) in drugi najnovejši prispevki po UDK 001.814:002. [selected papers from *Informatologija*, a Croatian information science journal]

Education for Cataloging
in Spanish Universities:
A Descriptive and Critical Study

Rafael Ruiz-Perez
Emilio Delgado López-Cózar

SUMMARY. Objective: This is a critical descriptive study of the situation of cataloging as an academic discipline within Library and Information Science studies in Spain. Material and methods: The descriptive analysis of the sectional contents of the general and specific guidelines of the degrees of *Diplomado* (three-year degree) and *Licenciado* (five-year degree) in LIS and the curricular programs of the Spanish university schools or departments. Variables analyzed: The denomination and content descriptors of the course offerings and credit hours. The test-retest method was used, with a qualitative processing of data. Results: General data is given about the studies in LIS: their introduction, the universities that offer them, and the degrees awarded. Cataloging is considered an obligatory core subject matter, and is represented by several

Rafael Ruiz-Perez, PhD, is Professor of Library and Information Science Documentation, Universidad de Granada, Facultad de Biblioteconomía y Documentación, Campus Universitario de Cartuja, 18071 - Granada, Spain (E-mail: rruiz@ugr.es). Emilio Delgado López-Cózar, PhD, is Professor of Library and Information Science Documentation, Universidad de Granada, Facultad de Biblioteconomía y Documentación, Campus Universitario de Cartuja, 18071 - Granada, Spain.

[Haworth co-indexing entry note]: "Education for Cataloging in Spanish Universities: A Descriptive and Critical Study." Ruiz-Perez, Rafael, and Emilio Delgado López-Cózar. Co-published simultaneously in *Cataloging & Classification Quarterly* (The Haworth Information Press, an imprint of The Haworth Press, Inc.) Vol. 41, No. 3/4, 2006, pp. 291-307; and: *Education for Library Cataloging: International Perspectives* (ed: Dajin D. Sun, and Ruth C. Carter) The Haworth Information Press, an imprint of The Haworth Press, Inc., 2006, pp. 291-307. Single or multiple copies of this article are available for a fee from The Haworth Document Delivery Service [1-800-HAWORTH, 9:00 a.m. - 5:00 p.m. (EST). E-mail address: docdelivery@haworthpress.com].

courses that present important differences insofar as their denominations, their credits, and their character from one curricular program to the next. The average credit requisite for obligatory courses in cataloging in Spain is 14 (1 credit = 10 class hours), and 19.7 if electives are also considered. At present, this discipline is undergoing a reform that will produce important changes as a result of the adaptation of university studies to the common framework of the European Union. *[Article copies available for a fee from The Haworth Document Delivery Service: 1-800-HAWORTH. E-mail address: <docdelivery@haworthpress.com> Website: <http://www.HaworthPress.com> © 2006 by The Haworth Press, Inc. All rights reserved.]*

KEYWORDS. Library and Information Science (LIS), Spain, cataloging, cataloging education, teaching, curricula, professional instruction

INTRODUCTION

The importance that cataloging has historically had in the context of the universal bibliographic control of publications cannot be underestimated. This was made quite clear by Michael Gorman in his paper presented at the 67th IFLA General Conference and Council, Boston, USA, August 16-25, 2001,[1] when he underlined the significance of the initiatives carried out over the last 30 years insofar as the international standardization of cataloging rules and formats (ISBD, AACR2, and MARC). It is only fair to acknowledge the meritorious role that cataloging continues to play in the preparation of professionals for library and documentary services.

During the first half of the 20th century, in the U.S., widespread consensus already existed that cataloging should be core material in the educational programs for Library and Information Science (LIS) professionals. More recently, a study by G. A. Marco in 1994 showed that only two subjects, one of them cataloging, are required as a core course in over 50% of the U.S. schools of LIS accredited by the ALA.[2] At present, most of the ALA-accredited programs[3] impart, to different degrees, contents related to cataloging and to the study of standards used in bibliographic control.

At the international level, organizations tied to the field of Libraries, Documentation and Information, such as IFLA, UNESCO, or FID, have worked intensely to elaborate standards, guidelines, and directives regarding instruction in LIS, with cataloging always occupying a basic modular position as an academic discipline.[4,5,6,7]

At this point in time, we would like to describe and assess the way that current curricula reflect this international recognition of cataloging officially, in the different studies that have formalized programs for Library and Information Science. We gladly contribute to this volume to offer an overview of cataloging in Spanish academic institutions.

As has occurred in other countries, a number of publications and studies here have tried to analyze the historic development of LIS academics on an international level,[8] as well as the evolution of the training of professional librarians.[9] There are also a number of studies on the gestation of LIS in Spain,[10,11] looking at the overall organization of its contents and its thematic characterization.[12] Finally, there are studies about the teaching of specific subjects such as Information Sources,[13] Information Technology,[14] Research Methods and Techniques[15] or Information Retrieval.[16] Yet, until now, no study has focused precisely on the in-depth analysis of cataloging as an academic discipline.

Therefore, the purpose of this study will be to bridge this gap with a critical and comparative analysis of how the subject matter "Descriptive Cataloging" is represented in the different curricular plans of the LIS degrees from Spanish institutions.

MATERIAL AND METHODS

First, we present a descriptive analysis of the sectional contents of Cataloging, as expressed in the general and specific guidelines for the degrees of *Diplomado* and *Licenciado* in Library and Information Science, and for the *Licenciatura* in Information Science alone. Secondly, we apply this analysis to the representation of cataloging in the different curricula of the schools and departments that offer LIS degrees. The data sources used include the aforementioned directives, which are published in the Official Bulletin of the Spanish Government (BOE), as well as the curricular plans consulted on the web pages of the Schools of Spanish Universities.

The general guidelines for the degrees and the curricular programs give information about the following variables: denomination and descriptors of the contents of subjects and the respective courses, the course credit load, and the area of knowledge where it is imparted. To control the reliability of the observations made, we used the test-retest method, and the data were processed qualitatively. It should be mentioned that one of the data sources used (the University School web sites) may introduce bias in the results obtained, given that this information is conditioned by the policy of each particular center. In other words, the programs on web pages, even when available, may not have been complete, or may not correspond exactly with what is actually imparted. In Spain it is obligatory to provide such programs in the departments, but it is not obligatory to put them on the Web. On the other hand, the age of the web information could also be variable. It is known that one indicator of the quality of a web page is its degree of currency. An unwritten law recommends that the latest date of revision of the contents be indicated at the foot of the page (screen).

RESULTS

General Data About the Studies of Library and Information Science in Spain

The official incorporation of studies in LIS into the Spanish University is fairly recent. The three-year degree known as *Diplomatura* was established by Royal Decree in 1978, and the first university initiative was set in motion in 1981. This first cycle consisted of basic instruction and formation in general, to prepare the student for professional activity. At present these studies are offered in 12 universities: Barcelona, Carlos III de Madrid, Complutense de Madrid, La Coruña, Extremadura, Granada, León, Murcia, Salamanca, Valencia, Vic, and Zaragoza. There were 4,734 students enrolled in these programs during the academic year 2002-2003.[17]

The *Licenciatura* in Information Science, which completes or complements university undergraduate education, was established in 1992 (*Real Decreto* 912/1992). This second cycle, with a duration of two years, is dedicated to specialization in the field and prepares students for exercising the profession in the direction of centers of documentation and the management of information. At present this degree is offered in 11 university schools: Alcalá de Henares, Autónoma de Barcelona, Barcelona, Carlos III de Madrid, Complutense de Madrid, Extremadura, Granada, Murcia, Oberta de Catalunya, Salamanca, and Valencia, with a total enrollment of 2,279 students for 2002-2003.[18]

The third cycle or Doctorate program is designed for preparing professors and researchers. There are now LIS Doctorate Programs in Spain at the universities of Alcalá de Henares, Carlos III de Madrid,

Complutense de Madrid, Granada, Murcia, Salamanca, Valencia, and Zaragoza, with some 100 graduates enrolled.

In all of these cycles, courses are counted by credits, with a credit the equivalent of ten hours of practical or theoretical instruction. As for contents, we will focus on the presence of core courses of obligatory inclusion all over Spain. The rest of the subjects taught are either obligatory courses that are specified by each university, or optional material specific to each university as well, but of free choice for the student.

Cataloging in the Specific Guidelines for the LIS Diplomatura: *A Critical Analysis*

In Spain the educational system, including higher education, is a public service and, therefore, the government is in charge of establishing its ground rules. University studies are subject to general directives and specific guidelines; these rules expound and regulate the basic curricular characteristics that each academic degree is to have in the entire national territory. In the specific guidelines for the elaboration of the plans of study of the *Diplomaturas* in LIS, whose latest reform was passed in 1991 (*Real Decreto* 1422/1991, August 30), there is a listing of the core courses that are obligatory for all centers that offer such a degree. The consideration of cataloging as core course content (Table 1) has led, as we shall see later, to its automatic inclusion in all of the curricula of the University LIS Schools and Departments.

A first look at Table 1 shows the area which includes Cataloging–Documentary Analysis and Languages–to be the most important in terms of material and credits. Moreover, among the descriptors of the material, most correspond to cataloging.

On the other hand, we concede that the very denomination of the subject matter is unfortunate. As J. A. Frias[19] points out, the clearest incoherence is seen in that one of the descriptors, "Information Management and Retrieval," is even more generic than the subject matter it is included in (and would, in fact, be a more appropriate name for the course). Indeed, the material it attempts to describe is that embracing all of the disciplines related to the techniques of information retrieval and processing, such as: Access to Description (Access Points), Elaboration of Catalogs, Theory and Structure of the Classification and Indexing Systems, and Analysis of Contents. In a future revision of the guidelines, therefore, it could be recommended that we change the denomination "Documentary Analysis and Languages" to "Information Processing and Retrieval."

TABLE 1. Specific Guidelines for the Curricula for the *Diplomatura* Degree in LIS in Spain: Core (Compulsory) Subjects

Core Course Title	Credits	Description of Contents
Análisis y Lenguajes Documentales	20	Introduction to cataloging and classification. Information management and retrieval. Bibliographic description of documents in different formats: access to the description and elaboration of catalogs. Theory and structure of classifications and indexing systems. Content analysis.
Archivística	10	Introduction to the study and organization of archives.
Bibliografía y Fuentes de Información	10	Nature, function, and typology of general and specific documentary sources.
Biblioteconomía	10	Organization and administration of libraries and information centers.
Documentación General	10	Study of the concept of documentary information.
Técnicas Historiográficas de la Investigación Documental	6	Applied paleography, diplomatics, and numismatics.
Tecnología de la Información	15	Technologies of conservation and retrieval of information.
Practicum	10	Professional practice in libraries and information centers or systems.

The descriptors that specify the contents of the subject must be qualified as scanty and indiscriminately formulated, but above all there is an obviously poor correspondence between the descriptors and the contents they attempt to describe. In following the Anglo-Saxon terminology and the logical order of the techniques for processing bibliographic information, in our opinion, the most correct denominations to designate all of the operations involved in cataloging and elaborating catalogs are: "Descriptive Cataloging" to refer to the bibliographic description of the documents, to the choice of access points and to their standardization as entries to the information in the catalog (Heading); and on the other hand, "Cataloging by Subject Matter" to refer to the formulation of the Subject Heading. The term "Classification or Classification Systems" would have been adequate as well for referring to systematic indexing or classificatory notations (Classification). Finally, the descriptor "Analysis of Contents" is possibly the best, though we might also directly use "Documentary Summary" (Abstract or Summary) to refer to the operation which consists of creating an abbreviated representation of the contents.

The credit load (20 credits = 200 hours) assigned to this subject calls for some clarification. Bearing in mind that each university can freely organize the core material into specific disciplines or subjects, we believe that the material within Documentary Analysis and Languages should be divided into at least four areas. But this would mean each subject ending up with five credits, a totally insufficient load in any case. For instance, for a course in "Descriptive Cataloging," it would be practically impossible to teach, in a total of 50 hours, the theoretical and practical contents of the International Standard Bibliographic Description (ISBD), the assignment and form of access points or "Headings" (*Reglas de Catalogación Españolas* or RCE and AACR2), the presentation of data in a computerized format (MARC and IBERMARC), and the formation of authority records (GARE, GSARE, and MARC Authorities). In our view, the student should acquire a critical scientific attitude about the need to change the standards used to create bibliographic records,[20] well aware of their importance for the development of future work in the field, and for the advancement of the methodologies and tools of bibliographic control in the context of new technologies.

Therefore, to properly develop the contents we have described, at least two courses in cataloging would be necessary, with the following characteristics: that they be part of the core curriculum, compulsory, and annual, with 10 credits corresponding to each.

Because time is also a factor, and this point admits no debate, we the professors must strive to reconcile two contrasting needs: on the one hand, to adapt contents of subjects to the time available, and on the other hand, to try not to sacrifice any fundamental aspects in our exposition of the material. Actually, these two interests cannot be made entirely compatible, and as the first is more impending than the second, we are left omitting contents as a partial solution. Or, perhaps, as the only possible solution.

Descriptive Cataloging in the LIS Curricula in Spain

Given that the directives regulating the awarding of degrees in Spain establish subject matter and not subjects per se, and that the principle of university autonomy is a cornerstone of the Spanish educational system, the different universities here enjoy freedom and a legal capacity to formalize the specific contents of the core curriculum into subjects, and also to create compulsory subjects specific to that university itself, along with a wide array of elective subjects. In fact, each center interprets the official directives in a slightly different manner, depending upon their own objectives, curricula, and–above all–the resources and faculty members that integrate the departments involved in teaching LIS.

In Table 2 we see the course designations that partly or fully develop the contents pertaining to Cataloging, distributed by university, and by the degree obtained. The contents of Subject Headings and those of Classifications have been excluded from this analysis because they appear associated with the curricula of Content Analysis (Indexing and Abstracting). On the other hand, note that only a general analysis could be made from the the denominations of the subjects and the credit hours assigned to each. A detailed analysis of the contents of the programs of each subject is not possible, as we cannot obtain that information on the Web in most cases, and even when it is available, all of the course syllabi may not be presented in a uniform manner, making it impossible to attempt a comparative study.

Before entering into the analysis of Cataloging, a general matter to be addressed, reflected in Table 2, is the consideration of LIS in Spain as a discipline associated with Human Sciences as opposed to Social Sciences. The universities where the degree is not offered in a separate school, but instead in a department pertaining to a broader discipline, often situates LIS among the Humanities (Philosophy, Literature, Geography, and History). We believe this has had a negative impact on the orientation of students and teachers, and has hampered the development of scientific research in our specialized field.

Generally speaking, cataloging is represented in all of the curricular plans, though with noteworthy differences or imbalances in its configuration or denomination from one center to the next. Six out of the 12 LIS programs (Carlos III, Complutense de Madrid, La Coruña, León, Murcia, and Vic) maintain the unfortunate name "Document Analysis" for the contents of Cataloging. This obliges them to dedicate ample introductions to the study in these courses, until now known as Documentary Processing, or to differentiate between Formal Analysis and Content Analysis. The latter is nowadays irrelevant in the context of bibliographic databases, as we know. The study programs of the other six centers use the denomination "Cataloging," though we applaud the fact that Salamanca and Barcelona prefer the denomination "Descriptive Cataloging."

As for the distribution of the three degrees offered (Table 2), it is evident that, in Spain, cataloging is understood as a discipline belonging to the first cycle. That is, it is fundamentally and specifically for the formation of *Diplomados*. Within this three-year program, cataloging is represented in all of the universities by two or more subjects, and in many

TABLE 2. Spanish Universities with Cataloging Curricula and Degrees

Universidad *Centro*	Degrees	Course Names (R) Required or (O) Optional	Length in Credit (T-P)
Universidad de Alcalá de Henares *Facultad de Ciencias de la* *Documentación*	L D	Gestión Evaluación de Catálogos Automatizados (O)	6 (2-4)
Universidad Autónoma de **Barcelona** *Facultat de Ciencies de la* *Comunicació*	L D		
Universidad de Barcelona *Facultad de Biblioteconomía y* *Documentación*	D B and D	Introducción a la Catalogación (R) Catalogación Descriptiva (R) Organización de Catálogos On Line (R) Publicaciones Seriadas (O)	7,5 (4-3,5) 7,5 (4-3,5) 6 (3-3) 4,5
	L B and D		
Universidad Carlos III (Madrid) *Facultad de Humanidades,* *Comunicación y Documentación*	D B and D	Análisis Documental I (R) Análisis Documental II (R) Catalogación Automatizada (R) Catalogación Materiales Especiales (O)	8 7 7 6
	L B and D	Mantenimiento de Catálogos Automatizados (O)	6
Universidad Complutense (Madrid) *Escuela Universitaria de* *Biblioteconomía y Documentación* *Facultad de Ciencias de la* *Información*	D B and D	Análisis Documental I (R) Análisis Documental II (R) Fondos Bibliográficos Antiguos (O) Catalogación Materiales Especiales (O)	9 (4,5-4,5) 6 (3-3) 6 6
	L B and D		
Universidad de La Coruña *Facultad de Humanidades*	D B and D	Análisis Documental I (R) Análisis Documental II (R)	12 (6-6) 9 (4,5-4,5)
Universidad de Extremadura *Facultad de Biblioteconomía y* *Documentación*	D B and D	Catalogación (R) Catalogación de Fondos Especiales (O)	5 (2-3) 6 (3-3)
	L B and D	Mantenimiento de Catálogos Automatizados (O)	6 (1-5)
Universidad de Granada *Facultad de Biblioteconomía y* *Documentación*	D B and D	Catalogación (R) Control de Autoridades (O) Catalogación de Materiales Especiales (O)	5 (0-5) 7,5 (2,5-5) 7,5 (2,5-5)
	L B and D	Gestión Automatizada de Catálogos (O)	4,5 (2-2,5)
Universidad de León *Facultad de Filosofía y Letras*	D B and D	Análisis Documental (R) Tratamiento Materiales Especiales (O)	10 (4-6) 6 (2-4)
Universidad de Murcia *Facultad de Ciencias de la* *Documentación*	D B and D	Introducción al Análisis Documental (R) Catalogación (R) Documentos Audiovisuales (O)	5 (3-2) 7 (4,5-2,5) 5 (3-2)
	L B and D		
Universidad Oberta de Catalunya	L D		
Universidad de Salamanca *Facultad de Traducción y* *Documentación*	D B and D	Catalogación Descriptiva I: impresos modernos (R) Organización de Catálogos en Línea (R) Catalogación Descriptiva II: Materiales Especiales O)	10 (3-7) 4,5 4,5
	L B and D	Evaluación de Catálogos en Línea (O)	4,5 (1,5-3)

TABLE 2 (continued)

Universidad *Centro*	Degrees	Course Names (R) Required or (O) Optional	Length in Credit (T-P)
Universidad de Valencia *Facultad de Geografía e Historia*	D B and D	Catalogación y Clasificación (R) Catalogación Automatizada (R)	9 (6-3) 4,5 (1,5-3)
	L B and D		
Universidad de Vic *Facultad de Ciencias Humanas,* *Traducción y Documentación*	D B and D	Análisis Documental (R) Formatos Bibliográficos y Catálogos en Línea (R) Catalogación de Materiales no Librarios (O)	9 12 6
Universidad de Zaragoza *Facultad de Filosofía y Letras*	D B and D	Catalogación (R)	12 (4-8)

L D = *Licenciado* in Information Science (2nd cycle). D B and D = *Diplomado* (3-yr. degree) in LIS. L B and D = *Licenciado* (5-yr. degree) in LIS. (T-P) = Theory-Practice. See Appendix for URL consulted.

cases by four, whose general characteristics may be summed up as follows: (1) In all curricular plans, the Cataloging of Serials and of Special Materials (Audiovisual Material, Music, Cartographic Material, and Computer Files) is considered a specific subject of an elective nature, separate from the Cataloging of Monographs; (2) Cataloging Electronic Resources and Internet Resources has not yet been incorporated into the contents of the study programs as an independent course; (3) of the 12 Universities, only five (42%) include as compulsory within this first cycle, the subjects of Computerized Cataloging or OnLine Cataloging (this situation forces us to acknowledge that, in Spain, there may be *Diplomados* in LIS who, aside from other formative gaps or weaknesses concerning the organization, use, and maintenance of the online catalogs, may not have technical training in the use of MARC format, or in the computerized systems of Authority Control); and (4) only one curricular program, that of the University of Granada, grants special treatment to Authority Control by giving it a specific course, albeit with an elective character, of 7.5 credits.

As for the credit load, and according to the data shown in Table 2, the average of obligatory credits (theory and practice) assigned to cataloging in the Spanish curricular prgrams of the first cycle is 14. There is a noteworthy difference between those universities that dedicate some 20 credits to the subject area (Barcelona, Carlos III de Madrid, La Coruña, and Vic) and the schools that lend it only five credits (Granada and Extremadura). Between these two extremes we see the rest of the universities with a range of 10-15 credits. If, however, we also take into account the elective credits pertaining to cataloging, the mean jumps to 19.7. Indeed, what is revealed by the data in Table 2 is that most curricular programs in LIS attempt to alleviate the lack of obligatory credit hours in cataloging by offering electives, mainly in the *Diplomatura* cycle but also in the *Licenciatura* in some cases. We should also point out that in the specific guidelines for the *Licenciatura* degree, cataloging is not represented in any of the core courses, and therefore, never generates obligatory subjects in the second cycle. In fact, one of the trademarks of the Spanish LIS *Licenciatura* degree (Table 2) is its scarcity. Out of the 11 universities that award this five-year degree, six (Autónoma de Barcelona, Barcelona, Complutense de Madrid, Murcia, Oberta de Catalunya, and Valencia) do not offer cataloging *per se*, and the others do so with only one course offering of the following characteristics: optional, of 5-6 class credit hours, and referring always to different aspects of the management or maintenance of computer catalogs or online catalogs.

The data on the obligatory subjects of the first academic cycle can be broken down as to theoretical or practical contents as shown in Table 2. The average number of credits with respect to the theoretical contents of cataloging (T) is 5.8, whereas the practical contents take up 6.6 credits. If we consider all courses together (obligatory and electives), these means are slightly different, with the increase seen on the side of the practical credits (6.9 T and 8.6 P). We may state in general terms that the theoretical/practical distribution in all of the study plans is around 50%, with the exception of universities such as Granada where cataloging has a predominantly practical orientation (5 T and 15 P).

Cataloging in Other Stages of Professional Instruction

In Spain, instruction in the first university-level cycle culminates with the practicum of students in libraries, documentation centers, or archives. This practicum has a quatrimestral duration, and is carried out in public and private centers with which the Schools or Departments of Library and Information Science have cooperative agreements. Logically, the practica in cataloging have an important role within this formative stage, and are directed by the persons responsible for the centers, while supervised by the LIS professors.

At the same time, in view of the mobility from one university to another allowed Spanish students, it is possible to enroll in the second cycle if holding a *Diplomatura* degree, even when it is not specifcally in LIS. For this purpose, it is necessary to finish a course known as "Adaptation" or "Complements of Formation," whose contents are practically identical in all of the universities listed in Table 2. This course involves 45 credits, and integrates all of the subject matter that is considered basic for formation; here, Cataloging and Classification are well represented as a general subject consisting of 10 credits.

The Immediate Future: LIS in the Context of the EU

In the ongoing academic year, the European universities, including those of Spain, are immersed in a process of convergence of the different national systems of higher education. In our case, the results of this process are far from definitive, and therefore, we cannot predict the situation that will be left for LIS studies, or the specific situation of cataloging therewithin. At this point in time, we can only describe the framework and the general directives of this convergence of the European Universities. The most important steps in the process of harmonization have been synthesized by L. Orera.[21] Foremost is the Declaration of Bologne, a document drawn up in June 1999 and undersigned by 29 European nations, including Spain. The meetings of the EUA (European University Association) (Salamanca, March, 2001) and, finally, the declaration of Prague (undersigned by 33 European countries) have only come to back up the Declaration of Bologne.[22] It addresses the creation of a common area for higher eduction in the framework of the European Union principles, as well as improved competitiveness of the European educational system in the broader international context. The year 2010 has been set for this undertaking, and the most important general principles to be achieved are:

- Organization of higher education into two cycles: a first cycle of three to four years of undergraduate education, and a second cycle leading to the degree of master or doctor, both with validity in the whole of the European Union workplace.
- The teaching system should take, as units of reference, the semester and the credit as implanted by the ECTS (European Credit Transfer System) in specific and consolidated programs such as "Erasmus" or "Socrates," where Spanish scholars have been participating for some years. Under this system, the credit does not only represent the time the student spends in class, but it computes the total volume of the work done (class attendance, practical tasks, work practicum, personal projects, exams, etc.). In this con-

text, 30 credits would represent the work volume of a semester, 60 of an academic course, and 20 in a trimester.

- The curricula and the corresponding degrees of each country should be legible and comparable in the framework of the European Union. The academic degree, the courses taken and their equivalence in credits, and the grades obtained should all be uniform or easily converted.

Consequently, in the case of Spain, the curricular changes needed are considerable. Although we have already implanted the credit system, it requires adaptation to the new European system, as at present it does not take into account the full work load of the student, but rather only the hours of class scheduled. As far as the organization of cycles is concerned, the three that currently exist should be reduced to two: an undergraduate cycle of four years of duration, and with a predominantly professional orientation, and a second graduate cycle of specialization, preparing the student to design, plan, and evaluate units and systems of information, as well as to carry out research and apply the results of research generated in the field of choice. From our vantage point, these changes will markedly affect LIS studies; and even if we cannot provide data for their evaluation, it can be foreseen that the professional orientation in our degree area will be reinforced with the adaptation to the common European framework. Therefore, basic subjects in the formation of librarians, as is cataloging, will no doubt wield greater relevance.

CONCLUSIONS

In the first place, we must positively appraise the consideration of cataloging as a core and compulsory subject within all of the curricular programs of Spain's schools of Library and Information Science. This means that it is upheld as fundamental material in achieving the objectives of the first cycle of formation of the professional librarian. Nonetheless, this does not take away from the important deficiencies that the present study identifies: the incorrect characterization and description of the subject matter, its limited obligatory class load, and its heterogeneous formulation.

At the same time, however, the diversity of the different programs has made it impossible to carry out an analysis of the precise contents of the subjects taught. Although this situation may seem logical or justifiable given the comparative "youth" of LIS studies in Spain, consensus among the different universities is urgently needed to strive toward homogeneity in the foundations, contents, and orientations of the subject. We might also hope that the adaptation to the common European framework will allow us to introduce modifications in the denomination of the subject matter, increase the corresponding number of credits, and reinforce contents that relate cataloging and bibliographic control with the latest technology.

REFERENCES

1. Gorman, M. "Bibliographic Control or Chaos: An Agenda for National Bibliographic Services in the 21st Century" *IFLA Journal* 27(2001): 307-313.
2. Marco, G.A. "The demise of the American core curriculum" *Libri* 44(1994): 175-189.
3. ALA. *Standards for accreditation of Master's programs in Library and Information Studies.* http://www.ala.org/alaorg/oa/standard.html [consulted 2003-10-04].
4. IFLA. Sección de Escuelas de Biblioteconomía. *Normas para Escuelas de Biblioteconomía.* (Madrid: ANABAD, 1977).
5. UNESCO. *Armonización de la capacitación en materia de Biblioteconomía, Ciencias de la Información y Archivística. PGI-87/WS/2.* (París: UNESCO, Programa General de Información, 1987).
6. Saunders, W.L. *Guidelines for curriculum development in information studies. PGI-78/WS/27.* (París: UNESCO. Programa General de Información, 1987).
7. Large, J.A. *Un programa modular de estudios de la información. PGI-87/WS/5.* (París: UNESCO. Programa General de Información, 1987).
8. Delgado López-Cózar, E. "La enseñanza de la biblioteconomía y documentación: una perspectiva global" *Boletín de la Asociación Andaluza de Bibliotecarios* 35(1994): 27-54.
9. Orera Orera, L. "La evolución en la formación de los bibliotecarios." *Documentación de las ciencias de la Información* 24(2002): 167-188.
10. Cid, P., Recoder, M.J. "La licenciatura de documentación: estudio de las propuestas formuladas en España para su realización." In: *IV Jornadas Españolas de Documentación.* (Gijón 1994). Gijón: FESABID, 1994. p. 611-615.
11. López Yepes, J. "La licenciatura en documentación, marco formativo de un nuevo profesional." *Revista General de Información y Documentación* 5(1995): 33-69.
12. Solano Macías, C.; López Pujalte, C. "Perfil multidisciplinar de los nuevos profesionales de la información: principales áreas de conocimiento en los estudios de Biblioteconomía y Documentación." *Actas de las VI Jornadas Españolas de Documentación. Los sistemas de información al servicio de la sociedad* (Valencia 1998). Valencia: FESABID, p. 855-871.
13. Carrizo Sainero, G.; Ayuso Sánchez, M.J.; Sánchez Domínguez, M.C. "Análisis comparativo de los diferentes programas docentes en Fuentes de Información en las universidades y escuelas de Biblioteconomía y Documentación en España." *Actas del V encuentro de EDIBCIC. La formación de profesionales e investigadores de la información para la sociedad del conocimiento.* (Granada 2000). Granada: Facultad de Biblioteconomía y Documentación, 2000, p. 82-94.

14. González Molina, A., Navarrete Cortes, J. "La enseñanza de las tecnologías de la información en las Escuelas Universitarias de Biblioteconomía y Documentación en España." *VIII Jornadas Bibliotecarias de Andalucía.* (Huelva 1994). Huelva: Asociación Andaluza de Bibliotecarios, Diputación Provincial, 1995, p. 387-396.

15. Delgado López-Cózar, E. "La enseñanza de metodología de la investigación en las Licenciaturas en Documentación en España" *Homenaje a J. A. Martín Fuertes: la documentación para la investigación.* León: Universidad, 2002, p. 145-167.

16. Salvador Olivan, J.A. "Formación en recuperación de información: análisis de los cursos y asignaturas en las escuelas de Biblioteconomía y Documentación de Norteamérica y España." *Documentación de las Ciencias de la Información* 25(2002): 189-215.

17. http://www.ine.es/inebase/cgi/um?M=%2Ft13%2Fp405&O=inebase&N=&L= [consulted 2003-10-29].

18. http://www.ine.es/inebase/cgi/um?M=%2Ft13%2Fp405&O=inebase&N=&L= [consulted 2003-10-29].

19. Frias, J.A. "Las relaciones entre análisis documental y catalogación: su representación en el plan de estudios de la Universidad de Salamanca." *Proceeding of the first ISKO-Spain Conference (Madrid 1993).* Edited by F. J. Garcia Marco. Zaragoza, 1995, p. 145-57.

20. Ruiz-Perez, R. "Consequences of Applying Cataloguing Codes for Author Entries to the Spanish National Library Online Catalogs." *Cataloging & Classification Quarterly* 32, 3(2001): 31-55.

21. Orera Orera, L. "La evolución en la formación de los bibliotecarios." p. 185.

22. Declaración conjunta de los Ministros Europeos de Educación, reunidos en Bolonia el 19 de Junio de 1999 <http://www.universia.es/contenidos/universidades/documentos/Universidades_docum_bolonia.htm>.

Docampo, D. La declaración de Bolonia y su repercusión en la estructura de las titulaciones en España <http://www.gts.tsc.uvigo.es/~ddocampo/galinbol.html>.

APPENDIX

URLs [Consulted, Nov. 2003]

Universidad de Alcalá de Henares:
http://www.uah.es/organ/facultades_escuelas/lstAsignaturas_v2.asp?
    CodCentro=109&CodPlan=640

Universidad Autónoma de Barcelona:
http://www.uab.es/estudis/dosframes.htm

Universidad de Barcelona:
http://www.ub.es/biblio/

Universidad Carlos III (Madrid):
http://www.uc3m.es/uc3m/gral/ES/ESCU/escu11b.html

Universidad Complutense (Madrid):
http://www.uc3m.es/uc3m/gral/ES/ESCU/escu51b.html
http://berceo.eubd.ucm.es/html/docs/estudios/plan/nuevo.html

Universidad de La Coruña:
http://www.udc.es/cap4c/

Universidad de Extremadura:
http://alcazaba.unex.es/

Universidad de Granada:
http://www.ugr.es/~fbd/Planes_de_estudio/Diplomatura.htm
http://www.ugr.es/~fbd/Planes_de_estudio/Licenciatura.htm

Universidad de León:
http://www.unileon.es/estudios/filosofia/plan_bibliot.htm

Universidad de Murcia:
http://www.um.es/fccd/

Oberta de Catalunya:
http://www.uoc.edu/web/esp/estudios/estudios_uoc/documentacion/
    documentacion_cuadro.htm

Universidad de Salamanca:
http://exlibris.usal.es

Universidad de Valencia:
http://www.uv.es/dise/estudi/plans/02bid.html

Universidad de Vic:
http://www.uvic.es/central/campus/gabinet/ca/guies/fchtd/biblioteconomia.pdf

Universidad de Zaragoza:
http://ebro3.unizar.es:8080/acad/FMPro?-db=w%5fcentros.fp5&-format=centro.
htm&-lay=cgi&-sortfield=cod%5fcentro&-recid=28&-findall=

Education and Training
for Cataloguing and Classification
in the British Isles

J. H. Bowman

SUMMARY. A survey of postgraduate education and training for cataloguing and classification in the British Isles in late 2003 was carried out by consulting websites and sending an e-mail request. Cataloguing and classification have become largely invisible in professional education, but it appears that most courses still include something about them, though not always as a compulsory module and usually without much practical work. The course at University College London is described. Views of recent graduates, and of chief cataloguers and other trainers, are included, and show that the general opinion is that not enough is being taught about cataloguing and classification. Finally, the article looks at training given by commercial providers. *[Article copies available for a fee from The Haworth Document Delivery Service: 1-800-HAWORTH. E-mail address: <docdelivery@haworthpress.com> Website: <http://www.HaworthPress.com> © 2006 by The Haworth Press, Inc. All rights reserved.]*

KEYWORDS. Education for cataloguing, training for cataloguing, cataloguers, Britain, United Kingdom

---

J. H. Bowman, MA, MA, PhD, MCLIP, FRSA, is Programme Director for Library and Information Studies, School of Library, Archive & Information Studies, University College London, Gower Street, London WC1E 6BT, England.

[Haworth co-indexing entry note]: "Education and Training for Cataloguing and Classification in the British Isles." Bowman, J. H. Co-published simultaneously in *Cataloging & Classification Quarterly* (The Haworth Information Press, an imprint of The Haworth Press, Inc.) Vol. 41, No. 3/4, 2006, pp. 309-333; and: *Education for Library Cataloging: International Perspectives* (ed: Dajin D. Sun, and Ruth C. Carter) The Haworth Information Press, an imprint of The Haworth Press, Inc., 2006, pp. 309-333. Single or multiple copies of this article are available for a fee from The Haworth Document Delivery Service [1-800-HAWORTH, 9:00 a.m. - 5:00 p.m. (EST). E-mail address: docdelivery@haworthpress.com].

Available online at http://www.haworthpress.com/web/CCQ
© 2006 by The Haworth Press, Inc. All rights reserved.
doi:10.1300/J104v41n03_07

INTRODUCTION

Education for the library and information professions in the United Kingdom is carried out in departments of seventeen institutions, which are listed in Appendix 1. There is one such department in the Republic of Ireland, at University College Dublin. Almost all of these institutions are now called "universities"; some have always been so, others only since 1992, when they converted from polytechnics. All of the departments offer education at the graduate level, and some also provide undergraduate courses, though the number of these has declined in recent years. In this article I intend to focus only on the postgraduate courses. Most courses in the United Kingdom are accredited by CILIP, the Chartered Institute of Library and Information Professionals, which is the professional association formed in April 2002 by the amalgamation of the Library Association and the Institute of Information Scientists. Both of those organizations had criteria for the accreditation of courses, and these have been carried forward into a combined document.[1] Accreditation is important, because without it a course, even though it may amount to a degree in its own right, is not necessarily accepted as a suitable qualification preliminary to becoming a Chartered Member of CILIP. This process need not concern us here, but it is important that candidates have the initial qualification before they can move on to it.

It has been remarked elsewhere that during the last twenty or so years there has been a considerable reduction in the amount of cataloguing[2] taught in American library schools.[3] I have no reason to believe that the situation is any different in the United Kingdom. A fairly recent collection of essays, for example, includes neither cataloguing nor classification in its index.[4] In fact there is some reference to it in the book, but only in discussing the question of what constitutes a core curriculum, the answer apparently being that cataloguing does not. A recent editorial in *Catalogue and Index*, the periodical of the Cataloguing and Indexing Group of CILIP, states that library schools "seem to have virtually abandoned formal cataloguing and classification teaching" as if this were a well-known fact.[5]

One might expect that CILIP would have something to say about the inclusion of cataloguing in the curriculum, yet in looking at their criteria for accreditation we find some ambiguity.[6] Item A4 is entitled "Knowledge Organization, Recording & Retrieval," and this is the closest the document comes to mentioning cataloguing or classification. There is in any case no indication of whether this item, or any other, is compulsory. So many subjects are listed that it would be impossible for any one course to cover all of them. In contrast it is heartening to find that CILIP's basic leaflet about the profession refers to cataloguing and classification in its first paragraph. In answer to the question "Is this the career for me?" it states: "It could be, if you want a career for life that would test your abilities in communication, budgeting, cataloguing and classifying information."[7]

THIS SURVEY

In order to try to discover the extent to which cataloguing is included in present-day British postgraduate courses, I have consulted the websites of several institutions. I also circulated a request for information on lis-link, which is an e-mail discussion list used by a wide range of library and information professionals in Britain. I asked particularly for responses from recent library and information studies graduates, from those engaged in cataloguing, and from those involved in cataloguing training. I received about twenty replies, including only two from other lecturers, but in all cases the replies were of interest.[8]

CATALOGUING EDUCATION IN POSTGRADUATE COURSES

It is not always easy to identify from the websites which module of a course might contain cataloguing or classification. A wide variety of names is used at the various institutions, giving the impression that it is a subject which almost "dare not speak its name." Only Bristol, Dublin, and University College London (UCL) have the words "Cataloguing and classification" in the module name; elsewhere the commonest titles are names like Organising knowledge or Information retrieval. It may be that the subject's reputation within the profession for being difficult, boring, and depressing has led departments to try to disguise it for fear that it will be unpopular with students. Sites where there is no mention of cataloguing or classification (with module titles that might include them in brackets) are: Aberystwyth (Information retrieval); City (Principles of knowledge organisation); Edinburgh (Information sources and retrieval); Leeds (Organisation and management of information); Sheffield (Information searching and retrieval); Northumbria (Information storage and retrieval).

Elsewhere various titles are used: Indexing and retrieval (Thames Valley); Information handling (Loughborough); Information organisation and retrieval (London Metropolitan); Information sources, organisation and services (Strathclyde); Organisation of information (Dublin); Organising knowledge (Brighton, where classification is specifically mentioned in the description, and University of Central England); Organisation of bibliographic data (Liverpool); Technical services (Robert Gordon).

Even assuming that one can identify courses containing cataloguing and classification it is not easy to find out what is actually covered or how much time is devoted to it. Nor is it always clear whether the relevant course is compulsory or optional, though it seems that in most cases it is compulsory (exceptions are mentioned below). Sometimes there seem to be far too many subjects included for them to be able to receive adequate treatment. The University of Central England refers to "catalogues, classification" as part of its Organising knowledge module. Is it significant that this does not actually say "cataloguing"?

Where it is possible to look in more detail at the modules we find considerable variation. At Liverpool, the module entitled Organisation of bibliographic data "provides a critical analysis of the important codes within international cataloguing and classification: AACR2 . . . , Dewey decimal classification and the MARC format for computerized data." Critical analysis is all very well, but it is not clear whether this includes any actual cataloguing.

At Loughborough, the Information handling module consists of:

> Bibliographic data management; methods of identifying bibliographic records in retrieval systems using national and international standards; cooperative cataloguing and networks; online public access catalogues; metadata; cataloguing (description, access points, authority control); library classification; classification in retrieval systems; taxonomies; practical classification (enumerative and faceted classified schemes, application of one major classification scheme).[9]

This seems a comprehensive coverage, but to achieve it in 11 hours' lectures and 17 hours' practicals seems a tall order.

The MA in Information and Library Management at Manchester formerly included a module called Documentation, which dealt with bibliographic records, catalogues, and classification schemes. Following a course review, this module has now been dropped and the material incorporated into a new module called Information retrieval and systems design. This course is taught jointly by two people, and Peter Lea, who teaches the part covering cataloguing and classification, is unhappy about the result. Moreover, he points out that all of the evidence, from CILIP, employment agencies, and employers, suggests that they should be teaching more cataloguing and classification rather than less.[10]

At the Robert Gordon University the module is called, unusually, Technical services, and includes the theory and structure of the bibliographic record; codes and standards; organization and administration; application of standards, as well as looking at OPACs, mark-up languages, and classification schemes. Contact time amounts to 36 hours overall, half of which are lectures, the rest tutorials, seminars, and practicals. There are two pieces of assessment, one of which is a critical appraisal and the other, a piece of practical cataloguing and classification work.[11] If it is not possible to provide a separate module, this combination seems to make the most sense, integrating as it does the creation of the catalogue records with the applications.

At London Metropolitan University, the MA in Information Services Management includes two modules relevant to this area: Information organisation and retrieval is compulsory, and Indexing for information retrieval is optional. The former includes reference to bibliographic record structures, but the course is mainly concerned with retrieval systems. The latter consists chiefly of cataloguing and classification, but the assessment appears to consist only of the creation and indexing of a faceted classification scheme, cataloguing not being tested at all.[12]

At Sheffield, although the subjects are invisible on the website, they do exist as an optional addition to the module Information searching and retrieval. The basic module includes "basic awareness of the notion of [and] need for cataloguing" and covers metadata and the idea of record description. The optional part is a more detailed series of lectures and practicals on AACR2, Dewey and MARC, with the intention of providing an introduction to the mechanics of using the codes.[13] It appears that little practical work is involved.

The MSc in Information and Library Management at Bristol is unusual in that it is taught entirely by practising librarians and information professionals rather than by permanent lecturers. What is interesting about this course is that a half-module on Cataloguing and classification has been introduced in response to student demand.[14] The other half of the module may be either Introduction to advanced information systems or Publishing. Prior to this, the only reference to cataloguing and classification was in the unit called Information and its users, and this includes only four lectures on these topics, one each on AACR2, MARC, classification, and subject headings. These have been retained because the new half-unit is only optional. The half-unit covers:

- structure and history of AACR2
- cataloguing monographs
- cataloguing other materials, e.g., maps, journals, AV items
- structure and history of MARC
- cataloguing monographs and other materials using MARC 21
- use of traditional skills in digital libraries
- the impact of automation on cataloguing, and subsequent issues for AACR2 and MARC
- use of library management systems, and the restrictions they may place on cataloguing standards
- reasons for, and consequences of, libraries varying the rules
- relevance of traditional skills in knowledge management, records management, etc.

There is one assignment, which takes the form of a report, with recommendations, on cataloguing standards written for a management team to consider.[15] It seems clear from this that there is hardly time for the students to do much *practical* cataloguing, and it is noteworthy that this is not included in the course assignment. Nevertheless, it is encouraging that the half-module has been introduced in response to student demand, and that in one recent year over half of the students chose it.

VIEWS OF RECENT STUDENTS

One should be very wary of generalizing from a self-selecting survey such as this, but it is probably significant that all of the recent students who responded were critical of their courses, and generally they do not feel that they were taught much about cataloguing or classification. (It is hardly surprising that no responses were received from former UCL students.) One respondent refers to a single session using Dublin Core as being the whole of what was provided, because it was not possible for part-time students to attend on the day when the cataloguing and classification module was taught. This person believes, however, that the amount has subsequently been increased. Another, on a different course, found "the cataloguing section of our course quite inadequate." It was part of an information retrieval module but consisted of an hour a week over four weeks. Another respondent from the same course implies that this was optional only.

On another course, there was "not so much as a mention of classifying or cataloguing," and this statement agrees with the information available via that department's website. This person felt that it took her at least eighteen months to gain a reasonable level of proficiency, and that all students ought to be given some basic training in these subjects. Another respondent says that they spent only an afternoon on each of the main classification schemes, and a similar amount of time on the elements of cataloguing. Altogether there was "nowhere near enough of it."

Looking further back, a graduate from 1991 says that he received "virtually no training in practical cataloguing at all," and that, according to his experience in supervising students from his local library school, this is still the case. Another respondent, who studied at Dublin ten years ago, describes the changes which have since taken place in the teaching there. At that time cataloguing and classification were taught by practising librarians who came in to do it. Later this changed and they were taught by an existing member of the department who was inexperienced in cataloguing. More recently the amount has been considerably reduced on the grounds that fewer libraries do original cataloguing nowadays, relying on imported records. This person feels that although those who have been taught cataloging at library school do not necessarily make the best cataloguers, it ought not to be possible to complete a professional qualification without knowing anything about it.

UNIVERSITY COLLEGE LONDON

Because I am a lecturer at University College London (UCL), I obviously know more about the course there than about other courses. I have been in post for ten years and have seen some changes to the curriculum. The School of Library, Archive & Information Studies (SLAIS) at UCL offers several MA degrees, but the one which concerns us here is the MA in Library and Information Studies. This includes the following compulsory modules (arranged here in alphabetical order):

- Cataloguing and classification 1
- Collection management and preservation
- Information sources and retrieval

- Management
- Principles of computing and information technology
- Professional awareness

Each of these should amount to a total of about 100 hours' study time on the part of the student; this is a UCL policy which is in line with national guidelines. The first five are specifically taught, and are assessed by coursework, while "Professional awareness" is designed to bring together the various taught courses, together with current professional issues. It is assessed by a written examination and by a case study in which students apply theoretical knowledge gained from the course to some real-life situation of their choice in a library or information unit. In addition, students choose two optional modules from a wide range which does not concern us here, but which includes Cataloguing and classification 2. Finally the students undertake a dissertation of about 12,000 words, which can be on any topic related to the field of library and information studies.

This structure was introduced in the academic year 2002/03, superseding a previous one which had been in place since 1993. UCL has always had a reputation for including rather more on cataloguing and classification than the other British library schools, and the syllabus revision was almost certainly unique in that it gave a *greater* allocation of time to Cataloguing and classification. It also made them more prominent, because during the previous ten years they had been combined in a single module with Information sources and retrieval. This separation was made because we felt that students were having to do a disproportionate amount of work in that module for the credit they gained for it, and we have been careful to ensure that in dividing the module into two we have not increased their workload. We have always believed at UCL that cataloguing and classification are fundamental to librarianship, and that everyone going to work in a library or information service needs to be familiar with them. How can someone working on an enquiry desk adequately help users without knowing something about how the catalogue is constructed?

The modules vary considerably as to the proportion of the 100 hours' study time that is occupied by class contact. Cataloguing and classification 1, as now taught, is the most labour-intensive of the courses for staff, because we decided at the outset that the students need plenty of supervised practice and that there is relatively little that they need to do in their own time. In the past we had tried to get them to practise more on their own, with the inevitable result that only the keenest actually did so.

The time allowed is divided more or less evenly between cataloguing and classification. Each of these has a one-hour lecture each week; there is a second one-hour lecture which is used for either cataloguing or classification in different weeks; and each student has two one-and-a-half-hour practical sessions every week, one for cataloguing and one for classification. The course lasts ten weeks. Because of student numbers, the full-time students are divided into two groups and all practical sessions are done twice, so that the teaching load is considerably more. Moreover, the part-time students are taught this module completely separately, which means that each year we do all of the practical work three times.

The Students

With one or two exceptions who are registered for the Diploma only, all of our students take the MA. They all have a first degree, in a non-librarianship subject, and have to have worked in some kind of library or information service for a year before admission to the course. This prerequisite has been in place for very many years, and is considered essential so that students have gained some idea of what library and information work is like and picked up some of the basic routines before they start their academic studies. Depending on the kind of library, this experience varies greatly, which is to the ultimate benefit of all students as they share their experiences. In some cases, students have spent a considerable proportion of their time cataloguing, while in other cases you would think they had never looked at a catalogue at all.

Curriculum Content: Cataloguing

There has been much debate generally in relation to professional education regarding the balance between theory and practice.[16] My aim, perhaps unusually, is to concentrate more on the practice and to try to ensure that all students acquire some of the fundamentals of basic cataloguing using AACR2. However, I think it is unhelpful to do this with no context at all, and I therefore devote a couple of lectures at the beginning to the development of cataloguing codes, and the students do some practical exercises illustrating the problems of filing. In looking at the codes, I do not go into detail except for the British Museum rules, which I still think it is useful for all librarians in Britain to know something about. For the rest, I try to point out peculiarities, and things which would be done differently now, always reminding the students that they are likely to find card catalogues everywhere which were compiled by older rules. Because some of the them invariably get jobs involved in retrospective conversion, it is particularly important for them to realize that cataloguing has not always been as it is now, but is in a constant state of development and flux.

Next I introduce the first edition of AACR, follow this with some brief information on International Standard Bibliographic Description, and then start on AACR2. Our department has a collection of some fifty books which were chosen to be used as examples for practical work in cataloguing and classification. All students are provided with a bundle of photocopies of the title-pages and other relevant parts, so that they can all look at the same examples for practical work. When it comes to the physical description area we look at enough of the books for all students to be able to work on them in groups and pass them round so as to cover a reasonable number in the time available. As we work through the areas of description, students gradually build up complete catalogue records for many of these books. All of the descriptive work is based on books, though reference is made, as appropriate, to other physical formats. I am of the view that if students can understand how to catalogue a book they should be able to apply this knowledge to other formats without undue difficulty. It also seems to me that there is rather more local variation in practice when dealing with non-book materials.

Towards the end of the term we look at MARC, and the students convert some of the previous exercises into MARC 21 format. It is always disappointing that much of what they have been taught disappears from their minds as soon as the MARC format is imposed, and it would be interesting to know whether this happens with students elsewhere. Some of the additional lectures are used to look at such topics as the importance and uses of MARC, authority control, and OPACs. I feel that it is very important that students put the practical cataloguing into context, and understand the relationship between the inputting side of cataloguing and the use of the catalogue by the library users.

Curriculum Content: Classification

Classification is taught largely by my colleague Vanda Broughton, with contributions from me on Dewey. This part of the course starts by discussing the theory of classification and its relationship to the physical arrangement of materials, leading to the problem of citation order. Next the structure of classification schemes is considered, including how relationships are displayed, notation, and the question of main class order. The students at this point do some practical work on content analysis, attempting to create objective summaries of the content of some of the sample books, considering particularly the terms that would be sought by users. A pervasive theme in considering subject headings, as it is in cataloguing, is an emphasis on the need for judgement in selecting terms, having always in mind the needs of the end-users. Content analysis leads on to consideration of the alphabetical approach to subject access, including Library of Congress Subject Headings. The remainder of the course is then devoted to practical work with the main classification schemes, Library of Congress, Dewey and UDC, and with LCSH. Throughout this, the students are encouraged to think about the effects that their choices will have on physical arrangement, and on retrieval by users. Finally they undertake some facet analysis, including analysis of a selection of terms from their chosen subjects (see next section).

Coursework

Over the years we have had much discussion of the best ways to test cataloguing and classification, given that it is not feasible to have a practical unseen examination in these subjects. Theoretical questions can be and are included in the general Professional awareness examination, but we have always wanted the assessed coursework to be as practical as possible. Students are therefore required to choose a subject, so that they can imagine that they are working in a specific subject area, perhaps as a subject librarian or else in a special library. They then choose ten items and produce catalogue records for them, using AACR2 punctuation. Between them the ten items have to exhibit certain features, which are:

- a personal author
- joint authors, with added entry
- an edited work (i.e., a collection of chapters by different people, with an overall editor)
- a revised edition (i.e., something that requires an edition statement)
- a corporate body main entry
- proceedings of a conference
- a work requiring a uniform title (e.g., a translation or other appropriate work)

For classification, they have to select from the ten titles and classify four of them by each of the main classification schemes used, at the same time providing Library of Congress Subject Headings; they must choose a different four each time. In addition, they do a brief exercise in document analysis, a short essay on subject analysis of their chosen subject, and a longer piece on the classification scheme which would best suit a special library devoted to the subject.

We find that the subject focus is quite successful. It gives them some reasonable way of restricting what would otherwise be an infinite choice of titles, and in the following term they are able to link it into their coursework for the module Information sources and retrieval. It might be objected that there is nothing to stop students from cheating, by copying from other catalogues. This is true, and it is inevitable as long as the work is not done under examination conditions. This is one reason why I insist on the AACR2 punctuation for the cataloguing, which is difficult to find in an OPAC. In practice, it is the hardest thing in the world to copy something correctly, and from the number of mistakes made by some of them it is clear that, if they are copying from elsewhere, they are not benefiting from it!

Most other coursework, when marked, is returned with a comment sheet attached, so that students have a reasonable amount of feedback. In the case of cataloguing and classification, as in some other subjects, it is more appropriate to annotate the work heavily and put very little on the comment sheet. I normally mark every error that I see, and write comments, some of which recur on many students' work. As for actual marks, we take the view that cataloguing could be 100% correct (it never is), and that, therefore, students should have the opportunity of achieving 100% if they can. This is very different from the situation in most modules, where 70% would be exceptionally good for an essay mark. Each year I look at the aspects which have caused the most difficulty and try to emphasize these even more to the next cohort of students.

Curriculum Content: Cataloguing and Classification 2

This module is offered as an option, and usually half a dozen or so students choose it. We use it as a means of exploring certain topics in more depth, and looking at special problems such as cataloguing maps, music, rare books, serials, videos, etc., in more detail than is possible in the compulsory course. About a third of the course is devoted to the construction of a faceted classification and associated thesaurus. We also have seminar discussions on topics related to cataloguing and classification, such as: the need for main entry; alternatives to traditional classification schemes; the role and future of the cataloguer; different types of subject approach. To some extent, the content is determined by the interests of the students in that year. Assessment allows a range of topics, some being more practice-based (and including compilation of a thesaurus) and others theoretical essays, and students must do one of each kind.

WORKPLACE TRAINING

Training in the workplace is even harder to generalize about than education leading to a qualification. There is tremendous variation in the number of cataloguers employed in libraries: from the British Library, which has some 50 cataloguers at its National Bibliographic Service, to the smallest one-person library. It should also be remembered that many quite large public library authorities nowadays may have only one cataloguer.

The respondent from the British Library National Bibliographic Service indicated that they treat all new cataloguers as novices in order to avoid overlooking any aspect of cataloguing. The training programme lasts for twelve months. The first four weeks are spent on intensive training in AACR2, DDC, LCSH and UKMARC, and in cataloguing systems. Then come six months of practical cataloguing, starting with batches of "straightforward" material. Gradually they move on to standard batches and, during this time, attend seminars on more complex areas of cataloguing (uniform titles, collections, exhibitions, conferences, etc.). After the first seven months, monitoring may be reduced to regular spot-checking depending on progress, but all cataloguers must achieve departmental targets for quality and output by the end of the training programme.

Another major creator of bibliographic records in Britain is a commercial organization, Bibliographic Data Services (BDS). Their records are created to the normal bibliographic standards, i.e., AACR2, UKMARC and MARC 21, the current edition of the Dewey Decimal Classification, Library of Congress Classification (for adult academic material only), and Library of Congress Subject Headings. In addition, genre headings are added for fiction, and a short descriptive annotation is included to aid selection. BDS are also the current suppliers of Cataloguing-in-Publication (CIP) data to the British Library. Records can be bought by libraries, either directly or through book suppliers, and the intention is that they can be used without further modification.[17] Their cataloguing manager indicates that they start from first principles, using an in-house manual which summarizes AACR2. As for classification, they start with Dewey, and move on to LCSH and Library of Congress classification later, after looking at authority control. Again there is an assumption that beginners will not have learnt much about cataloguing at library school.

Other responses illustrate two perhaps typical situations, both in quite large libraries, and also represent the opinions of cataloguers who have to do the training. One respondent coordinates the cataloguing and classification training for new professionals in one of the larger (ex-polytechnic) metropolitan universities. The trainees receive between 5 and 7 hours' training a week, over a period of up to a year. This starts with working through textbooks such as Eric J. Hunter's *Introduction to AACR2*, Bowman's *Essential Cataloguing*,[18] and an in-house workbook on Dewey. They then move on to creating simple records from scratch, and progress to more difficult items before moving on to validating existing MARC records. Finally they learn about non-book materials.

The other respondent, this time at a major "old" university, comments that he would expect it to take between six and nine months for a new cataloguer to be fully trained in his section. In this case, there is a mixture of on-the-job training and courses which are offered generally to library staff across the university, which has many colleges and faculties. He comments that, from recent experience, it appears that library schools are not teaching even the most basic aspects of cataloguing and classification, and that it is "frustrating for employers looking for cataloguers."

A third respondent was until recently chief cataloguer at one of the major colleges of the University of London. There the training was based on a manual prepared for the Bodleian Library, Oxford, which was itself based on some Library of Congress manuals. In his opinion, most library schools are not doing enough to teach students either the principles or the practice of cataloguing.

The chief cataloguer of one of London's main public library authorities has considerable experience of recruiting for cataloguers, and says that good cataloguers are very rare. This response is worth quoting at some length because it raises several interesting points:

When we recruit we are asking for professionally-qualified staff with a couple of years' experience in bibliographical services (we found that asking for specifically cataloguing experience was too restrictive) and we select on the basis of an interview and also a practical test. In interview I find that a majority of candidates think that the only important qualities of a good cataloguer are accuracy and a love of detail (disregarding entirely the necessity for good judgement and an understanding of the purposes of the catalogue and the needs of its users). I have seen blank faces when I have asked what the uses are of a bibliographic record or what a catalogue is for, and I have been told that Dewey is a cataloguing code and that the conversion to MARC 21 will involve moving all the stock in the library. My simple test involves asking the candidates to catalogue three (varied but not especially difficult) books to AACR level 2 within 30 minutes, on paper and without any need for MARC coding–and most candidates, even those already in cataloguing jobs or who have spent time cataloguing, find this difficult, since they are used to filling in templates on a screen or downloading records from external databases. Even though they have access to AACR during the test, they prove themselves ignorant of the basic rules and principles of cataloguing and indexing.

This seems to show that many candidates, even those fairly familiar with cataloguing, may be unfamiliar with its context, and at a loss when outside the confines of their own system. This respondent feels that it would be unfair to blame just the library schools for these shortcomings:

> There is an extraordinary belief in the profession as a whole that there is no connection between the construction of a database and the ability to carry out an effective search. . . . Chief librarians have been encouraged to think the same and to believe that the technology will make good any failings in input, which is why there aren't many cataloguers at all any more. Until the profession as a whole recognises the value of good cataloguing . . . there will be no demand for library schools to provide a proper education in cataloguing.

As for the qualities of a good cataloguer:

> . . . even when faced with a prospective cataloguer who is lamentably ignorant of cataloguing, it is possible to undertake on-the-job

training and to supply the lack of a cataloguing education provided at library school–as long as the candidate has the right cast of mind. Here again I find myself at odds with many in the profession who think that someone who is fussy and pedantic is therefore a natural born cataloguer. What I want in a cataloguer is someone who is capable of logical and analytical thought, who has got a sense of balance and perspective, who can make sensible judgements about what is worth time and effort and what is not.

COMMERCIAL TRAINING PROVIDERS

For those who wish to attend short courses in this subject area there are four main providers in the United Kingdom: CILIP, Aslib (the Association for Information Management), TFPL, and Allegro Training. TFPL runs a course on thesaurus construction, but apart from this it is not involved in this area. The other three all run one- or two-day courses on cataloguing or classification at least twice a year, and the continuance of these must be an indication that there is a demand.

CILIP

The main course in this subject area offered by CILIP is called "Cat and class: it's OK for anyone!"–OK standing in this case for "organization of knowledge." This is a two-day course, a mixture of lectures and practical exercises, and covers both descriptive and subject cataloguing, including AACR2, MARC, and Dewey. There is also the more specialized one-day course "Library of Congress Subject Headings: an introduction," which is described in the publicity as "not suitable for anyone who is new to cataloguing and classification."

Aslib

Aslib offers three one-day courses relevant to this area:

- Basic cataloguing and indexing
- Cataloguing practice
- Classification practice

Outlines of these are given in Appendices 2-4 of this article. The "Cataloguing practice" course is described as "a practical course, for people with cataloguing experience, on using AACR2 . . . and the MARC . . . Manual." It is clear from the outlines that all of the courses cover very much the kind of material which would at one time have been normal in most library schools.

Allegro Training

Allegro Training is run by Ian Ledsham and, as its name implies, specializes in aspects of music librarianship, but also includes courses on cataloguing using MARC and on using Dewey. Initially aimed at music librarians, these courses seem to have been broadened in their target audience, and include three in this subject area:

MARC 21: An Introduction

This is intended primarily for staff of libraries which are migrating from UKMARC to MARC 21, but presumably it will be possible to change its emphasis in the future to make it more of an introduction to MARC in general.

Number Crunching: A Guide to Classifying with Dewey

This course is a new one, recently introduced, and considers:

• the history and structure of Dewey
• how to define the subject content of an item
• number building
• strategies for deciding between alternative classifications
• using Dewey in MARC 21.

Word Games: Library of Congress Subject Headings in Practice

This course covers:

• the principles of subject cataloguing
• how to create basic headings in LCSH
• the use of subdvisions to refine headings
• provision for the use of LCSH in MARC 21
• provision for special categories of material such as periodicals, literature, music, etc.

A fourth course was added for 2004: *An introduction to cataloguing.*

It is noticeable that all of these providers' courses operate at quite a basic level, covering topics which cataloguers would need to know to get them started. Ledsham says that he has received a number of requests for cataloguing training from recently qualified professional librarians.[19] There seems to be no advertised provision for more advanced work. Presumably by this stage the demand is catered for largely by in-house training.

CONCLUSION

What conclusions can we draw from this? There is certainly a general perception that cataloguing and classification are not being taught as much as they were. Examination of the courses, however, appears to show that something *including* these subjects does appear in almost every course, even if in some cases it is optional. My impression, though, is that most of it merely provides a broad overview, with very little practical content. It is rather like the difference between a degree in Classics and a degree in Classical Studies; the latter will not include any language work. Without considerable practical work one can never really learn how to use a cataloguing code or classification scheme. It is probably this fact that is causing both former students and their employers to believe that, with one or two exceptions, library schools are not doing enough to prepare their students for the world of cataloguing.

The reason why they are not doing enough is less clear. It seems likely that there is much truth in Gorman's remarks, referring to the American situation, that "ill-informed library administrators" are unaware of the importance of cataloguing and that they have allowed it to decline in the mistaken belief that the catalogue records will be created by someone else. This is borne out by the comments from the public library chief cataloguer mentioned earlier. Because library administrators no longer require recent graduates to have a sound knowledge of cataloguing, there is no incentive for the library schools to teach it.[20] What they seem to be ignoring is that even graduates in posts where most work is done by copy-cataloguing need to know how to identify good and bad catalogue records, and be able to make informed decisions when choosing between them. It is ultimately the catalogue users who will be disadvantaged by poor catalogues.

Another long-standing problem is the perception that cataloguing and classification are old-fashioned and boring. This is a myth which, in my experience, is perpetuated by most information professionals, to the extent that anyone who expresses an interest in cataloguing, or who actually enjoys it, is regarded as something of a freak. Perhaps some library schools therefore feel a sense of "shame" if they confess to teaching it, because they want to be seen as doing things which are more "modern." Meanwhile, they probably take refuge in the excuse that so much of cataloguing depends on local practice, which cannot be taught, that it is not worth giving more than a superficial overview. While there may be some truth in this, it does not excuse the failure to teach the fundamental principles and basic techniques of these processes. It also ignores the fact, emphasized by Hill in the American context, that many graduates who in their first professional posts find themselves cataloguing will have no one to teach them but themselves.[21]

I suspect, too, that some of those teaching cataloguing and classification are not experts in the subjects and are doing so reluctantly. It is not within the scope of this article to investigate this, as it would be difficult to do so tactfully, but if it is true, it would explain why the courses show a tendency to be superficial.

All of this leaves out of account the fact that cataloguing and classification are fundamental to library and information work, not just incidental. They are at the heart of the profession, and it is essential that *all* librarians, not just cataloguers, are taught them.[22] If these subjects are not taught, what will be? Computing and management skills can be learnt anywhere, but not cataloguing and classification. There seems to have been too much dilution of the skills which are specific to the profession in favour of other skills, which although important, are not specific. It would be encouraging if CILIP would give clearer guidance as to what subjects should be included in the curriculum and which of them should be compulsory. The current growing interest in metadata and in cataloguing the Web ought to make this an appropriate time to do so.

There is also clearly a pressing need to educate senior library managers in the importance of catalogues and cataloguers, because without a change of view on their part it seems unlikely that any major change can be effected. The chief cause for hope lies in the fact that students themselves are realizing that the treatment of these subjects is inadequate, and demanding more.

NOTES

1. CILIP, *Accreditation Instrument: procedures for the accreditation of courses.* Approved October 1999, revised March 2002 ([London]: CILIP, 2002).

2. A note on terminology here: I shall initially use "Cataloguing" to include classification, though classification will also receive some separate mention. I shall use "library school" as an old-fashioned shorthand term for "institution teaching library or information science or management." I was tempted to use the term "LIS department," but this is sometimes cumbersome and inappropriate. Moreover, most of my respondents used the term "library school," and it was used throughout the special issues of *Cataloging & Classification* (34, no. 1/2 and 3) that dealt with this topic. See also John Feather, "Whatever Happened to the Library Schools?" *Library & Information Update* 2, no. 10 (Oct. 2003): 40-41.

3. See, for example, Michael Gorman, "Why Teach Cataloguing and Classification," *Cataloging & Classification Quarterly* 34, no. 1/2 (2002): 1-13; Jerry D. Saye, "Where Are We and How Did We Get Here?, or, The changing place of cataloging in the library and information science curriculum: causes and consequences," *Cataloging & Classification Quarterly* 34, no. 1/2 (2002): 121-143.

4. Judith Elkin and Tom Wilson (eds.), *The Education of Library and Information Professionals in the United Kingdom* (London: Mansell, 1997).

5. *Catalogue and Index* 148 (summer 2003): 13.

6. CILIP, *Accreditation instrument* (note 1).

7. CILIP, *When information goes wild–take cover or take control!* (London: CILIP, 2002). Leaflet.

8. Most respondents wished to remain anonymous, and I have respected their wishes.

9. Loughborough University, Dept. of Information Science, *Module specification: Information handling.* Available at: http://cisinfo.lboro.ac.uk:8081/ci/wr0015.module_spec?select_mod=03ISP402 [accessed 15 Sept. 2003].

10. Information from Peter Lea (e-mail, 1 October 2003).

11. Information from website, at http://www.rgu.ac.uk/prospectus/modules/disp_moduleview.cfm [accessed 17 October 2003].

12. Information from website at http://www.unl.ac.uk/postgradline/ME82P.html and http://www.unl.ac.uk/postgradline/ME95P.html [accessed 29 September 2003].

13. Information from Nigel Ford, who teaches the module (e-mail, 18 September 2003).

14. "Graduates the Market Needs," *Library & Information Update* 2, no. 5 (May 2003): 48-50, at p. 50.

15. Information from Mary Jane Steer, who teaches the course (e-mail, 2 October 2003).

16. In relation to cataloguing, see Sheila S. Intner, "Persistent Issues in Cataloging Education: Considering the Past and Looking Toward the Future," *Cataloging & Classification Quarterly* 34, no. 1/2 (2002): 15-29.

17. Information from BDS website, http://www.bibdsl.co.uk [accessed 10 October 2003].

18. Eric J. Hunter, *An Introduction to AACR 2: a programmed guide to the second edition of the Anglo-American cataloguing rules, 1988 revision,* Rev. ed. (London: Bingley, 1989); J. H. Bowman, *Essential Cataloguing* (London: Facet, 2003).

19. Personal communication (e-mail, 12 September 2003).

20. Gorman, "Why Teach Cataloguing and Classification?" pp. 2-3.

21. Janet Swan Hill, "What Else Do You Need to Know? Practical skills for catalogers and managers," *Cataloging & Classification Quarterly* 34, no. 1/2 (2002): 245-61, at p. 248.

22. See again Gorman, "Why Teach Cataloguing and Classification?" pp. 10-11.

APPENDIX 1. List of Institutions Offering Courses in Library and Information Studies

City	Institution	Department
Aberdeen	Robert Gordon University	School of Information and Media
Aberystwyth	University of Wales	Department of Information Studies
Birmingham	University of Central England	School of Information Studies
Brighton	University of Brighton	School of Information Management
Bristol	University of Bristol	Department of Continuing Education
Edinburgh	Queen Margaret University College	Department of Communication and Information Studies
Glasgow	University of Strathclyde	Department of Information Science
Leeds	Leeds Metropolitan University	School of Information Management
Liverpool	Liverpool John Moores University	Centre for Information and Library Management, Liverpool Business School
London	City University	Department of Information Science
London	University College London	School of Library, Archive and Information Studies

APPENDIX 1 (continued)

City	Institution	Department
London	London Metropolitan University	Department of Applied Social Sciences
London	Thames Valley University	Faculty of Professional Studies
Loughborough	Loughborough University	Department of Information Science
Manchester	Manchester Metropolitan University	Department of Information and Communications
Newcastle upon Tyne	Northumbria University	Division of Information and Communication Studies, School of Informatics
Sheffield	University of Sheffield	Department of Information Studies

APPENDIX 2. Outline of Aslib's "Basic Cataloguing and Indexing" Course

Introduction

- order from chaos–the purpose and principles and practice of cataloguing and indexing

The starting point

- the collection–what is in and what is out
- the material–from books to Internet pages

The cataloguing and indexing process

- the description
- access by title, creator, series . . .
- access by subject

The products

- the catalogue
- the collection, organised
- the authority control files

Automation aspects

- the computerised catalogue
- user interfaces (OPACs)

Practical exercises

- making simple records
- representing subjects
- building the computerised catalogue
- locating records in online OPACs

APPENDIX 3. Outline of Aslib's "Cataloguing Practice" Course

Introduction

- the essential principles and purposes of cataloguing

The tools available

- AACR2
- MARC (UKMARC, USMARC, MARC 21)
- authority files

The tools in use, 1

- AACR2 descriptions
- AACR2 access points

The manual product

- physical formats
- guides

APPENDIX 3 (continued)

The tools in use, 2

• MARC coding

The automated product

• OPACs as the output user interface
• adding further data to increase user access through the OPAC

Practical exercises including

• making simple and complex records for different types of material
• building an authority file
• developing Local Practice Notes
• accessing and using records in online OPACs via the Internet

APPENDIX 4. Outline of Aslib's "Classification Practice" Course

Introduction

• basic principles and objectives
• summarising versus in-depth indexing
• pre-coordination and post-coordination
• alphabetical and classified schemes

General schemes

• the alphabetical subject heading approach
• the classified approach
• the alphabetical subject index

Special schemes and thesauri

• the alphabetical subject heading approach
• the classified approach

Build-your-own subject heading or classification scheme

- controlled and uncontrolled language indexing
- authority files

Practical exercises

- identification of subject content of an item
- establishing subject index terms for an item
- establishing classification codes for an item
- making appropriate entries for the alphabetical index
- choosing your own terms and cross-references

LATIN AMERICA

The Teaching
of Information Processing
in the University of Buenos Aires,
Argentina

Elsa E. Barber
Silvia L. Pisano

SUMMARY. The article broadly describes the current curriculum in the Departamento de Bibliotecología y Ciencia de la Información at the Facultad de Filosofía y Letras of the Universidad de Buenos Aires. The Information Processing area, including cataloging and classification is introduced: its composition, theoretical background, strategies, and teaching techniques used in the teaching process/learning, relationship

Elsa E. Barber is Professor of Classification of Knowledge (E-mail: elsabarber@ciudad.com.ar); and Silvia L. Pisano is Professor of Cataloging of Non-Print Materials (E-mail: filolog@dd.com.ar), both at Departamento de Bibliotecología y Ciencia de la Información, Universidad de Buenos Aires.

[Haworth co-indexing entry note]: "The Teaching of Information Processing in the University of Buenos Aires, Argentina." Barber, Elsa E., and Silvia L. Pisano. Co-published simultaneously in *Cataloging & Classification Quarterly* (The Haworth Information Press, an imprint of The Haworth Press, Inc.) Vol. 41, No. 3/4, 2006, pp. 335-351; and: *Education for Library Cataloging: International Perspectives* (ed: Dajin D. Sun, and Ruth C. Carter) The Haworth Information Press, an imprint of The Haworth Press, Inc., 2006, pp. 335-351. Single or multiple copies of this article are available for a fee from The Haworth Document Delivery Service [1-800-HAWORTH, 9:00 a.m. - 5:00 p.m. (EST). E-mail address: docdelivery@haworthpress.com].

Available online at http://www.haworthpress.com/web/CCQ
doi:10.1300/J104v41n03_08

with other areas in the curriculum, the mode of connection between theory and practice, as well as the main existing research areas. *[Article copies available for a fee from The Haworth Document Delivery Service: 1-800-HAWORTH. E-mail address: <docdelivery@haworthpress.com> Website: <http://www.HaworthPress.com> © 2006 by The Haworth Press, Inc. All rights reserved.]*

KEYWORDS. Information processing, cataloging, cataloging education, teaching, Universidad de Buenos Aires, Argentina

INTRODUCTION

The Departamento de Bibliotecología of the Universidad de Buenos Aires was founded in 1922. It has gone through several clearly defined stages that have been documented in several previous publications.[1]

From its beginnings, the Department wanted ongoing revision of its curriculum in order to provide instruction that responded to the needs of the country and the professional trends.

The education of the library science professional at the Universidad de Buenos Aires has been performed by means of diverse programs of study that emphasized the first cycle of basic professional education, in preference to the second cycle leading to the Licenciatura.

The new curriculum, approved on November 24, 1999, by the Superior Board of the University, attempts to undo this history, since it conceives of the program as a complete professional cycle concluding with the Licenciatura. This curricular design aims to adequately achieve the relationship between undergraduate and graduate studies. It also adjusts to the general orientation inspired by the "Acuerdo de Gobierno para la Reforma de la Universidad de Buenos Aires"[2] and the "Programa de Reforma Curricular de la Universidad de Buenos Aires."[3]

This article describes broadly the current curriculum[4] with a focus in the Information Processing area. To this aim, it introduces the composition, theoretical background, strategies, and teaching techniques used in the teaching process/learning, relationship with other areas in the curriculum, the mode of connection between theory and practice, as well as the main existing research areas.

CURRICULUM

The scientific and technological changes that have taken place in the information field in recent years have had an effect not only on the concept itself, but also on the procedures, techniques, and strategies for its collection, organization, conservation, transfer, and dissemination. To this, we must add the evolution of contemporary society towards a post-industrial society, whose information needs and the importance this attains made it impossible to postpone the development and implementation of a training program that would allow continuing development to the graduates from the Departamento de Bibliotecología y Ciencia de la Información.

For this reason, we worked concurrently in two programs:

1. Curriculum change.
2. Empowerment of the program towards the implementation of the new curriculum.

In the first case, the three governing bodies, professors, students, and graduates, discussed and analyzed the project. After a thoughtful analysis that made it possible to obtain consensus among the different actors, the plan was approved and submitted to the Board of the Facultad de Filosofía y Letras. The Superior Board of the University later endorsed the plan. Implementation began in 2001. As opposed to the previous one, this is a flexible plan, which has characteristics that challenge its management, unprecedented until then.

The plan is divided into two cycles:

1. Professional Training, which is comprised of General Training and Basic Professional Training. Upon completion, the student gets a Diploma in Library Science.
2. Specialized Training. Upon completion, the student gets a Degree in Library and Information Science, with one of six orientations:
   • Information Processing
   • Information Resources and Service
   • Management of Information Centers
   • Information Technology
   • Archives
   • Preservation and Conservation

The student can also choose to pursue the Teaching path or the PhD in Philosophy and Letters with a specialization in Library and Information Science. Keeping in mind the desire to respond to the needs stated in the beginning of this section, the Department developed a Master's in Information Science (MIS) with two orientations, "Management of Information Resources" and "Analysis and Design of Information Systems." As of the writing of this paper, the MIS plan was going through the different stages of approval within the University.

In the second case, in order to empower the program, we worked together with the University of Texas at Austin, with the financial support of the Lampadia Foundation (Antorchas Foundation in Argentina), in a program that allowed us:

1. To grant scholarships to get a Master's degree in Library and Information Science in a United States university.
2. A professors' interchange program (professors from UT teaching graduate courses in the University of Buenos Aires and professors from the University of Buenos Aires who attended courses at UT to observe teaching methods).
3. Getting a computing laboratory dedicated to the Department of Library and Information Science.
4. The acquisition of bibliographic material.
5. The establishment of a complete conservation laboratory.

Having obtained a computer lab of our own, we started with the necessary procedures to get OCLC services for educational purposes for free in mid-1998. This had a great impact since, until then, OCLC was known only in theory. Students still have few chances of working in institutions with a subscription to these services, but we understand that they will be future users of them and they will start using them according to the possibilities of the institutions where they work. Although the use of LCSH, LCC, and MARC 21 is not widespread, they have been included in the curriculum. Obviously, this means having to learn them in an environment where almost no one uses them.

Cataloging teachers took courses on authority control offered by the LC Program for Cooperative Cataloging (PCC) during 2000 and 2001 in order to transmit this knowledge to future information professionals, so that they can, in turn, create awareness in authority control at the institutions where they work, and thereby make effective the change our country needs so much regarding bibliographic control. It is a complicated challenge . . . but we are working on it from our teaching.

INFORMATION PROCESSING AREA

Since the interdisciplinary library and information science field requires varied and imaginative curricula, professionals need intellectual tools that make it easy for them to adapt their thinking to social change and the technological environment. It looks into information processing, aiming towards standardization, access to information, and information management.[5]

The positivist pragmatics (rules that solve concrete problems) constitutes the theoretical background on which the area is based. Great theorists such as Bliss and Ranganathan, among others, worked with this approach. Nowadays, a theoretical reformulation is taking place. This shift looks for input from different disciplines like Linguistics. The general principles guiding these theories are inscribed within the so-called Knowledge Organization.

On this basis, the Professional Training cycle strives for a general training that provides:

- philosophical, linguistic, and epistemological knowledge, fundamental for the comprehension and future development of the core courses in the area,
- training in the use of systems designed for the organization of knowledge,
- knowledge of cataloging standards and international formats for recording information.

The Specialized Training cycle, given the complexity and diversification of the disciplines, requires the deepening of aspects such as:

- research methods applied to library and information science, identification and definition of research areas, design and implementation of the most appropriate policies and projects,
- effective use of tools to produce original cataloging of non-print materials (electronic resources, microforms, films, and so on),
- methods for the selection, evaluation, processing, and dissemination of the great variety of non-print materials available,
- knowledge to expand local services through cooperative networks,
- techniques for the construction and modification of online public access catalog,
- application of indexing and abstracting techniques to all types of materials,
- preparing of coordinated indexes and keywords,
- ability to set up technical services routines and procedures.

From the theoretical background described, we continue to specify area courses in each cycle (see Table 1), minimum content requirements, and basic required readings. However, there are some limitations: the article will not provide information about the additional readings that the professor supplies during the course and it will also cite instruments used to do the cataloging and subject analysis in the courses of the first cycle, since they also apply to the area as a whole. It is worth mentioning that even though students are exposed to the main changes in the Anglo American Cataloging Rules, 2002 revision and 2003 update, this work is not used for the corresponding practice, given the lack of a Spanish version of the cited tool.

Professional Training Cycle

The **General Training** section is comprised of six courses corresponding to the so called "Common Basic Cycle" of the Universidad de Buenos Aires (college stage that includes basic knowledge of: Introduction to scientific thinking, Introduction to the knowledge of society and state, Economy, Philosophy, Sociology, and Semiology).

Basic Professional Training section

It consists of nine required courses, two electives to choose out of six, a period of professional practice, and three levels of English. Within this section, the courses belonging to the area described are:

Cataloging Principles (required)

Minimum contents:

Study of the theory and application of organizational principles to information entities. Cataloging standards and their application. Selection and form of access points, bibliographic description, and description formats.

Required readings:

Hagler, Ronald. *The Bibliographic Record and Information Technology*. 3rd ed. Chicago: American Library Association, 1997.
MARC 21 Format for Bibliographic Data: Including Guidelines for Content Designation. 1999 ed. Washington: Library of Congress, 1999.

TABLE 1. Courses of the Information Processing Area

Information Processing Area	
Professional Training Cycle **Basic Professional Training**	**Specialized Training Cycle**
Cataloging principles	Cataloging services
Classification of knowledge	Indexing and Abstracting
	Organization of non-print materials
	Technical services in information units
	Seminar: Advances in information processing

"The MARC 21 Formats: Background and Principles." Revised November 1996. WWW Home page. [cited March 5, 2003]. Available on the Internet at: http://lcweb.loc.gov/marc796principl.html.

Reglas de Catalogación Angloamericanas. 2nd ed., rev. 1988, amended 1993 and 1997. Santafé de Bogotá: Rojas Eberhard, 1998.

Taylor, Arlene G. *Wynar's Introduction to Cataloging and Classification.* 9th ed. Englewood: Libraries Unlimited, 2000.

Classification of Knowledge (required)

Minimum contents:

Introduction to the principles and systems used in the organization of knowledge of all types of library and information materials. Origins and philosophical and historical development of library classification schemes. Analysis, comparison, and evaluation of different systems.

Required Readings:

American Library Association. Filing Committee. *ALA Filing Rules.* Chicago: American Library Association, c1980.

CDU: Clasificación Decimal Universal: Norma UNE 50 001. [CD-ROM]. Madrid: AENOR, 2000.

CDU–Clasificación Decimal Universal: Norma UNE 50 001. Madrid: AENOR, 2000. 3 v.

Cutter, Charles Ami. *Tabla de Tres Números para Autores: Revisión de Swanson-Swift,* 1969, arranged in the Spanish alphabet by María Rosa del V. Andreozzi. Montevideo: Cinterfor, 1977.

Dewey, Melvil. *Sistema de Clasificación Decimal Dewey.* 21st ed. Santa Fe de Bogotá, Colombia : Rojas Eberhard Editores, 2000. 4 v.

Lista de Encabezamientos de Materias para Bibliotecas. 3a. ed. Santa Fe de Bogota, Colombia: Rojas Eberhard Editores, 1998. 2 v.

Sears. *Lista de Encabezamientos de Materia.* Translated and adapted by Carmen Rovira, from the 12th ed. in English edited by Bárbara Wetsby. New York: H. W. Wilson, 1984.

Taylor, Arlene G. *Wynar's Introduction to Cataloging and Classification.* 9th ed. Englewood, CO: Libraries Unlimited, 2000.

Tesauro de la Unesco: Lista Estructurada de Descriptores para la Indización y la Recuperación Bibliográficas en las Esferas de la Educación, la Ciencia, las Ciencias Sociales, la Cultura y la Comunicación. Prepared by Jean Aitchison. Paris: Unesco, 1984. 2 v.

Specialized Training Cycle

In order to get the Licenciatura in Library and Information Science, it is a prerequisite to have passed the Professional Training cycle.

This state requires taking eight courses (four from the selected orientation; two to choose from the courses from the other orientations; two required of research, common to all orientations), an internship or field work, and three levels of a latin language: Portuguese, French, or Italian. Courses related to information processing are:

Cataloging Services (required)

Minimum contents:

Study of automated cataloging and cataloging services. Analysis and comparison of different bibliographic formats. Constitution, structure, and form of online catalogs. Cooperative and networking cataloging. Organization of a cataloging service.

Required readings:

Byrne, Deborah J. *Manual de MARC: Cómo Interpretar y Usar Registros MARC.* Translated and adapted from the 2nd ed. in English in GREBYD by Nicolás Rucks. Buenos Aires: GREBYD, 2001.

Fernández Molina, Juan Carlos, and Félix de Moya Anegón. *Los Catálogos de Acceso Público en Línea: El Futuro de la Recuperación de*

Información Bibliográfica. [s.l.]: Asociación Andaluza de Bibliotecarios, [1998].

Garduño Vera, Roberto, ed. *Control Bibliográfico Universal: El Control Bibliográfico en América Latina y el Caribe hacia el Tercer Milenio: Memoria.* México, D.F. : Universidad Nacional Autónoma de México, 1999.

Garduño Vera, Roberto. *Modelo Bibliográfico Basado en Formatos de Intercambio y en Normas Internacionales Orientado al Control Bibliográfico Universal.* México, D.F. : Universidad Nacional Autónoma de México, 1996.

Taylor, Arlene G. *Wynar's Introduction to Cataloging and Classification.* 9th ed. Englewood: Libraries Unlimited, 2000.

Gorman, Michel, ed. *Technical Services Today and Tomorrow.* 2nd ed. Englewood, Colo.: Libraries Unlimited, 1998.

Indexing and Abstracting (required)

Minimum contents:

Theory and methods of analysis of information for retrieval. It stresses subject analysis, including abstracting, vocabulary control methods and resources, specialized indexing systems, automatic and computer-assisted indexing. Techniques and special problems of the indexing of different types of recorded information, with special attention to new methods. Study of the structural characteristics of printed and electronic databases indexes.

Required readings:

American National Standards Institute. *American National Standard for Library and Information Sciences and Related Publishing Practices–Basic Criteria for Indexes. (Z39.4-1984).* New York: American National Standards Institute, 1984.

American National Standards Institute. *American National Standard for Writing Abstracts (Z39.14-1979).* New York: American National Standards Institute, 1979.

American National Standards Institute. *Guidelines for the Construction, Format and Management of Monolingual Thesauri (Z39.19-1993).* New York: American National Standards Institute, 1993.

Chicago Manual of Style. 14th ed. Chicago: University of Chicago Press, 1993.

Cindex. Rochester, NY: Indexing Research.

Cleveland, Donald B., and Ana D. Cleveland. *Introduction to Indexing and Abstracting*. 3rd ed. Englewood, CO: Libraries Unlimited, 2001.

Lancaster, Frederick W. *Indización y Resúmenes: Teoría y Práctica*. Translated by Elsa Barber. Buenos Aires: EB Publicaciones, 1996.

Lancaster, Frederick W. *Indexing and Abstracting in Theory and Practice*. 2nd ed. Champaign, IL: University of Illinois, 1998.

Mulvany, Nancy C. *Indexing Books*. Chicago: University of Chicago Press, 1994.

Organization of Non-Print Materials (required)

Minimum contents:

Non-print materials collection development. Principles of selection of logical and technical support. Problems of cataloging and classification of non-print materials (films, maps, videos, audio recordings, CD-ROMs, etc.), both as separate and integrated collections.

Required readings:

Byrne, Deborah J. *Manual de MARC: Cómo Interpretar y Usar Registros MARC*. Translated and adapted from the 2nd ed. in English in GREBYD by Nicolás Rucks. Buenos Aires: GREBYD, 2001.

Federación Internacional de Asociaciones de Bibliotecarios y Bibliotecas. *ISBD (CM): Descripción Bibliográfica Internacional Normalizada para Materiales Cartográficos*. Ed. rev. [Madrid]: ANABAD: Arco/Libros, 1993.

Federación Internacional de Asociaciones de Bibliotecarios y Bibliotecas. *ISBD (NBM): Descripción Bibliográfica Internacional Normalizada para Materiales no Librarios*. Ed. rev. [Madrid]: ANABAD: Arco/Libros, 1993.

Federación Internacional de Asociaciones de Bibliotecarios y Bibliotecas. *ISBD (PM): Descripción Bibliográfica Internacional Normalizada para Música Impresa*. Ed. rev. [Madrid]: ANABAD: Arco/Libros, 1994.

Hsieh-Yee, Ingrid. *Cómo Organizar Recursos Electrónicos y Audiovisuales para su Acceso: Guía para la Catalogación*. Translated and adapted from the original English in GREBYD by N. Rucks. Buenos Aires: GREBYD, 2002.

International Federation of Library Associations and Institutions. *ISBD (CR): International Standard Bibliographic Description for Serials and Other Continuing Resources.* [cited March 5, 2003]. Available on the Internet at: http://www.ifla.org/VII/s13/pubs/isbd.htm.

International Federation of Library Associations and Institutions. *ISBD (ER): International Standard Bibliographic Description for Electronic Resources.* [cited December 7, 2000]. Available on the Internet at: http://www.ifla.org/VII/s13/pubs/isbd.htm.

Olson, Nancy B. *Cataloging of Audiovisual Materials: A Manual Based on AACR2.* 3rd ed. DeKalb, Ill.: Minnesota Scholarly Press, 1992.

Taylor, Arlene G. *Wynar's Introduction to Cataloging and Classification.* 9th ed. Littleton, Co.: Libraries Unlimited, 2000.

Technical Services in Information Units (optional)

Minimum contents:

Organization of information units to acquire, organize, store, keep, preserve, and circulate collections. Principles of selection of the technical and logical support. Status of online systems in the current practice of technical services. Research and evaluation of available and developing systems, and examination of its use and functions.

Required readings:

Evans, G. Edward, Sheila S. Intner, and J. Weihs. *Introduction to Technical Services.* 7th ed. Englewood, CO: Libraries Unlimited, 2002.

Godden, Irene P., ed. *Library Technical Services: Operations and Management.* 2nd ed. San Diego, CA: Academic Press, 1991.

Kaplan, Michael, ed. *Planning and Implementing Technical Services Workstations.* Chicago: American Library Association, 1997.

Taylor, Arlene G. *The Organization of Information.* Englewood, CO: Libraries Unlimited, 2003. (Library and information science text series).

Yee, Martha M., and Sara Shatford Layne. *Improving Online Public Access Catalogs.* Chicago: American Library Association, 1998.

Seminar: Advances in Information Processing (optional)

Trend issues will be selected each semester the course is offered.

Professional Practice

This aspect is absolutely novel compared with the previous plans of study in the Universidad de Buenos Aires; it aims to introduce the graduate student to the professional reality he or she will find when he or she enters the work field, uniting the academic and professional domains. The curriculum determines the number of credit hours students must devote to this ruled teaching. The period of professional practice accumulates at the end of the corresponding courses. This avoids distraction from the regular course of academic work, and students are better prepared for their practice. These internships do not imply, in any case, financial compensation, nor a job relationship with the different information units; this activity has only an academic goal. A set of regulations was created that includes: goals, candidates, interns' obligations, choice of institutions where the internships will take place, constitution and functions of the faculty body, intern activities, intern evaluation, activity of the institutional advisor, and agreements with public and private information units.

Teaching Strategies and Techniques

The organization and treatment of information is a complex area which builds on a substantial body of knowledge of theories, disciplines, professions, and cultures. This diversity requires a particular teaching plan for the development of competencies in the field. The main characteristics of the plan are:

- approach to the real world,
- analysis of the critical incident,
- work in interdependent areas as a method of problem solving,
- implementation of solutions,
- continual evaluation.

We agree with the international literature in the area that identifies at least three important issues for a basic teaching-learning plan:

1. The process must be very open from the beginning. It is essential to start by creating awareness of the problem, then to proceed to identify and structure specific issues for students.
2. In the learning situation, the perspective of application to the "real world" is paramount. Routines and strategies must be developed.

Difficulties emerging later and necessary revisions of the first solutions are significant aspects of the learning process and they require supervision and/or support during the translation phase.
3. The learning process, as any open process, is based on problems
taken from the learner's own context. The student performs a double action: on the one hand, he or she provides knowledge from
his or her experience; on the other hand, he or she works on his or
her own learning, assimilating the knowledge taught.

Courses in the area develop through theoretical, theoretical-practical,
and practical classes. In theoretical classes, topics are introduced (with
or without visual support), each of which will receive treatment later in
practical classes. Theoretical-practical classes aim to the practical application of concepts previously explained and the discussion and exchange of experiences related to the readings. We strive to provide
students with active participation. In practical classes, different types of
cases that can be found are introduced; practical problems are identified, defined, and structured; information for a solution is obtained, alternative solutions are developed, choosing one or several of them: they
are implemented, verified, and revised if necessary. In all cases, the integration of information technology is important.

Finally, the Department encourages the integration and relationship
with other areas by means of formal and informal ways, for instance,
workshops on the curriculum, area meetings, gathering with other areas, and so on. This aims to avoid unwanted overlapping among different courses.

Theory vs. Practice

Students need information organization theories and principles in order to understand that professional practice is more than a routine application of different tools, and that allows them to adapt to changes. There
is a strong interconnection between theory and practice. Every practice
is based on a theory, and this is what must be researched at the academic
level. The relationship theory-practice in the teaching of this area is reflected in the continuing exchange of ideas, opinions, and information
in the course of the classes. On the other hand, a guided schedule for the
development of the different topics is established in order to avoid dis-
association between theory and practice, as well as to contribute to
creating and strengthening in the student the concept of the importance
of theory in the practical application.

In many cases, theoretical-practical classes have been implemented which allow: reading and comprehension of texts, exposition of topics, group debate, reports written by students under faculty supervision, and application of knowledge to real cases. Aiming to reinforce the relationship described, the new course of studies includes a professional practice instance or field work in the area at the end of both cycles.

Research Trends

Research is key in order to build and develop theories, test hypothesis, introduce new practices, and take advantage of the interdisciplinary nature of library and information science. Regarding this area, literature is mainly focused on case studies, format and language projects, and description. Mentioning of updates and/or theoretical instruments which have a specific application is scarce. In recent years, contributions came from mathematics, computational linguistics, business administration, computer science, engineering systems, sociology, artificial intelligence, and cognitive studies, among others.

New professionals must often guide inexpert users in the use of electronic and Internet databases, as well as online public access catalogs. The potential use of classification schemes to search and retrieve sources on the Internet is also a fast-growing area, with meaningful implications for classification systems and theory. Cataloging of Internet electronic resources through new description schemes such as metadata, its impact on traditional information control tools, such as bibliographic description standards, cataloging rules, and bibliographic formats, is a significant issue in the practice of this area. Thus, students must be aware of current research on these topics.

International trends in research during recent years have focused on: universal classification systems, cognitive processes, thesauri, structure and relationships, terminology, and natural language processing (including clusters analysis, semantic classification, and automatic indexing). Smaller groups of documents include works on concepts and categories, semantics, semiotics, linguistics, images classification, taxonomy, and ontology. Some research areas are not as new as they seem to be. Topics such as hypermedia and structure-based systems were studied since 1988, though with more complexity each time given the increasing sophistication of technology. Options for the organization of the Internet are, for obvious reasons, relatively new. Likewise, alternatives to solve cataloging of electronic resources are studied, suggesting different metadata schemes adapted to the specific characteristics of such resources (Dublin Core, Text Encoding Initiative, Warwick Framework, and Resource Description Framework). Application of coding languages such as SGML, HTML, and XML are researched as a common base for these suggested schemes.

Thus, we can also name other research topics that have not been studied in Argentina (except, more than 20 years ago, the introduction of AACR2 and thesauri construction). In recent years, a bibliographic revision on subject searching and content description in online catalogs was made, making a brief mention of the situation in the country. On the other hand, we are working on a research approach closely related to information technology, information resources and services, and management.

Several research projects were launched: "Automation processes of Argentine academic libraries" (Scientific Programming, 1995-1997), "The Automation of Argentine academic libraries facing the new millennium" (Scientific Programming 1998-2000), and "Libraries, information society, and technology: an approach to automation and public library services in Argentina" (Scientific Programming, 2001-2003). All projects were approved and financed by UBACYT (Universidad de Buenos Aires. Ciencia y Tecnología), after an internal and external evaluation. They have their headquarters at the Instituto de Investigaciones Bibliotecológicas of the Facultad de Filosofía y Letras, Universidad de Buenos Aires. The first work produced, "Los procesos de automatización de las bibliotecas universitarias argentinas: Capital Federal y Gran Buenos Aires" was published in 1999. It allows comparison of the information units situation in issues such as: automation of cataloging, circulation, public catalogs, periodicals management, reference services, administration, among others. The second work, published in 2003, "Tiempos y contratiempos de la automatización en las bibliotecas universitarias argentinas," is closely related to the first one, and it extends the geographical area of study to the whole country. It deals with retrospective conversion and some aspects of standardization: cataloging standards used, bibliographic formats, and tools used for subject analysis.

The third research project was carried out, applying the same methodology adopted in the previous ones, to public libraries in Buenos Aires city and surrounding areas. Thus, as for information processing, fundamental indicators were considered in order to describe the situation regarding bibliographic control. Given the magnitude of the challenges these libraries face in the information society, the project attempts to evidence the relationship between the automation level achieved and the use of new technologies to proven value-added services. At present, data obtained is being tabulated for the preparation of the final report.

After eight years of research in the field of information units automation in the country, the importance of the use of online public access catalogs (OPACs) related to access to information in different environments and levels is recognized. Thus, a new project that analyzes the problem of web OPACs at national, academic, special, and public libraries in the Mercosur countries (Argentina, Brazil, Paraguay, and Uruguay) has been introduced. From the initial presumption that OPACs do not follow international trends and that they are currently in an initial stage of implementation, we study aspects related to: (a) how bibliographic description is made; (b) how subject analysis is made, (c) the way in which help messages for the user are provided, and (d) the procedure used for the visualization of bibliographic information.

From what has been explained, it can be inferred that in Argentina there are different topics in the area that require a scientific approach. There is an imperical need to promote the development of more concrete research topics on the organization and treatment of information.

CONCLUSION

The Departamento de Bibliotecología y Ciencia de la Información of the Facultad de Filosofía y Letras of the Universidad de Buenos Aires has introduced, with the curricular change, a comprehensive and flexible design according to the needs of contemporary society.

This means a broad challenge, since the present situation of libraries in Argentina is without any doubt complex, made evident through tangible problems, diffused policies, and multiple restrictions. But the information processing area has committed with proposals that attempt to look to the future from an international viewpoint.

ENDNOTES

1. For further information on the last curricular changes at the Departamento de Bibliotecología of the Universidad de Buenos Aires, see the following articles by Elsa Barber, "Carrera de Bibliotecología y Documentación, Facultad de Filosofía y Letras, Universidad de Buenos Aires," in *Anales del Congreso Internacional de Información INFO'95*, La Habana, Cuba, 1995; "Carrera de Bibliotecología y Documentación. Facultad de Filosofía y Letras. Universidad de Buenos Aires. Vol. 1: Cursos da Argentina," in *Encontro de Dirigentes dos Cursos Superiores em Biblioteconomia do*

Mercosul. A Formaçao Profissional em Biblioteconomia no Mercosul, Porto Alegre, BR, Associaçao Brasileira de Ensino de Biblioteconomia e Documentaçao (ABEBD), 1996: 1-41; "Panorama de la enseñanza y la investigación en el área de Bibliotecología y Ciencia de la Información en las escuelas universitarias argentinas," in *Reunión de Investigadores y Educadores de Iberoamérica y del Caribe en el área de la Bibliotecología y Ciencia de la Información*, México: UNAM, Centro Universitario de Investigaciones Bibliotecológicas, 1996: 220-233; "La Formación Profesional en Bibliotecología y Ciencia de la Información en los Países del Mercosur," in *IV Encuentro de Educadores e Investigadores de Bibliotecología, Archivología y Ciencia de la Información de Iberoamérica y el Caribe*, Maracaibo, Venezuela, 1998; "Estudios de Bibliotecología y Ciencia de la Información, Facultad de Filosofía y Letras, Universidad de Buenos Aires," in *Actas del V Encuentro de EDIBCIC*, Granada, España: Universidad de Granada, 2000; "Adecuación de los planes de estudio del profesional de la Bibliotecología y Ciencia de la Información," in *I Congreso Internacional de Bibliotecología y Ciencia de la Información*, Lima, Perú: Colegio de Bibliotecólogos del Perú, 2002.

2. *Acuerdo de Gobierno para la Reforma de la Universidad de Buenos Aires*. Colón, ER: Universidad de Buenos Aires, 1995.

3. *Programa de Reforma de la Universidad de Buenos Aires. Reforma curricular. Borrador para la discusión*. Buenos Aires: Secretaría de Publicaciones del C.E.F. y L., 1996.

4. See Elsa Barber and Susana Romanos de Tiratel, "Diseño Curricular de la Licenciatura en Bibliotecología y Ciencia de la Información," in *IV Encuentro de Educadores e Investigadores de Bibliotecología, Archivología y Ciencia de la Información de Iberoamérica y el Caribe*, Maracaibo, Venezuela, 1998.

5. See Elsa Barber [et al.], "Bases conceptuales y metodológicas de la enseñanza de las disciplinas Bibliotecología/Ciencia de la Información. Síntesis de las principales tendencias y enfoques de cada área. Área Organización y Tratamiento de la Información," Paper presented at the IV Encuentro de Directores y III de Docentes de Escuelas de Bibliotecología y Ciencia de la Información del Mercosur, Montevideo, Uruguay, 2000.

Education
for Cataloging and Classification
in Mexico

Filiberto Felipe Martínez Arellano

SUMMARY. The main objective of this paper is to provide an overview about education for cataloging and classification in Mexico. Mexican Library and Information Science (LIS) schools have traditionally featured a strong emphasis on cataloging and classification learning, which continues to be an important part of their curricula. Additionally, as in other countries, education for cataloging and classification in Mexico has been influenced by the changes that libraries and Library Science have experienced as a result of new technological developments. General trends in education for cataloging and classification in Mexico are seen by comparing the different Mexican LIS schools and their program curricula. *[Article copies available for a fee from The Haworth Document Delivery Service: 1-800-HAWORTH. E-mail address: <docdelivery@haworthpress.com> Website: <http://www.HaworthPress. com>* © 2006 by The Haworth Press, Inc. All rights reserved.]

Filiberto Felipe Martínez Arellano, PhD, is Director, University Center for Library Science Research, National Autonomous University of Mexico, Torre II de Humanidades, Piso 12, Circuito Interior, Ciudad Universitaria, C. P. 04510, Mexico, D. F. (E-mail: felipe@servidor.unam.mx).

[Haworth co-indexing entry note]: "Education for Cataloging and Classification in Mexico." Martínez Arellano, Filiberto Felipe. Co-published simultaneously in *Cataloging & Classification Quarterly* (The Haworth Information Press, an imprint of The Haworth Press, Inc.) Vol. 41, No. 3/4, 2006, pp. 353-388; and: *Education for Library Cataloging: International Perspectives* (ed: Dajin D. Sun, and Ruth C. Carter) The Haworth Information Press, an imprint of The Haworth Press, Inc., 2006, pp. 353-388. Single or multiple copies of this article are available for a fee from The Haworth Document Delivery Service [1-800-HAWORTH, 9:00 a.m. - 5:00 p.m. (EST). E-mail address: docdelivery@haworthpress.com].

doi:10.1300/J104v41n03_09

353

KEYWORDS. Cataloging teaching in Mexico, cataloging education, classification in Mexico, Mexican library schools, technical services in Mexico, library education in Mexico

One of the main problems that Mexican libraries have faced over time is the organization of their collections. Therefore, Mexican Library and Information Science (LIS) schools have traditionally featured a strong emphasis on cataloging and classification learning, which continues to be an important part of their curricula. At the present time, there are eight Library and Information Science schools in Mexico that prepare professionals. Unlike LIS education in the United States, professional librarian training in Mexico is at the undergraduate level, which is called "licenciatura." LIS graduate programs also exist but these are only for those librarians that want to specialize, or as a first step for those who wish to prepare to conduct research.

The first Mexican LIS schools, founded approximately fifty years ago in the country's capital, were the National School of Library and Archive Sciences [Escuela Nacional de Biblioteconomía y Archivonomía (ENBA)] in 1945, and the College of Library Science at the National Autonomous University of Mexico in 1956. At the present time, there are six other LIS schools or "licenciatura" programs in different Mexican universities that provide LIS education in Mexico, which have their own characteristics and curricula: the School of Library and Information Sciences at the Autonomous University of San Luis Potosí [Universidad Autónoma del Estado de San Luis Potosí (UASLP)], College of Library Science at the Autonomous University of Nuevo León [Universidad Autónoma de Nuevo León (UANL)], Documental Information Sciences Program at the Autonomus University of Mexico State [Universidad Autónoma del Estado de México (UAEM)], Library Science Program at the Autonomous University of Chiapas [Universidad Autónoma de Chiapas (UACH)], School of Information Sciences at the Autonomous University of Guadalajara (UAG)], and the Information Sciences Program at the Autonomous University of Chihuahua (UACh). Two universities offer LIS master's degrees: the National Autonomous University of Mexico [Universidad Nacional Autónoma de México (UNAM)] and the Monterrey Technological Institute of Higher Studies [Instituto Tecnológico de Estudios Superiores de Monterrey (ITESM)].

LICENTIATE SCHOOLS AND PROGRAMS

National School of Library and Archive Sciences (Escuela Nacional de Biblioteconomía y Archivonomía, ENBA)

ENBA, founded in 1945, is the oldest Mexican institution dedicated to providing professional training for librarians. ENBA is an institution that depends on the Mexican Department of Education. Moreover, it is really remarkable that ENBA is the only Mexican Library Science school that at the present time offers a distance education program with students enrolled from different parts of the country. The school's population is around 1,000 students of which 60 percent are distance students (El quehacer . . . , 2003). ENBA has 48 professors on the faculty teaching LIS courses of whom only eight are full-time, with most being lecturers (Docentes . . . , 2003).

The main objective of ENBA's "licenciatura" is: "to form librarians able to interpret, to plan, to administer, to direct, to supervise, and to evaluate the programs, projects and professional tasks in libraries and information entities and centers, applying manual and automatized techniques to take care of the information needs that diverse society sectors demand" (Escuela Nacional de Biblioteconomía y Archivonomía, 2000).

ENBA's curriculum includes 45 required courses within the following areas: Technical organization, Services, Administration, Collection development, Social, Methodology, and Automation (Table 1). The Technical organization area includes eight courses. Objectives for the courses included in Technical organization are:

- Technical organization foundations
  To know the theoretical foundations that will allow students to understand the function and importance of diverse elements that entail bibliographic organization, as well as the main activities and procedures involved in it.

- Cataloging codes I
  To understand the norms and principles to carry out adequate document description as well as to set up access points for its retrieval.

- Cataloging codes II
  To apply the Anglo-American Cataloguing Rules to organize non-book materials.

- Dewey Decimal Classification
  To understand and to apply Dewey Decimal Classification to organize bibliographic materials.

- Library of Congress Classification
  To understand and to apply Library of Congress Classification to organize bibliographic materials.

- Subject headings
  To understand and to utilize different subject headings and thesauri as tools for the conceptual organization of documents.

- Indexing
  To select and to apply indexing terms from different subject headings and thesauri as elements for the conceptual organization of documents.

- Automated cataloging
  To identify and to apply elements involved in the planning process of automated cataloging.

Library Science College at the National Autonomous University of Mexico (Universidad Nacional Autónoma de México, UNAM)

In March 1956, the University Council of the National Autonomous University of Mexico (UNAM) approved the foundation of the UNAM Library and Archive Sciences College, which in 1975 became the UNAM Library Science College.

During the Fall 2003 term, there were 64 newcomers and 242 students who applied for continuing their program at the UNAM Library Science College. One peculiarity of the UNAM Library Science College is that its renowned faculty includes professors with an outstanding career in Library Science research and prominent Library Science practitioners. Currently, the UNAM Library Science College faculty has five full-time professors and 69 lecturers. Nevertheless, it is important to point out that eight of them are full-time researchers from the University Center for Library Science Research of UNAM. Likewise, 15 lecturers have higher administration positions in the UNAM library system, the largest Mexican library system. Seven of the remaining lecturers also have high ranking positions in other important Mexican libraries. Moreover, UNAM's Library Science College is the only Mexican

LIS school whose faculty includes several professors with a PhD degree.

A revised curriculum for the UNAM Library Science College was approved in September 2002 with the main objective: "to form Library Science professionals able to select, organize, retrieve, and deliver information as well as promote its use in diverse sectors of the Mexican Society to contribute to its scientific, technological, cultural and educational development" (Universidad Nacional Autónoma de México, 2002).

With the purpose of facing the challenges implicit in current Library Science practice, the UNAM Library Science College complies with the current professional necessities, but without leaving aside the basic functions of the LIS discipline. The main trend of its renewed curriculum is providing professional training to form librarians able to select, acquire, and appropriately organize all kinds of information resources, regardless of their format; professionals who can adequately administrate and manage libraries and other information units; librarians who can manage information resources of any kind and use them to provide high quality services to any user; librarians able to apply information technology in his/her professional activities; and librarians able to apply research methods to solve practical and theoretical problems within the LIS field.

This is why the new curriculum includes 42 mandatory courses placed in six areas: Bibliographic and documental organization, Information services administration, Bibliographic and information resources, Library services, Information technology, and Research and teaching (Table 2). Additionally, it includes four elective courses in Humanities, two in diverse LIS areas, and three more in any other discipline.

Objectives for the seven courses that compose the Bibliographic and documental organization area are:

- Documental organization foundations
  To distinguish basic elements involved in the documental organization process as well as its importance for bibliographic control.

- Cataloging I
  To understand descriptive cataloging theory and apply it in the record creation for different material types to get adequate information storage and retrieval using bibliographic control approaches.

- Cataloging II
  To set up main and secondary entries in records for different material types and to establish their correct form to get adequate information storage and retrieval using bibliographic control approaches.

- Subject cataloging
  To understand content representation theory using control vocabularies, subject headings, and thesauri to organize documents.

- Dewey Decimal Classification
  To understand Dewey Decimal Classification principles and to apply this classification in documental organization.

- Library of Congress Classification
  To understand Library of Congress Classification principles and to apply this classification in documental organization.

- Indexing
  To know indexing evolution and theory to apply it in information storage and retrieval.

Library and Information Sciences School at the Autonomous University of San Luis Potosí (Universidad Autónoma de San Luis Potosí, UASLP)

The origins of the UASLP Library and Information Sciences School date back to 1980 when the University established a Librarianship major. Currently, UASLP Library and Information Sciences School has 238 students enrolled. Its faculty includes 9 full-time professors and 21 lecturers.

The mission of the UASLP Library and Information Sciences School is: "to form qualified information professionals to select, organize, systematize, analyze, preserve and deliver documental information." Then, its objective is to "form information professionals to be able to support the construction of an informed society through the administration of documental resources together with a social orientation, to satisfy the growing information needs of users by giving them pertinent and timely information access and retrieval." The [UASLPL] Library and Information Sciences program intends to train information professionals capable of managing documental resources and who have strong skills to act as a guide in library services, archives, and information and documentation centers. Not just a provider of pertinent resources for users or an aide for accessing Internet resources, but also a social counselor in using hardware and software resources, so the information fits within logical sense and meaning in people's daily life" (Martínez Rider, 1998).

The UASLP Library and Information Science School curriculum includes 56 required courses, based in four core areas: Social, Humanistic, Methodological, and Professional. The Professional area includes five subordinate tracks: Foundations, Information analysis and organization, Information services, Information economy and administration, and Information technology (Table 3). In the Information analysis and organization track, there are nine courses dealing with cataloging and classification issues. Objectives for each course are as follows:

- Cataloging I
  To catalog bibliographic materials using AACR2, with a special emphasis on the second level of description and entries for author, titles, and uniform titles, to create catalog records for information entities.

- Cataloging II
  To catalog bibliographic materials using AACR2, with a special emphasis on the second level of description and entries for corporate bodies, titles, and uniform titles, to create catalog records for information entities.

- Cataloging III
  To catalog different types of nonbook materials (audiovisual, three-dimensional, and graphic materials, etc.) using AACR2, with a special emphasis on the second and third level of description and entries for author and titles, to create catalog records for information entities.

- Cataloging IV
  To catalog cartographic materials using AACR2, with a special emphasis on the third level of description, to create catalog records for information entities.

- Cataloging V
  To catalog serials using AACR2 and ISDS.

- Classification I
  To introduce students to the use of classification concepts; the necessity of its application to organize the recorded human knowledge; the representation of that knowledge using subject headings; its role as a basic language to organize information from all kinds of bibliographic materials; and the understanding of bibliographic classification systems.

- Classification II
  To generate classification numbers, taking into account content documents and Dewey Decimal Classification, as well as author numbers and other elements to shelve materials.

- Classification II
  To give the students knowledge about the organization and structure of Library of Congress Classification, as well as the skills to classify any bibliographic and documental material using it.

- Indexing and languages for information searching
  The student can create indexes as well as use language and searching procedures to retrieve information according to systems and standards. Tools for information storage and retrieval of documents, databases, and databanks will become the core knowledge.

Library Science College at the Autonomous University of Nuevo León (Universidad Autónoma de Nuevo León, UANL)

The UANL Library and Information Sciences Program is within the Library Science College, an entity of the Philosophy and Letters School. It was founded in August 1984 although its curriculum was recently renewed. Thirty-seven students currently attend this program (Asociación Nacional de Universidades e Instituciones de Educación Superior, 2004).

The mission of the UANL Library and Information Sciences licentiate is "to form professionals able to satisfy the society requirements by means of an efficient management of information entities, applying learned knowledge and scientific and technological development to benefit the community" (Universidad Autónoma de Nuevo León, 2004).

The UANL Library and Information Sciences renewed curriculum includes 55 required courses grouped in three wide areas: General studies, Fundamental concepts, and Co-curricular (Table 4). The nine courses and their objectives in the UANL Library and Information Sciences curriculum dealing with cataloging and classification topics are:

- Introduction to cataloging
  Theoretical-practical course to give students an overview of the processes and tools involved in documental organization.

- Descriptive cataloging
  It intends that students become familiar with the Anglo-American Cataloguing Rules (AACR2) to identify those applicable to books, pamphlets, and printed sheets. Access points for these material types will be analyzed as well as the MARC tags, indicators, and subfield codes to manage their surrogates in automated systems.

- Dewey Decimal Classification
  This course intends to introduce students to library classification concepts, with a particular emphasis on Dewey Decimal Classification.

- Library of Congress Classification
  This course intends that students become acquainted with Library of Congress Classification.

- Special materials cataloging I
  It intends that students become familiar with Anglo-American Cataloguing Rules (AACR2) to identify those applicable to cartographic materials, manuscripts, music, sound recordings, motion pictures, and videorecordings. Access points for these material types will be analyzed as well as the MARC tags, indicators, and subfield codes to manage their surrogates in automated systems.

- Special materials cataloging II
  It intends that students become familiar with Anglo-American Cataloguing Rules (AACR2) to identify those applicable to graphic materials, computer files, three-dimensional artefacts, and realia. Access points for these material types will be analyzed as well as the MARC tags, indicators, and subfield codes to manage their surrogates in automated systems.

- Subject headings and thesauri
  This course begins with the understanding and comprehension of documental language. It reviews concepts, typology, components, and representative examples of documental language. Subject headings and some principles for their application are studied. Thesauri are reviewed as part of the indexing theory. Also, subject authority control is studied: its function, operation, and how libraries cooperate in this specialized field.

- Indexing and abstract elaboration
  This course intends to train students for document indexing and abstract elaboration. There will be an analysis of processes, methods, automation, and normalization of these activities, which are fundamental for the control and use of information.

- Cataloging and classification workshop
  Practical course to reinforce understanding and skills that students acquired in the previous courses of cataloging and classification.

Documental Information Sciences Program at the Autonomous University of Mexico State (Universidad Autónoma del Estado de México, UAEM)

The UAEM Documental Information Sciences Program is one of the Humanities School programs which was established in 1992 and modified in 1999. The number of students enrolled in this program is 157 (Asociacion Nacional de Universidades e Instituciones de Educación Superior, 2004).

The main objective of this program is "to train those professionals that our country requires to safeguard, organize, preserve, administer, and deliver documental information by means of a critical and reflexive attitude toward the innovation of the present information structures. Likewise, this program intends to give students the knowledge that supports the development of their capacities, skills and attitudes for the documental information process in order to take care and to solve inherent problems of their profession" (Universidad Autónoma del Estado de México, 1999).

The UAEM Documental Information Sciences Program includes 59 required courses grouped in the following six areas: Foundations, Humanities, Research, Administration, Technology, and Discipline. This last one includes three tracks: Archives, Library Science, and Documentation (Table 5). Most of the courses dealing with cataloging and classification are part of the Library Science tracks, and one of them is part of the Documentation track. The objectives for courses dealing with cataloging and classification matters are:

- Classification systems I
  To determine when it is right to use the Dewey Decimal Classification in libraries.

- Classification systems II
  To determine the utility of the Library of Congress Classification.

- Cataloging I
  To elaborate the descriptive component of catalog records using the first part of the Anglo-American Cataloguing Rules.

- Cataloging II
  To elaborate the descriptive and subject components of catalog records using the Anglo-American Cataloguing Rules.

- Analytic abstracts, indexing, and thesauri
  To elaborate abstracts, indexes, and thesauri as result of the documental analysis.

Library Science Program at the Autonomous University of Chiapas (Universidad Autónoma de Chiapas, UACH)

The UACH Library Science Program, established in September 1992, is one of the newest Library Science programs in Mexico and is sponsored by the Humanities School. At the present time, this program has 260 students. Its faculty has 24 professors of whom five are full-time professors and the rest are lecturers.

The UACH Library Science Program's main objective is to train library professionals who, by means of an understanding of the philosophical, scientific, and technical foundations of the discipline, as well as some other ones from related disciplines, and with the reasonable application of theories and techniques, can satisfy the documental information needs of users altogether with their implicit recreational and educational concerns (Universidad Autónoma de Chiapas, 1992).

Likewise, this program intends that its graduates will be able to plan, design, and administer information systems, either manual or automated, such as libraries, documentation centers, archives, and other information entities. Additionally, they will generate appropriate strategies to promote the use of information systems. Anticipating the use of information systems, he/she will keep a permanent communication with those ones demanding these services. They also should have the capacity to fulfill the local, regional, and national information necessities (Universidad Autónoma de Chiapas, 1992).

The 49 required courses included in this program are grouped in six areas: Information users, Information services, Information technology, Information units organization, Research, and Documental classification systems (Table 6). Courses dealing with cataloging and classification matters are placed in the Documental classification systems area. Additionally, there are three other courses from the Information technology area approaching issues on cataloging automation. Objectives for all of these courses are:

- Knowledge classification systems
  To educate students in the comprehension of diverse theoretical, philosophical, and sociological trends related to knowledge classification to understand library classification systems structures.

- Library classification systems
  To provide students with an understanding of the logical foundations of library classification systems and the differences with knowledge classification.

- Information analysis and representation I (description)
  To teach students to analyze the components that integrate a document in order to identify and represent them using standards for document description.

- Information analysis and representation II (subject content)
  To lead students in the understanding of the intellectual process to identify subject content of documents in order to represent it using principles and notations from library classification systems.

- Resources classification
  To help students acquire the knowledge to understand and to apply library classification systems to organize documents.

- Catalog classification
  To educate students in understanding the logical foundations for the organization of elements that integrate a catalog.

- Abstracts
  To educate students in understanding the nature and types of abstracts and their use in information systems.

- Thesauri
  To provide students with an understanding of thesauri foundations and their use as tools for subject classification. To identify potential information services derived from these library classification systems.

- Bibliographic information automated systems workshop
  To involve students in the understanding and management of automated systems for bibliographic information available on the market.

- Bibliographic databases design I
  To train students in the design and organization of bibliographic databases.

- Bibliographic databases design II
  Taking into consideration knowledge acquired in bibliographic databases design I, to apply it to solving difficult problems using database programming.

School of Information Sciences at the Autonomous University of Guadalajara (Universidad Autónoma de Guadalajara, UAG)

The School of Information Sciences at the Autonomous University of Guadalajara was founded in August 2002.

The "licenciatura" in Information Sciences "is a career that answers to the current challenges dealing with information organization in Mexico." The main objective of the UAG Information Sciences School is to train a professional to manage and to use documental information structured in an effective and efficient way, as well as to promote its systematic retrieval and transfer, by print and electronic means, to support development of public and private entities. Therefore, training of professionals focuses on: "(1) Selection of pertinent information for work, social, and personal settings, (2) Information organization,

(3) Information delivery, and (4) Information commercialization" (Universidad Autónoma de Guadalajara, 2004).

The curriculum of the UAG Information Sciences School includes 53 required courses grouped in five areas: Information Sciences, Business, Science and Technology, General humanistic education, and Professional practices (Table 7). The UAG Information Sciences curriculum does not include a particular area for information organization; however, six required courses dealing with cataloging and classification issues are placed in the Information Sciences area and their objectives are:

- Documental organization (cataloging)
  This program involves diverse cataloging systems for documents, elaboration of catalogs for distinct information entities, and catalog access.

- Content analysis
  Study of content analysis theory. To teach students to identify information trends, to analyze content creators, forms, and users, as well as to identify information appropriateness, truthfulness, veracity, and pertinence.

- Documental organization (classification)
  This course includes a review of diverse classification systems to obtain information access. Also, elaboration of an authority catalog to unify access points to documental material.

- Content analysis (documental languages)
  To identify different documental languages, their structure, typology, and common uses.

- Indexes and abstracts (theory and elaboration)
  General, theoretical, and practical principles for indexes and abstracts elaboration, content description, documental languages, controlled and non-controlled vocabulary, indexing, and elaboration of thesauri and controlled vocabularies, using printed and electronic means.

- Thesauri construction
  Fundamental concepts on thesauri construction, application of concepts and technological standards, thesauri structures, general and specialized thesauri, and document retrieval by means of thesauri.

Information Sciences Program at the Autonomous University of Chihuahua (*Universidad Autónoma de Chihuahua, UACh*)

The UACh Library Science Program is the newest one since it was established in January 2003 in the Philosophy and Letters School at the Autonomous University of Chihuahua (UACh). At the present time, about 40 students are enrolled in this program. Researchers from the University Center for Library Science Research (CUIB) participate as lecturers giving some courses.

One of the main goals of the UACh Information Sciences Program is to train professionals able "to store and retrieve all kind of documents by means of their cataloging, classification, indexing, and abstracting" (Universidad Autónoma de Chihuahua, 2002). This program includes 50 required courses grouped in six areas: Information Sciences foundations, Information resources and media, Organization of information, Information centers and systems, Complementary information services, and Science knowledge (Table 8). Courses dealing with cataloging and classification matters are placed in the Organization of information area and have the following objectives:

- Print documents cataloging
  Theory and practice applying the Anglo-American Cataloguing Rules, MARC format, and ISO 690 to cataloging diverse types of print documents.

- Non-print and electronic documents cataloging
  Theory and practice applying the Anglo-American Cataloguing Rules, MARC format, and ISO 690 to catalog diverse types of non-print and electronic documents.

- Classification systems
  Application of Dewey Decimal Classification and Library of Congress Classification, in traditional and electronic format, according to particular information settings.

- Documental languages
  Role and features of natural language for the information transfer. Semiotic, Syntax, and Pragmatic foundations for language analysis. Techniques for text analysis. Main documental languages, use, meaning, and practical applications.

- Thesauri creation
  Analysis of available thesauri. Development of conceptual maps for thesauri elaboration. Differences with other tools for information management.

- Indexes and abstracts
  Procedures to indexing and abstracting documents in information centers, information storage and retrieval systems, online searching, and catalogs. Information retrieval basic tasks, theories, techniques, and applications. Use behavior, retrieval systems, and technological impact.

MASTER'S PROGRAMS

National Autonomous University of Mexico (Universidad Nacional Autónoma de México, UNAM)

In January 1972, the University Council of the National Autonomous University of Mexico (UNAM) approved the establishment of graduate studies in Library Science. Since that time, until the beginning of the 21st century, UNAM was the only Mexican institution offering a master's degree in Library Science. During the '90s, the UNAM University Center for Library Science Research (Centro Universitario de Investigaciones Bibliotecológicas, CUIB) proposed a new curriculum for graduate studies in Library Science and Information Studies, including master's and doctoral degrees that the University Council approved in November 1998. This graduate studies program is part of the University Center for Library Science Research and the Philosophy and Letters Faculty of UNAM.

During the 2004 Spring term, the program had 65 students enrolled at the master's level and 15 at the doctoral level. Faculty of this program consists of 18 full-time CUIB researchers, 2 full-time professors of the Philosophy and Letters Faculty and 10 lecturers.

The main objective of the Master's in the Library Science and Information Studies curriculum is: "to prepare Library Science professionals at the highest level, with a solid education to be able to research, generate, and transmit new knowledge in universities and higher education institutions, as well as to support the design and development of modern information systems, using technology, in government institutions, businesses, and industries" (Universidad Nacional Autónoma de México, 2004).

To obtain a Master's in Library Science and Information Studies, students have to take four courses and eight seminars of which one course and three seminars are mandatory. The remaining courses and seminars can be elected by the student according to his/her interests. There is a wide supply of courses and seminars placed in five areas: Information, knowledge, and society; Organization of documental information; Information technology; Library and information systems and services; Information users (Table 9).

Objectives for the required seminar, and for elective courses and seminars included in the Organization of documental information that students can elect, are:

- Documental analysis (required seminar)
  To study the foundations, methods, and processes of documental analysis.

- Documental classification (elective seminar)
  To analyze the principles and foundations of documental classification as well as its current issues and trends.

- Documental languages (elective seminar)
  To analyze the principles and foundations of documental languages used for information storage and organization.

- Information normalization (elective seminar)
  The students will be able to understand the theoretical and practical foundations of bibliographic control with a particular emphasis in the national library settings. Likewise, the students will acquire the knowledge to participate easily in automation of documental information.

- Linguistics and information (elective seminar)
  To study the fundamental concepts of Linguistics. To analyze language as a cognitive and social matter.

- Textual databases theory (elective seminar)
  To analyze the principles and methods that information technologies offer to process electronic texts documental languages used for information storage and organization.

Monterrey Technological Institute of Higher Studies (Instituto Tecnológico de Estudios Superiores de Monterrey, ITESM)

The Monterrey Technological Institute of Higher Studies [Instituto Tecnológico de Estudios Superiores de Monterrey (ITESM)] established an LIS master's program supported by the University Texas at Austin in 1999. This graduate program originally was called Master's in Library and Information Science and recently became Master's in Information Sciences and Knowledge Administration.

At this writing the program has 11 students (Asociacion Nacional de Universidades e Instituciones de Educación Superior, 2004), most of them ITESM library workers. Since this program is within the Graduate School of Education, most of the faculty are professors of that school.

The objective of the ITESM Master's in Information Sciences and Knowledge Management is: "to prepare Library Science professionals at the highest level, with a solid education to be able to research, generate, and transmit new knowledge in universities and higher education institutions, as well as to support the design and development of modern information systems, using technology, in government institutions, businesses, and industries" (Instituto Tecnológico y de Estudios Superiores de Monterrey, 2004).

To receive the Master's in Library Science and Knowledge Management, students have to take eight required courses and four elective courses (Table 10). Only one course approaches organization of information matters and its objective is: "To study theory and application of principles to organize library and other informative materials. It includes cataloging and classification with an emphasis on cataloging interpretation and providing an introduction to descriptive and subject cataloging, selection of entries and its forms, and Library of Congress Classification. Also, it covers a review of automated cataloging using the Internet, indexing, metadata, and search engines."

CONCLUSIONS

The previous discussion gives a general overview of education for cataloging and classification in Mexican Library Science schools. Definitely, in Mexican Library Science education, matters dealing with cataloging, classification, subject analysis, and indexing have had an important role. The Mexican LIS schools have considerable diversity. However, independent of their names, most of them have included in their curriculum an area for courses dealing with cataloging and classification issues. Almost all of the programs include learning AACR2. Moreover, the study of DDC and LCC is part of the students' education. Likewise, subject control, subject headings and thesauri knowledge constitute an important part of the LIS programs. Notwithstanding this fact, Mexican LIS schools face a series of challenges for improving education for cataloging and classification. One of the most important challenges, perhaps, is determining the basic knowledge and skills core that any librarian must posses in the cataloging and classification area. At the same time, Mexican LIS schools should look for uniformity in naming the areas and courses dealing with cataloging and classification, since some schools have used different names for the same course and have unavoidably contributed to confusion among employers. Moreover, it is necessary to establish similar objectives and contents for these courses. Achieving more uniformity in names, objectives, and contents undoubtedly will help in establishing a distinct identity as a profession in which information organization is an important and unique feature.

REFERENCES

Asociación Nacional de Universidades e Instituciones de Educación Superior (2004). Población escolar de licenciatura por entidad, institución y carrera [Licenciate student population by state, institution, and career]. [cited 27 January 2004]. Available from World Wide Web: (http://www.anuies.mx).

"Docentes de la ENBA" [ENBA faculty] (2003). *Carta Informativa: Gaceta Informativa y Cultural de la Escuela Nacional de Biblioteconomía y Archivonomía*, no. 56-57: 22.

"El quehacer académico de la ENBA en números" [ENBA academic work in numbers] (2003). *Carta Informativa: Gaceta Informativa y Cultural de la Escuela Nacional de Biblioteconomía y Archivonomía*, no. 56-57: 23.

Escuela Nacional de Biblioteconomía y Archivonomía (2000). *Plan y programas de estudio 2000 [Curriculum and courses programs 2000]*. México: n. p.

Instituto Tecnológico y de Estudios Superiores de Monterrey (2004). *Maestría en Ciencias de la Información y Administración del Conocimiento (MIK) [Master in Information Sciences and Knowledge Administration (MIK)]*. [cited 27 January 2004]. Available from World Wide Web: (http://www.ruv.itesm.mx/portal/promocion/oe/m/mik/infoacademica/descripcion.htm).

Martínez Rider, R. M. (1998). *Proyecto de reestructuración curricular para la Escuela de Bibliotecología e Información de la Universidad Autónoma de San Luis Potosí. [Curriculum redesign project for the Library and Information Sciences School at the Autonomous University of San Luis Potosí]*. San Luis Potosí, S.L.P.: n. p.

Universidad Autónoma del Estado de México (1999). *Currículo de la Licenciatura en Ciencias de la Información Documental 1999* [*Curriculum of the licenciate in Documental Information Sciences 1999*]. Toluca, Edo. de México: n. p.

Universidad Autónoma de Chihuahua (2002). *Licenciatura en Ciencias de la Información: propuesta de diseño curricular 2002* [*Licentiate in Information Sciences: curriculum design proposal 2002*]. Chihuahua, Chihuahua: n. p.

Universidad Autónoma de Chiapas (1992). *Licenciatura en Bibliotecología: Plan de estudios* [*Currículum of the licentiate in Library Science*]. Tuxtla Gutiérrez, Chiapas: n. p.

Universidad Autónoma de Guadalajara (2004). *Escuela de Ciencias de la Información* [*School of Information Sciences*]. [cited 27 January 2004]. Available from World Wide Web: ⟨http://www.uag.mx/eci/default.htm⟩.

Universidad Autónoma de Nuevo León (2004). *Licenciaturas: Bibliotecología y Ciencias de la Información* [*Licenciates: Library and Information Sciences*]. [cited 27 January 2004]. Available from World Wide Web: ⟨http://www.filosofia.uanl.mx/default.asp⟩.

Universidad Nacional Autónoma de México (2000). *Proyecto de modificación del Plan de estudios de la Licenciatura en Bibliotecología y Estudios de la Información* [*Project to modify the licentiate in Library Science and Information Studies*]. México: n. p.

Universidad Nacional Autónoma de México (2004). *Programa de Maestría y Doctorado en Bibliotecología y Estudios de la Información* [*Master and Doctorate Programs in Library Science and Information Studies*]. [cited 27 January 2004]. Available from World Wide Web: ⟨http://www.filos.unam.mx/POSGRADO/programa/biblio.htm⟩.

APPENDIX

TABLE 1. Courses by Areas of the National School of Library and Archive Sciences Curriculum (ENBA)

Technical organization
    Technical organization foundations
    Cataloging codes I
    Cataloging codes II
    Dewey Decimal Classification
    Library of Congress Classification
    Subject headings
    Indexing
    Automated cataloging

Services
    Public services
    Information sources
    Use and management of information sources
    Information users
    Services promotion

Administration
    Administrative process
    Administration functional areas
    Library planning
    Public and children's libraries
    University and school libraries
    Specialized libraries

Collection development
    Serials
    Bibliography
    Information resources acquisition
    Preventive preservation
    Mexican bibliography
    Collection development

Social
    Introduction to library science
    Book and libraries history I
    Book and libraries history II

APPENDIX (continued)

TABLE 1 (continued)

Information policies
Information industry
Seminar on profession prospective
Didactics

Methodology
Introduction to knowledge organization
Documental research
Field research
Descriptive statistics
Introduction to bibliometrics
Research seminar I
Research seminar II

Automation
Computing practice tools
Networks in information settings
Information entities automation
Information conversion and migration
Information storage and retrieval
Seminar on library automation

TABLE 2. Courses by Areas of the UNAM Library Science College Curriculum

Bibliographic and documental organization
    Documental organization foundations
    Cataloging I
    Cataloging II
    Subject cataloging
    Dewey Decimal Classification
    Library of Congress Classification
    Indexing

Information services administration
    Administration foundations
    Library and information services administration
    Human resources administration
    Information marketing
    Information entities evaluation

Bibliographic and information resources
    Book and libraries history I
    Book and libraries history II
    Information resources
    Bibliography theory and technique
    Publishing and information industries
    Collection development
    Mexican bibliography, XVI-XIX century
    Contemporary Mexican bibliography

Library services
    Information services foundations
    Social library science
    Read, readers and libraries
    Library and information services
    Reference I
    Reference II
    Information users

Information technology
    Library science computing
    Information technology for libraries
    Databases

APPENDIX (continued)

TABLE 2 (continued)

Library automation systems and programs
Automated systems administration
Digital resources and multimedia

Research and teaching
Library science foundations
Library science in Mexico
Introduction to research
Quantitative research methods
Qualitative research methods
Thesis seminar I
Thesis seminar II
Library science didactics

TABLE 3. Courses by Areas of the UASLP Library and Information Science School Curriculum

Social
Introduction to psychology
Introduction to pedagogy
Communication theory
Human relationships
General administration
Human resources administration
Legislation and regulations
Information context in Mexico I, II
Building design for information entities

Humanistic
Introduction to philosophy
Reading and writing workshop
Culture history I, II
Science history

Book and libraries history
Seminar on history of Mexico

Methodological

Mathematics
Probabilities and statistics
Research methodology
Seminar on library science research

Professional

Foundations

Introduction to library science
Archive science
Information and library knowledge theory
Comparative library science

Information analysis and organization

Cataloging I, II, II, IV, V
Classification I, II, III
Preservation and restoration workshop
Indexing and languages for information searching
Scientific papers writing
Information processing workshop
Bibliography I, II
Mexican bibliography

Information services

Information sources I, II, III
Information users
Information and reference resources
Information services I, II, III

Information economy and administration

Information entities administration
Information entities strategic planning
Information economy

Information technology

Computing
Systems analysis
Information entities automation
Information networks and systems
Information new technologies

APPENDIX (continued)

TABLE 4. Courses by Areas of the UANL Library Science School Curriculum

General studies
    Oral and writing communication
    Creative thinking
    Scientific methodology
    Psychology and professional development
    Computing
    Art appreciation
    Sociology and profession
    Professional practice ethics
    Environmental sciences
    Sociologic process in the XX century
    Philosophy problems
    Education and development
    Text analysis and interpretation
    Current society theory

Fundamental concepts
    Bibliographic foundations
    Introduction to cataloging
    Introduction to library science
    Information users
    Information services I
    Communication theory and models
    Information services II
    Descriptive cataloging
    Dewey Decimal Classification
    Information sources I
    General administration
    Special materials cataloging I
    Library of Congress Classification
    Information sources II
    Human resources administration
    Special materials cataloging II
    Bibliography
    Introduction to informatics
    Information entities administration
    Subject headings and thesauri
    Mexican bibliography

Telematics and information networks
Serials
Indexing and abstract elaboration
Cataloging and classification workshop
Automated systems
Information trends overview
Processes and services evaluation
Collection development
Mathematics for library science
Automated processes
Library science research
Statistics for library science
Legislation and normalization
Introduction to information systems analysis

Co-curricular
English I, II, III, IV, V, VI

TABLE 5. Courses by Area of the UAEM Documental Information Sciences Program Curriculum

Foundations
Introduction to documental information sciences
Document transfer history
Administrative systems in Mexico
Documental legislation
Philosophical foundations of documental information sciences

Humanities
Introduction to humanities
Reading and writing workshop
Mexican political institutions history
Novohispanic political institutions history
Cultural patrimony
Scientific thought history
Literature judgment
Pedagogy techniques for documental information sciences
Information sociology

APPENDIX (continued)

TABLE 5 (continued)

Research
Applied statistics to documental information sciences
Research methods I
Research methods II
Thesis seminar I
Thesis seminar II
Thesis seminar III
Information metric studies

Administration
Introduction to administration
Organizational communication theory
Systems general theory
Documental entities administration
Documental services planning
Building design for documental entities

Technology
Computing workshop
Documental collections automation workshop I
Documental collections automation workshop II
Reprography
Theoretical foundations of documental preservation
Preventive preservation
Restoration workshop

Discipline

Archives
Paleography workshop I
Paleography workshop II
Archives classification
Diplomatics
Archivistic
Documental disposition I
Documental disposition II
Organization and management of active and semi-active documents
Organization and management of inactive documents

Library Science
Collection development
Classification systems I
Classification systems II
Cataloging I
Cataloging II
Periodicals
General bibliography
Mexican bibliography

Documentation
Documental analysis
Analytic abstracts, indexing and thesauri
Cartographic collections
Information resources
Museology
User formation
Information marketing

TABLE 6. Courses by Areas of the UACH Library Science Program

Information users
Reading and writing workshop I
Reading and writing workshop II
Communication theory I
Communication theory II
Didactics
Instrumental and critical didactics
Users I
Users II

Information services
Historical development of library science
Current problems of Mexico
The Southern borderline and its current problems
Technological knowledge
Public libraries
Collection development

APPENDIX (continued)

TABLE 6 (continued)

Comparative library science
Information services philosophy and praxis

Information technology
Computing instruction workshop
Information services automation workshop
Bibliographic information automated systems workshop
Information economy
Information automated banks
Bibliographic databases design I
Bibliographic databases design II
Document preservation and restoration workshop

Information entities organization
Introduction to administration studies
Human resources administration
Library administration
Library cooperation
Library services
Archives I
Archives II
Specialized information units

Research
Statistics
Research methodology seminar I
Research methodology seminar II
Library science research seminar
Information retrieval
Special libraries
University libraries
Information resources
Thesis seminar

Documental classification systems
Knowledge classification systems
Library classification systems
Information analysis and representation I (description)

Information analysis and representation II (subject content)
Resources classification
Catalogs classification
Abstracts
Thesauri

TABLE 7. Courses by Areas of the UAG Information Sciences School

Information Sciences
Information sciences theory
Information entities
Comparative information science
General information sources
Information products and services
Documental organization (cataloging)
Information sources in humanities and social sciences
Content analysis
Documental organization (classification)
Information sources in science and technology
Collection development
Archival process
Content analysis (documental languages)
User training
Information sources in health sciences
Information users
Indexes and abstracts (theory and elaboration)
Thesauri construction
Information agencies
Research seminar

Business
Information administration
Information marketing
Information products and services design
Information products and services lines
Information agencies
Information business organization
Knowledge management

APPENDIX (continued)

TABLE 7 (continued)

Finances management
Information projects

Science and Technology
　Informatics
　Information technology
　Information systems
　Information systems design
　Databases
　Networks
　New information technologies
　Telematic networks
　Statistics

General humanistic education
　Documental linguistics
　Philosophy of science
　Philosophical anthropology
　Information legislation and regulation
　Information ethics
　Reading theory
　Research methodology

Professional practices
　Introduction to professional job
　Professional job
　Introduction to information skills
　Information skills development
　Introduction to professional competencies
　Professional competencies application
　Professional practices

TABLE 8. Courses by Areas of the UACh Information Sciences Program

Information Sciences foundations
    Information sciences theory
    Library science and documentation

Information resources and media
    Information technology
    Periodicals
    Information sources and services
    Adminstration of network information services
    Software for information sciences evaluation
    Technological development of products

Organization of information
    Printed documents cataloging
    Non-printed and electronic documents cataloging
    Classification systems
    Document languages
    Thesauri creation

Information centers and systems
    General administration
    Information centers
    Intellectual capital development
    Strategic planning
    Information legislation
    Knowledge management
    Documental products
    Organizational intelligence
    Information mapping
    Information retrieval strategies
    Documentation processes
    Indexes and abstracts

Complementary information services
    Information products and services marketing
    Infometrics
    Document preservation and conservation
    User analysis and formation
    Collection development and evaluation

APPENDIX (continued)

TABLE 8 (continued)

Science knowledge
Text analysis
Advanced Spanish
Contemporary culture
Philosophy of culture
Geopolitics
Professional ethics
Knowledge theory
Research methodology
Document writing
Oral communication

TABLE 9. Seminars and Courses by Areas of the UNAM Master in Library Science and Information Studies Curriculum

Information, knowledge, and society
Library science and information theory (required seminar)
Information and society (elective seminar)
Library science and information studies education (elective seminar)
Specialized libraries collections and services (elective course)
Evaluation theory (elective course)

Organization of documental information
Documental analysis (required seminar)
Documental classification (elective seminar)
Documental languages (elective seminar)
Information normalization (elective seminar)
Linguistics and information (elective seminar)
Textual databases theory (elective seminar)

Information technology
Information services automation (required course)
Telecommunications and information services (elective seminar)
Bibliographic databases design (elective course)

Operative systems and platforms (elective course)
Information policies (elective seminar)
Information retrieval languages (elective course)
Electronic information and documentation (elective seminar)

Library and information systems and services
Library science and information studies in Mexico (required seminar)
Specialized information resources (humanities, social sciences, or science
and technology) (elective course)
Information management (elective course)
Buildings and information services (elective course)
Economy and information commercialization (elective course)
Cost analysis (elective course)
Statistical evaluation (elective seminar)
Metric studies (elective course)

Information users
Information technology and society (required seminar)
User studies (elective seminar)
User training (elective seminar)
Scientific communities and information (elective seminar)
Scientific communication (elective seminar)
Communication and human relations (elective seminar)

APPENDIX (continued)

TABLE 10. Courses of the ITESM Master in Library Science and Knowledge Management Curriculum

Required courses
    Use of information technology for distance learning
    Information organizations and services administration
    Information needs and resources acquisition (Printed and electronic)
    Information resources and reference services
    Value systems based in knowledge
    Organization of information
    Human capital administration
    Bases and flow of information and knowledge

Elective courses
    Elective I
    Elective II
    Project I
    Project II

Education for Cataloging and Related Areas in Peru

Ana María Talavera Ibarra

SUMMARY. This paper presents the situation of library education in Peru during the last decades of the 20th century, particularly education in the area of cataloging and bibliographic control. Both an historical view and the current situation are explained to give a general panorama of education in the areas of cataloging, classification, organization of electronic materials, cataloging networks, and the like. A short panorama of the near future is also given. At the same time, not only professional education is presented, but also nonprofessional, continuing, and on-the-job education in Library and Information Science (LIS) in Peru. *[Article copies available for a fee from The Haworth Document Delivery Service: 1-800-HAWORTH. E-mail address: <docdelivery@haworthpress.com> Website: <http://www.HaworthPress.com> © 2006 by The Haworth Press, Inc. All rights reserved.]*

KEYWORDS. Cataloging education, Library and Information Science (LIS) education, Peru, nonprofessional education, on-the-job education, continuing education

Ana María Talavera Ibarra, PhD Candidate, is Lecturer, Pontificia Universidad Católica del Perú, Departamento de Humanidades, Apdo. 1761, Lima 1, Peru (E-mail: atalave@pucp.edu.pe).

[Haworth co-indexing entry note]: "Education for Cataloging and Related Areas in Peru." Talavera Ibarra, Ana María. Co-published simultaneously in *Cataloging & Classification Quarterly* (The Haworth Information Press, an imprint of The Haworth Press, Inc.) Vol. 41, No. 3/4, 2006, pp. 389-406; and: *Education for Library Cataloging: International Perspectives* (ed: Dajin D. Sun, and Ruth C. Carter) The Haworth Information Press, an imprint of The Haworth Press, Inc., 2006, pp. 389-406. Single or multiple copies of this article are available for a fee from The Haworth Document Delivery Service [1-800-HAWORTH, 9:00 a.m. - 5:00 p.m. (EST). E-mail address: docdelivery@haworthpress.com].

INTRODUCTION

Library education in Peru began in 1943 with the creation of the Escuela Nacional de Bibliotecarios (National School of Librarians), although courses began to be taught in 1944. This School gradually moved, between 1944 and 1980, from a 6-month program to a 4-year program. All of this time, library education was considered an undergraduate program but not a university one. In 1980 it was transferred, as a University program, to the Universidad Nacional Mayor de San Marcos, Faculty of Arts and Human Sciences, with the official name Escuela Académico Profesional de Bibliotecología y Ciencias de la Información. The University assumed all active and passive structures of the previous School, including faculty members, students, and grades and other materials from former students. Courses at the University began in 1981, and from that time to now, there have been five different study programs which will be discussed later.

At the same time, a private University, the Pontificia Universidad Católica del Perú (Pontifical Catholic University of Peru), created a new program on Library and Information Science within the Faculty of Human Sciences. The official name is Especialidad de Bibliotecología y Ciencia de la Información. From its creation to now, there have been three study plans which will be also discussed later.

University-level studies are taken by students after completing an 11-year school education (primary and secondary) and after passing a required entrance exam. In the case of San Marcos University, students enter directly to the School they have selected, which means they occupy the number of seats available each year for each School. In the School of LIS, the number of vacancies has been increased from 35 to 80 students in recent years. During the first year, students take some general courses together with other students from the Human Sciences Faculty (i.e., Philosophy, Linguistics, Communication, and the like). After that (from their 2nd year), they take only LIS courses. On the other hand, students at the Catholic University enter the "General Studies Program," which lasts two years. There, students mix with all students from the Humanities and select study programs from the Human, Social, and Administrative Sciences, or Law, or Communication Studies. This means that, at that level, they have not yet selected their career, LIS being one option. Another particular difference between the two programs, is the fact that, at the Catholic University, the LIS study plans consider a number of credits from other study programs. This number has varied from 24 to 16 in recent years; students are free to select these credits from any program or Faculty at the University.

1. PROFESSIONAL CATALOGING EDUCATION IN PERU

Education for cataloging in Peru had different levels and subjects covering the field. Because of this, we prefer to explain the professional education according to each institution that offers it. For each one, we will specify degrees, names of courses, contents, credit hours, practicum, and other related areas. The presentation will be chronological beginning with the National School of Librarians to the present programs.

1.1 Escuela Nacional de Bibliotecarios

The National School of Librarians functioned within the National Library for 36 years, during which time it graduated approximately 600 students.[1] Study plans have varied greatly during all of those years, not only on the subjects taught, but particularly on the number of years of study: as told, from an initial urgent program required to graduate professionals to "rebuild" the National Library destroyed by a big fire, to a graduate-level program of 4 years. All cataloging and classification courses were compulsory, including theoretical and some practical classes. Apart from the practical classes for each course, there was a Practicum taken by students at the end of their studies, lasting 10-11 months at the different departments of the National Library.

According to McKee (1966), the study plan of that time considered the following courses dealing particularly with cataloging and classification topics: Library Classification, Classification and cataloging of periodical and official publications, Classification of maps, music photographs and engravings, and Cataloging. After that time, courses dealing with Library of Congress Classification, Universal Decimal Classification, and Documentation were added in the 3rd year of studies.

In relation to contents, the course on Library Classification (2nd year) dealt almost exclusively with Dewey Decimal Classification (2 semesters), including National Library expansions and particular applications. It also included filing techniques for authors and subjects, LC Subject Headings, and other notations (like Peruvian Malaga's notation instead of Cutter's). The other courses related to periodicals, official publications, and audiovisual materials, and included both classification and cataloging topics with hours of practice with those materials. Dewey Decimal was applied to the classification of those materials as well as ALA cataloging rules. The general course on Cataloging also used the ALA rules, including descriptive cataloging and access points. No evidence has been found about teaching AACR1.

Approximately by the beginning of the 1970s, a change in the study plan occurred, other courses were added, including some technical and some dealing with state of the art topics. In relation to Library classification from the 2nd year, it continued the same, but in the 3rd year, Library of Congress Classification (LC) and Universal Decimal Classification (UDC) were added, each one lasting half a year (one semester). Both included theoretical and practical classes. In addition, the Cataloging course was modified to include special materials–that course disappeared–and the course on Periodicals and Official publications suffered a decrease in the number of hours. In relation to Documentation, it was fairly new, and the lecturer was a librarian who just came from specialized courses in Brazil and Russia. Topics related to post-coordinated information retrieval (manual and some online) and thesaurus construction, and some automated services were introduced in this course.

By the time the School was transferred to San Marcos University (1980) and it became a 4-year program, some new courses had been added, and the hours of Practicum were extended. No further changes were found in the area of cataloging and classification, apart from those mentioned above. The School issued the professional degree of "Bibliotecario," the only one in the country during its existence.

1.2 Universidad Nacional Mayor de San Marcos

As mentioned, classes began in this University in 1981 when the first enterance exam was scheduled. There were only two full-time lecturers who came from the previous School, with most lecturers hired just to teach one or two courses. The new program was in a transitory stage. We can say in poor condition: poor infrastructure, lack of faculty, few students, and the like. In that year, the first study plan was issued, which unfortunately is not available at this time, although a general paper (Claustro Pleno, 1992), issued in 1985 as the basis for a study plan reform to be implemented in 1986, gives us a general view of that first study plan. That plan established a program of 10 semesters leading to an academic degree of *Bachiller* in Human Sciences, and a *Licenciado* in Library and Information Sciences after submitting and receiving approval for a Dissertation. The whole program included 207 credits (192 required and 15 electives). An area called Information processing had courses offered mainly from the 3rd to the 5th semesters. Also, the last semester had a Practicum requiring the students to do work at an information unit, including technical processing of library materials.

With the approval of the new plan of 1986, a better age began for the program. On one hand, there was a better infrastructure, including a specialized library, more lecturers (6 newly appointed), a greater number of students, and the like; and on the other hand, a new study plan with more coherence and experience. Five courses dealt with topics related to cataloging: Information processing 1, 2 and 3; and Information retrieval and transfer 1 and 2. Information processing 1 dealt with bibliographic description, ISBD rules, and AACR2; Information processing 2, with the major classification systems: Dewey, UDC, and LC; and the third one with indexing, thesauri construction, and abstract elaboration and analysis. According to F. Miyagi (1992), lecturer for the different Information processing courses from 1987 to 1991, there were acute problems in offering them, particularly because of the lack of teaching materials for classes, i.e., just one copy of *AACR2*, the classification schedules, and so on. The courses Information retrieval and transfer 1 and 2 dealt, in the first course, with the concepts of retrieval, Boolean search, user studies, and services to them; and in the second, with more personalized services to users, such as SDI, manual and automated searches, document delivery, and the like.

The Practicum was extended to four semesters A, B, C, D; the first two were planned as a basic level of practice, particularly dealing with acquisitions and initial cataloging. The last two covered all different library processes including administration and services.

Effective in 1993, a new study plan[2] restructured the courses of Information Processing 1 to 3, and added a workshop to put more emphasis on the practical area. It left the principles of cataloging and bibliographic description in the first course, and placed in the second the topics related to classification and the main classification schemes, including LC subject headings. The Information processing workshop, dealing particularly with hands-on cataloging and classification work, included the practical components for both. A new course, Special materials processing, covered the *AACR2* chapters related to non-book materials. In relation to Information retrieval and transfer 1 and 2, their contents were joined in two new courses: Information analysis and retrieval and Information analysis and retrieval workshop. The concepts of indexing, retrieval, and thesauri construction and use, including Boolean logic, were taught in these courses, as well as a comparison between Subject headings and descriptors. Finally, this plan considered another new course, called Bibliographic standardization, that dealt with topics related to the preparation and publishing of bibliographies, journals, technical articles, etc., and in-depth study of bibliographic standards, national and international, such as ISO and ISBD, among others.

By adding the new workshops, the Practicum was also restructured. Only two were continued: Pre-professional practicum 1 and 2, dealing with all general principles of the profession and practice of cataloging and classification.

From 1998 to the present, small changes were applied to the study plan in the area of cataloging and classification. The Information processing 1 course changed to "Bibliographic description," with the same contents plus some description of non-book materials. Information processing 2 became just "Information Processing," and the Special materials processing course disappeared, creating a new workshop. Thus, Information processing workshop 1 dealt with a practical approach to the first part of AACR2, MARC format, and Dewey and UDC classification schedules, while Information processing workshop 2, dealt with the second part of AACR2 (access points) and LC classification. Information analysis and retrieval and the Information analysis and retrieval workshop remained the same, with some emphasis on practicing LC schedules and LC Subject headings. The Bibliographic standardization course also remained the same.

The School has a total population of approximately 380 students, with nearly 60 students take the cataloging courses in the corresponding semester. All courses and workshops are compulsory, and the number of faculty and teaching assistants vary. Normally there is a faculty member in charge of the course, and the same lecturer takes one group in the workshop, while an assistant takes the other. Generally, two faculty members and one assistant provide the instruction on these topics.

According to the head of the Library School,[3] no more changes have been implemented in current years, though automation at the University Main Library created a need for stronger emphasis on MARC formats, and for practical work on an automated system. Thus, apart from the known software Micro CDS/ISIS and its new version for Windows (WinISIS), which students use in practical work at the School, students are taken to the Main Library to practice on the automated system

SABINI. No notice on the introduction of metadata or description of electronic or Internet resources were reported.

1.3 Pontificia Universidad Católica del Perú

Courses leading to a degree of *Bachiller* in Human Sciences (up to the 4th semester) and to the *Licenciado* in LIS (up to the 6th semester) began at this University in 1985, although the program officially opened in 1986 with the name of "Especialidad de Bibliotecología y Ciencia de la Información." It was one of the programs offered by the Faculty of Human Sciences, such as Philosophy, Literature, History, and the like. The program began with the support of the British Council, which offered scholarships for the Coordinator and 3 lecturers to get a Master's degree in that country. The British Council also brought British lecturers to the University and provided bibliographic support for books and periodicals. The program has always attracted few students though its contents and lecturers always remained in good status.

In relation to the cataloging areas, the first study plan from 1986 and the second one from 1992 included the course Knowledge systems in the first semester, and the courses Information organization and retrieval 1 to 3 in the following ones. The Knowledge systems course included philosophical and logical reasoning, the legacy of philosophers to the organization of information, and their classification attempts and related topics. These contents prepare students for the classification course. Information organization and retrieval 1 dealt with cataloging and bibliographic descriptions, different standards, AACR2, standardization, and the like. Information organization and retrieval 2 dealt with classification, including the most known schedules, such as Dewey, UDC, and LC, subject headings, and access points. Both courses had theory and practice classes. The third course, was devoted to post-coordinated systems, faceted classification, automation (including MARC format), and evaluation of retrieval systems.

In 1997 a curricular reform proposed a new study plan, first offered in 1998. With this plan, the Knowledge systems course disappeared, and parts of its content were included in Information organization and retrieval 1, which changed its content to cover knowledge systems, classification concepts, major classification systems, indexing, and faceted classification. Information organization and retrieval 2 incorporated the following contents: Information representation and retrieval, natural and controlled retrieval languages, subject headings, thesauri, evaluation of retrieval, and the like. This study plan added a new course, Information organization and retrieval workshop, which included the entire area of cataloging and bibliographic description, with special emphasis on the organization of different materials, the automation of cataloging, AACR2 and new standards and changes, metadata, and Web resources.

Since 2001, despite no changes to the study plan, there have been some changes in the contents of these courses, as we can see on their syllabi. Those changes have been incorporated in the new study plan submitted for approval, to begin in 2004. In this new plan, the course's name changed slightly to Information analysis and retrieval. The changes included for the first course are: an introduction to the philosophical concepts of organization of knowledge, classification, major classification systems–Dewey and LC–and an introduction to cataloging which includes: bibliographic description, standards, AACR2, automation of cataloging, MARC bibliographic, cataloging of electronic resources, metadata, and the like. Students have the opportunity to practice with the *Classification Plus* tool available online in the University Main Library. The second course deals with subject representation of documents, including faceted classification, subject headings, and the second part of AACR2, that is, normalization of headings, access points, authority files, and particularly, MARC Authority and Holdings files. Practical work is also done as a part of this course, with demonstrations of cataloging on the Library's integrated system: Unicorn.

The third course, the workshop, is devoted to automated systems for organization and retrieval, post-coordinated systems, content analysis, natural and controlled information retrieval, thesauri, evaluation of information retrieval, evaluation of integrated library automated systems, and retrieval in automated systems: bibliographic databases vs. Internet browsers, new advances in information organization, full-text retrieval, metadata, Internet resources, and the like. This third course has a practical component. Students use the Unicorn system, and computer laboratories to perform Internet retrieval.

A final Practicum has been part of all of the study plans. They require practical work in two different information units which the students select; they perform different library duties, including organization and analysis of information, abstracting and indexing, and in some cases, preparation of an information retrieval system or a bibliographic database.

2. OTHER PROFESSIONAL EDUCATION AT UNIVERSITIES

2.1 Diploma Course at Pontificia Universidad Católica del Perú[4]

Since 1998, the Catholic University is offering a Diploma course particularly addressed to people from other subject areas, who can take core courses for entering the Library and Information Science field. Also, librarians from the ex-School of Librarians, or San Marcos University, have taken this Diploma (in a shorter version) as a refresher course. They complete 35 credit-hours from the current study plan to get the Diploma. Information organization and retrieval 1 and 2 are among the compulsory courses. Since 1998, the *Especialidad* has graduated 28 people from the Diploma course.

A Diploma course offered as distance education became available in February 2004. It will last 11 months and is addressed to people with professional (*Bachiller* or *Licenciado*) degrees or librarians needing an updating course. It is completely online except for 2-3 days of sessions on site at the beginning, middle, and end of the program. There are two courses on organization and analysis of information, dealing with different topics of cataloging, classification, automated cataloging, MARC formats, thesauri, research and retrieval, and the like. The objective is to review some general topics and present the new and up-to-date bibliography of the area.

2.2 Updating Courses to Obtain a Licenciatura Degree at Both Universities

The Peruvian University law gives the University programs the freedom to devise other graduate options besides the dissertation in order to get the *Licenciatura* degree. Thus, Universities have created different courses called updating courses, degree courses, or professional report preparation, to allow the students to fulfill the requirements for their degree.

Since 2000, San Marcos University opened the option of obtaining the *Licenciado* degree by preparing a "professional report" in a course designed for students who finished classes 3 years ago. During a five-month period, students took updating courses together with practical research and a literature review, in order to prepare a final report. Five versions have been offered since that time, particularly during summer or weekends. Few courses on the area of Information organization have been scheduled in those courses, although in its first version, an updating course on automated systems (including cataloging and retrieval) was taught.

Since 2002, the Catholic University also began an updating program leading to a *Licenciatura* degree; its name is "Updating course in LIS" and it lasts five months. In this University, the program is run by the Office of Continuing Education. The program (in its first version) offered an updating course called "Advances in information organization and retrieval," where topics such as organization of knowledge in automated environments, metadata, retrieval of information on the Internet vs. bibliographic databases, and the like, were introduced. Both scenarios also had a practical component doing information retrieval. In 2004, the University offered another version of this course.

3. NON-PROFESSIONAL EDUCATION (SUPPORT STAFF TRAINING)

3.1 National Library

The National Library has a regular program for library technicians and school teachers which is called the "Program of Continuing Education." It offers 7 different modules, each one having from 120 to 180 class hours. After completing module 1 and 2 and electives totaling 400 hours, students can get a certificate for the basic module. Successful completion of modules 3, 4, and 5 allows the students to obtain the certificate of the intermediate module, and after finishing the 6th one, they can obtain a certificate for "Application assistant of library services." After completing the whole program (7 modules), they can receive a Diploma for "Technician in library organization and services." All of these courses are progressive and can be taken by anyone, but particularly by people already working in a library. Courses are offered on a demand basis, and are normally taught in the evenings and weekends.

Basic modules cover a variety of topics such as, Module 1: Organization of library collections; Module 2: Information services; Module 3: Organization of periodicals and special materials; Module 4: Management and planning of information promotion; and Module 5: Information technology. The intermediate Module 6 deals with Organization of library services and the elective Module 7 offers different courses, such as Paleography, Organization of historical archives, Document preservation, and the like.

In relation to the area of classification and cataloging, we can mention that, within the first module, courses offered include: Introduction to library organization, Introduction to bibliographic description, where foundations of AACR2 are taught; Introduction to bibliographic classification, dealing with Dewey and notation; Introduction to bibliographic analysis, where subject headings and thesauri are included; Introduction to automated cataloging, which offers a reinforcement of cataloging principles using the software CDS/ISIS micro. This module totals 180 hours. The second module has two courses on information search and retrieval, the first dealing with general searching on databases, the second with searching on the Internet. Both include developing search strategies, coordination, and Boolean searching. Within the third module, courses on the organization of periodicals, organization of audiovisual materials, and analytic indexing of periodicals and newspapers are offered. These three courses deal with physical organization, arrangement, acquisitions, and the like, plus classification, cataloging, and indexing of these materials. No mention is made of the rules or bibliographic tools in use for these courses. The third module covers 120 hours. Within the elective module, we can find some other related courses, such as the organization of a vertical file and the organization of historical archives.

3.2 San Marcos University

The Universidad Nacional Mayor de San Marcos (UNMSM) offers courses in two different departments: one is the Library School and the other is the Main Library. The Library School has offered summer courses addressed to everybody, including Library School students. These are not offered on a regular basis and the school has offered courses in the area of bibliographic control only a few times. For example, two years ago it offered an introduction to AACR2 for special materials.

In relation to the Main Library, courses on MARC 21 were offered twice a year during the last two years; they are open to librarians from the University and outside, and to library technicians. We consider them in the area of continuing education.

3.3 Lima Municipality

During the last two years, the Lima local government or Major, through its Public Library, has offered a regular program of 1-2 lectures a month covering different aspects of Library Science. They offered lectures dealing mostly with library services, but some aspects of cataloging, as well as library automation and library software, were also presented.

3.4 Other Institutions

Apart from the three institutions mentioned, there are distance education programs being offered by two Universities in the northern part of the country, the Universidad Nacional del Santa and the Universidad Santiago Antúnez de Mayolo, both in the Ancash Province. Both offer weekend sessions and reading materials for self-training. Although it is known that some professional librarians are teaching those courses, complete program descriptions are not available.

Apart from these, we can find two other examples, also outside Lima, one at Cusco and the other at Piura, though no recent news was found about them. The Cusco program was prepared by the University in order to qualify its staff, and then opened to the general public. It lasted almost two years, with courses offered by librarians from Lima who went there during weekends. The Piura program has been offered by librarians working in that province, and was organized by an NGO and an Association of library technicians in that area who attended the classes.

In general, the courses offered to non-professionals or support staff deal with basic cataloging and classification. In places where there are professional librarians (like Universities or specialized libraries), support staff are expected to perform circulation and other user-service processes, such as registration IDs and other paperwork, and also complementary processes to the collection, such as labeling, covering, basic repairing, or reshelving. Sometimes they enter bibliographic information into the computer (previously cataloged by the librarian), add copies, prepare the inventory, and do basic searching. Most support staff are not experienced when beginning the job; they are trained on the job under the close supervision of a librarian. Normally they are selected if they have good typing skills, demonstrate attention to detail, have the ability to file by letters and numbers, and communicate well. On the other hand, in libraries with no professional librarians (mostly school and public libraries), support staff perform all of the above, including basic cataloging and classification.

4. ON-THE-JOB EDUCATION

Universities, both public and private, have issued on-the-job education courses in order to stay current with cataloging rules and international trends in the area. In 1994-95, the Pontificia Universidad Católica del Perú began its process of automation, acquiring Unicorn software from Sirsi. They received training from the vendor, and also organized courses for staff, mostly related to AACR2 and MARC formats as well as circulation and information retrieval. Updating courses have been devised when a new module of the software was implemented or new staff was hired. A recent course related to the cataloging of electronic resources (the new approved chapter in *AACR2*) was offered last year.

In the case of the Universidad Nacional Mayor de San Marcos, regular training began in 1999 when the integrated system SABINI, a Spanish software, was installed at the Main Library. Training began in the year 2000, when the vendor offered courses on cataloging and MARC bibliographic and holdings format; a later course dealt with Authority files. In addition to cataloging training, the professional and technical staff also received training in circulation and information retrieval, both at the command level and the Web-based OPAC. After the initial implementation of the cataloging sub-module, other sub-modules dealing with periodicals, audiovisual materials, music, and manuscript cataloging were added, and training on cataloging of those materials was also offered. By the middle of 2004, the libraries of Arts and Humanities, Education, Belles Arts, and a special research institute began to work with the software, so special training for the staff was also provided by the vendor. Besides the courses offered by the vendor, the Main Library also offered some courses which were addressed mainly to its personnel, but also open to library school students and some qualified technicians. These courses are explained in the following section.

The National Library is offering permanent training to its staff, apart from the courses explained in the section on non-professional education, which are courses open to everybody. These courses are internal and deal particularly with cataloging rules and Authorities, especially on special criteria adopted by the National Library as the national bibliographic center in charge of the National Bibliography. The National Library also uses the SABINI software, and the vendor offered the same kind of courses that were given at San Marcos University. Particular emphasis was put on Authorities (personal, institutional, subjects, etc.), periodicals, audiovisual materials, and manuscripts; they do no use the module for circulation nor the acquisitions modules.

A group of University Libraries formed a consortia called Altamira, most of them private Universities from Lima and provinces. They have organized some courses, particularly dealing with information retrieval and the evaluation of bibliographic databases. They have also invited other library automation software vendors in order to have multiple options from which to choose. Some of those vendors have provided training on MARC and automated cataloging in a one-day workshop or demonstration.

5. CONTINUING EDUCATION

Although there are no regular programs of continuing education, those relating to the *Licenciatura* degree mentioned in 2.2 are similar. Furthermore, some courses offered on an irregular basis by San Marcos University and the Professional School of Librarians (like the National Professional Association) deal with different topics, and can sometimes be related to cataloging and classification.

The ones devised by the San Marcos University Main Library (not the Library School) were offered twice a year during the last two years and covered the use of MARC 21, including an introduction to MARC bibliographic records for monographs, and sometimes, for periodicals, and analytic indexing of periodical articles. Classes were theoretical and practical, using the library's automated system SABINI, mentioned in point 4.

Courses offered by the Professional Association dealt more with management of information resources, automated systems, and similar topics, although some of them discussed information retrieval on the Internet and on bibliographic databases.

Overall, most of the informal education in Peru has been offered as on-the-job education not as a continuing education program scheduled on a regular basis.

6. OTHER TOPICS

Some other opportunities to gain awareness of new trends on bibliographic control or cataloging could be the National or International conferences scheduled in the country almost every two years. Both the

Professional Education School and the Peruvian-American Cultural Institute (ICPNA) have been offering conferences from 1998 to the present. Apart from the papers submitted, automated systems representatives and vendors of bibliographic databases were present to show their products, thus offering demonstrations and some workshops within the conferences, and letting the professionals know about new features. The conferences normally have good attendance, and libraries normally provide support for three or four members of their staff to attend.

In terms of residence programs or self-training, there are no examples in this country. Just one or two times, some libraries, like the Catholic University, have received a librarian from a province, but it is not a regular program. No tutorial or self-training programs are available either.

In Peru there is a general discussion list called "Biblio" (biblio@ listas.rcp.net.pe), which discusses different topics related to professional development, not just cataloging or bibliographic control topics. Problems with language prevent most of the librarians from participating actively on international lists. Few examples were found, and cataloging is not a very attractive topic among professional librarians.

Regarding cooperation between library schools and libraries, the relationship lies mostly in temporary positions the University libraries offer to School students to work part-time jobs during their study years. Both University Libraries with library schools are offering students opportunities to work in cataloging and circulation, which will give the students good experience before graduation. Another relationship exists when University libraries offer their space for practical cataloging in their automated system, or as mentioned in the Catholic University, to use the *Classification Plus* tool. Also, in the area of cataloging, a professional librarian frequently can become a lecturer, or a teaching assistant, depending on the number of students for each semester.

In terms of qualifications, most of the people working or looking for a job in cataloging need to prove experience in the area. Both the Catholic and San Marcos Universities ask for experience in LC classification, MARC format, and automated cataloging; other libraries using CDS/ISIS ask for experience in this software, and also with AACR2. No particular requirements are set in relation to languages or metadata, though they are a plus.

Finally, library automation can be traced from the middle 1980s when CDS/ISIS began to be used to create OPACs, although a general awareness of rules and authorities began with the introduction of library automation integrated systems at the National Library and at Peru's two main Universities. Since then, there have been some initiatives to create more OPACs, to put them on the Web, and to collaborate in the creation of digital libraries and information networks. For example, Peru is the center of the Biblioteca Andina (Andean Library) (http://www.comunidadandina.org/bda/home_biblio.htm), the Biblioteca Virtual de Salud Ambiental (http://www.cepis.ops-oms.org), and a member of other Latin American projects, including the Biblioteca Virtual de Salud (BVS) (http://www.bireme.br). A good directory of Peruvian libraries can be found at http://quelcas.rcp.net.pe and also on the Professional School web site, http://www.cbp.org.pe.

In terms of publications, the San Marcos Library School published a journal called *Claustro Pleno* which devoted some papers to the evaluation of the School and different courses. Apart from that, the National Library publishes the journal *Fénix*, which sometimes publishes articles on bibliographic control. The Professional School of Librarians publishes *Bibliotecólogos*, and San Marcos publishes a new journal called *Infobib*. There is also an electronic journal named *Biblios*. In terms of monographs published on the topic, San Marcos Library School published a posthumous book last by Erlinda Chávez[5] (their first lecturer) on classification and indexing. This year the Main Library has published the second edition of a book on MARC 21.[6]

CONCLUSIONS

Few lines can be added as a conclusion to what has been stated already. In general, library education in Peru continues to be traditional in terms of teaching methodology, contents, number of students, and the like. It is not sufficient to meet demand, particularly for the rest of the country, as the only two schools are located in Lima. The real situation is that many positions related to technical services are occupied by paraprofessionals or people without qualifications, being perhaps the area where it is easiest to find non-professionals. On the other hand, automated systems and on-the-job training are giving paraprofessionals more skills to develop those functions. Generally, professional librarians are working more and more on original cataloging, developing of cataloging criteria and tools, and supervising technical staff work. In addition, areas like Management, Information services, Internet searching, and the like, are more attractive to recent graduates and students than bibliographic control; thus, no real innovations can be found in the country in this field. Very few people are confident with the new revision of *AACR2*, or MARC 21 changes, or the new Electronic Resources chapter of *AACR2*, or metadata, and the like, even though these are taught at the Library School. There is no real interest in developing them because of the interest in, and emphasis on, creating digital libraries by digitizing original documents.

NOTES

1. The number differs according to different sources. Silva Santisteban (1984) considers an approximate of 600, though only 302 graduated, p. 8, while Hurtado Galván (1995) mentions 462, p. 102.

2. Study plan explained in "50 años de Enseñanza Bibliotecológica en el Perú 1943-1993" published by the UNMSM in 1993, p. 51-80.

3. McKee de Maurial, Nelly. Personal interview November 2003.

4. A complete description of the Diploma course can be reviewed at: http://www. pucp.edu.pe/acad/pucvirtual/difaci/. Cf. Biblioteca Nacional del Perú. Centro de Investigaciones y Desarrollo Bibliotecológico. Programa de Capacitación Continua para bibliotecarios y docentes; Programa técnico formativo en organización y servicios bibliotecarios. Lima, agosto 2003.

5. Chávez Barriga, Erlinda. Clasificación e indización. Lima: Universidad Nacional Mayor de San Marcos Escuela Académico Profesional de Bibliotecología y Ciencias de la Información, 2002. 140 p.

6. Universidad Nacional Mayor de San Marcos. Biblioteca Central Pedro Zulen. Formato MARC 21 para monografías y folletos. / trad-adaptación y elaboración Gloria Samamé Mancilla [et al.]. Lima: UNMSM, 2003.

BIBLIOGRAPHY

Biblioteca Nacional del Perú. Centro de Investigaciones y Desarrollo Bibliotecológico. Programa de Capacitación Continua para bibliotecarios y docentes: programa técnico formativo en organización y servicios bibliotecarios. Lima: BNP, 2003. 8 p.

Curriculum de la Escuela Académico Profesional de Bibliotecología y Ciencias de la Información de la Universidad Nacional Mayor de San Marcos. p. 5-24. En: *Claustro Pleno*, No. 6, agosto 1992.

Hurtado Galván, L. (1995). Desarrollo desde arriba y desde abajo. Piura: Cipca; Cusco: Centro Bartolomé de las Casas.

MacKee de Maurial, N. (1966). La Escuela Nacional de Bibliotecarios del Perú. p. 243-270. En: *Fénix*, No. 16, 1966.

Miyagi M., F. (1992). Informe y evaluación de los cursos: Procesos técnicos y Bibliotemetría impartidos en la EAPBCI de la UNMSM. p. 25-27. En: *Claustro Pleno*, No. 6, agosto 1992.

Pontificia Universidad Católica del Perú. Facultad de Letras y Ciencias Humanas. Plan de Estudios de la Especialidad de Bibliotecología y Ciencia de la Información. Lima, PUCP, 1986. 19 p.

_____. Plan de Estudios de la Especialidad de Bibliotecología y Ciencia de la Información, aprobado en Consejo Universitario en enero de 1992. Lima, PUCP, 1992. 9 p.

_____. Plan de Estudios 2001: Plan de Estudios de la Especialidad de Bibliotecología y Ciencia de la Información, aprobado por Consejo Universitario el 11 de febrero de 1998. Lima, PUCP, 1998. p. 25-36.

Silva Santisteban, T. (1984). Indice de tesis de la Escuela Nacional de Bibliotecarios. Lima: BNP, 1984.

Universidad Nacional Mayor de San Marcos. Facultad de Letras y Ciencias Humanas. Escuela Académico Profesional de Bibliotecología y Ciencias de la Información. 50 años de enseñanza de la Bibliotecología en el Perú 1943-1993. Lima: UNMSM, 1993. 80 p.

Universidad Nacional Mayor de San Marcos. Facultad de Letras y Ciencias Humanas. Escuela Académico Profesional de Bibliotecología y Ciencias de la Información (037). Plan de Estudios 1986-1992. Lima: UNMSM, 1992.

_____. Plan de Estudios 1995. Lima: UNMSM, Secretaría Académica, 1995. 6 p.

_____. Plan de Estudios 1998. Lima: UNMSM, Dirección Académica, 1998. 6 p.

_____. Plan de Estudios 2001–EPA de Bibliotecología y Ciencias de la Información. Lima: UNMSM, 2001. 15 p.

Cataloging and Classification Education in Egypt: Stressing the Fundamentals While Moving Toward Automated Applications

Mohammed Fat'hy Abdel Hady
Ali Kamal Shaker

SUMMARY. This paper concentrates on the current state of cataloging and classification education in Egypt. The authors highlight the changes which have occurred in the past five years and also envision expected changes for the near future. All courses related inclusively to cataloging

Mohammed Fat'hy Abdel Hady, PhD, is Professor, Department of Library and Information Science, Cairo University, Egypt (E-mail: mfhady@maktoob.com).

Ali Kamal Shaker, PhD, is affiliated with the Department of Library and Information Science, El-Minia University, Egypt (E-mail: akshaker2003@yahoo.com).

[Haworth co-indexing entry note]: "Cataloging and Classification Education in Egypt: Stressing the Fundamentals While Moving Toward Automated Applications." Abdel Hady, Mohammed Fat'hy, and Ali Kamal Shaker. Co-published simultaneously in *Cataloging & Classification Quarterly* (The Haworth Information Press, an imprint of The Haworth Press, Inc.) Vol. 41, No. 3/4, 2006, pp. 407-429; and: *Education for Library Cataloging: International Perspectives* (ed: Dajin D. Sun, and Ruth C. Carter) The Haworth Information Press, an imprint of The Haworth Press, Inc., 2006, pp. 407-429. Single or multiple copies of this article are available for a fee from The Haworth Document Delivery Service [1-800-HAWORTH, 9:00 a.m. - 5:00 p.m. (EST). E-mail address: docdelivery@haworthpress.com].

Available online at http://www.haworthpress.com/web/CCQ
doi:10.1300/J104v41n03_11

(both descriptive and subject) and classification of library materials have been examined. Research design includes analyzing curricula, distributing a written questionnaire, and interviewing library and information science faculty from different departments throughout the country. The paper reveals a number of findings that are of particular relevance to current and near-future cataloging and classification education in Egypt. Among these findings are the increasing focus on machine-readable cataloging, cooperation in cataloging, improving the practical part of cataloging and classification education, the need for continuing education of instructors, and continuing development of cataloging courses. *[Article copies available for a fee from The Haworth Document Delivery Service: 1-800-HAWORTH. E-mail address: <docdelivery@haworthpress.com> Website: <http://www.HaworthPress.com> © 2006 by The Haworth Press, Inc. All rights reserved.]*

KEYWORDS. Cataloging and classification education, LIS (Library and Information Science) education, LIS curricula, descriptive cataloging, subject cataloging, classification, Egypt

INTRODUCTION

This paper focuses on the current state of cataloging and classification education in Egypt. It also moves back and forth in time to highlight the changes which have occurred in the past five years and also to envision anticipated changes within the next five years. The authors examine all of the courses related inclusively to cataloging (both descriptive and subject) and classification of library materials. This, therefore, excludes courses such as indexing and abstracting, since many of the academic staff in Egypt tend to consider that these courses–in addition to cataloging and classification–fall inside the technical services' frame.

In order to document the current state of cataloging and classification education in library and information science (LIS) departments in Egypt, the authors analyzed curricula, distributed a written questionnaire, and interviewed many LIS faculty members from different departments throughout the country. The paper provides information on the number of courses, levels of courses (basic vs. advanced), course descriptions (based on syllabi), and available facilities (such as bibliographic labs and fieldwork). The following departments have participated in the study:

1. LIS Department in Cairo University
2. LIS Department in Ain Shams University
3. LIS Department in Monoufia University
4. LIS Department in Minia University
5. LIS Department in Helwan University
6. LIS Department in Cairo University (Bani Swif Branch)
7. LIS Department in South Valley University (Sohaj Branch)
8. LIS Department in Banha University
9. LIS Department in Alexandria University
10. LIS Department in October 6 University

LIS EDUCATION IN EGYPT

This section provides an overview of the historical development of LIS education in Egypt. The beginnings go back to the 1950s when Law number 9, in 1951, had been issued to establish the "Archives and Librarianship Institute" in Cairo University (then called First Found University). That Institute continued as an independent entity within Cairo University until 1954 when Law number 116 was issued to transform the Institute into a department in the Faculty of Arts [the school of languages, literature, and some other social and humanities sciences]. Since then, the LIS curriculum has been changed many times, and the current curriculum was developed in 1993 when the name of the department changed to the Department of Librarianship, Archives, and Information to keep abreast of current and ongoing developments in the field (Abdel-Hadi, 1994).

The LIS Department in Cairo University was the only one in the country until the early 1980s, when another department was opened in Alexandria University in 1981. That was followed by two LIS departments in Bani Swif (1985) and Tanta (1986).

The last decade of the 20th century has seen a proliferation in LIS education in Egypt. Table 1 shows the openings of LIS departments.

To enroll in an LIS undergraduate program in Egypt, students must have the secondary school general certificate. The study takes four academic years, and upon successful completion, students are honored with the bachelor's degree in Arts (BA). Each academic year is divided into two semesters from September to May, and summer is always off. Every program is based on fixed 'obligatory' courses, each lasting 4 hours/week. However, new curricula developed recently do provide some 'optional' courses.

TABLE 1. Development of LIS Education in Egypt

Name of the Department	Year Opened
LIS Department in Cairo University	1951
LIS Department in Alexandria University	1981
LIS Department in Bani Swif	1985
LIS Department in Tanta University	1986
LIS Department in Monoufia University	1990
LIS Department in South Valley University	1995
LIS Department in Minia University	1997
LIS Department in Asuit University	1997
LIS Department in Banha University	1997
LIS Department in Ain Shams University	1999
LIS Department in October 6 University	1999

In addition to undergraduate programs, many departments also offer graduate studies that include:

1. Diploma (two years)–for BA or BS holders other than LIS graduates. Upon completion with a 'very good' GPA, students can continue their graduate studies in LIS, as follows:
2. Master's degree–open for 'good' GPA students with BA in LIS and also for 'very good' GPA diploma students (see 1 above).
3. Doctoral degree–open only for LIS Master's degree holders.

Faculty must have their doctoral degrees in LIS before taking teaching responsibilities. Each department has its own assistant faculty who usually teach lab sessions and oversee fieldwork while preparing their Master's and doctoral degrees. Therefore, in order to fulfill the requirements, LIS departments usually have faculty from other specializations teach some courses, especially related to information technology.

The facilities available for LIS departments include specific lecture rooms in addition to lecture rooms that are shared with other departments in the school or university; bibliographic labs (details on this appear later in this paper); computer labs; and a special library for LIS faculty and graduate students.

LITERATURE REVIEW

Generally, there are very few research papers related to cataloging and classification education in Egypt. The oldest study was published by Nabila Khalifa Gomaa in 1990, which gave highlights on teaching cataloging courses in the western world and new trends in that area. She then focused on cataloging and classification practices in Arab countries, which was mostly original cataloging. She explained that the reason for that might be the unavailability of bibliographic data in machine-readable format and of a formal program for cataloging in publication. Hence came the persistent need for qualified catalogers (Gomaa, 1990).

Another important study was published by Abdel Wahab Abonnour about teaching classification in LIS departments in the Arab world. It generally covered the main objectives for teaching classification, and related issues such as a classification curriculum. The study (Abonnour, 1998) suggested a complete teaching plan for classification that could be used as guidelines by anyone teaching that course.

Two other studies were Master's theses in 1999. The first one was written by Magdy Abdel Badea (Ain Shams University) and tried to determine the required skills for descriptive cataloging that should be possessed by catalogers. Abdel Badea also constructed an educational schema to develop skills in using cataloging rules for non-print materials (Abdel Badea, 1999).

The second Master's thesis was written by Emad Aisa Saleh (Cairo University) about computer-aided instruction (CAI) in LIS in general, and classification in particular. Saleh aimed to find out the effect of CAI on teaching classification for undergraduate students by employing an experimental research methodology. The study concluded that CAI could save up to 40% of the time required for learning classification, and increase the educational outcome (Saleh, 1999).

ANALYSIS OF LIS CURRICULA

The following section highlights the number and nature of cataloging and classification courses in LIS departments in Egypt. The focus is on undergraduate programs; graduate studies are excluded.

LIS Department in Cairo University

All students take the same courses in the first three years. However, in the fourth year (senior students), students are divided into three areas of study: Librarianship, Archives, and Information Technology.

There are a total of 44 courses throughout the four-year program, with a total of 176 teaching hours for theoretical lectures and 15 practical hours.

The cataloging and classification courses make up 9% of the curriculum; the proportion of teaching hours is 9% and 26.7% of the practical hours. Please refer to Table 2 below.

LIS Department in Alexandria University

All students take the same courses in the four-year program, and there is no division in the last year as in Cairo University. There is a total of 37 courses, with 156 teaching hours and 12 practical hours.

The cataloging and classification courses make up 13.5% of the curriculum. The percentages are 12.8% of the lecture hours and 50% of the practical hours. See Table 3.

LIS Department in Cairo University (Bani Swif Branch)

As in Alexandria University, students in Bani Swif take all courses and there is no division. There are 45 courses, with 166 lecture hours and 20 hours for practice. The cataloging and classification courses make up 6.7% of the curriculum, with 6.6% of the hours on lectures and 20% of the hours on practice. See Table 4.

LIS Department in Monoufia University

All students take the same courses throughout the four-year program. There are 42 courses with 162 teaching hours and 26 practical hours.

TABLE 2. Cataloging and Classification Courses in Cairo University

Course Title	Year	Number of Hours	
		Lecture	Practice
Descriptive Cataloging (basic level)	Second year	4	1
Classification	Second year	4	1
Subject Cataloging	Third year	4	1
Descriptive Cataloging (advanced level)	Third year	4	1
Number of courses (4)		16	4

TABLE 3. Cataloging and Classification Courses in Alexandria University

Course Title	Year	Number of Hours	
		Lecture	Practice
Descriptive Cataloging	Second year	4	2
Classification	Second year	4	2
Cataloging Audiovisual Materials	Third year	4	2
Comparative Classification	Third year	4	0
Subject Cataloging	Third year	4	0
Number of courses (5)		20	6

TABLE 4. Cataloging and Classification Courses in Bani Swif University

Course Title	Year	Number of Hours	
		Lecture	Practice
Descriptive Cataloging	First year	4	2
Classification	First year	4	2
Subject Cataloging	Second year	3	0
Number of courses (3)		11	4

The cataloging and classification courses make up 7.1% of the curriculum, 7.4% of lecture hours, and 23% of practical hours. See Table 5.

LIS Department in South Valley University (Sohaj Branch)

Students take the same courses and there is no division. There are 40 courses with a total of 156 lecture hours and 26 practical hours. The cataloging and classification courses make up 12.5% of the curriculum, 12.8% of teaching hours, and 30.7% of practical hours. See Table 6.

LIS Department in Zakazik University (Banha Branch)

Students take the same courses and there is no division. There are 46 courses with a total of 180 lecture hours and only 4 practical hours. The cataloging and classification courses make up 10.9% of the curriculum, 11.1% of teaching hours, and there are no practical hours. See Table 7.

TABLE 5. Cataloging and Classification Courses in Monoufia University

Course Title	Year	Number of Hours	
		Lecture	Practice
Descriptive Cataloging	Second year	4	2
Classification	Second year	4	2
Subject Cataloging	Third year	4	2
Number of courses (3)		12	6

TABLE 6. Cataloging and Classification Courses in South Valley University

Course Title	Year	Number of Hours	
		Lecture	Practice
Bibliographic Description (basic level)	Second year	4	2
Classification (basic level)	Second year	4	2
Subject Cataloging	Third year	4	0
Bibliographic Description (advanced level)	Third year	4	2
Classification (advanced level)	Third year	4	2
Number of courses (5)		20	8

TABLE 7. Cataloging and Classification Courses in Banha University

Course Title	Year	Number of Hours	
		Lecture	Practice
Basic Cataloging (printed materials)	Second year	4	-
Decimal Classification	Second year	4	-
Subject Analysis	Third year	4	-
Advanced Cataloging (non-book materials)	Third year	4	-
Classification Theories	Third year	4	-
Number of courses (5)		20	-

LIS Department in Ain Shams University

The program here is almost similar to Cairo University's LIS program, with some minor differences in some courses. Students take the same courses for the first three years, and then they are divided into three specializations: Librarianship, Archives, and Information Technology. There are 47 courses, with a total of 188 lecture hours and 15 practical hours.

The proportion of cataloging and classification courses (4 courses) is 8.5% of teaching hours, and 26.7% of practical hours. See Table 8.

LIS Department in October 6 University

Students take the same courses in the first year as all other students in the school. This means that in the Faculty of Social Sciences, of which the department of LIS is a part, the first year consists of courses taught to the whole student population in the school. Specialization then begins in the second year, when students can select to proceed in the LIS department or any other departments. And the program is based on the credit-hour system. LIS students take 47 courses with a total of 150 credit hours. These courses are distributed as 91 lecture-type credit hours and 59 practical-type credit hours.

The cataloging and classification courses make up 6.4% of the curriculum, with 6.6% of lecture hours and 10.2% of practical hours. The ratio of credit hours (9 credits) to the total is 7.5%. See Table 9.

TABLE 8. Cataloging and Classification Courses in Ain Shams University

Course Title	Year	Number of Hours	
		Lecture	Practice
Descriptive Cataloging (1)	Second year	4	1
Classification	Second year	4	1
Subject Analysis	Third year	4	1
Descriptive Cataloging (2)	Third year	4	1
Number of courses (4)		16	4

TABLE 9. Cataloging and Classification Courses in October 6 University

Course Title	Year	Number of Hours		
		Lecture	Practice	Credit
Bibliographic Description (obligatory course)	Second year	2	2	3
Classification Systems (obligatory course)	Fourth year	2	2	3
Subject Analysis (obligatory course)	Fourth year	2	2	3
Number of courses (3)		6	6	9

DATA ANALYSIS

Number of Courses

The authors noticed that the number of cataloging and classification courses is generally low compared to the total number of courses in each curriculum. See Table 10.

As shown in Table 10, cataloging and classification courses are between three and five (6.4%-13.5%). The average is 9.3%.

Theoretical and Practical Components

The theoretical portion is more common than practice when teaching cataloging and classification courses, despite the severe need for practical training. See Table 11.

Table 11 illustrates the wide divergence between theoretical and practical hours (0%-100%). While there is no practical training at all in Banha, the LIS program in October 6 University achieves the maximum percentage without even having a bibliographic lab. We find the best percentage achieved was in Monoufia. We also notice the few number of hours in October 6 University (6 hrs.) compared to the highest number in three other departments (Alexandria, Sohaj, and Banha). Furthermore, we find out that there is no practical training in some courses, like subject analysis (Sohaj, Bani Swif, Alexandria) and comparative classification (Alexandria).

Distribution of Courses

Table 12 below shows that cataloging and classification courses are mainly distributed between the 2nd and 3rd years of the undergraduate

TABLE 10. Number of Cataloging and Classification Courses in LIS Curricula

Department	Cat. And Class. Courses	Total Number of Courses	Percentage
Cairo	4	44	9%
Alexandria	5	37	13.5%
Bani Swif	3	45	6.7%
Monoufia	3	42	7.1%
Souhaj	5	40	12.5%
Banha	5	46	10.9%
Ain Shams	4	47	8.5%
October 6	3	47	6.4%

TABLE 11. Theoretical vs. Practical Hours

Department	Theoretical Hours	Practical Hours	Percentage
Cairo	16	4	25%
Alexandria	20	6	30%
Bani Swif	11	4	39%
Monoufia	12	6	50%
Souhaj	20	8	40%
Banha	20	0	0%
Ain Shams	16	4	25%
October 6	6	6	100%

TABLE 12. Distribution of Cataloging and Classification Courses

Department	1st year	2nd year	3rd year	4th year	Total
Cairo	0	2	2	0	4
Alexandria	0	2	3	0	5
Bani Swif	2	1	0	0	3
Monoufia	0	2	1	0	3
Souhaj	0	2	3	0	5
Banha	0	2	3	0	5
Ain Shams	0	2	2	0	4
October 6	0	1	0	2	3
Total	2	14	14	2	32

program. Only one department offers cataloging courses in the first year (Bani Swif), and only one department offers these courses in the last year of the program (October 6 University). The authors believe that it is not suitable to offer cataloging courses either in the first or the last year. Students who just enter the program may not yet be ready for technical details and, similarly, students who have almost finished most of their courses cannot gain the required skills in the last year.

Course Categories

Analysis of LIS curricula in Egypt indicated that the most dominant area in cataloging and classification courses is the category of descriptive cataloging. This is followed by courses in classification, and then subject cataloging courses. See Table 13.

However, we should mention that, in most LIS departments in the country, there is a course in "indexing and abstracting," which is considered an advanced level of the subject cataloging course. One also should notice that there is no introductory course that combines both cataloging and classification. Furthermore, LIS curricula in Egypt are missing–so far–a course that deals with automated applications in cataloging and classification. The absence of such a course reflects the 'traditional' view of cataloging and classification courses. We finally should say that all of these courses are obligatory in the undergraduate program.

Course Titles

Table 14 shows wide use of the title "descriptive cataloging" in LIS curricula in Egypt. Sometimes that title is augmented by the word "basic" or "advanced," indicating the level of the course. Titles of subject cataloging courses are shown in Table 15. It is obvious that the title "subject analysis" is more common than "subject cataloging." Now we turn to the titles of classification courses. Table 16 illustrates how classification courses differ in titles among LIS programs in Egypt.

The most common title–as shown in Table 16–is classification. But, it is worth mentioning the two classification courses in Banha University: decimal classification and classification theories, and also the comparative classification course in Alexandria. These are considered advanced courses in classification.

TABLE 13. Categories of Cataloging and Classification Courses

Department	Descriptive Cataloging	Subject Cataloging	Classification	Total
Cairo	2	1	1	4
Alexandria	2	1	2	5
Bani Swif	1	1	1	3
Monoufia	1	1	1	3
Souhaj	2	1	2	5
Banha	2	1	2	5
Ain Shams	2	1	1	4
October 6	1	1	1	3
Total	13	8	11	32

TABLE 14. Titles of Cataloging Courses

Department	Bibliographic Description	Descriptive Cataloging	Introductory Cataloging and Advanced Cataloging	Processing Audiovisual Materials
Cairo		√		
Alexandria		√		√
Bani Swif		√		
Monoufia		√		
Souhaj	√			
Banha			√	
Ain Shams		√		
October 6	√			

TABLE 15. Titles of Subject Cataloging Courses

Department	Subject Cataloging	Subject Analysis
Cairo	√	
Alexandria		√
Bani Swif		√
Monoufia	√	
Souhaj		√
Banha		√
Ain Shams		√
October 6		√

TABLE 16. Titles of Classification Courses

Department	Classification	Comparative Classification	Decimal Classification	Classification Theories	Classification Systems
Cairo	√				
Alexandria	√	√			
Bani Swif	√				
Monoufia	√				
Souhaj	√				
Banha			√	√	
Ain Shams	√				
October 6					√

LIS FACULTY AND AVAILABLE FACILITIES

The following section details information about faculty members in terms of their qualifications and responsibilities. Also covered are the facilities available in LIS departments, such as bibliographic and computer labs.

Faculty and Assistant Faculty

Lectures are given only by PhD holders in LIS departments. These are mainly the faculty of the department. Sometimes, the department contracts with other departments or with the faculty of other schools to have a visiting professor teach a course. This happens mostly in the area of information technology courses. In addition to faculty members, each department has its own assistant faculty whose main resposibility is providing the practical training sessions.

Assistant faculty normally teach lab sessions, which are a series of practical exercises on cataloging different information resources. The faculty member teaches the rules in a lecture room, and then the role of teaching assistants is to help students with practice on real-life materials. The assistants are also responsible for following up on the homework exercises.

Training in automated cataloging systems is held in computer labs. Usually, there is a demo of a common automated system used in libraries in the country to illustrate an example of cataloging modules. However, most departments still train students in preparing catalog cards (traditional methods), as the majority of libraries are still not automated yet.

Available Facilities

Table 17 shows bibliographic and computer labs available for LIS programs.

The computer lab in Cairo University is considered to be the best lab among LIS departments. It consists of 25 PCs linked in a LAN, with an Internet connection. Bibliographic lab consists of cataloging rules (mostly AACR), subject heading lists (LC and Arabic ones), and classification schemes (mostly DDC and translated (into Arabic) DDC with modifications). Bibliographic labs usually contain different kinds of library materials, mainly in Arabic, but also in English and a few in French and other European languages.

One department has a bibliographic lab as part of the school's library, and materials are brought in for the practice of students. But this is a temporary situation until the department creates its own bibliographic lab. Most departments usually share a common problem, that is, obtaining recent editions of classification schemes, subject heading lists, and cataloging rules. One faculty member indicated, "DDC 20th edition is the most recent edition available. It was even a gift from the British Council in Cairo." Another faculty member pointed out that "only one

TABLE 17. Facilities of LIS Departments

Name of the department	Bibliographic lab	Computer lab
LIS Department in Cairo University	Yes	Yes
LIS Department in Alexandria University	No	No
LIS Department in Tanta University	No	No
LIS Department in Monoufia University	Yes	Yes
LIS Department in Helwan University	Yes	Yes
LIS Department in El-Minia University	No	Yes (for all the school)
LIS Department in Asuit University	No	No
LIS Department in South Valley University	No	No
LIS Department in Ain Shams University	No	Yes (for all the school)
LIS Department in October 6 University	No	No

version of DDC (v. 21) is available, in addition to a translation of the 12th abridged edition."

Fieldwork

There is no specific fieldwork related mainly to cataloging and classification. In all of the departments, there is a course called "Field Training" in the fourth year [senior students]. In that course, students work 4 hours/week for one semester in selected libraries, and go around to all of the different divisions within the library, including the cataloging department.

CONTENT ANALYSIS OF CATALOGING AND CLASSIFICATION COURSES

The information which follows is based on the course descriptions provided by faculty members who responded to the distributed questionnaire.

Descriptive Cataloging

Normally there are two courses for descriptive cataloging: one is basic and the other is advanced. The basic-level course normally covers the Anglo-American Cataloging Rules. Topics addressed include: definition of cataloging, types of cataloging, types and formats of catalogs, bibliographic records, description of books, entries. The advanced course usually focuses on topics such as cataloging of periodicals, maps, and atlases, computerized cataloging, bibliographic utilities, and cooperative cataloging.

Subject Cataloging

This course provides students with skills required to describe the subject(s) of library materials (books, periodicals, audiovisual, etc.). Also, students are trained in the correct use of subject heading lists (LCSH, and the Greater List of Arabic Subject Headings created by Professor Sha'ban Khalifa).

Topics covered in subject cataloging usually include: definition of subject cataloging, the difference between subject headings and classification and the relationship between them, advantages and disadvantages of alphabetical subject catalogs, rules or principles of selecting subject headings, types or forms of subject headings, subdivisions in subject headings, cross-references, punctuation, notes, arrangement of subject headings, selected examples of Arabian and foreign subject heading lists. Also covered are thesauri and the difference between thesauri and subject headings.

Classification

Some departments have two courses for classification; one is basic and the other is advanced. However, most departments now are moving toward only one course for classification in the curriculum. Normally, topics covered in classification courses include: definition of classification, common classification systems (DDC, LCC, and UDC), and DDC (in detail): main tables, auxiliary tables, constructing classification numbers, etc. Other topics covered include: development of classification systems, characteristics of a good classification system, narrow vs. broad classification, components of a classification system, and Arabic modifications of the DDC scheme.

CHANGES IN CATALOGING AND CLASSIFICATION EDUCATION

The questionnaire shown in Appendix C was constructed to collect information about changes in cataloging and classification education in Egypt during the last five years, as well as changes expected for the next five years. The results are summarized.

Descriptive Cataloging

Changes over the past five years can be summarized as follows:

- Cataloging materials other than books. Before, the concentration was on book cataloging, but other materials have been considered during the past five years. These materials include audiovisual materials and electronic resources.
- Automated cataloging systems, with practical application on one system as an example.
- In the advanced course level, the comparative study of Arabic and translated automated systems. Also, MARC format.

Changes expected for the next five years can be summarized as follows:

- This is generally based on new technology and developments in automated systems, and cataloging rules.
- Increasing the focus on copy cataloging as a result of the expansion of automated systems.
- More on characteristics and applications of automated cataloging modules.
- Training students in using computerized cataloging and integrated library systems.

Subject Cataloging

Changes over the past five years can be summarized as follows:

- Use of natural language in subject analysis.
- Teaching of subject cataloging tools has been always affected by automated systems.
- Use of thesauri as important tools in automated applications, which are expanding in Egyptian libraries and information systems nowadays.

Changes expected for the next five years can be summarized as follows:

- Use of expert systems in subject analysis (practically, not just theoretically).
- Automatic preparation of thesauri.
- The difference of automated applications and search strategies and how they are developed in an automated environment has been reflected in how subject headings or keywords are formulated, and how librarians select them to adapt to the online environment. All of this will be reflected in the teaching of this course.

Classification

Changes over the past five years can be summarized as follows:

- Changes were always related to new editions of classification schemes. Focus was, and still is, on DDC.

- Students have been trained on the electronic DDC version once it became available on CD-ROM. Currently, the educational Web site of DDC was introduced to students. But this is mostly theoretical with little practice, depending on the availability of an Internet connection in the computer lab, and it also depends on students' familiarity with the Internet, and on whether they can log on on their own (from outside the school). Students' financial ability must be considered here.

Changes expected for the next five years can be summarized as follows:

- This is also related to the changes in the classification scheme (DDC) itself.
- More on LCC.
- Classification in an online environment.
- Classification of Internet resources.

CONCLUSIONS AND RECOMMENDATIONS

A number of findings have been revealed during the course of this study. These are of particular relevance to the current and near-future of cataloging and classification education in Egypt.

1. Increasing the focus on machine-readable cataloging to fulfill the need for qualified catalogers who possess skills suitable for automated applications that are currently spreading in all types of libraries throughout the country.
2. Stressing the benefits of cooperation in cataloging, especially the partenership with the major bibliographic utilities such as OCLC and RLIN.
3. Making available the required facilities to improve the practical part of cataloging and classification education, such as bibliographic labs and training on cataloging modules in automated systems.
4. Continuing education for instructors to follow up with new trends in the field.
5. Developing cataloging and classification courses to reflect new trends and needs, such as machine-readable cataloging in automated environments.

6. Assuring the importance of utilizing new educational technology, such as the Internet and distance education, and computer-aided instruction.
7. Establishing a fomal program for cataloging in publication (CIP) to lessen the burden upon LIS departments. This means that major libraries in the country (e.g., the national library and the big university libraries) should do some work in cataloging so that original cataloging is minimized.
8. Updating textbooks to include–not only the theoretical background–but also the practical applications of cataloging rules.

REFERENCES

Abdel Badea, Magdi. 1999. *Designing an Educational Schema for Teaching Cataloging Non-Printed Materials.* Cairo: Ain Shams University. (Master's thesis).

Abdel Hadi, Mohamed Fathy and Abdel Majed Bouazza. 1994. A Survey of Education for Library and Information Science in Egypt, the Maghreb, and Sudan. In: *Information and Libraries in the Arab World.* London: Library Association. Pp. 26-27.

Abonnour, Abdel Wahab. 1998. Teaching Classification in Arabia LIS Programs: A Study on Objectives and a Suggested Syllabus. *Arab Journal for Library and Information* (Reyadh). Vol. 18, issue 3 (July). Pp. 5-28. and Vol. 19, issue 1 (January 1999). Pp. 76-105.

Alexandria University. Faculty of Arts. 1993. *Dalil Al-Altaleb* [Student Guide]. Alex.: The Faculty.

Cairo University. Bani Swif Branch. Faculty of Arts. 1993. *Al-La'eha Al-Dakhelia Le-Kolliat Al-Adab* [Faculty of Arts Directory]. Cairo: The University. Press.

Cairo University. Faculty of Arts. 1997. *Dalil Kolliat Al-Adab* [Faculty of Arts Directory]. Cairo: The Faculty Press.

Gomaa, Nabila Khalifa. 1990. New Trends in Teaching Cataloging and Their Effects in Arab Countries. *Alam El-Kotob* (Reyadh). Vol. 11, issue 4 (November). Pp. 489-498.

Helwan University. Faculty of Arts. 199? *La'ehat Kolliat Al-Adab* [Faculty of Arts Directory]. Cairo: The Faculty.

Monoufia University. Faculty of Arts. 199? *Dalil Kolliat Al-Adab* [Faculty of Arts Directory]. Shibin El-Kom(Monoufia): The Faculty.

Saleh, Emad Aisa. 1999. *Computer-Aided Instruction in LIS: An Experimental Study of Undergraduate Students in Cairo University and Helwan University.* (Master's thesis, Cairo University).

Tanta University. Faculty of Arts. 199? *Dalil Kolliat Al-Adab* [Faculty of Arts Directory]. Tanta: The Faculty.

APPENDIX A. Cataloging and Classification Course Descriptions (Cairo University)

Descriptive cataloging   2nd year–1st semester   (4 hrs./week + one hour training)
Gives students theoretical and practical skills in bibliographic description of printed materials and manuscripts (physical description). Topics covered are: entries selection and format, elements of description, preparing main card and additional cards [for the card catalog environment], filing rules, types [author, title, subject . . . catalogs] and forms (book, card, microfiche) of catalogs.

Classification   2nd year–2nd semester   (4 hrs./week + one hour training)
Students study the difference between philosophical and bibliographic classification, and characteristics of good bibliographic classification. Topics covered are: famous classification systems with particular focus on Dewey Decimal Classification [DDC], Universal Decimal Classification [UDC], and their applications.

Subject cataloging   3rd year–1st semester   (4 hrs./week + one hour training)
Students learn theories and philosophies of subject analysis and use of subject heading lists. Topics covered are: the anatomy of subject headings, notes and cross-references, and subdivisions. Also covered are practical training on subject analysis.

Descriptive cataloging (advanced level)   3rd year–1st semester   (4 hrs./week + one hour training)
Students study bibliographic description of non-printed materials, such as audiovisual materials, microforms, computer files, and compact discs [CDs]. This course is an extension of topics covered in the basic course in the 2nd year.

APPENDIX B. New Curriculum of LIS in Cairo University

The following courses are included in the newly developed program in Cairo University, and are planned to start in the 2004-2005 academic year. Students will take the same course in the first two years of the program, and then will be divided into three specializations: library science, archives, and information technology (during the last two years of the program).

Library science students take 46 courses for a total of 184 hours, including 30 hours for practical training. The following courses are relevant to this paper:

- Descriptive cataloging   2nd year   4 hrs.
- Classification   2nd year   3 hrs. lecture + 1 hr. training
- Computerized cataloging   3rd year   1 hr. lecture + 2 hrs. training
- Subject cataloging   3rd year   3 hrs. lecture + 2 hrs. training

Information technology students take the following relevant course in the last two years of the program:

- Automated technical   3rd year   1 hr. lecture + 2 hrs. training
  processing of
  information
- Automated authority   3rd year   3 hrs. lecture + 2 hrs. training
  control systems

Thus, we can easily notice the addition of new courses related to new trends in cataloging and classification.

APPENDIX C. The Questionnaire

Questionnaire for Study on
"Cataloging and Classification Education in LIS Departments in Egypt"

1. Personal data:
   - name: ....
   - tel.: ....
   - e-mail: ....

2. Please circle the course that you teach:
   - descriptive cataloging
   - classification
   - subject cataloging

3. In which University do you teach that course? ....

4. Would you please describe the content of that course (e.g., cataloging rules, classification systems, subject heading lists . . . etc.)
   ....
   ....

5. What is the level of that course?   ( ) Basic   ( ) Advanced

6. Please determine the changes which have occurred in that course during the past five years.
   ....

7. Please determine the anticipated changes in that course for the following five years.
   ....

8. What is the role of assistant faculty members (e.g., teaching assistants)?
   ....

9. Is there a bibliographic\computer lab for practical training?
   ....

10. Does the department provide fieldwork for students in cataloging facilities?
    ....

An Account
of Cataloging and Classification Education
in Iranian Universities

Mortaza Kokabi

SUMMARY. This paper presents a brief account of cataloging and classification education in Iran. The number of universities with library and information science departments is given, along with content of the courses taught on cataloging and classification. Cataloging rules, subject heading lists, and classification schedules taught are discussed. Changes to the curricula over the past 5 to 10 years, as well as anticipated changes over the next 5 to 10 years, are enumerated. Degrees awarded, number of faculty teaching in the area of cataloging and classification, and the number of students taking cataloging-related coursework for a year or semester are the other topics covered by the paper. The role of teaching assistants and the practicum of students in library cataloging and/or cataloging-related departments are also discussed. *[Article copies available for a fee from The Haworth Document Delivery Service: 1-800-HAWORTH. E-mail address: <docdelivery@haworthpress.com> Website: <http://www.HaworthPress.com> © 2006 by The Haworth Press, Inc. All rights reserved.]*

Mortaza Kokabi is Associate Professor, Department of Library and Information Science, Shaheed Chamran University of Ahwaz, POB 61355-139, Iran (E-mail: kokabi80@yahoo.com).

[Haworth co-indexing entry note]: "An Account of Cataloging and Classification Education in Iranian Universities." Kokabi, Mortaza. Co-published simultaneously in *Cataloging & Classification Quarterly* (The Haworth Information Press, an imprint of The Haworth Press, Inc.) Vol. 41, No. 3/4, 2006, pp. 431-441; and: *Education for Library Cataloging: International Perspectives* (ed: Dajin D. Sun, and Ruth C. Carter) The Haworth Information Press, an imprint of The Haworth Press, Inc., 2006, pp. 431-441. Single or multiple copies of this article are available for a fee from The Haworth Document Delivery Service [1-800-HAWORTH, 9:00 a.m. - 5:00 p.m. (EST). E-mail address: docdelivery@haworthpress.com].

doi:10.1300/J104v41n03_12

431

KEYWORDS. Cataloging, classification, cataloging education, Iran, cataloging code, subject heading list, classification schedules, degrees

INTRODUCTION

Cataloging and classification are taught both in short-term non-university courses and in universities as formal courses. These subjects are taught in courses mostly entitled "Organization of Materials." They are required courses and comprise 12 credits (20%) of 58 special required credits (not considering 12-credit Internship courses that consist of more than 50% practical cataloging and classification, which bring the number of credits actually allocated to cataloging and classification to 18, or more than 31%) in the B.A. syllabus of library and information science in Iranian universities. What follows is a brief account of some aspects of cataloging and classification education in Iranian universities.

UNIVERSITIES WITH LIBRARY
AND INFORMATION SCIENCE DEPARTMENTS

There are no curricula or degrees specific to cataloging and/or classification in Iranian universities that have library and information science programs. Cataloging and classification courses are taught in the context of library and information science curricula. According to recent statistics, at the beginning of the academic year 1999, some twenty-four departments of library and information science, including 19 general librarianship and 5 medical librarianship departments, have been active in Iranian universities and institutions of higher education. Some of these have been involved in two-year undergraduate, some in B.A., some in master's, and some in doctoral programs (Kiani, 2002, 67). Some of these departments, such as Shaheed Chamran University of Ahwaz (SCUA), are simultaneously involved in undergraduate and graduate courses. In the academic year beginning on Sept 23, 2004, SCUA will have its first doctoral students. These statistics exclude library and information science departments in Islamic Azad Universities (IAU) all through the country, non-governmental institutions that act apart from the Ministry of Science, Research and Technology (MSRT). These IAUs that are sometimes more active in higher education quantitatively than the institutions of higher education of MSRT, are also very active in the field of library and information science. The first doctoral program in library and information science in Iran was established in IAU.

CONTENT OF THE COURSES TAUGHT ON CATALOGING AND CLASSIFICATION

Cataloging Rules

The cataloging rules taught in cataloging courses are not standard. The Farsi translation of *AACR2* published in 1992 is taught in some universities while, in others, a *Manual of Cataloging Rules* published by the National Library of the Islamic Republic of Iran in 1996 is used. The latter, which claims to be based on Iranian bibliographic circumstances, is in fact the accumulation of decisions made on designating main entries and making *AACR* compatible with Farsi language from 1969 up to the time it was published.

Subject Heading Lists

The List of Persian Subject Headings (LPSH), first published in 1983 by the National Library of Iran, is used for teaching subject cataloging in cataloging courses. It is in fact the compilation of the subject headings used in TEBROC (Tehran Book Processing Center, a pre-Islamic Revolution organization that was transferred to the National Library of Iran after the revolution) from 1969 to 1981. LPSH is very similar in form to LCSH but is different in many aspects, including subject headings specific to Islamic as well as Iranian subjects. The third edition of LPSH has been published in 2002. It is also available in CD-ROM.

Classification Schedules

The classification systems most frequently taught in Iranian universities are Dewey Decimal Classification (DDC) and Library of Congress Classification (LCC). Due to the fact that English versions of these classification systems are both expensive and in English, which is not the mother tongue of the Iranian student, the teaching staff usually prefers to use the Farsi expansions of these systems expanded by the NLI. The DDC Farsi expansions include Iranian languages, Iranian literature, Islam, History of Iran, and Geography of Iran. The last one is, in fact, the expansion of the geographic area numbers allocated to Iran in Table 2 (Areas) in the DDC.

The LC Farsi expansions include PIR for Persian language and literature, Class DSR: History of Iran, BP: Islam, BBR: Islamic Philosophy, PJA: Arabic literature, and some other expansions.

WHETHER A CATALOGING COURSE IS REQUIRED OR OPTIONAL FOR A LIBRARY SCIENCE MAJOR

In all of the undergraduate programs, cataloging and classification courses that are called "Organization of Materials" are required. In the two-year programs, students must pass two 54-hour courses in two consecutive semesters. The courses are called: "Organization of Materials 1" and "Organization of Materials 2." This length of time is doubled in four-year programs to 108 hours comprising four "Organization of Materials." Each cataloging and/or classification course is presented in three credits, theoretical and practical. The teaching staff is obliged to attend the theoretical sessions and to allocate some time to visit the students individually in their offices for the practical sessions, though they sometimes prefer to be present at group practical sessions. The length of the practical sessions is double the time allocated in syllabi to theoretical ones.

The students with a non-librarianship background who are accepted into a master's program are required to pass a preliminary three-credit course called "Organization of Materials (Preliminary)," along with some other courses, in order to be eligible for the program. The students with a librarianship background need not pass this course.

CHANGES IN THE CURRICULA OVER THE PAST 5-10 YEARS

There have been no formal changes to curricula on classification and cataloging during the past 5-10 years. In fact, there has been no formal change to the curricula since 1988 when the High Council of Planning of MSRT approved the four-year undergraduate library and information science program. But the library and information departments have themselves made changes to the curricula, informally, to be compatible with the fast developments in the field. The changes made in Shaheed Chamran University of Ahwaz are examples of such informal changes.

When the author returned home from his doctoral program in 1995, as the head of the Department of Library and Information Science and as a lecturer in both cataloging and classification courses, he felt the need to change the contents of the courses and reflected his ideas in an article entitled: "A Glance at the 'Organization of Materials'" (Kokabi, 1997). The contents of four "Organization of Materials" courses were studied critically in that article and then modified to suggest new contents for each. The four modified "Organization of Materials" courses are as follows:

Organization of Materials 1: Cataloging

The definition of cataloging, the aim of cataloging, a brief history of cataloging, identification of parts of a book, familiarity with cataloging terms, the study of the specifications of a catalog card, descriptive cataloging using the translation of *AACR2*, designating main entry and its form using "The Name Authority List of Authors and Famous People" and *AACR2* (when the former is not applicable), corporate bodies, uniform titles, multi-volume books and sophisticated cases, and visiting a modern library.

Organization of Materials 2: Cataloging

The aims of subject cataloging, familiarity with the List of Persian Subject Headings (LPSH) and working with it, familiarity with some other list of subject headings (LCSH and SEARS), filing, the aims of filing, styles and principles of filing, the problems filing Farsi entries, and practical filing.

The rest of the semester, if any remains, will be allocated to practical descriptive and subject cataloging.

Organization of Materials 3: Classification

Classification and its necessity, principles of classification, classification in science, classification of Islamic sciences, Dewey Decimal Classification (DDC), familiarity with the Farsi translation of Abridged DDC, the Iranian expansions to DDC (Iranian literature, Islam, Iranian history, Geography of Iran, Iranian languages), and practice with these expansions.

Organization of Materials 4: Classification

Library of Congress Classification (LCC) and practice with some of its subclasses; the Iranian expansions to LCC (Iranian languages and literature, Islam, Iranian history, French language and literature, Arabic literature) and practice with these expansions; a brief familiarity with Colon, Cutter's Expansive, and Universal Decimal Classifications; Author number and some of its types (Cutter-Sanborn and LC); shelf list filing; how to search the resources such as union catalogs, etc.; and printed NLI catalog cards and how to obtain them.

And the author suggested, for the first time in that article, the addition of a new course called "Organization of Materials 5: Computerized Cataloging." The content of the suggested course was familiarity and practice with cataloging softwares. Since this course was suggested for the first time, the author could not present any syllabus for it, but anticipated that after one or two semesters, the teaching staff would offer the appropriate syllabus. The four "Organization of Materials" courses and also "The Basics of Computers and Programming" were considered as the prerequisites for this new course. Although this course has not been presented formally, its content has been merged with the contents of four "Organization of Materials" courses in practice.

As mentioned earlier, these modifications to the "Organization of Materials" courses are peculiar to the Department of Library and Information Science of SCUA. The author does not have any idea if any other university has accepted the suggested modifications. Also, in SCUA, the Farsi translation of *AACR2* is taught instead of the *Manual of Cataloging Rules*.

ANTICIPATED CHANGES OVER THE NEXT 5-10 YEARS

There are some factors that are going to affect the curricula of cataloging and classification over the next 5 to 10 years. The development of IRANMARC format (IRANMARC National Committee, 2002), with its manual published in 2002, is considered one of these factors. The Iranian Library Association (ILA) held the first workshop on IRANMARC in Tehran in Summer 2003. The workshop received a high degree of acceptance by librarians and teaching staff so that ILA plans to hold more workshops in the near future in different cities.

MSRT has commissioned revising the whole syllabus of the B.A. program to the Department of Library and Information Science of SCUA, and the job is in process. The author, as the present head of that department, anticipates that there will be a great number of modifications, and that the modifications will include more use of computers and other new information retrieval tools such as the Internet and other online and offline means of information retrieval. Greater emphasis on the English language is another change that will happen to the syllabus. The argument is that since English is the scientific language of the world, students must be more familiar with this language to be able to retrieve information more efficiently and rapidly. A move toward computerized cataloging and classification and use of IRANMARC format is another definite modification to the syllabus. IRANMARC is based on UNIMARC, due to the fact that the Iranian National MARC Committee (INMC) had, as one of its main objectives, greater compatibility with the rest of the world. This will probably result in some modifications in cataloging and classification rules now being studied and employed in Iranian universities and libraries; that fact will have its reflections on cataloging and classification education in Iranian universities.

The implementation of IRANMARC, especially in the Iranian National Bibliographic Network, requires highly standardized cataloging all through Iran. The author, both in his doctoral dissertation and other articles, has shown the need for a National Cataloging Committee (NCC). This committee, about to be established, will have its impact on both cataloging and classification in Iranian libraries and its education in Iranian universities.

Another factor that will affect the future of education for cataloging and classification in Iranian universities is the decision-making by the Iranian Library Association Committee on Revision of Library and Information Science Undergraduate Syllabus. This committee has had ten sessions so far, and decided in one of its sessions to modify cataloging and classification courses and to add "Organization of Materials 5: Computerized Cataloging" to the syllabus.

The Iranian Library Association and its local branches will probably affect the future of cataloging and classification education in Iranian universities. So far, cataloging and classification education has been deeply influenced by NLI through its cataloging and classification decisions and its training courses. Although NLI is an authorative institution, it runs the risk of neglecting the cataloging needs of local library communities. This fact has also been neglected in Farsi literature dealing with cataloging and classification issues. It is anticipated that local branches of ILA will provide the opportunity to study these local needs and reflect them in future cataloging education, although compatibility with the rest of the world in terms of bibliographic control and exchange of cataloging information has always been a major concern of Iranian libraries.

ILA itself will hold some seminars on all aspects of cataloging and classification and this will most probably modify the present status of the topic.

Pressures imposed by the teaching staff and students to modify the syllabus of library and information science in general, and that of cataloging and classification in particular, can be considered as another factor changing the present situation.

DEGREES AWARDED

There are no degrees specific to cataloging and classification in Iranian universities. The degrees are the formal degrees awarded at the completion of a formal program. As mentioned earlier, the programs include two-year undergraduate, B.A., master's, and doctoral programs.

NUMBER OF FACULTY TEACHING
IN THE AREA OF CATALOGING AND CLASSIFICATION

According to a table in an article entitled "Survey on Scientific and Research Activities of the Library and Information Sciences Academic Staff of the University and Research Centers of Iran Up to the End of the Year 1378," there have been 74 staff involved in teaching cataloging and classification courses in Iran up to 19 March 2000 (Horri, 2000, 18). According to the same table, cataloging and classification have been the second most important courses among others. The 74 faculty members represent 12 institutions, including 8 universities and 4 research centers (Horri, 2000, 14). A simple calculation of these figures indicates that there are about 50 of these faculty members teaching cataloging and classification in universities (two-thirds of 74 equals 49.2 or 50 when rounded up). According to another statistic, there are at least 24 universities having departments of library and information science (Kiani, 2002, 67). That increases the estimate of teaching faculty from 50 to 150 (the multiplication of 50 by 3 equals 150). Another, not very recent, statistic indicates a total of 109 faculty members teaching cataloging and classification in 20 universities (Kiani, 1997, 44). These figures collected by Kiani in two different years have shown a logical, similar increase in the number of university faculty members who teach cataloging and classification. And since the figure 109 reflects the statistics up to September 22, 1996, the figure 150 seems to be a realistic estimate for the year 2002. Due to the rapid increase in the number of graduates who become involved in the task of teaching cataloging and classification in Iranian universities, the number of teaching faculty members has definitely grown larger than 150 in the year 2005.

NUMBER OF STUDENTS
TAKING CATALOGING-RELATED COURSEWORK
FOR A YEAR OR SEMESTER

Kiani in 1997 stated that in the period 1991-96, some 1,760 students had been enrolled in 12 universities in B.A. programs (Kiani, 1997, 41). In another research, he counted the number of universities having departments of library and information science as at least 24. A very simple calculation then doubles the figure 1,760 and brings it to 3,520. Due to the fact that the number of departments of library and information science has increased, and that the number of students has also increased, the figure was most probably about 4,000 in the period 1997-2003. Therefore, the number of students enrolling is about some 666 per annum in B.A. programs. The figure will be about 750 considering the number of enrollments in two-year undergraduate programs. Since the cataloging and classification courses must be taken in four consecutive semesters, which is half the total length of any librarianship program, the number of students taking cataloging and classification courses in a semester is, at the very least, some 375 students. But the figure is most probably more than that.

ROLE OF TEACHING ASSISTANTS

There are no teaching assistants in the sense that exists in western librarianship teaching traditions. When students are doing their internship courses in the libraries, some librarians who are usually superior to them qualitatively, teach them practically; these librarians play the role of teaching assistants. Interaction between the teaching staff and these librarians on the progress made by the students usually results in a deeper understanding of the subject.

PRACTICUM OF STUDENTS IN LIBRARY CATALOGING AND/OR CATALOGING-RELATED DEPARTMENTS

As mentioned above, the practicum of cataloging and classification is partly done in individual or group sessions. The students can discuss their problems with the teaching staff in their offices. If the problem of an individual student suggests a possible problem for other students as well, the lecturer might then decide to address the students' question additionally in group sessions. Students particularly interested in cataloging and classification (this usually happens, since the topic has proven to be of special interest to some students) are also directed to some library to practice cataloging and classification in real circumstances.

But the most important and formal part of practical cataloging and classification is the "Internship" course. There are four "Internship" courses: Internships (Parts one to four). Internship (Part one) consists of 272 hours, of which cataloging is 136 hours. "Organization of Materials 1: Cataloging" is the prerequisite for Internship (Part one). Internship (Part two) consists of 272 hours, with 166 hours for classification, and "Organization of Materials 2: Classification" is its prerequisite. The length of Internship (Part three) is 204 hours, including 96 hours of cataloging, and it has "Organization of Materials 3: Cataloging" as its prerequisite. The length is the same for Internship (Part four), except that the 96 hours are for classification, and its prerequisite is "Organization of Materials 4: Classification."

Some universities such as SCU have, for some reason, divided the length of time allocated to each Internship and, therefore, the length of time allocated to cataloging and classification included in each Internship, in half.

CONCLUSION

Cataloging and classification in Iranian universities is experiencing deep modifications. The modifications, which are mostly qualitative, move these topics toward greater compatibility with internationally accepted standards, greater use of computers and electronic media, and greater reliance on the Internet.

The future of cataloging and classification in Iranian universities looks exciting and intoxicating!

REFERENCES

حري، ع. 1379. "بررسي فعاليت هاي علمي و پژوهشي اعضاي هيئت علمي رشته كتابداري و اطلاع رساني تا پايان سال
1378" فصلنامه كتاب، 11 (2): 9 – 36.

Horri, A. 2000. "Survey on Scientific and Research Activities of the Library and Information Sciences Academic Staff of the University and Research Centers of Iran Up to the End of the Year 1378." *Faslname-ye Ketab (Book Quarterly)*, 11(2): 9-36.

كميته ملي مارك ايران. 1381. *مارك ايران.* تهران. كتابخانه ملي جمهوري اسلامي ايران.

IRANMARC National Committee. 2002. *IRANMARC*. Tehran: National Library of the Islamic Republic of Iran.

كياني، ح. 1381. "آموزش كتابداري و اطلاع رساني"، در: *دائرة المعارف كتابداري و اطلاع رساني،* تهران: كتابخانه ملي جمهوري اسلامي ايران، ج. اوّل: 55 – 67.

Kiani, H. 2002. "Education of Library and Information Science," in: *Encyclopedia of Library and Information Science*. Tehran: National Library of the Islamic Republic of Iran, vol. 1: 55-67.

كياني، ح. 1376. "نظام آموزش كتابداري در دانشگاههاي ايران، در دو دوره قبل و بعد از انقلاب اسلامي و نكات لازم در اصلاح و بهبود وضعيت موجود، فصلنامه پيام كتابخانه، 7 (2): 35 – 49.

Kiani, H. 1997. "Library Education System in Iranian Universities in Pre- and Post-Islamic Revolution Periods: Some Points to Improve the Current Status," *Faslname-ye Payam-e Ketabkhaneh (Library Message Quarterly)*, 7(2): 35-49.

كوكبي، م. 1376. "نگاهي به دروس "سازماندهي مواد"، فصلنامه كتاب، 8 (3): 57 – 69.

Kokabi, M. 1997. "A glance at the 'Organization of Materials,'" *Faslname-ye Ketab (Book Quarterly)*, 8(3): 57-69.

Cataloging Instruction in Israel

Snunith Shoham

SUMMARY. Despite its young age compared to similar programs in the United States, cataloging instruction in Israel has also been transformed to reflect the changes in the work done in libraries based on technological innovations and conceptions held by those involved in academia. Cataloging instruction in Israel is marked by a number of factors:

- There has always been a division, carried through to today, between distinct and independent courses on various aspects of cataloging: a course on classification, a course on descriptive cataloging, and a course on indexing. Even today, these courses are requirements in all of the instructional frameworks, though the length of the course has been reduced over the years.
- Over the years additional courses have been introduced as a reflection of the technological developments and work in the field.
- The majority of courses are now taught in computer labs.
- There has been a switch to instruction by academics and not by librarians, workers in the field, as was customary for many decades.
- Focus of instruction in university departments is on theory and understanding of concepts.

Snunith Shoham, PhD, is Chair, Department of Information Science, Bar-Ilan University, Ramat Gar 52900, Israel.

[Haworth co-indexing entry note]: "Cataloging Instruction in Israel." Shoham, Snunith. Co-published simultaneously in *Cataloging & Classification Quarterly* (The Haworth Information Press, an imprint of The Haworth Press, Inc.) Vol. 41, No. 3/4, 2006, pp. 443-460; and: *Education for Library Cataloging: International Perspectives* (ed: Dajin D. Sun, and Ruth C. Carter) The Haworth Information Press, an imprint of The Haworth Press, Inc., 2006, pp. 443-460. Single or multiple copies of this article are available for a fee from The Haworth Document Delivery Service [1-800-HAWORTH, 9:00 a.m. - 5:00 p.m. (EST). E-mail address: docdelivery@haworthpress.com].

doi:10.1300/J104v41n03_13

KEYWORDS. Education for cataloging, library school curricula, theory vs. practice dilemma, Israel

INTRODUCTION

Cataloging is defined here based on Turvey & Letarte[1] as the spectrum of intellectual activities relating to the provision of bibliographic control, from traditional cataloging, classification, and indexing to the use of metadata schema.

Cataloging has been an important subject in the curriculum of American library education. In the first period, since Dewey's time and for decades thereafter, the emphasis was on the practical aspect of cataloging.

This practical approach was the rule in all fields of library science studies. Dewey viewed library technical services as the operational backbone of the library. Instruction was provided through apprenticeship programs, complemented by lectures which reviewed the various techniques and discussed their implementation. The following topics were taught in this manner during the period under discussion:

- *Library handwriting:* Penmanship exercises to ensure that handwriting conformed to the accepted standard.
- *Cataloging:* Recitation by rote of cataloging principles.
- Accessioning: Acquisition of materials for the library and inventory management.
- *Shelf listing:* Creation of a shelf list that could be used as a limited classified catalog.
- *Classification:* Classification according to the Dewey Decimal System.

For years, students had to learn Dewey's *Library School Rules*, Cutter's *Rules for a Dictionary Catalog*, and the American Library Association's *List of Subject Headings*.[2]

Williamson's study in the early 1920s revealed some variety in the length of the cataloging courses among the different library schools, however, the practical approach remained dominant at all of the schools. Furthermore, about half of the students' time was devoted to four subjects: cataloging, book selection, reference work, and classification.[3] In 1926 the Graduate Library School of Chicago was the first to offer more theoretical content as part of its focus on research.[4] During the 1930s, cataloging course work was reduced. Now, new courses have been introduced into the curriculum, and many libraries use the LC cataloging service, which reduces cataloging work in libraries.

Margaret Mann, at the University of Michigan, integrated descriptive cataloging, classification, and subject cataloging assignments into one course, and this approach has been popular in library schools for many years. Since that time, theoretical understanding of knowledge organization has become the main focus, and this has come at the expense of practical work. At the same time, criticism started coming in from the field stating that new graduates were not ready for the duties of catalogers. Employers expected to get new graduates of academic departments that would be immediately capable of performing cataloging work without the need for them to invest in training.

When automation began to take hold, it was predicted that there would be even less call for catalogers, as most of the original cataloging would be done by the Library of Congress. This led a number of library schools to drop cataloging from the required course curricula and to offer this subject as an elective course. In the 1980s, cataloging courses were still being offered at all schools, however, in some it became an elective course and only one school (UCLA) offered students the option of specializing in cataloging.[5] Whereas in 1986, 78% of the introductory cataloging courses were required, in 1998 the percentage dropped to 55%.[6] The cataloging courses also began teaching computerized cataloging, including the use of OCLC.

Another response was the addition of new courses such as *automated cataloging* that taught the MARC format and later added instruction on the use of OCLC or RLIN systems.

Vellucci,[7] in her survey of 52 ALA-accredited library schools, found that courses in the organization of information are still a strong part of the curricula. Ninety-two percent offered an introductory course in cataloging and classification, and 63% of these are a required course. She noted changes in the title of many introductory courses to include *Organization of . . . , Information Resources, Knowledge, Library Materials,* or *Bibliographic Control.* Furthermore, 38% of the programs offered a more general introductory level course with broader content and tended to be more theoretical than practical. These course labels are *Theory of Organization of Information, Information Structure,* and *Organization and Representation of Knowledge and Information.* Seventy-three percent of the schools also offered an advanced cataloging course that covered descriptive cataloging, subject cataloging, and classification.

LIBRARY SYSTEMS IN ISRAEL

In Israel there are seven universities plus the Open University (all of which are public institutions that receive financial support from the government via The Council for Higher Education), as well as a large number of colleges. Some of these colleges are also funded by The Council for Higher Education (similar to the universities), and others are independent. In addition, there are about 42 teachers colleges, some of which also offer bachelor's degrees in other subjects as well. Two out of the seven universities have central libraries, and others have decentralized libraries across the campus. At the beginning of the 1980s, the university libraries switched from card catalogs to computerized catalogs, and all of them now use the same software and are on the same network. Furthermore, Israel also has approximately 220 public library systems, hundreds of school libraries, as well as special libraries and information centers that service public bodies, institutions, and private enterprises.

Different classification systems are in use at the various libraries in Israel. At school libraries and public libraries, the most common system is the Dewey Classification System (DDC). The special libraries frequently use the Universal Decimal Classification system (UDC) and classification systems that they have developed independently. Even at university libraries, there is no uniform system in place. Some use the Dewey, others LC, and even the UDC system (at the Technion–Israel Institute of Technology library). The subject catalogs, for the most part, utilize LC Subject Headings.

With regard to descriptive cataloging, AACR2 is the accepted norm, although many different versions and editions are used. Even then, many libraries set rules that are quite different. This is an indicator of the lack of standardization of the library collections in Israel. Perhaps the primary reason for this is that an insufficient amount of copy cataloging was done here, that is to say, less than could be expected, and many libraries are doing original cataloging for their collections. This is the case despite the fact that all of the university libraries and many of the college libraries (26), as well as 8 other libraries and 5 archives use the same library software and are part of the ALEPH system on a uniform network, and is also despite the fact that the ALEPH system holds the LC MARC and LC Name Authorities files.

At university libraries, most of the material in Hebrew and Arabic is processed originally. One reason for this is that the Jewish National Library does not meet the schedule required by the academic world, which is in a rush to prepare books and put them on the shelves to serve readers; occasionally, this is due to the various approaches taken with regard to Hebrew writing guidelines. That said, when processing the material in other languages, at least 70% of it has been copy cataloged according to LC MARC or OCLC's WorldCat databases.

Approximately 600 libraries, the majority of which are public libraries and the remainder being school libraries and small college libraries, receive cataloging records from the Israeli Center for Libraries in a format suitable to the library software used (there are five different library management systems). Among other services provided by the Center, it catalogs the majority of Hebrew books published in Israel and distributes a weekly update via e-mail or diskette. The records are prepared by the Center's cataloging department and are based on the AACR2 descriptive cataloging guidelines, Dewey classification numbers, and keywords from the Hebrew Thesaurus of Indexing Terms.[8] Despite this, hundreds of libraries catalog their collections independently. Less than 60% of the librarians in public libraries have received professional training in librarianship, and even then, it is rarely academic librarianship training (under 20%).

As a matter of fact, Israel has no supreme body involved in setting standards. (Israel has no leading body that drives this issue, such as the Library of Congress in the United States.) That said, since 1983 the interuniversity subcommittee on cataloging was established by the Standing Committee of the National Library and University Libraries (SCONUL).[9] It deals solely with descriptive cataloging and was established to contribute to uniformity and identical standards among libraries. However, professional resolutions adopted by this committee are not fully implemented by the university member libraries, not to mention the other libraries in Israel (including those that also work with the ALEPH system) that are not represented there and are virtually not reported at all. The committee meets 3-4 times a year. In 2001, a discussion group was even set up, though it is not very active.

The ALEPH system used by university libraries and developed at the end of the 1970s and early 1980s was not based on the MARC format. Only at the end of the '90s did they come to the conclusion that the decision of the founders had been incorrect, and they decided to switch to MARC format, which is based on the LC MARC 21 format with a limited number of local modifications. The shift to working according to MARC was done to enable the product to be sold abroad and to enable copying from international bibliographic sources and participation in international bibliographic systems.[10] In June 1999 the first Israeli library switched to MARC, and since then, most of the university libraries, with the exception of a small number of small libraries, have also made the switch.

The university libraries in Israel are currently facing the challenge of upgrading to the new version of ALEPH–ALEPH 500. This process is only in its most initial stages, with the exception of several national databases on the ALEPH network and two university libraries. All of the remaining libraries are in various stages of the process. Some have already performed a test migration and some have already set a date for the final cutover (in another few months). Others still have not begun at all. This constitutes a professional challenge. Not every college has staff trained to support this, or the resources to cover the high costs. In light of the above, an initiative has recently been proposed by several colleges: to unite and set up a central system with a number of central servers on which the various library systems would reside and trained staff would provide support for ALEPH 500. This would, without a doubt, reduce the costs involved.

Cataloging Departments

Cataloging departments in university libraries have undergone structural changes as a result of technological developments. At a large number of university libraries, classification, indexing (subject cataloging), and descriptive cataloging are all handled by a single department, and there are even libraries where the same people perform all of these tasks. Other libraries have added acquisition to the tasks of those departments (a trend which took hold many years ago in the United States). In contrast, there are universities where the work is distributed among departments based on language: a department for Hebrew cataloging and a department for cataloging in non-Hebrew scripts. Even in the serials departments, changes have occurred: first of all, there has been a reduction in the number of employees due to the recent massive shift to e-journals and reduced use of printed periodicals. Many libraries do not classify periodicals and only record the details of the journal. This means that the substantial part of the work performed by these departments is no longer related to processing the material, but to ordering, agreements, contracts, and coordination with faculties or departments.

Cataloging Department Personnel

Whereas in the United States there are generally different categories of catalogers (professional/original catalogers; non-professional/library technician catalogers; and student assistants), in Israel there is very little use of library technicians. In the States the tasks are divided among the different catalogers as follows: the professionals assume leadership roles as team leaders and project planners; non-professionals do copy cataloging and sometimes even perform original cataloging, as is the case at Ohio State University Libraries;[11] student assistants sometimes do the searching part of the copy cataloging, while the high-level copy cataloging is done by the non-professional staff.

At some Israeli university libraries, there are a small number of students working on a hourly basis in the cataloging departments. They generally perform the routine non-professional assignment of checking for details in the university catalog, or they help with retrospective cataloging (done by using the OCLC module), or add holding information to an existing record. However, there are virtually no paraprofessional librarians in the libraries; and even the hourly work done by students is limited and can only be found in a few of the libraries.

In the university library departments, the entire staff consists of professional librarians with master's degrees or at least with post-graduate diplomas. Only very rarely are there staff members with non-academic library training, and they do not employ individuals without professional training. In contrast, at public libraries and school libraries, much of the staff has undergone non-academic training or no training in librarianship at all.

TEACHING CATALOGING IN ISRAEL

The professional training system is definitely influenced by the situation in Israel, as outlined in the first part of this article, as well as by the way in which the fields of librarianship and information are perceived by academics.

In Israel there are three academic frameworks that offer different types of curricula. The largest academic center in this field is the Department of Information Science at Bar-Ilan University, which awards a BA, MA, and PhD in information science. Approximately 500 students are currently enrolled in the department. In addition, the School of Library, Archive and Information Studies at The Hebrew University of Jerusalem offers a master's program (though this program is currently undergoing changes), and a very limited certificate program is offered at the University of Haifa. Beyond these programs, 4 teachers colleges offer 2-3 year programs in Library/Information Studies. These programs do not grant academic degrees, and most of the graduates are later employed by public libraries and school libraries.

In Israel, as in the rest of the world, the cataloging curriculum has undergone changes which, for the most part, are in keeping with the changes implemented at the information and library studies departments at American universities. The main changes are in the reduction in the number of hours dedicated to traditional cataloging courses, though recently, innovative courses in the field are being added to the programs. For years the curricula offered traditional introductory courses in cataloging which were requirements and were generally year-long courses, two academic hours a week. Further in the past, these courses were even two years long. The traditional courses were given as two distinct courses: *Descriptive Cataloging* and *Classification Methods*, each one year long. This is in contrast to many American departments, where it is generally acceptable to teach both of these subjects together, at least in the introductory course, which may be given different names but is always some version of *Organizing Information*. However, there are American departments, such as the department at the University of Pittsburgh, where the two subjects (subject access and descriptive cataloging) are taught as two separate subjects in advanced courses.[12]

Furthermore, in Israel, unique additional courses in cataloging were offered on occasion. This explains why the librarianship curriculum at Bar-Ilan University also offered a separate course in cataloging and organization of rare books (a year-long course) until the beginning of the '90s.

There is much room for thought and consideration in this matter. However, the author of this article, who herself is the chair of the largest department of information science in Israel and who researches information organization, is sure that teaching both fields separately enables students to gain more insight into the area (indexing is also taught as an independent course). All students are required to take the basic introductory course, *Introduction to Information Science*, in their first year. In this course and also in the first lectures in the classification course, titled *Information Classification Methods*, the students are presented with a common theoretical foundation that links the two areas of information organization.

Today, too, these cataloging courses are required courses at all of the academic and non-academic departments in Israel. The number of students enrolled in the course is naturally related to the number of students in the program and to the capacity of the lab (number of computer stations). Thus, at Bar-Ilan there are four parallel groups (for a total of 170 students in the 2003-2004 academic year) for descriptive cataloging, two groups for BA students and two as part of the supplemental program for students who received their BAs in fields other than library and information science and who are now working on MAs.

The main topics taught in the descriptive cataloging courses include: the purpose of cataloging and familiarity with the different types of cataloging; familiarity with the basic structure of bibliographic description; entries in catalogs for people, corporations, uniform title, and more; management of authority files and creating references in the catalog. These also include the most current issues in the field: core records, copy cataloging, and Internet cataloging. Some instructors allocate several classes to MARC records. Basically, the students learn the AACR2 cataloging guidelines.

The main topics covered in classification courses include: introduction to organization of information by subject, and classification theory, including facet analysis. Courses also introduce students to the following classification systems: the Dewey Decimal System which generally takes up 40%-50% of the course, a maximum of two lessons on UDC, and Library of Congress, to which 2-4 lessons are dedicated. Some lecturers (and then only in courses that are longer than two hours in a single semester) also briefly discuss special classification systems or expand on the Dewey Decimal system for Judaic fields (Shalom system).

About 20 years ago, some of the educational institutions also added indexing courses. At Bar-Ilan this course is currently taught to BA students. It is a very basic and required course (37 students are currently enrolled in this course). At the MA level, students take a course titled, *Indexing and Creating Thesauri*. The course is given by a different instructor at a higher level, and a part of the course is dedicated to creating thesauri. This reflects the current market demand at various organizations for development of thesauri and organizational ontologies. This is a required course in some of the department tracks (organizational information science, knowledge management, and intellectual property). This year 55 students are enrolled in this course, which is offered in two parallel groups. The issues covered in the course span the fundamentals of indexing, covering basic concepts in indexing, the international standard for examining and indexing documents, Library of Congress Subject Headings, and indexing research, as well as creation of thesauri, including hierarchical indexing language, creation and maintenance, and the international standard for thesaurus creation. However, it should be noted that a course on indexing is not offered at the University of Haifa, for example, nor is it offered at all of the colleges.

The proliferation of computers led to the development of courses in the 1980s titled *Computer Applications in Libraries*, which, to a great extent, taught students to use the various library management systems, including the computerized cataloging system. Students were also given practical cataloging exercises within ALEPH (the library system used by university libraries in Israel). Some departments also introduced students to the library management systems used primarily at public libraries and school libraries. At Bar-Ilan University this is a required course for BA students and for those in the "Information Science for Cultural and Educational Institutions" track. A total of 58 students are enrolled in this course in the 2003-2004 academic year.

With regard to the current curriculum in Israel, it would be incorrect to claim that a consensus exists and that there is uniformity in conceptions. Thus, differences between the university departments exist. At Bar-Ilan University, since the middle of the '90s, the department has offered cataloging and classification as semester-long courses (14 weekly meetings of two hours each). These are required courses for both BA students and MA students who received BAs from other departments. In contrast, Haifa University offers, as part of its certificate studies program, a semester course on classification and a year-long course on descriptive cataloging. Hebrew University of Jerusalem offers semester-long courses on classification and cataloging, though at three hours a week. Up through 1999 they taught classification as a year-long course.

In recent years, two of the universities have begun offering new courses in this field to MA students. These include: *Advanced Information Organization*, a new elective at Bar-Ilan University (approximately 16 MA students) designed to respond to the need to manage new non-book materials. The course provides a more in-depth look at new conceptions, for example, integrating resources, continuing resources, and new cataloging guidelines. This course currently discusses cataloging of Internet materials and cataloging of electronic materials.

Another innovative course in this area is *Digital Preservation and Metadata*, which has now been offered for three years at the Hebrew University of Jerusalem and is only required in certain tracks, though many students in other tracks take it as an elective (approximately 35 students). Here students gain familiarity with metadata engines, metalanguage, and digital preservation. This course has taken the place of a course that had been offered for many years on bibliographic networks. The instructor of the course, indeed, believes that students are lacking in knowledge of bibliographic consortia and networks.

In terms of librarianship studies at colleges that do not award an academic degree, they continue to hold fast to the more traditional approach of cataloging instruction. They all offer classification and descriptive cataloging courses. Only at some of these schools is indexing taught. Three of them also offer a course on applying computerized services, where part of the course is dedicated to computerized descriptive cataloging, including a brief look at MARC and gaining familiarity with how to work in a computerized cataloging environment using the library management systems in use in Israel.

A central point that is quite marked in librarianship studies at the colleges, as opposed to at university departments, is the longer length of instruction in the majority of the introductory courses in descriptive cataloging and classification. Most of them do not offer innovative courses, and some do not even teach indexing. Thus, their cataloging curricula reflect the traditional approach. This may be due to their view of the program as one that trains librarians for work in the field and they therefore strive to provide them with practical knowledge.

Standing in direct contrast to this approach is that guiding the Department of Information Science at Bar-Ilan University. The guiding precept there is to be a purely academic department and to take on a greater role than merely being a vocational school. This approach is part of the department's struggle for its place within the university system and its place vis-à-vis other academic departments at the university. The department proactively encourages research and fosters thought on the various subjects in information science. The department does not view itself as being involved solely in libraries, but also in information in the broadest sense, explaining why it offers tracks in *organizational information science, social information, knowledge management, information technologies* and *intellectual property*.

It is interesting to note that, at each of the universities, several instructors teach these courses. One instructor teaches descriptive cataloging, another teaches classification, and yet another teaches indexing. This is done to ensure that each instructor teaches in his/her area of expertise. At Bar-Ilan University all of the instructors of the aforementioned courses are academics who are also involved in research (though some have worked in a library for many years). At the other universities, these courses are taught both by faculty members and by librarians who work in this area. At the colleges (in the non-academic programs), most of the instructors in this field are librarians who work in this area. The background of the instructors clearly reflects the focus that each of them has in the course and their view on the theory vs. practice dilemma.

In all of the courses discussed in this article, students are required to hand in exercises on a regular basis. In some, assignments must be handed in each week and, in others, several times a semester along with a final exam.

DILEMMAS

The main dilemmas concerning instruction of cataloging are: (1) the teaching of theory versus practice; (2) formal education versus on-the-job training; (3) integration of technology within the cataloging curriculum.[13]

The Teaching of Theory versus Practice

Seymour Lubetzky[14] stated in 1964 that "it is proper to treat the subject of cataloging not as a how-to-do-it routine outlined in so many rules, but rather as a problem in the design of a methodological system to facilitate the exploitation of the library's resources by its users."

Educators more frequently support the position that a firm grounding in the principles underlying the organization of information will educate students to become informed decision-makers able to adapt to changing environments in their future career. Practitioners and employers often adopt the more pragmatic view, wanting to hire recent graduates with practical knowledge of the existing cataloging process.[15] Fallis & Fricke[16] also asserted that training in practical skills is not appropriate in graduate-level programs. At the other side of the spectrum is Michael Gorman,[17,18] a library director who believes that bibliographic control is central to librarianship and "while it is not necessarily important for librarians to know individual cataloging rules or the bases of the major classification . . . it is vital that [they] understand the ways in which knowledge and information are organized for retrieval." He would like library school to provide a cataloging course to prepare the students for the work in libraries.

However, there are also other voices; for example, Professor Arlene Taylor,[19] in a 2002 article written by her and a doctoral student, Daniel N. Joudrey, stated her belief in a bi-level approach to teaching subject cataloging: teaching the practical skills and also the theoretical foundation, as it is important for the students to know "how," but also to know "why."

The majority of instructors teaching classification, who were interviewed as part of a survey taken for the purpose of this article, view classification as an expertise that cannot be properly taught within the framework of a single semester-long course.

Given the above, then, the purpose of the course is to provide students with an understanding of the fundamentals and theories of classification, so that they can, on the one hand, understand how libraries are organized–and be able to find their way around a library–and on the other hand, gain additional knowledge of information organization, where classification conceptions provide the foundation of the new approaches. Anyone who chooses to work in this field will have to learn it in-depth through on-the-job training.

The instructors of the descriptive cataloging courses are aware of the fact that the course is too short to turn out skilled catalogers. The goal, however, is to provide students with basic knowledge of the process of document cataloging and the preparation of bibliographic records, and to give them an understanding of the importance of standard recording guidelines as the foundation of the information system.

Formal Education versus On-the-Job Training

The majority of instructors interviewed for this article explained that they are aware of the fact that the course is insufficient for producing expert catalogers. That said, instructors at the colleges want to prepare the graduates to work in libraries. This can be seen in the fact that the courses are longer and there is a lack of emphasis on research. At the universities, departments work first of all to provide students with a theoretical background and an understanding of concepts, so that they have a strong foundation that allows them to understand other complex aspects of information organization, even in a future environment where the picture is not yet completely clear.

Heads of cataloging departments all clearly stated that they are aware of the fact that the graduates they hire are not expert catalogers and will need to undergo on-the-job training.

Integration of Technology Within the Cataloging Curriculum

Technology has affected both the methods and location of instruction, as well as course content.

As opposed to the situation in the past, today most courses are given in computer labs, with the exception of some of the descriptive cataloging courses. Even traditional courses such as classification are currently taught in computer labs at most departments, as most of today's classification systems are computerized, either on CDs or on the Web. This reality places restrictions on the number of participants, as most labs have a maximum of 25-35 workstations. Given these constraints, there are courses given using presentations, with students using the lab to do the exercises.

Computerization of catalogs and the switch made by university libraries in Israel in the '80s to OPAC systems, and in the '90s, the massive switch of many public libraries to computerized systems, changed the content of descriptive cataloging courses so that the focus is now on computerized cataloging. They relate to computerized cataloging records and no longer relate to cataloging cards.

In the classification courses, which still teach the classification systems developed in the 19th century (Dewey) and the beginning of the twentieth century (LC and UDC), instruction is also provided on classification in computerized systems and where they fit in the Internet reality.

In indexing courses, computerized indexing is taught as well as automated computer indexing.

Technological developments are what led to the development of new courses such as metadata and a course on advance information organization which, for the most part, deals with nontextual information, electronic resources, and metadata.

CONTINUING EDUCATION

Most of the continuing education programs in Israel are taught by the Israeli Center for Libraries, and they appeal mainly to the staff at public libraries. Furthermore, most of the courses offered are in the area of Internet resources. However, once a year they offer a course in the use of library software, and one part of it deals with indexing and familiarity with the *Thesaurus of Indexing Terms*,[20] which is the tool for the subject cataloging of books in Israeli public libraries.

As for courses in cataloging, these were rare for many years. However, over the last few years, a demand for instruction on the MARC format has led to an emergence of courses in this area. This is due to the adoption of the MARC format in the ALEPH system. University departments have provided few courses in this area. The Department of Information Science at Bar-Ilan University has offered this topic to some libraries in Israel that have asked for the courses to be given on their premises. The Israeli Association of Librarians and Information Professionals also provided several additional courses on this topic. In addition, during the previous academic year, Bar-Ilan University taught two courses on advanced cataloging to two groups of librarians (about 20 participants in each), one group being university library staff, and the second group, librarians at teachers colleges. Most of the participants were catalogers. The focus was on the changes in AACR2, cataloging of non-book materials, and cataloging of digital resources and Internet sites. Each course lasted 20 hours.

RESEARCH

In Israel, librarians deal very little with research, as it is not a condition or requirement for professional advancement. Consequently, they publish very little, with the exception of occasional project descriptions.

Very few academics in Israel are involved in research on cataloging, explaining why the number of publications in this field is minimal. When articles are written, a good portion is published outside of Israel. From 1990 to date, 14 articles on descriptive cataloging were published in Hebrew in Israel, 6 on subjects related to indexing (only one of which was a research paper), and 6 on classification. During the same period, a number of articles by Israeli researchers on cataloging were published in English outside of Israel (a sample appears as an appendix to this article). A portion of these studies are related to the unique issues faced by libraries and catalogs in Israel, such as multilingual and multiscript systems; others are on topics of universal appeal.

CONCLUSION

Cataloging instruction in Israel is marked by a number of factors:

- There has always been a division, carried through to today, between distinct and independent courses on various aspects of cataloging: a course on classification, a course on descriptive cataloging, and a course on indexing.

- Another characteristic is the introduction of additional courses over the years. In the 1980s a course was added to familiarize students with the automated library management systems used in Israel. In this course, students also learn how computerized cataloging works. A course on indexing was also added. Recently, at the beginning of the 21st century, additional courses on metadata and advanced information organization were also introduced into the curricula.
- The courses on classification and descriptive cataloging are still required courses for students in all tracks and in all of the librarianship programs in Israel.
- Certain differences exist in the instruction of these topics at universities and non-academic frameworks at colleges: the length of the courses is frequently longer at the colleges, and lecturers there are, for the most part, librarians. The focus of instruction there is more practical.

The main changes that have taken place in instruction in these fields are as follows:

- Reduced length of courses–from year-long courses to semester courses
- Location of the majority of courses has now moved to computer labs
- Switch to instruction by academics and not by librarians, workers in the field, as was customary for many decades
- Introduction of instruction on MARC in recent years, as a reflection of market demand, along with the shift of universities to MARC-based cataloging.

In the instruction of the various cataloging-related subjects, various dilemmas regarding the practice vs. theory approaches come to the fore. While most instructors recognize that the material taught is insufficient to introduce skilled catalogers into the workforce and realize that graduates who choose a career in cataloging will need to undergo a great deal of on-the-job training, what goes on in the field still impacts significantly on the curriculum. This can be seen in courses, such as *Computer Applications in Libraries*, which were added in the 1980s as a result of the migration of library collections in Israel to computerized catalogs and, lately, the addition of teaching the MARC format.

REFERENCES

1. Michelle R. Turvey and Karen M. Letarte, "Cataloging or Knowledge Management: Perspectives of Library Educators on Cataloging Education for Entry-Level Academic Librarians," *Cataloging & Classification Quarterly*, 34: 1/2 (2002), p. 164-165.

2. Roxanne Sellberg, "The Teaching of Cataloging in U.S. Library Schools," *LRTS*, 32: 1 (1988), p. 31.

3. Desretta McAllister-Harper, "An Analysis of Courses in Cataloging and Classification and Related Areas Offered in Sixteen Graduate Library Schools and Their Relationship to Present and Future Trends in Cataloging and Classification and to Cognitive Needs of Professional Academic Catalogers," *Cataloging & Classification Quarterly*, 16: 3 (1993), p. 101.

4. Sellberg, 1988, p. 31.

5. Sellberg, 1988, p. 35.

6. Jodi Lynn Spillane, "Comparison of Required Introductory Cataloging Courses, 1986 to 1998," *Library Resources and Technical Services*, 43: 4 (1999), p. 227.

7. Sherry L. Vellucci, "Cataloging Across the Curriculum: A Syndetic Structure for Teaching Cataloging," *Cataloging & Classification Quarterly*, 24: 1/2 (1997), p. 45-47.

8. *Thesaurus of Indexing Terms*. Jerusalem: Center for Libraries, 1996.

9. Elhanan Adler, "Cataloging Decisions and Rule Changes in Israeli University Libraries," *Yad-Lakore*, 25: 2 (1991), p. 69. [Hebrew].

10. Elhanan Adler, "The MARC Standard and Israeli Cataloging," *Yad-Lakore*, 33 (Dec. 2000), p. 4. [Hebrew].

11. Magda El-Sherbini and George Klim, "Changes in Technical Services and Their Effect on the Role of Catalogers and Staff Education: An Overview," *Cataloging & Classification Quarterly*, 24: 1/2 (1997), p. 31.

12. Arlene G. Taylor and Daniel N. Joudrey, "On Teaching Subject Cataloging," *Cataloging & Classification Quarterly*, 34: 1/2 (2002), p. 223.

13. Vellucci, 1997, p. 36.

14. Seymour Lubetzky, "On Teaching Cataloging," *Journal of Education for Librarianship*, 5: 1 (Summer 1964), p. 257.

15. Vellucci, 1997, p. 37.

16. Don Fallis and Martin Fricke, "Not by Library School Alone," *Library Journal*, 124 (October 15, 1999), p. 44-45.

17. Michael Gorman, "How Cataloging and Classification Should be Taught," *American Libraries*, 23: 8 (1992), p. 694.

18. Michael Gorman, "Why Teach Cataloguing and Classification?" *Cataloging & Classification Quarterly*, 34: 1/2 (2002), p. 1-13.

19. Taylor and Joudrey, 2002, p. 222-223.

20. *Thesaurus of Indexing Terms*, 1996.

APPENDIX. Research Publications by Israeli Authors

S. Shoham and S. Lazinger, "The No-Main-Entry Principle and the Automated Catalog," *Cataloging & Classification Quarterly*, 12: 3/4 (1991): 51-67.

S. Lazinger "ALEPH: Israel's Research Library Network: Background, Evolution, Implications for Networking in a Small Country," *Information Technology and Libraries*, 10: 4 (Dec. 1991): 275-291.

S. Lazinger, "To Merge and Not to Merge: Israel's Union List of Monographs in the Context of Merging Algorithms," *Information Technology and Libraries*, 13: 3 (Sept. 1994): 213-219.

S. Shoham and M. Yitzhaki "Classification Systems and the Online Catalog," *Advances in Knowledge Organization*, 4 (1994): 312-319.

S. Lazinger and E. Adler: *Cataloging Hebrew Materials in the Online Environment: A Comparative Study of American and Israeli Approaches.* Englewood, Colo.: Libraries Unlimited, 1998.

S. Lazinger, "MARCing Time: Information Flow and Inevitability in Non-MARC Israel." In *International Librarianship: Cooperation and Collaboration.* Frances Laverne Carroll and John F. Harvey with the assistance of Susan Houck. Lanham, MD: Scarecrow Press, Inc., 2001.

S. Lazinger, *Digital Preservation and Metadata: History, Theory, Practice.* Englewood, CO: Libraries Unlimited, 2001.

S. Shoham and R. Kedar, "The Subject Cataloging of Monographs with the Use of Keywords." *Cataloging & Classification Quarterly*, 33: 2 (July 2002): 29-54.

S. Shoham and R. Kedar, "The Subject Cataloging of Monographs with the Use of a Thesaurus." *Advances in Knowledge Organization*, 8 (2002): 173-180.

There are additional publications on cataloging that refer to the unique problems faced in Israel, including multilingual systems and multiscript issues. Many of these articles were authored by Elhanan Adler.

Continuing Education for Catalogers in Saudi Arabia

Zahiruddin Khurshid

SUMMARY. Studies have revealed that LIS programs of the four library schools in Saudi Arabia are traditional, and their cataloging courses do not cover new trends and issues in the organization of information. As a result, graduates of these schools lack the required skills for various cataloging positions, especially in an electronic library environment. Once hired, they need to embark on a continuing education program to develop these skills. The paper aims to review continuing education programs for catalogers offered by various library schools, human resource development institutions, automation vendors, and professional associations in Saudi Arabia. Several other continuing education opportunities available to catalogers, such as Web-based training, professional reading, and electronic discussions lists, are also discussed. *[Article copies available for a fee from The Haworth Document Delivery Service: 1-800-HAWORTH. E-mail address: <docdelivery@haworthpress.com> Website: <http://www.HaworthPress.com> © 2006 by The Haworth Press, Inc. All rights reserved.]*

Zahiruddin Khurshid, MSLIS, is Senior Manager, Cataloging Operations Division, King Fahd University of Petroleum & Minerals Library, Dhahran, 31261, Saudi Arabia (E-mail: khurshid@kfupm.edu.sa). He is also responsible for supervising the Library Systems Division.

[Haworth co-indexing entry note]: "Continuing Education for Catalogers in Saudi Arabia." Khurshid, Zahiruddin. Co-published simultaneously in *Cataloging & Classification Quarterly* (The Haworth Information Press, an imprint of The Haworth Press, Inc.) Vol. 41, No. 3/4, 2006, pp. 461-470; and: *Education for Library Cataloging: International Perspectives* (ed: Dajin D. Sun, and Ruth C. Carter) The Haworth Information Press, an imprint of The Haworth Press, Inc., 2006, pp. 461-470. Single or multiple copies of this article are available for a fee from The Haworth Document Delivery Service [1-800-HAWORTH, 9:00 a.m. - 5:00 p.m. (EST). E-mail address: docdelivery@haworthpress.com].

Available online at http://www.haworthpress.com/web/CCQ
© 2006 by The Haworth Press, Inc. All rights reserved.
doi:10.1300/J104v41n03_14

KEYWORDS. Cataloging, cataloging education, catalogers, library education, continuing education, Saudi Arabia

INTRODUCTION

Celli observed back in 1981 that "while Saudi Arabia's vast wealth can build beautiful new libraries and furnish them with comfortable accoutrements and the full panoply of library technology, and while that wealth can also purchase the support services of international vendors and the experience of professional librarians, library and information science will not take root in Saudi Arabia until these libraries are staffed and administered by Saudi professionals fully trained in twentieth century methodology."[1] It is not that the government was not aware of the need for well-educated and trained professionals to run government and private institutions and agencies, including libraries, it had its own limitations. According to Namlah, "the government had only two alternatives. The first was to postpone planning and wait until the manpower was available and simply concentrate on educating populace. This could be a very time-consuming effort. The second alternative was to hire both a professional and non-professional manpower force from abroad and continue planning and developing."[2] The government decided to go with the second alternative. Two decades later, the Kingdom is in a much better position to recruit locals and is seriously working on a national plan of Saudization (a term meaning replacing the expatriate manpower with Saudi nationals) of the job market. A number of categories of jobs, including library jobs, have been targeted for this purpose. Many Saudis with professional degrees in library and information science are now taking library jobs.

Library schools are producing hundreds of graduates each year. However, the quality of education they receive does not prepare them enough for entry-level positions. Upon hiring, they require a comprehensive induction and on-the-job training to be able to perform their daily jobs. Positions like those in cataloging become a big challenge for new recruits. Having little or no knowledge of new trends in cataloging, it becomes very difficult for them to perform in an electronic library environment in which cataloging tools are also used in electronic format. The employers are extremely concerned about catalogers lacking competencies and encourage them to improve their knowledge and skills through continuing education. A variety of continuing education programs for catalogers are available in the Kingdom and elsewhere in the region. The paper aims to review those programs offered by library schools, human resource development institutions, automation vendors, and professional associations. Several other continuing education opportunities available to catalogers, such as Web-based training, professional reading, and electronic discussion lists, are also discussed.

LIBRARY EDUCATION

There are four library schools in the Kingdom offering professional degrees in library and information science from BLS to Ph.D. The first library school with a 4-year degree program was established at King Abdulaziz University in Jeddah in 1973. The school now offers degrees from BLS to Ph.D. Three other schools are located at King Saud University in Riyadh (BLS program), Imam Muhmammad Ibn Saud University in Riyadh (MLS and Ph.D programs), and Umm Al-Qura University in Makkah (BLS program). In addition to the four degree programs, the Institute of Public Administration (IPA) offers a diploma program at the undergraduate level. In fact the IPA program is the oldest in Saudi Arabia; it was started in 1968.[3] Librarians coming out of these programs are taking both paraprofessional and professional positions in all types of libraries in Saudi Arabia. However, studies have revealed that the quality of these programs is not up to the desired level. They are traditional and have not been updated for years. Library employers were asked in a survey to comment on the quality of library education programs in the Arabian Gulf region (including Saudi Arabia). "Their comments show that they are very critical of these programs. They stated that the programs were traditional and not oriented to the needs of the local community. Furthermore, the employers thought that library schools lacked adequate facilities and resources."[4] Another problem is that new trends in information technology are not adequately covered.[5] Some of the new concepts and trends in cataloging, such as Dublin Core, SGML, XML, CORC, Listservs (Autocat, Coopcat, and Serialst), etc., are not taught at all or discussed briefly at one or two schools.[6] Graduates of these schools do not even get enough knowledge of primary cataloging tools. One of the reasons is the language problem. While most of the cataloging tools are in English, the language of instruction is Arabic, which makes it extremely difficult for students to fully understand them. Only a few tools have been translated into Arabic, such as the Anglo-American Cataloguing Rules and Sears List of Subject Headings but, they are not updated regularly. All of this shows that the education received from library schools is not enough and must be supplemented by continuing education programs if catalogers are to perform quality work in a modern library. Intner believes "cataloging education has to be an ongoing process over a professional's entire career, not a one-time exposure followed by practice alone. One must learn about and absorb the implications of the application of new and changed cataloging rules, new materials, and new policies formulated to account for new types of searching tools, technologies, and services."[7]

CONTINUING EDUCATION

Continuing education is defined as "all learning activities and efforts, formal and informal, by which individuals seek to upgrade their knowledge, attitudes, competencies, and understanding in their special field of work (or role) in order to: (1) deliver quality performance in the work setting, and (2) enrich their library careers."[8] Different types of continuing education opportunities are available to catalogers in Saudi Arabia, including formal course work (outside of a library degree), workshops, seminars, conferences, short courses, Web-based training, professional reading, discussion lists, etc. Each of these programs will be discussed in the context of Saudi Arabia and its relevance to catalogers.

LIS Courses (Outside of a Library Degree)

Of the four library schools in Saudi Arabia, three also offer continuing education programs. The LIS department at King Saud University is the only one that does not have such a program. However, the continuing education courses offered by LIS departments, which both Ashoor and Chaudhry[9] and Marghalani[10] have listed in their studies, do not include any worthwhile course on cataloging or a related topic and, therefore, have little or no value to catalogers. They should feel obligated to have programs of continuing education for all members of the profession.

Workshops

Workshops are generally organized by the Arabian Gulf Chapter of the Special Libraries Association (AGC-SLA), automation vendors, libraries, and several governmental and non-governmental organizations. They address various topics of current interest including cataloging and related subjects.

The AGC-SLA organizes a pre-conference workshop and a mid-year workshop each year as part of their professional development program. Some of these workshops are either entirely or in part related to cataloging, such as the workshop on the *Use of Electronic Utilities for Knowledge Organization*, held at the Arabian Gulf University in Manama, Bahrain, in November 1998. The topics covered in the workshop included Library of Congress Subject Headings, Library of Congress and Dewey Decimal Classification systems, CD-ROM-based bibliographic databases, and OCLC cataloging services. Instructors are invited from OCLC, overseas libraries, and also from libraries in the region. These workshops are great success and run to full capacity. Because of limited seats, some applicants who apply late fail to get accommodated. Because of the value of these workshops, most libraries send their employees to attend them as part of their continuing education and training.

Some of the automation vendors also organize workshops as part of vendor services. The Arabian Advanced Systems (AAS), the local vendor of Horizon, offers a series of workshops and training courses for librarians each year. Some of their programs are specifically designed for catalogers, such as a 5-day workshop on MARC 21 held in Riyadh in May 2003. Others deal with the management and administration of the Horizon library system, which also includes the cataloging module. Edutech Middle East, the local vendor of VTLS/Virtua and Q-Series, is another vendor which organizes workshops with regularity. They are also renowned for their workshops on the OCLC Arabic Cataloging Software, which they organize in coordination with OCLC.[11]

The King Fahd University of Petroleum & Minerals (KFUPM) Library in Dhahran also held several workshops not only for its own staff, but also for librarians of other libraries in the region.[12] These workshops also included cataloging components.

Short Courses

The KFUPM Library is organizing short courses of 5 days duration since 1985. In the beginning, only one course was offered each year. Beginning with 1988, the number of courses offered has increased to two per year. Most of these courses have one to two lectures related to cataloging, such as *Online Cataloging, Cataloging on Microcomputer, TQM Applications in Cataloging, Using CD-ROM for Cataloging*, etc. For the first time, an entire course on *Electronic Tools for Knowledge Organization* was offered for catalogers in 2003. Another course on *Cataloging Using Horizon Library Automation System* was scheduled for April 2004. These courses attract a large number of librarians and information professionals from the Kingdom as well as from other countries of the region. Those local library staff whose work is related to the course topics are also encouraged to attend. According to Chaudhry, Ashoor, and Rehman, "short courses turned out to be a very valuable experience for the KFUPM Library. In addition to a marked improvement in the skills of the library staff, these courses have also had a tremendous impact on building confidence amongst staff."[13] Emphasis is given on the practicum so that the participants have hands-on experience, which is important to their jobs. Participants are asked to evaluate the course at the end. Their input about the content, course material, lab facilities, and instructors help in improving future short courses. Marghalani observes that the KFUPM Library is playing a leading role in the training of librarians, not only from Saudi Arabia, but also from the other Arabian Gulf states.[14]

The Institute of Public Administration is also famous for their training courses covering a wide range of topics, including library and information science. Their latest brochure of 2002/03 includes a four-week course on the organization of documents and manuscripts, held three times in January, April, and June 2003 in Riyadh.

Seminars

In addition to workshops and short courses, the KFUPM Library training program also includes local seminars given both by the library staff and visiting librarians and vendors from different parts of the world. These seminars have included some topics of interest to catalogers, such as *Library of Congress Services, Authority Control, Horizon Library System*, etc. Seminars are also held at other libraries, but are not so much a part of the library training program as at KFUPM.

Conferences

The AGC-SLA organizes annual conferences in each of the six Arabian Gulf states (Saudi Arabia has not yet organized any conference. However, many Saudi librarians and expatriate librarians working in Saudi Arabia serve on the Chapter board and on the organizing and papers committees) by rotation. These conferences provide an excellent opportunity for practicing librarians, including cataloging librarians to share their knowledge and discuss issues of common interest. Cataloging librarians from Saudi Arabia participate in these conferences both as paper presenters and as listeners. The topics of some papers presented by them include *Cataloger's Workstation, Cooperative Cataloging, MARC and the Arabic Language, Arabic Authority Control, Preparing Catalogers for the Electronic Environment, The Impact of IT on Job Requirements and Qualifications for Catalogers.* The KFUPM Library presented a proposal for developing ARABMARC for discussion in one of the special sessions of the 2nd conference held in Bahrain in January 1994, which drew a lot of interest among participants. Unfortunately no further progress has been made on this proposal since then. At these conferences, catalogers also have the opportunity to meet with colleagues as well as resource persons from the region and around the world, and to discuss issues related to cataloging, especially to Arabic cataloging. They also obtain information about new trends and developments. One of the conference events is vendor presentations, which may also include talks on topics of interest to catalogers, such as authority control, Arabic cataloging, MARC, etc. These conferences thus provide good opportunities for the continuing education of catalogers.

Web Sites

A number of libraries, institutions, and individuals are maintaining Web sites with documents and tools of interest to catalogers, such as Cataloger's Reference Shelf, Cataloger's Toolbox, and Technical Processing Online Tool (TPOT). These Web resources provide valuable information on the availability of both primary and secondary cataloging tools and how to make better use of them. Other sites include documents and manuals for training. Notable among them are the *Cataloger's Desktop Web-Based Training* document from the Library of Congress (http://loc.gov.cds/desktop/wbt/default2.htm) and *Cataloging Internet Resources: A Manual and Practical Guide*, 2nd ed. from OCLC (http://www.purl.org/oclc/cataloging-internet). The KFUPM Library is the only library in Saudi Arabia providing access to these Web sites through its cataloging division home page (http://www.kfupm.edu.sa/library/cod-web/cod-new.htm) as tools for the continuing education of catalogers.

INFORMAL CONTINUING EDUCATION

Subscribing to discussion lists, memberships in professional organizations, and reading library science journals are considered methods of informal continuing education. Discussion lists are available in many subject areas, but we are concerned here with those related to cataloging only, such as AUTOCAT, Passport for Windows list, Coopcat, Serialst, etc. These lists help catalogers in two areas: "general current awareness (of trends, new tools, policy changes at LC or the utilities, etc.) and specific (and immediate) current awareness. (How do I catalog this particular item? How do I choose among these classes when classifying a work on this topic? What is the meaning of this class number which I found on a CIP record but which isn't in the edition of the classification schedule which my library has?)"[15] Similar focused lists may also be maintained at national and regional levels. However, no such lists are available in Saudi Arabia. A very small number of catalogers (2-3) subscribe to AUTOCAT and they, too, hardly post any questions or provide answers, but they read those that others have posted and learn from them.

With regard to professional reading, catalogers of the KFUPM Library have access to journals such as *Cataloging & Classification Quarterly, Cataloging Service Bulletin, Library Resources and Technical Services, Information Technology and Libraries, Library Hi Tech,* etc. These journals have been a source of continuing education for them. Some of the catalogers have even contributed articles to these journals. Catalogers of other libraries generally read *Library Journal,* as their libraries do not subscribe to journals with a focus on cataloging.

Librarians, including catalogers, in Saudi Arabia are generally sponsored by their employers to attend conferences. Catalogers, therefore, like to have memberships in several national and regional professional organizations, such as the Saudi Library and Information Science Association (SLIA), AGC-SLA, and the Arab Federation for Libraries and Information (AFLI), to be able to get sponsorships to attend their conferences.

CONCLUSION

Intner recommends three types of education for catalogers. First, advanced level coursework, including laboratories, taken in an academic program; second, on-the-job-training; and third, continuing education to augment training.[16] Cataloging courses taught in library schools in Saudi Arabia are not up-to-date and lack the training component. As a result, new hires require on-the-job training to learn everything from the use of cataloging tools to original cataloging. However, what they learn from on-the-job training are mostly routine things. To broaden the scope of their cataloging knowledge and to learn about new concepts and trends in cataloging, catalogers need continuing education. Unfortunately, library schools in Saudi Arabia are doing very little in the continuing education of catalogers by not offering cataloging and related courses outside of their degree programs. Whatever small-level activities we see in this area are due to the efforts of AGC-SLA, library automation system vendors, KFUPM Library, and IPA. Other professional organizations, libraries, and especially LIS departments, need to play their part in enhancing continuing education programs in the Kingdom. Employers should continue to provide all kinds of support to catalogers to participate in conferences, workshops, short courses, and seminars, and should also encourage them to engage in informal continuing education activities, including subscribing to focused lists on cataloging, reading library science journals, and seeking membership in professional associations.

REFERENCES

1. John P. Celli, "Saudi Arabian Libraries Revisited," *Leads* 23, no. 1 (Spring 1981): 8.

2. Ali I. Namlah, "Manpower Deficiency in Saudi Arabia: Its Effect on the Library and Information Profession," *International Library Review* 14, no. 1 (January 1982): 7.

3. Mohammad M. Aman, "Arab countries: Saudi Arabia." In, Miles M. Jackson, (Ed.), *International Handbook of Contemporary Developments in Librarianship*, (Westport, CT: Greenwood Press, 1981): 126-9.

4. Mohammed Saleh Jamil Ashoor and Abdus Sattar Chaudhry. *The Education of Library and Information Professionals in the Arabian Gulf Region*, (London: Mansel, 1999): 93.

5. Abdulghafoor A. Qari, "Electronic Library and Library and Information Science Departments in the Arabian Gulf Region," *Journal of Education for Library and Information Science* 39, no. 1 (Winter 1998): 32.

6. Zahiruddin Khurshid, "Preparing Catalogers for the Electronic Environment: An Analysis of Cataloging and Related Courses in the Arabian Gulf Region," *Journal of Education for Library and Information Science* 39, no.1 (Winter 1998): 10-11.

7. Sheila S. Intner, "Present Issues in Cataloging Education: Considering the Past and Looking Toward the Future," *Cataloging & Classification Quarterly* 34, no. 1/2 (2002): 25.

8. Elizabeth W. Stone, "The Growth of Continuing Education." *Library Trends* 34, no. 3 (Winter 1986): 489-90.

9. Ashoor and Chaudhry, *The Education of Library and Information Professionals in the Arabian Gulf Region*, p. 114-5.

10. Mohammad A. Marghalani, "Continuing Education for Librarians and Information Specialists in Saudi Arabia." In, Blanche Woolls, (Ed.), *Continuing Professional*

Education and IFLA: Past, Present, and a Vision for the Future (Munchen: K. G. Saur, 1993): 123-4.

11. "OCLC Arabic Cataloging Software: A Complete Solution for Arabian Gulf Libraries," *The Arabian Gulf Chapter Newsletter* 8, no. 3 (October 2000): 7.

12. Ashoor and Chaudhry, *The Education of Library and Information Professionals in the Arabian Gulf Region*, p. 104-9.

13. Abdus Sattar Chaudhry, Mohammad Saleh Ashoor, Sajjad Ur Rehman, "Development and Implementation of an In-House Continuing Education Program in an Academic Library," *Education for Information* 11, no. 1 (March 1993): 53.

14. Marghalani, "Continuing Education for Librarians and Information Specialists in Saudi Arabia," p. 124.

15. Judith Hopkins, "The Community of Catalogers: Its Role in the Education of Catalogers," *Cataloging & Classification Quarterly* 34, no. 3 (2002): 377.

16. Intner, "Present Issues in Cataloging Education," p. 26.

Index

AACR versions, 9-11,16,27-32,58,
  60-61,95,110-115,124-131,
  154-168,174-182,199-200,
  220-223,278,292-293,297,
  312-314,318-324,349-350,
  359,361,363,367,392-405,
  421-423,433-436,446-449,
  463-464
Abdel Hady, Mohammed Fat'hy,
  407-430
Academic Library Center North
  Rhine-Westphalia, 195
AFLI, 468
African perspectives, 5-70. *See also*
  under individual topics
  Botswanan, 5-26
  Nigerian, 27-52
  overviews and summaries, 1-4
  South African, 53-70
AGC-SLA, 464-465
AGRIS, 10
Aichi Shukutoku University, 128-129
Ain Shams University, 415
ALEPH system, 446-449
Alexandria University, 412-413
ALIA, 152,174-176
Allegro Training, 325-326
American National Standards Institute.
  See ANSI
Anglo-American Cataloging Rules
  versions. *See* AACR versions
ANSI, 343
APPM, 175
Arabian Federation for Libraries and
  Information. *See* AFLI
Arabian Gulf Chapter-Special
  Libraries Association. *See*
  AGC-SLA

Arabic Subject Headings, 422-423
Argentinean perspectives, 335-352.
  See also Latin American
  perspectives
  future contexts, 350
  historical contexts, 336
  overviews and summaries,
    335-336,350
  reference resources, 350-351
  standards and tools, 338-350
    AACR versions, 349-350
    ANSI, 343
    Dublin Core, 349-350
    ISBDs, 344-345
    LCC, 338
    LCSH, 338
    MARC versions, 338,340-343
    SGML, 349-350
    TEI, 349-350
    Warwick Framework, 349-350
    XML, 349-350
  university programs, 336-350
    curricula, 336-338
    information processing areas,
      338-350
    practicums, 346
    research trends, 348-349
    teaching strategies, 346-347
    University of Buenos Aires,
      335-406
ASB, 201
Asian perspectives, 71-148. *See also*
  under individual topics
  Chinese, 71-104
    current status, 85-104
    development-related issues, 71-84
  Indian, 105-120
  Japanese, 121-134

471

overviews and summaries, 1-4
South Korean, 135-148
AsLib, 324-325
Association of Information
    Management. *See* AsLib
Australian Library and Information
    Association. *See* ALIA
Australian perspectives, 149-192. *See
    also under individual topics*
New South Wales, 173-192
overviews and summaries, 1-4
Queensland, 149-172
Austrian and German perspectives,
    193-226. *See also* European
    perspectives
Austrian-specific, 222-225
careers, 195-196
consortia, networks, and systems,
    195-196
    Academic Library Center North
        Rhine-Westphalia, 195
    Bavarian Library Network, 195
    Common Library Network, 195
    ekz.bibliotheksservice GmbH,
        195
    Hessian Library Consortium, 195
    OCLC, 195
    South West German Library
        Consortium, 195
degrees, 195-196
future contexts, 224-225
German National Library, 195
German-specific, 193-222
historical contexts, 193-197
name authorities, 201
overviews and summaries, 193-195
qualification levels and typical jobs,
    219
reference resources, 225
standards and tools,
    199-201,220-222
    AACR versions, 199-200,220-223
    ASB, 201
    current status, 220-222

DDC, 200-201
descriptions, 199
KAB, 201
LCC, 200-201
MAB, 220-223
MARC versions, 220-223
RAK, 199-223
RAK-Musik, 199-201
RAK-NBM, 199-201
RAK-OB, 199-201
RAK-UW, 199-201
RAK-WB, 199-201
RSWK, 199-201
UDC, 200-201
university programs, 196-199,
    202-219,223-225
    Austrian-specific, 223-225
    continuing education centers,
        198-199,217-219,225
    descriptions, 196-197
    German-specific, 196-199,
        202-219
    mid-level service, 198,216-217
    public librarian, 198
    senior-level service, 197,209-216
    upper-level service, 197-198,
        202-209

Banha Branch (Zakazik University),
    413-414
Bani Swif Branch (Cairo University),
    412-413
Barber, Elsa E., 335-352
Basic Subject Headings. *See* BSH
Basic topics. *See* Overviews and
    summaries
Bavarian Library Network, 195
BDS, 321-326
Bibliographic Data Services. *See* BDS
Bliss classification, 11,277
Bodleian Library, 322-323
Bologna Declaration, 270-271

Botswanan perspectives, 5-26. *See also*
    African perspectives
consortia, networks, and systems, 11
databases, 10-11
    AGRIS, 10
    PADIS, 10
    UNESCO, 10
future contexts, 22-23
historical contexts, 7
overviews and summaries, 5-7,22-23
reference resources, 23-25
SABINET, 11
standards and tools, 8-18
    AACR versions, 9-11,16
    Bliss classification, 11
    DDC, 8-11,17-18
    LCC, 8-11
    UDC, 11
university programs, 5-26
    cataloging activity impacts, 18-19
    cataloging and classification, 8-11
    certificate, 8
    descriptions, 5-7
    diploma, 8-11
    faculty contexts and statistics, 11
    formal training options, 5-26
    in-service training, 20
    junior *vs.* senior staff, 5-8
    library-university cooperation, 14
    local *vs.* outside training, 19-22
    on-the-job education and
        training, 14-18
    practicums, 13-14
    seminars, 16-17
    student contexts and statistics,
        12-13
    TINlib system, 19
    University of Botswana, 7-26
    workshops, 16-17
Bowman, J. H., 309-334
British Library, 321-324
British perspectives, 309-334. *See also*
    European perspectives
BDS, 321-326
Bodleian Library, 322-323

British Library, 321-324
commercial training providers,
    324-326,330-333
    Allegro Training, 325-326
    AsLib, 324-325
    CILIP, 310-313,324-326
    TFPL, 324,330-333
future contexts, 326-327
historical contexts, 310-311
on-the-job training, 321-324
overviews and summaries,
    309-311,326-327
reference resources, 328-329
standards and tools, 312-324
    AACR versions, 312-314,
        318-324
    CIP data, 321-322
    DDC, 312-313,319,321-324
    LCC, 319
    LCSH, 319,321-324
    MARC versions, 312-314,318,
        321-324
    UDC, 319
university programs, 311-326
    curricula, 315-321
    postgraduate courses, 311-314
    student contexts and statistics,
        314-315
    UCL, 315-321
BSH, 125-131

Cairo University, 407-430
CALIS, 95-97
Carter, Ruth E., 1-4
Cataloging education (international
        perspectives). *See also under*
        individual topics
    African perspectives, 5-70
        Botswanan, 5-26
        Nigerian, 27-52
        South African, 53-70
    Asian perspectives, 71-148
        Chinese (current status), 85-104
        Chinese (development-related
            issues), 71-84

Indian, 105-120
Japanese, 121-134
South Korean, 135-148
Australian perspectives, 149-192
New South Wales, 173-192
Queensland, 149-172
European perspectives, 193-334
Austrian and German, 193-226
British, 309-334
Polish, 227-268
Slovenian, 269-290
Spanish, 291-308
future contexts. *See* Future contexts
historical contexts. *See* Historical
contexts
Latin American perspectives,
335-406
Argentinean, 335-352
Mexican, 353-388
Peruvian, 389-406
Middle Eastern perspectives, 407-470
Egyptian, 407-430
Iranian, 431-442
Israeli, 443-460
Saudi Arabian, 461-470
overviews and summaries, 1-4. *See
also* Overviews and
summaries
reference resources. *See* Reference
resources
Cataloging standards and tools. *See*
Standards and tools
Cataloging-in-Publication data. *See*
CIP data
CatSkill training software, 156-166
CC, 77,94-95,112-115,127,277
CCC, 77,110-115
CDS/ISIS software, 111
CEBID, 232-233
Center for Library, Information and
Documentation Education.
See CEBID
Chartered Institute of Library and
Information Professionals.
See CILIP

China National Library System. *See*
CALIS
Chinese Cataloging Rules, 76-77
Chinese Classified Thesaurus, 77-79,94
Chinese Library Classification, 77,91-95
Chinese perspectives. *See also* Asian
perspectives
current status, 85-104
CALIS, 95-97
course content, 86-95
facilities, 98
faculty contexts and statistics, 97
future contexts, 100-101
historical contexts, 85-86
master's programs, 86-91
materials development, 95-97
methodologies, 98,101
overviews and summaries, 85-86
practicums, 98-100
problems, 97-100
reference resources, 101-103
standards and tools, 91-95
teaching assurance systems, 100
undergraduate programs, 87-90
university programs, 86-91
Wenhua Library Science School,
85-86
development-related issues, 77-80
change-related issues, 77-80
course content, 74-77
education types and levels, 72-74
future contexts, 80-81
historical contexts, 71-84
Ministry of Education, 73-84
Northeast Normal University,
73-84
overviews and summaries,
71-72,80-81
Peking University, 72-84
reference resources, 82-83
standards and tools, 75-77
Wuhan University, 72-84
overviews and summaries, 1-4
standards and tools, 75-80,91-95
AACR versions, 95
CC, 77,94-95

CCC, 77
Chinese Cataloging Rules, 76-77
Chinese Classified Thesaurus,
  77-79,94
Chinese Library Classification,
  77,91-95
Classification of the Chinese
  Academy of Sciences
  Library, 94-95
Classification of the Library of
  the People's University of
  China, 94-95
DDC, 77,94-95
Dublin Core, 77-80,95
LCC, 94-95
LCSH, 77
MARC versions, 75-77,95
UDC, 77,94-95
CILIP, 310-313,324-326
CIP data, 321-322,468
Classification for General Libraries.
  See KAB
Classification of the Chinese Academy
  of Sciences Library, 94-95
Classification of the Library of the
  People's University of China,
  94-95
Classification standards and tools. *See*
  Standards and tools
Classified Catalog Code. *See* CCC
Cloete, Linda M., 53-70
COBISS, 282-283
College-level programs. *See* University
  programs
Colon Classification. *See* CC
Commercial training providers,
  324-326,330-333
Common Library Network, 195
Consortia, networks, and systems. *See
  also under individual topics*
  Academic Library Center North
    Rhine-Westphalia, 195
  African perspectives, 11,33-34
    Botswanan, 11
    Nigerian, 33-34
  Asian perspectives, 95-97,124-132
    Chinese, 95-97
    Indian, 107-119
    Japanese, 124-132
  Australian perspectives,
    Queensland, 150-151
  Bavarian Library Network, 195
  CALIS, 95-97
  COBISS, 282-283
  Common Library Network, 195
  DELNET, 107-108,118-119
  ekz.bibliotheksservice GmbH, 195
  European perspectives, 195-196,
    249-250,282-283
    Austrian and German, 195-196
    Polish, 249-250
    Slovenian, 282-283
  Hessian Library Consortium, 195
  INFLIBNET, 111,114-115,118-119
  Kinetica, 150-151
  Middle Eastern perspectives, Saudi
    Arabian, 465-467
  NACSIS-CAT, 124-132
  NII, 132
  NUNet, 33-34
  OCLC, 125,150-151,195,282,
    465-467
  RLN, 150-151
  SABINET, 11
  South West German Library
    Consortium, 195
  TINlib system, 19
  VSAT, 33-34
  WLN, 150-151
Continuing education, 116-118,
  198-199,217-219,225,402,
  464-468. *See also under
  individual topics*
  Austrian and German perspectives,
    198-199,217-219,225
  Indian perspectives, 116-118
  Peruvian perspectives, 402
  Saudi Arabian perspectives,
    464-468

Co-operative Online Bibliographic
     Information System &
     Services. *See* COBISS
CORC, 463-464
Course content and curricula. *See also
     under individual topics*
     Argentinean perspectives, 336-338
     Austrian and German perspectives,
          196-199,202-219,223-225
     Botswanan perspectives, 8-11
     British perspectives, 315-321
     Chinese perspectives, 74-77,86-95
     Egyptian perspectives, 411-420
     Indian perspectives, 108-119
     Iranian perspectives, 433-436
     Israeli perspectives, 449-457
     Japanese perspectives, 122-132
     Mexican perspectives, 373-388
     New South Wales perspectives,
          177-178
     Polish perspectives, 229-233
     Slovenian perspectives, 272-282
     South African perspectives, 55-70
     Spanish perspectives, 297-301
Cross River State, 27-52
Curricula and course content. *See*
     Course content and curricula

DDC, 8-11,17-18,58,60-61,77,94-95,
     125-129,154-155,176-182,
     200-201,277-280,312-313,
     319,321-324,358,360,363,
     367,392-395,421-425,
     433-434,465
DELNET, 107-108,118-119
Descriptive cataloging standards and
     tools. *See* Standards and tools
Developing/Delhi Library Network.
     See DELNET
Dewey Decimal Classification. *See*
     DDC
Distance education, 55-70
Dublin Core, 77-80,95,114-115,
     176-182,349-350

EBIB, 229-233,258-259
ECTS, 302-303
Education for cataloging (international
     perspectives). *See also under
     individual topics*
     African perspectives, 5-70
          Botswanan, 5-26
          Nigerian, 27-52
          South African, 53-70
     Asian perspectives, 71-148
          Chinese (current status), 85-104
          Chinese (development-related
               issues), 71-84
          Indian, 105-120
          Japanese, 121-134
          South Korean, 135-148
     Australian perspectives, 149-192
          New South Wales, 173-192
          Queensland, 149-172
     European perspectives, 193-334
          Austrian and German, 193-226
          British, 309-334
          Polish, 227-268
          Slovenian, 269-290
          Spanish, 291-308
     future contexts. *See* Future contexts
     historical contexts. *See* Historical
          contexts
     Latin American perspectives,
          335-406
          Argentinean, 335-352
          Mexican, 353-388
          Peruvian, 389-406
     Middle Eastern perspectives,
          407-470
          Egyptian, 407-430
          Iranian, 431-442
          Israeli, 443-460
          Saudi Arabian, 461-470
     overviews and summaries, 1-4
     reference resources. *See* Reference
          resources
Educator contexts and statistics. *See*
          Faculty contexts and statistics

Egyptian perspectives, 407-430. *See also* Middle Eastern perspectives
Cairo University, 407-430
future contexts, 425-426
historical contexts, 409-411
overviews and summaries, 407-409, 425-426
reference resources, 426
standards and tools, 421-425
AACR versions, 421-423
DDC, 421-425
Greater List of Arabic Subject Headings, 422-423
LCC, 423-425
LCSH, 422-425
MARC versions, 423-424
UDC, 423
university programs, 408-429
Ain Shams University, 415
Alexandria University, 412-413
Banha Branch (Zakazik University), 413-414
Bani Swif Branch (Cairo University), 412-413
Cairo University, 407-430
change-related issues, 423-425
course analyses, 422-423
course descriptions and statistics, 416-420
curricula, 411-420
descriptions, 408-410
faculty contexts and statistics, 420-422
fieldwork and practicums, 422
Monoufia University, 412-414
October 6 University, 415-416
recommendations, 425-426
Sohaj Branch (South Valley University), 413
South Valley University, 413-414
Zakazik University, 413-414
Ekz.bibliotheksservice GmbH, 195
Electronic Information Bulletin for Librarians. *See* EBIB

ENBA, 355-356,373-374
Escuela Nacional de Biblioteconomía y Archivonomía. *See* ENBA
European Credit Transfer system. *See* ECTS
European perspectives, 193-334. *See also under individual topics*
Austrian and German, 193-226
British, 309-334
overviews and summaries, 1-4
Polish, 227-268
Slovenian, 269-290
Spanish, 291-308
European Union, 270-271
European Union contexts, 302-303
Experiential learning contexts, 56-57
EXtensible Mark-up Language. *See* XML

Faculty contexts and statistics, 11,97, 112-116,182-185,420-422, 438-439. *See also under individual topics*
Botswanan perspectives, 11
Chinese perspectives, 97
Egyptian perspectives, 420-422
Indian perspectives, 112-116
Iranian perspectives, 438-439
New South Wales perspectives, 182-185
Farsi expansions (LCC), 434-436
FGDC, 175
Fieldwork, 422. *See also* Practicums
FRBR, 249-250
Functional Requirements for Bibliographic Records. *See* FRBR
Fundamental topics. *See* Overviews and summaries
Future contexts. *See also under individual topics*
African perspectives, 22-23,44-45, 67-68
Botswanan, 22-23
Nigerian, 44-45
South African, 67-68

Asian perspectives, 80-81,118-119,
    132-133,146-147
    Chinese (current status), 100-101
    Chinese (development-related
        issues), 80-81
    Indian, 118-119
    Japanese, 132-133
    South Korean, 146-147
Australian perspectives, 166-168,190
    New South Wales, 190
    Queensland, 166-168
European perspectives, 224-225,
        249-250,285,303-304,326-327
    Austrian and German, 224-225
    British, 326-327
    Polish, 249-250
    Slovenian, 285
    Spanish, 303-304
Latin American perspectives, 350,
        370-371,405-406
    Argentinean, 350
    Mexican, 370-371
    Peruvian, 405-406
Middle Eastern perspectives, 425-426,
        436-441,457-458,468-469
    Egyptian, 425-426
    Iranian, 436-441
    Israeli, 457-458
    Saudi Arabian, 468-469

GARE and GSARE, 297
General Classification Schedule for
        Libraries. *See* ASB
General Slovene Subject Headings. *See*
        GSSH
German and Austrian perspectives,
        193-226. *See also* European
        perspectives
    Austrian-specific, 222-225
    careers, 195-196
    consortia, networks, and systems,
        195-196
        Academic Library Center North
        Rhine-Westphalia, 195

Bavarian Library Network, 195
    Common Library Network, 195
    ekz.bibliotheksservice GmbH, 195
    Hessian Library Consortium, 195
    OCLC, 195
    South West German Library
        Consortium, 195
degrees, 195-196
future contexts, 224-225
German National Library, 195
German-specific, 193-222
historical contexts, 193-197
name authorities, 201
overviews and summaries, 193-195
qualification levels and typical jobs,
        219
reference resources, 225
standards and tools, 199-201,
        220-222
    AACR versions, 199-200,
        220-223
    ASB, 201
    current status, 220-222
    DDC, 200-201
    descriptions, 199
    KAB, 201
    LCC, 200-201
    MAB, 220-223
    MARC versions, 220-223
    RAK, 199-200,220-223
    RAK-Musik, 199-201
    RAK-NBM, 199-201
    RAK-OB, 199-201
    RAK-UW, 199-201
    RAK-WB, 199-201
    RSWK, 199-201
    UDC, 200-201
university programs, 196-199,
        202-219,223-225
    Austrian-specific, 223-225
    continuing education centers,
        198-199,217-219,225
    descriptions, 196-197
    German-specific, 196-199,
        202-219
    mid-level service, 198,216-217

public librarian, 198
senior-level service, 197,
  209-216
upper-level service, 197-198,
  202-209
German National Library, 195
GILS, 175
Graduate-level programs. *See*
  University programs
Greater List of Arabic Subject
  Headings, 422-423
Grycz rules, 235-236
GSARE and GARE, 297
GSSH, 277

Hallam, Gillian, 149-172
Harvey, Ross, 173-192
Hauke, Petra, 193-226
Hebrew Thesaurus of Indexing Terms,
  447-449
Hessian Library Consortium, 195
Historical contexts. *See also under*
  individual topics
  African perspectives, 7,27-34,
    37-38,53-56
    Botswanan, 7
    Nigerian, 27-34,37-38
    South African, 53-56
  Asian perspectives, 71-84,106-107,
    121-124,135-138
    Chinese (current status), 85-86
    Chinese (development-related
      issues), 71-84
    Indian, 106-107
    Japanese, 121-124
    South Korean, 135-138
  Australian perspectives, 150-151,
    173-176
    New South Wales, 173-176
    Queensland, 150-151
  European perspectives, 193-197,
    228-233,270-271,292-293,
    310-311
    Austrian and German, 193-197
    British, 310-311

Polish, 228-233
Slovenian, 270-271
Spanish, 292-293
Latin American perspectives, 336,
  353-356,390-391
  Argentinean, 336
  Mexican, 353-356
  Peruvian, 390-391
Middle Eastern perspectives, 409-411,
  431-433,444-446,462-464
  Egyptian, 409-411
  Iranian, 431-433
  Israeli, 444-446
  Saudi Arabian, 462-464
HTML, 175
HyperText Mark-up Language. *See*
  HTML

IFLA, 29-34,110-111,292-293
  Standards for Library Schools
    (1976), 29-34
  UBC program, 27-28,110-111
ILA, 436-437
Indian perspectives, 105-120. *See also*
  Asian perspectives
  consortia, networks, and systems,
    107-119
    DELNET, 107-108,118-119
    INFLIBNET, 111,114-115,
      118-119
  future contexts, 118-119
  historical contexts, 106-107
  IFLA UBC program, 110-111
  organization-program
    interrelationships, 107-108
  overviews and summaries, 105
  Ranganathan, S. R., 106-119
  reference resources, 119
  standards and tools, 110-115
    AACR versions, 110-115
    CC, 112-115
    CCC, 110-115
    CDS/ISIS software, 111
    Dublin Core, 114-115

ISBDs, 110-111,115
ISO 2709, 111
LCSH, 112,114-115
MARC versions, 110-115
POPSI, 110-115
PRECIS, 110-115
Sears List of Subject Headings,
    112-115
UCC, 103-119
UNESCO, 108-111
university programs, 108-119
    continuing education, 116-118
    current status, 112-116
    curriculum revision
        mechanisms, 110-112
    descriptions of, 108-110
    faculty contexts and statistics,
        112-116
    recommended courses, 109,112
INFLIBNET, 111,114-115,118-119
In-service training, 140-142
Institute of Information Science. *See*
    IZUM
Instituto Tecnológico de Estudios
    Superiores de Monterrey. *See*
    ITESM
Integrated training resources programs,
    62-66
International perspectives (cataloging
    education). *See also under*
    individual topics
    African perspectives, 5-70
        Botswanan, 5-26
        Nigerian, 27-52
        South African, 53-70
    Asian perspectives, 71-148
        Chinese (current status), 85-104
        Chinese (development-related
            issues), 71-84
        Indian, 105-120
        Japanese, 121-134
        South Korean, 135-148
    Australian perspectives, 149-192
        New South Wales, 173-192
        Queensland, 149-172

European perspectives, 193-334
    Austrian and German, 193-226
    British, 309-334
    Polish, 227-268
    Slovenian, 269-290
    Spanish, 291-308
future contexts. *See* Future contexts
historical contexts. *See* Historical
    contexts
Latin American perspectives,
    335-406
    Argentinean, 335-352
    Mexican, 353-388
    Peruvian, 389-406
Middle Eastern perspectives,
    407-470
    Egyptian, 407-430
    Iranian, 431-442
    Israeli, 443-460
    Saudi Arabian, 461-470
overviews and summaries, 1-4
reference resources. *See* Reference
    resources
International standard bibliographic
    description formats. *See*
    ISBDs
International Standards Organization.
    See ISO standards
Introductory topics. *See* Overviews and
    summaries
Iranian Library Association. *See* ILA
Iranian perspectives, 431-442. *See also*
    Middle Eastern perspectives
    future contexts, 436-441
    historical contexts, 431-433
    ILA, 436-437
    NLI, 433-434
    overviews and summaries,
        431-432,440-441
    standards and tools, 433-438
        AACR versions, 433-436
        DDC, 433-434
        LCC, 433-436
        LCC (Farsi expansions),
            434-436

LCSH, 435-436
LPSH, 433-434
Manual of Cataloging Rules
(National Library of Islamic
Republic of Iran), 433-434
MARC versions, 436-438
Sears List of Subject Headings,
435-436
UDC, 436
university programs, 432-440
cataloging course requirements,
434
course content, 433-434
curricular changes, 434-436
degrees, 438
descriptions, 432-433
faculty contexts and statistics,
438-439
practicums, 440
student contexts and statistics,
439
teaching assistant roles, 439
ISBDs, 31-32,110-111,115,124-125,
174-176,234-236,277-280,
292-293,297,344-345
ISDS, 359
ISIS/CDS software, 111
ISO standards, 111,277-278,367
690, 367
2709, 111
descriptions, 227-278
Israeli perspectives, 443-460. *See also*
Middle Eastern perspectives
future contexts, 457-458
historical contexts, 444-446
Jewish National Library, 446-447
overviews and summaries,
443-445,457-458
reference resources, 458-459
research-related issues, 457
standards and tools, 446-449
AACR versions, 446-449
ALEPH system, 446-449
DDC, 446-449
Hebrew Thesaurus of Indexing
Terms, 447-449
LCSH, 446-449
UDC, 446-449
university programs, 449-457
ITESM, 370,388
Iwe, J. I., 27-52
IZUM, 281-284

Japan Library Association. *See* JLA
Japanese perspectives, 121-134. *See
also* Asian perspectives
consortia, networks, and systems,
124-132
NACSIS-CAT, 124-132
NII, 132
OCLC, 125
current status (cataloging
education), 122-132
Aichi Shukutoku University,
128-129
career development impacts,
123-124
change-related impacts, 129
descriptions, 122
education quality impacts,
122-123
employment system impacts, 123
Keio University, 127-128
LIS-specific schools, 125-130
master's and doctoral programs,
129-130
non-LIS-specific schools, 130-132
on-the-job training, 132
University of Tsukuba, 126-127
current status (cataloging practice),
124-125
future contexts, 132-133
historical contexts, 121-124
JLA, 124-125,131
NDL, 124-125
overviews and summaries, 121-122,
132-133

reference resources, 133
standards and tools, 124-131
AACR versions, 124-131
BSH, 125-131
CC, 127
DDC, 125-129
ISBDs, 124-125
LCC, 125
LCSH, 128-129
MARC versions, 124-129
NCR, 124-131
NDC, 125-129
NDLSH, 128-129
UDC, 128-129
university programs, 122-132
Jewish National Library, 446-447
JHP BN, 238-239
JLA, 124-125,131

KAB, 201
KABA, 238-240
Keio University, 127-128
Kenya School of Professional Studies.
See KSPS
KFUPM Library, 465-469
Kgosiemang, Rose Tiny, 5-26
Khurshid, Zahiruddin, 461-470
Kinetica, 150-151
King Fahd University of Petroleum &
Minerals Library. *See*
KFUPM Library
Kokabi, Mortaza, 431-442
Korean perspectives. *See* South Korean
perspectives
KSPS, 56
Kwak, Chul-Wan, 135-148

Latin American perspectives, 335-406.
*See also under individual
topics*
Argentinean, 335-352
Mexican, 353-388

overviews and summaries, 1-4
Peruvian, 389-406
LCC, 8-11,58,61,94-95,125,154-155,
200-201,277,319,338,358,
360,363,392-395,423-425,
433-436,465
LCC (Farsi expansions), 434-436
LCSH, 58,77,112,114-115,128-129,
154-155,176-182,279-280,
319,321-324,338,394,422-425,
435-436,446-449,465
Library cataloging education
(international perspectives).
*See also under individual
topics*
African perspectives, 5-70
Botswanan, 5-26
Nigerian, 27-52
South African, 53-70
Asian perspectives, 71-148
Chinese (current status), 85-104
Chinese (future development),
71-84
Indian, 105-120
Japanese, 121-134
South Korean, 135-148
Australian perspectives, 149-192
New South Wales, 173-192
Queensland, 149-172
European perspectives, 193-334
Austrian and German, 193-226
British, 309-334
Polish, 227-268
Slovenian, 269-290
Spanish, 291-308
future contexts. *See* Future contexts
historical contexts. *See* Historical
contexts
Latin American perspectives, 335-406
Argentinean, 335-352
Mexican, 353-388
Peruvian, 389-406
Middle Eastern perspectives, 407-470
Egyptian, 407-430
Iranian, 431-442

Israeli, 443-460
Saudi Arabian, 461-470
overviews and summaries, 1-4
reference resources. *See* Reference
resources
Library of Congress Classification. *See*
LCC
Library of Congress Subject Headings.
See LCSH
List of Persian Subject Headings. *See*
LPSH
Local *vs.* outside training, 19-22
López-Cózar, Emilio Delgado,
291-308
LPSH, 433-434

Ma, Zhanghua, 71-84
MAB, 220-223
MAchine-Readable Cataloging format
versions. *See* MARC versions
Manual of Cataloging Rules (National
Library of Islamic Republic
of Iran), 433-434
MARC versions, 58,60-61,75-77,95,
110-115,124-129,156,
166-168,174-176,220-223,
236-237,277,312-314,318,
321-324,338,340-343,361,
367,394-399,423-424,
436-438,466-469
Martínez Arellano, Filiberto Felipe,
353-388
Mexican perspectives, 353-388. *See
also* Latin American
perspectives
future contexts, 370-371
historical contexts, 353-356
overviews and summaries,
353-354,370-371
reference resources, 371-372
standards and tools, 359-367
AACR versions, 359,361,363,
367
DDC, 358,360,363,367

ISDS, 359
ISO 690, 367
LCC, 358,360,363
MARC versions, 361,367
university programs, 355-388
course descriptions, 373-388
ENBA, 355-356,373-374
ITESM, 370,388
licentiate, 355-368
master's, 356-370
UACH, 363-365,381-383
UACh, 367-368,385-386
UAEM, 362-363,379-381
UAG, 365-366,383-384
UANL, 360-362,378-379
UASLP, 356-360,376-377
UNAM, 356-358,368-369,
375-376,386-387
Middle Eastern perspectives, 407-470.
*See also under individual
topics*
Egyptian, 407-430
Iranian, 431-442
Israeli, 443-460
overviews and summaries, 1-4
Saudi Arabian, 461-470
Monoufia University, 412-414
Münnich, Monika, 193-226

NACSIS-CAT, 124-132
National and University Library. *See*
NUK
National Diet Library. *See* NDL
National Diet Library Subject
Headings. *See* NDLSH
National Library (Warsaw), 237-250
National Library of Iran. *See* NLI
National Library of Islamic Republic
of Iran (Manual of
Cataloging Rules), 433-434
National Library of Medicine
classification. *See* NLM
classification
National School of Librarians, 390-392

NCR, 124-131
NDC, 125-129
NDL, 124-125
NDLSH, 128-129
Networks. *See* Consortia, networks,
    and systems
New South Wales perspectives,
    173-192. *See also* Australian
    perspectives
ALIA, 174-176
future contexts, 190
historical contexts, 173-176
overviews and summaries,
    173-176,190
reference resources, 190-191
standards and tools, 174-182
    AACR versions, 174-182
    APPM, 175
    DDC, 176-182
    Dublin Core, 176-182
    FGDC, 175
    GILS, 175
    HTML, 175
    ISBDs, 174-176
    LCSH, 176-182
    MARC versions, 174-176
    SGML, 175
    TEI, 175
    XML, 175
    Z39.50, 174-182
university programs, 176-192
    course offerings, 177-178
    faculty contexts and statistics,
        182-185
    paraprofessional contexts and
        statistics, 179-182
    professional practitioner
        contexts and statistics,
        185-189,191-192
Nigeria Universities Network. *See*
    NUNet
Nigerian perspectives, 27-52. *See also*
    African perspectives
consortia, networks, and systems,
    33-34

NUNet, 33-34
    VSAT, 33-34
Cross River State, 27-52
future contexts, 44-45
historical contexts, 27-34,37-38
IFLA Standards for Library Schools
    (1976), 29-34
overviews and summaries,
    27-34,44-45
reference resources, 45
research studies, 34-51
standards and tools, 27-32
    AACR versions, 27-32
    ISBDs, 31-32
    UAP, 27-28
    UBC, 27-28
    UNESCO, 37-38
University of Calabar, 27-52
university programs, 27-52
NII, 132
Nippon Cataloging Rules. *See* NCR
Nippon Decimal Classification. *See*
    NDC
NLI, 433-434
NLM classification, 58
Northeast Normal University, 73-84
NUK, 273-282
NUNet, 33-34

OCLC, 125,150-151,195,282,465-467
OCLC (Dublin Core), 77-80,95,
    114-115,176-182
October 6 University, 415-416
On-the-job training,
    14-18,132,140-141,321-324,
    401-402. *See also under*
    individual topics
Botswanan perspectives, 14-18
British perspectives, 321-324
Japanese perspectives, 132
Peruvian perspectives, 401-402
South Korean perspectives,
    140-141

Outcomes-based education and
    training, 57-58
Outside *vs.* local training, 19-22
Overviews and summaries, 1-4. *See
    also under individual topics*
    African perspectives, 5-7,22-23,
        27-34,44-45,53-55,67-68
        Botswanan, 5-7,22-23
        Nigerian, 27-34,44-45
        South African, 53-55,67-68
    Asian perspectives, 71-72,80-81,
        105,121-122,132-133,
        135-136,146-147
        Chinese (current status), 85-86
        Chinese (development-related
          issues), 71-72,80-81
        Indian, 105
        Japanese, 121-122,132-133
        South Korean, 135-136,146-147
    Australian perspectives, 149-151,
        166-168,173-176,190
        New South Wales, 173-176,190
        Queensland, 149-151,166-168
    European perspectives, 193-195,
        227-229,249-250,269-271,
        285,291-293,303-304,
        309-311,326-327
        Austrian and German, 193-195
        British, 309-311,326-327
        Polish, 227-229,249-250
        Slovenian, 269-271,285
        Spanish, 291-293,303-304
    Latin American perspectives,
        335-336,350,353-354,
        370-371,389-391,404-405
        Argentinean, 335-336,350
        Mexican, 353-354,370-371
        Peruvian, 389-391,404-405
    Middle Eastern perspectives,
        407-409,425-426,431-432,
        440-441,443-445,457-458,
        461-463,468-469
        Egyptian, 407-409,425-426
        Iranian, 431-432,440-441

        Israeli, 443-445,457-458
        Saudi Arabian, 461-463,468-469

PADIS, 10
Paraprofessional contexts and
    statistics, 179-182
Peking University, 72-84
Peruvian perspectives, 389-406. *See
    also* Latin American
    perspectives
    cataloging trend awareness, 402-404
    continuing education, 402
    future contexts, 405-406
    historical contexts, 390-391
    non-professional education,
        398-400
    on-the-job training, 401-402
    overviews and summaries,
        389-391,404-405
    reference resources, 405-406
    standards and tools, 392-405
        AACR versions, 392-405
        DDC, 392-395
        LCC, 392-395
        LCSH, 394
        MARC versions, 394-399
    university programs, 391-396
        National School of Librarians,
          390-392
        Pontifical Catholic University of
          Peru, 390,395-397
        San Marcos University, 390,
          392-395,402
Pilot projects, 155-159
Pisano, Silvia L., 335-352
Polish perspectives, 227-268. *See also*
    European perspectives
    consortia, networks, and systems,
        249-250
    curricula, 234-249,260-267
        cataloging and classification,
          242-248
        document description, 234-242,
          260-267

future contexts, 249-250
historical contexts, 228-233
National Library (Warsaw), 237-250
overviews and summaries, 227-229,
    249-250
reference resources, 250-257
standards and tools, 234-250
    FRBR, 249-250
    Grycz rules, 235-236
    ISBDs, 234-236
    JHP BN, 238-239
    KABA, 238-240
    MARC versions, 236-237
    Two Bibliographic Tomes,
        228-229
    Z39.50, 237-238
university programs, 229-233,
    258-259
    CEBID, 232-233
    descriptions, 229-233
    EBIB, 229-233,258-259
    study levels and forms, 258-259
Pontifical Catholic University of Peru,
    390,395-397
POPSI, 110-115
Postulate-based Permuted Subject
    Indexing. *See* POPSI
Practicums, 98-100,422,440. *See also*
    under individual topics
    Chinese perspectives, 98-100
    Egyptian perspectives, 422
    Iranian perspectives, 440
PRECIS, 110-115
Preserved Context Index System. *See*
    PRECIS
Programs (university). *See* University
    programs

Queensland perspectives, 149-172. *See*
    also Australian perspectives
    ALIA, 152
    CatSkill training software, 156-166
    consortia, networks, and systems,
        150-151
        Kinetica, 150-151
        OCLC, 150-151
        RLN, 150-151
        WLN, 150-151
    future contexts, 166-168
    GDLIS, 149-172
    historical contexts, 150-151
    overviews and summaries,
        149-151,166-168
    pilot projects, 155-159
    professional contexts, 152
    QUT, 149-172
    reference resources, 168-171
    standards and tools, 154-168
        AACR versions, 154-168
        DDC, 154-155
        LCC, 154-155
        LCSH, 154-155
        MARC versions, 156,166-168
    student learning outcomes, 159-166
    university programs, 152-155
Queensland University of Technology.
    See QUT
QUT, 149-172

Raghavan, K. S., 105-120
RAK, 199-223
    RAK-Musik, 199-201
    RAK-NBM, 199-201
    RAK-OB, 199-201
    RAK-UW, 199-201
    RAK-WB, 199-201
Ranganathan, S. R., 106-119
RCE, 292-293,297
Reference resources. *See also under*
    individual topics
    African perspectives, 23-25,45,
        68-69
        Botswanan, 23-25
        Nigerian, 45
        South African, 68-69

Asian perspectives, 82-83,119,
133,147
Chinese (current status),
101-103
Chinese (development-related
issues), 82-83
Indian, 119
Japanese, 133
South Korean, 147
Australian perspectives, 168-171,
190-191
New South Wales, 190-191
Queensland, 168-171
European perspectives, 225,250-257,
285-286,304-307,328-329
Austrian and German, 225
British, 328-329
Polish, 250-257
Slovenian, 285-286
Spanish, 304-307
Latin American perspectives, 350-351,
371-372,405-406
Argentinean, 350-351
Mexican, 371-372
Peruvian, 405-406
Middle Eastern perspectives, 426,
458-459,469-470
Egyptian, 426
Israeli, 458-459
Saudi Arabian, 469-470
Relas de Catalogación Españolas. *See*
RCE
Research trends, 348-349
Research-related issues, 457
Reynolds, Susan, 173-192
RLN, 150-151
RSWK, 199-201
Ruiz-Perez, Rafael, 291-308

SABINET, 11
San Marcos University,
390,392-395,402
SAQA, 58-60

Saudi Arabian perspectives, 461-470.
See also Middle Eastern
perspectives
AFLI, 468
AGC-SLA, 464-465
consortia, networks, and systems,
465-467
continuing education, 464-468
conferences, 466-467
descriptions, 464
informal options, 467-468
non-LIS degree courses, 464
seminars, 466
short courses, 465-466
Web sites, 467
workshops, 464-465
future contexts, 468-469
historical contexts, 462-464
KFUPM Library, 465-469
OCLC, 465-467
overviews and summaries,
461-463,468-469
reference resources, 469-470
SLIA, 468
standards and tools, 463-469
AACR versions, 463-464
CIP data, 468
CORC, 463-464
DDC, 465
Dublin Core, 463-464
LCC, 465
LCSH, 465
MARC versions, 466-469
Sears List of Subject Headings,
463-464
SGML, 463-464
XML, 463-464
university programs, 463-464
Saudi Library and Information Science
Association. *See* SLIA
Šauperl, Alenka, 269-290
Saye, Jerry D., 269-290
Sears List of Subject Headings, 60-61,
112-115,435-436,463-464
Self-training options, 142-147

SGML, 175,349-350,463-464
Shaker, Ali Kamal, 407-430
Shoham, Snunith, 443-460
Si, Li, 85-104
Sitarska, Anna, 227-268
SLIA, 468
Slovenian perspectives, 269-290. *See
     also* European perspectives
consortia, networks, and systems,
     282-283
     COBISS, 282-283
     OCLC, 282
EU, Bologna Declaration, 270-271
future contexts, 285
historical contexts, 270-271
NUK, 273-282
overviews and summaries,
     269-271,285
reference resources, 285-286
standards and tools, 277-280
     AACR versions, 278
     Bliss classification, 277
     CC, 277
     DDC, 277-280
     GSSH, 277
     ISBDs, 277-280
     ISO standards, 277-278
     LCC, 277
     LCSH, 279-280
     MARC versions, 277
     UDC, 277-280
university programs, 272-282
     descriptions, 272
     formal education programs,
          272-273
     higher education contexts, 272
     IZUM, 281-284
     master's programs, 281
     national infrastructure support,
          281-283
     texts and readings, 280,287-289
     undergraduate programs,
          273-280
ZBDS, 283

Sohaj Branch (South Valley University),
     413
South African perspectives, 53-70. *See
     also* African perspectives
distance education, 55-70
     advantages, 64-65
     B Tech, 59-60
     considerations, 65-66
     descriptions, 53-55
     disadvantages, 65
     education and training methods,
          62
     experiential learning contexts,
          56-57
     flexible higher education
          contexts, 56
     integrated training resources
          programs, 62-66
     M Tech, 59
     National Certificate, 59-60
     National Diploma, 59-60
     National Higher Certificate,
          59-60
     outcomes-based education and
          training, 57-58
     programs and qualifications,
          59-62
     qualification, knowledge, and
          skill set requirements, 57-58
     student contexts and statistics,
          55-56
     TSA COOL, 62-66
     virtual cataloging training
          classroom, 66-67
future contexts, 67-68
historical contexts, 53-56
KSPS, 56
overviews and summaries,
     53-55,67-68
reference resources, 68-69
SAQA, 58-60
standards and tools, 58-61
     AACR versions, 58,60-61
     DDC, 58,60-61
     LCC, 58,61

LCSH, 58
MARC versions, 58,60-61
NLM classification, 58
Sears List of Subject Headings,
60-61
UDC, 61
university programs, 55-70
UNSIA, 55-70
South African Qualifications
Authority. *See* SAQA
South Korean perspectives, 135-148.
See also Asian perspectives
academic libraries, 136-138
future contexts, 146-147
historical contexts, 135-138
in-service training, 140-142
automated system training,
141-142
on-the-job training, 140-141
requirements, 141
overviews and summaries,
135-136,146-147
practitioner contexts and statistics,
138-140
reference resources, 147
self-training options, 142-147
content requirements, 145-146
educational support, 144-145
materials, 142-143
project cooperation, 146-147
work-related journals, 143-144
university programs, 136-138
South Valley University, 413
South West German Library
Consortium, 195
Spanish perspectives, 291-308. *See
also* European perspectives
future contexts, 303-304
historical contexts, 292-293
IFLA, 292-293
overviews and summaries, 291-293,
303-304
reference resources, 304-307
standards and tools, 292-301
AACR versions, 292-293,297
GARE and GSARE, 297

ISBDs, 292-293,297
MARC versions, 292-293,
297-301
RCE, 292-293,297
UNESCO, 292-293
university programs, 294-303
descriptions, 294-303
descriptive cataloging curricula,
297-301
diploma programs, 295-303
ECTS, 302-303
EU contexts, 302-303
license programs, 301-303
materials and methods, 293-294
professional instruction stages,
301-302
Standards and tools. *See also under
individual topics*
AACR versions, 9-11,16,27-32,58,
60-61,95,110-115,124-131,
154-168,174-182,199-200,
220-223,278,292-293,297,
312-314,318-324,349-350,
359,361,363,367,392-405,
421-423,433-436,446-449,
463-464
African perspectives, 8-18,27-32,
58-61
Botswanan, 8-18
Nigerian, 27-32
South African, 58-61
ALEPH system, 446-449
ANSI, 343
APPM, 175
ASB, 201
Asian perspectives, 75-77,91-95,
110-115,124-131
Chinese (current status), 91-95
Chinese (development-related
issues), 75-77
Indian, 110-115
Japanese, 124-131
Australian perspectives, 154-168,
174-182
New South Wales, 174-182
Queensland, 154-168

Bliss classification, 11,277
BSH, 125-131
CC, 77,94-95,112-115,127,277
CCC, 77,110-115
CDS/ISIS software, 111
Chinese Cataloging Rules, 76-77
Chinese Classified Thesaurus,
    77-79,94
Chinese Library Classification,
    77,91-95
CIP data, 321-322,468
Classification of the Chinese
    Academy of Sciences
    Library, 94-95
Classification of the Library of the
    People's University of China,
    94-95
CORC, 463-464
DDC, 8-11,17-18,58,60-61,77,
    94-95,125-129,154-155,
    176-182,200-201,277-280,
    312-313,319,321-324,358,
    360,363,367,392-395,
    421-425,433-434,446-449,
    465
Dublin Core, 77-80,95,114-115,
    176-182,349-350
European perspectives, 199-201,
    220-222,234-250,277-280,
    292-301,312-324
    Austrian and German, 199-201,
        220-222
    British, 312-324
    Polish, 234-250
    Slovenian, 277-280
    Spanish, 292-301
FGDC, 175
FRBR, 249-250
GARE and GSARE, 297
GILS, 175
Greater List of Arabic Subject
    Headings, 422-423
Grycz rules, 235-236
GSSH, 277

Hebrew Thesaurus of Indexing
    Terms, 447-449
HTML, 175
ISBDs, 31-32,110-111,115,
    124-125,174-176,234-236,
    277-280,292-293,297,
    344-345
ISDS, 359
ISO 690, 367
ISO 2709, 111
ISO standards, 277-278
JHP BN, 238-239
KAB, 201
KABA, 238-240
Latin American perspectives,
    338-350,359-367,392-405
    Argentinean, 338-350
    Mexican, 359-367
    Peruvian, 392-405
LCC, 8-11,58,61,94-95,125,
    154-155,200-201,277,319,
    338,358,360,363,392-395,
    423-425,433-436,465
LCC (Farsi expansions), 434-436
LCSH, 58,77,112,114-115,128-129,
    154-155,176-182,279-280,
    319,321-324,338,394,422-425,
    435-436,446-449,465
LPSH, 433-434
MAB, 220-223
Manual of Cataloging Rules
    (National Library of Islamic
    Republic of Iran), 433-434
MARC versions, 58,60-61,75-77,
    95,110-115,124-129,156,
    166-168,174-176,220-223,
    236-237,277,312-314,318,
    321-324,338,340-343,361,
    367,394-399,423-424,
    436-438,466-469
Middle Eastern perspectives,
    421-425,433-438,446-449,
    463-469
    Egyptian, 421-425
    Iranian, 433-438

Israeli, 446-449
Saudi Arabian, 463-469
NCR, 124-131
NDC, 125-129
NDLSH, 128-129
NLM classification, 58
POPSI, 110-115
PRECIS, 110-115
RAK, 199-223
    RAK-Musik, 199-201
    RAK-NBM, 199-201
    RAK-OB, 199-201
    RAK-UW, 199-201
    RAK-WB, 199-201
RCE, 292-293,297
RSWK, 199-201
Sears List of Subject Headings,
    60-61,112-115,435-436,
    463-464
SGML, 175,349-350,463-464
TEI, 175,349-350
Two Bibliographic Tomes, 228-229
UAP, 27-28
UBC program, 27-28,110-111
UDC, 11,61,77,94-95,128-129,
    200-201,277-280,319,423,
    436,446-449
Warwick Framework, 349-350
XML, 175,349-350,463-464
Z39.50, 174-182,237-238
Student contexts and statistics, 12-13,
    55-56,314-315,439. *See also*
    under individual topics
Botswanan perspectives, 12-13
British perspectives, 314-315
Iranian perspectives, 439
South African perspectives, 55-56
Subject cataloging standards and tools.
    See Standards and tools
Subject Headings by the National
    Library in Warsaw. *See* JHP
    BN
Summary topics. *See* Overviews and
    summaries

Sun, Dajin D., 1-4
Systems. *See* Consortia, networks, and
    systems

Talavera Ibarra, Ana María, 389-406
Taniguchi, Shoichi, 121-134
Teacher contexts and statistics. *See*
    Faculty contexts and statistics
Teaching assistant roles, 439
Teaching assurance systems, 100
Teaching strategies, 346-347
TEI, 175,349-350
Text Encoding Initiative. *See* TEI
TFPL, 324,330-333
TINlib system, 19
Tools and standards. *See* Standards and
    tools
Trend awareness, 402-404
TSA COOL, 62-66
Two Bibliographic Tomes, 228-229

UACH, 363-365,381-383
UACh, 367-368,385-386
UAEM, 362-363,379-381
UAG, 365-366,383-384
UANL, 360-362,378-379
UAP, 27-28
UASLP, 356-360,376-377
UBC program, 27-28,110-111
UCC, 103-119
UCL, 315-321
UDC, 11,61,77,94-95,128-129,
    200-201,277-280,423,436,
    446-449
UNAM, 356-358,368-369,375-376,
    386-387
Undergraduate-level programs. *See*
    University programs
UNESCO, 10,37-38,108-111,292-293
Union of Associations of Slovene
    Librarians. *See* ZBDS
United Kingdom perspectives. *See*
    British perspectives

Universal Availability of Publications.
    See UAP
Universal Bibliographic Control
    program. *See* UBC program
Universal Decimal Classification. *See*
    UDC
Universidad Autónoma de Chiapas.
    See UACH
Universidad Autónoma de Chihuahua.
    See UACh
Universidad Autónoma de
    Guadalajara. *See* UAG
Universidad Autónoma de Nuevo
    León. *See* UANL
Universidad Autónoma de San Luis
    Potosí. *See* UASLP
Universidad Autónoma del Estado de
    México. *See* UAEM
Universidad Nacional Autónoma de
    México. *See* UNAM
University College London. *See* UCL
University Grants Commission. *See*
    UCC
University of Botswana, 7-26
University of Buenos Aires, 335-406
University of Calabar, 27-52
University of South Africa. *See*
    UNSIA
University of Tsukuba, 126-127
University programs. *See also under*
    individual topics
    African perspectives, 5-26,55-70
        Botswanan, 5-26
        Nigerian, 27-52
        South African, 55-70
    Asian perspectives, 86-91,108-119,
        122-132,136-138
        Chinese, 86-91
        Indian, 108-119
        Japanese, 122-132
        South Korean, 136-138
    Australian perspectives, 152-155,
        176-192
        New South Wales, 176-192
        Queensland, 152-155

European perspectives, 196-199,
    202-219,223-225,229-233,
    258-259,272-282,294-303,
    311-326
    Austrian and German, 196-199,
        202-219,223-225
    British, 311-326
    Polish, 229-233,258-259
    Slovenian, 272-282
    Spanish, 294-303
Latin American perspectives,
    336-350,355-388,391-396
    Argentina, 336-350
    Mexican, 355-388
    Peruvian, 391-396
Middle Eastern perspectives,
    432-440,449-457,463-464
    Egyptian, 408-429
    Iranian, 432-440
    Israeli, 449-457
    Saudi Arabian, 463-464
UNSIA, 55-70

Virtual cataloging training classroom,
    66-67
VSAT, 33-34

Warwick Framework, 349-350
Wenhua Library Science School,
    85-86
WLN, 150-151
Workshops, 16-17

XML, 175,349-350,463-464

Z39.50, 174-182,237-238
Zakazik University, 413-414
ZBDS, 283
Zotter-Straka, Heidi, 193-226